Also by Wolfgang Schivelbusch

In a Cold Crater: Cultural and
Intellectual Life in Berlin, 1945–1948

Tastes of Paradise: A Social History of Spices,
Stimulants, and Intoxicants

Disenchanted Night: The Industrialization
of Light in the Nineteenth Century

The Railway Journey: The Industrialization of
Time and Space in the Nineteenth Century

THE CULTURE OF DEFEAT

The

CULTURE

of

DEFEAT

ON NATIONAL TRAUMA,
MOURNING, AND RECOVERY

WOLFGANG SCHIVELBUSCH

Translated by Jefferson Chase

METROPOLITAN BOOKS
Henry Holt and Company · New York

m

Metropolitan Books
Henry Holt and Company, LLC
Publishers since 1866
115 West 18th Street
New York, New York 10011

Metropolitan Books™ is a registered trademark
of Henry Holt and Company, LLC.

Originally published in Germany in 2001 under the title
Die Kultur der Niederlage by Alexander Fest Verlag, Berlin.

Library of Congress Cataloging-in-Publication Data

Schivelbusch, Wolfgang, 1941–
    [Kultur der Niederlage. English]
    The culture of defeat : on national trauma, mourning, and
recovery / Wolfgang Schivelbusch ; translated by Jefferson Chase.
        p.   cm.
    Includes bibliographical references and index.
    ISBN 0-8050-4421-3 (hc.)
    1. United States—History—Civil War, 1861–1865—Psychological aspects.
2. Southern States—Social conditions—1865–1945.   3. Franco-Prussian War,
1870–1871—Psychological aspects.   4. France—Social conditions—19th century.
5. World War, 1914–1918—Psychological aspects.   6. World War, 1914–1918—
Germany.   7. Germany—Social conditions—1918–1933.   8. Defeat
(Psychology)—Case studies.   9. National characteristics—Case studies.
10. Military history—Case studies.   I. Title.

E468.9 .S35   2003
303.6'6—dc21   2002026515

Henry Holt books are available for special promotions and
premiums. For details contact: Director, Special Markets.

First American Edition 2003
Designed by Victoria Hartman
Printed in the United States of America

1   3   5   7   9   10   8   6   4   2

ancor'una volta per Emma

with thanks to Sara, Stephen, Riva, and Roslyn

Contents

THE CULTURE OF DEFEAT

Introduction:
On Being Defeated

The vanquished are the first to learn what history holds in store.
Heinrich Mann

In the beginning was the fall of Troy, the prototype for all Western defeats. The ancient myths attest to how little the Greeks gained from their conquest: the victorious captains meet the death they escaped in battle (Ajax), are strewn about the globe for years (Menelaus, Odysseus), or return to their homes only to be murdered (Agamemnon). Troy is lost, it's true—but with one crucial exception. The myths allow Aeneas and his family to escape and, after an odyssey of their own, to land on Italian soil and become the ancestors of the founders of Rome. Trojan lineage was an established part of Roman mythology even before Virgil used it as the basis for his national epic, the *Aeneid*, and after Rome's own demise the founding myths of early medieval Western Europe adopted it as well. According to a sixth-century legend, France was founded by Francio, one of Priam's sons, while England, if we believe Geoffrey of Monmouth's *Historia Regum Britanniae*, owed its existence to Brutus, one of Aeneas's grandsons and an early ancestor of King Arthur.[1]

The myth of Troy as both an end and a new beginning is one of the many expressions of the ancient idea, common to all the world's great cultures, that war, death, and rebirth are cyclically linked. The major myths of death and rebirth do not allow for absolute eradication. Life goes on in the afterworld much as it had in the realm of the living; it merely "changes venue," as the philosopher Ernst Cassirer puts it.[2] In many contemporary Western versions of the death-rebirth dynamic, negation appears as the driving force behind all progress. Without the eternally negating spirit of Mephistopheles, or the Hegelian antithesis, or the Freudian reality principle, there can be no Faustian bargain, no dialectical understanding of history, and no construction of the ego from the id. Defeat, at its most abstract, is nothing more than the negation of a will that has proven unable to realize its aims, despite using all the means at its disposal. Hegel's maxim that world history is the court of world justice regards victory as a verdict—the end result of a previous struggle—that remains in force only until an opponent's challenge begins a new struggle. Similarly, another Hegelian precept—the real is the rational—applies only for as long as the victorious side is able to assert its power. In the classical liberal system, the winners at any one point in history must always be prepared to face challenges from rivals, who are often yesterday's losers, whether the contest occurs in industry or the marketplace, in the world of fashion or ideas, in sports competitions or political elections.

To give up illusions of permanent triumph, to understand world history as a series of rises and falls, is to adopt the outlook of the jester Till Eulenspiegel, who relished the difficult path up the mountainside because of the easy downward slope that was sure to follow. The recognition that what triumphs today will be defeated tomorrow does more than just reverse the traditional tendency to identify with the great and powerful. Whereas the concept of hubris is primarily concerned with the demise of a supercilious and arrogant power, an empathetic philosophy of defeat seeks to identify and appreciate the significance of defeat itself.

There are two types of defeat empathy: the "interested" reflection of the vanquished themselves and the "disinterested" observations of third parties. A good example of the first is Carl Schmitt. Hitler's leading legal expert, Schmitt ended up as a defendant before a de-nazification tribunal. In the summer of 1946, he wrote an essay about Alexis de Tocqueville, whom he characterized as the paradigmatic loser: "Every sort of defeat was crystallized in his person, and not just accidentally but as a kind of existential destiny. As an aristocrat, he lost out in the revolution. . . . As a liberal, he anticipated the revolution of 1848 and its divergence from liberalism, and he was cut to the core by the onset of the terror he knew it would bring. As a Frenchman, he belonged to a nation that was defeated after twenty years of coalition warfare. . . . As a European, he was again in the role of the defeated since he foresaw the development of two new powers, America and Russia, . . . that would push Europe to the margins. Finally, as a Christian, . . . he was overwhelmed by the scientific agnosticism of his era."

For Schmitt in 1946, Tocqueville was a great historian because he "did not, like Hegel and Ranke, seat himself next to God Almighty in the royal box in the theater of the world" but rather took his place among the ranks of the losing side.[3] In 1934, when Schmitt, who drafted the legal justifications for the Night of the Long Knives, shared the box with Hitler, he no doubt saw things differently.

Some forty years later, Reinhart Koselleck drew a comparison between the historiography of victors and of the vanquished that reads like a paraphrase of Schmitt's commentary on Tocqueville. "While history may be temporarily made by the victors, who hold on to it for a while," Koselleck writes, "it never allows itself to be ruled for long." Koselleck goes on to characterize victors' history as "short-term, focused on the series of events that, thanks to one's merits, have brought about one's victory. . . . The historian who stands on the side of the victorious is easily tempted to interpret triumphs of the moment as the lasting outcomes of an ex post facto teleology." As examples, Koselleck cites Johann Gustav Droysen and Heinrich von Treitschke in Germany and François Guizot in France. The historiography of the defeated is another matter entirely: "Their defining experience is that everything turned out other than they hoped. They labor under . . . a greater burden of proof for having to show why events turned out as they did—and not as planned. Therefore they begin to search for middle- or long-term factors to account for and perhaps explain the accident of the unexpected outcome. There is something to the hypothesis that being forced to draw new and difficult lessons from history yields insights of longer validity and thus greater explanatory power. History may in the short term be made by the victors, but historical wisdom is in the long run enriched more by the vanquished. . . . Being defeated appears to be an inexhaustible wellspring of intellectual progress."[4]

The Frondists, who opposed French absolutism and, after their defeat, traded the sword for the pen, were typical "losers" of this reflective sort. The memoirs and aphorisms of Saint-Simon and La Rochefoucauld were ultimately both a sublimated form of revenge and a social critique that led directly to the Enlightenment and the French Revolution.[5] In the twentieth century, Russell Jacoby made a similar point about West European Marxism. Stumbling from one political defeat to the next, it retained a critical potential—a flexibility, an openness, and a humanity—that Soviet Marxism, its twin brother, lost while triumphantly marching forward.[6]

DISINTERESTED OBSERVERS OFFER another kind of defeat empathy. Most prominently, these oberservers include the minority within the victorious nation who recognize the danger of hubris. The best-known expression of such a view is Nietzsche's 1871 warning that great victories pose great dangers and that the triumph of the German empire would entail the demise of German culture. Arnold Toynbee, too, credits defeat with mobilizing the energies of a nation. In his system of "Challenge and Response," defeat represents the "stimulus of blows," one of the five stimuli that set historical action in motion.[7]

DEFEAT FOLLOWS WAR as ashes follow fire. At the heart of both defeat and war lies the threat of extinction, a threat that resonates long past the cessation of hostilities. From prehistoric tribal feuds through the wars of antiquity and the Middle Ages, this threat was directed at all members of the enemy people, not just its soldiers.[8] While the cabinet wars of the eighteenth and nineteenth centuries restricted violence to the direct participants on the battlefield, the scorched-earth policies of twentieth-century total war once more universalized the threat. Limited warfare, conducted by a professional military apparatus and carrying no real or imagined peril to the populace at large, was thus a phenomenon that lasted a mere two centuries—or only one, if we narrow our definition of cabinet warfare to the pre-1792 period. For though the nineteenth century continued the tradition of limited warfare militarily, in that the forces of destruction were contained within the armies doing battle, emerging mass societies in the age of nationalism returned, in psychological terms at least, to an earlier epoch of collective threat. While the actual consequences for civilians were relatively mild, war and defeat nevertheless took on the dimensions of a social Darwinist struggle for national survival. With war imagined as a battle of life and death, not only between armies but between entire populations, defeat became tantamount to the nation's death agony.[9] Jakob Burckhardt was one of the first to recognize this changed aspect of war: "A people only becomes acquainted with its full national strength in warfare, in tests of strength against other peoples, for it is only in war that such strength emerges."[10] He also identified the next step in the ongoing escalation, namely politicians' adoption of this annihilationist psychology. Of the Franco-Prussian War of 1870–71,

Burckhardt wrote, "A novel element has arisen in politics, an additional level, of which earlier victors knew nothing or at least made no conscious use. One seeks to humiliate the vanquished enemy as much as possible *in his own eyes* so that he henceforth lacks any confidence whatsoever."[11]

The passions excited in the national psyche by the onset of war show how deeply invested the masses now were in its potential outcome. Propaganda had reinforced their conviction that "everything was at stake," and the threat of death and defeat functioned like a tightly coiled spring, further heightening the tension. The almost festive jubilation that accompanied the declarations of war in Charleston in 1861, Paris in 1870, and the capitals of the major European powers in 1914 were anticipatory celebrations of victory—since nations are as incapable of imagining their own defeat as individuals are of conceiving their own death. The new desire to humiliate the enemy, noted by Burckhardt, was merely a reaction to the unprecedented posturing in which nations now engaged when declaring war.[12]

The deployment of armies on the battlefield is the classic manifestation of collective self-confidence. If both sides are not convinced of their military superiority, there will be no confrontation; rather, those who lack confidence will simply flee the field. Accordingly, the battle is decided the moment the confidence of one side fails. The will to fight ("morale") evaporates, the military formation collapses, and the army seeks salvation in flight or, if it is lucky, in organized retreat. The Greek term for this point in space (on the battlefield) and time (the course of the battle) was *trope*.[13] The victors demarcated the spot with the weapons of the vanquished and later with monuments, yielding the term *tropaion*, from which we get our word *trophy*. The nineteenth-century German military theorist Carl von Clausewitz, who defined battle as the "bloody and destructive measuring of strength, physical and moral, between enemies," characterized the *trope* from the perspective of the defeated: "The spirit of the whole is broken, nothing is left of the original obsession with triumph or disaster that made men ignore all risks; for most of them danger is no longer a challenge to their courage but harsh punishment to be endured."[14]

The outcome of each confrontation—down to a single hand-to-hand skirmish—exerts a subtle cumulative influence on the course of the battle as a whole. If individual defeats accrue to the point where they reach a critical mass, the experience of defeat is communicated to the collective and the entire battle is lost. A similar relationship exists between individual battles and wars: a critical mass of lost battles results in a lost war. In wars of attrition, this critical mass is reached not through decisive battles but through the gradual exhaustion of national resources. Aside from the dynamics of defeat, however, the outcome in both cases is the same.

Just as skirmishes affect battles and battles affect wars, defeat at the front has repercussions on the home front. Clausewitz, who witnessed the aftermath of Napoleon's defeat of Prussia at Jena-Auerstedt in 1806, again provides a memorable commentary: "The effect of all this outside the army—on the people and on the government—is a sudden collapse of the most anxious expectations, and a complete crushing of self-confidence. This leaves a vacuum that is filled by a corrosively expanding fear, which completes the paralysis. It is as if the electric charge of the main battle had sparked a shock to the whole nervous system of one of the contestants."[15]

As the news is conveyed to the home front, the fact of defeat takes on a monstrous and overwhelming dimension that was missing on the battlefield. Whereas soldiers experience lost battles, even lost wars, as painful but comprehensible outcomes given their firsthand experience and exhaustion, the news of defeat, as Clausewitz writes, plunges the home front into "panicked terror." The home front has lived, in the words of a Paris commentator after Sedan, *en plein roman*, or under an illusion, in the unshaken conviction of certain victory.[16] The intensity of the shock increases in direct proportion to the distance from the actual site of defeat, a phenomenon that stems from the experiential and psychological differences between battlefront and home front. This discrepancy may lead to nervous breakdowns, such as have frequently been recorded among otherwise hard-bitten politicians in response to their troops' defeat, or alternatively to a mobilization of the home front to continue the fight at the very moment that its war-weary army has surrendered. In 1792, after a series of setbacks inflicted by invading foreign armies, the revolutionary government raised an army of volunteers to meet the growing threat. This development, which since 1792 has been known as the *levée en masse* (mass mobilization), or people's war, is the spontaneous self-deployment of the entire nation as the last line of defense. The *levée en masse* thus represents the end of the cabinet-war era, with its strict separation of military and civilian populations, and points the way toward total warfare. In terms of psychology, the *levée en masse* appears to be a mechanism for restoring equilibrium between the military front line, which has collapsed, and a civilian society as yet untouched by the consequences of war, in that it replaces the troops' exhausted morale with the still vital spirit of the nation itself.

This psychological dynamic is the national equivalent of what Clausewitz calls "the instinct for retaliation and revenge" among troops who have suffered setbacks. "It is a universal instinct," writes Clausewitz, "shared by the supreme commander and the youngest drummer boy; the morale of troops is never higher than when it comes to repaying that kind of debt. . . . There is thus a natural propensity to exploit this psychological factor in order to recapture what has been lost."[17] Mass mobilization on the home front and political revolution usually go hand in hand—a significant conjunction since the new regime, having arisen from external defeat and internal coup d'état, may well require a surge of popular support to deflect accusations of illegitimacy and to prevent the spread of a legend of betrayal. The comparison between France in September 1870 and Germany in November 1918 is particularly instructive in this regard.

AFTER THE BATTLE of Sedan in 1870, the provisional republican government continued the war as *levée en masse*, something that was viewed by most contemporaries as crucial to the survival of the Third Republic and by later historians as the positive counterexample to the failed postdefeat Weimar Republic in Germany. Colmar von der Goltz, himself a soldier and later the author of the influential pamphlet *Das Volk in Waffen* (The People under Arms), was the first German to recognize that the military importance of the *levée en masse* was secondary to its political and psychological significance. "Above all, the spectacle was intended to impress," he wrote about the *défense nationale* organized by Léon Gambetta. "The German barbarians were to be defeated not by armed force but by their amazement at free France's tremendous capacity for sacrifice." The final sentence of Goltz's 1877 study of Gambetta reads: "Should it come to pass that, God forbid, our German fatherland suffers a defeat like that of the French at Sedan, I would wish that a man emerges who knows how to inspire the sort of absolute resistance Gambetta tried to organize."[18]

Industrialist Walther Rathenau's call for a German *levée en masse* in October 1918 echoed such sentiments, as did Adolf Hitler's reverential appraisal of the Third Republic, which he regarded, unlike the despised "November Republic" of Weimar, as a shining example of patriotic nationalism: "With the collapse of France at Sedan," Hitler proclaimed, "the people rose in revolution to *save* the fallen tricolor! The war was continued with new energy! The revolutionaries bravely fought countless battles. The will to defend the state created the French republic in 1870. It was a symbol not of dishonor but of the upstanding will to preserve the nation. French national honor was revived by the Third Republic. What a contrast to our republic!"[19] These words were part of a speech Hitler gave on September 12, 1923, two months before his attempted Munich putsch, when the Weimar Republic seemed on the brink of disintegration. The crisis was provoked by France's military occupation of the Ruhr region as leverage for its receipt of reparations payments. Moderate nationalists considered the passive resistance organized by the government as a German version of the *levée en masse*, a necessary if belated means of restoring the honor of the nation.[20] But Hitler dismissed the "Ruhr War," as it was commonly called, as ineffectual and dishonorable. "[The politicians] want to turn Germany into India, a people of dreamers," he said, ". . . so that it can be peacefully bounded under the yoke of slavery."[21]

Only wars that mobilize the nation to a high degree but end too abruptly for the losing side to adapt emotionally result in true *levées en masse*. In the American South and Wilhelminian Germany, both of which had exhausted the home front as well as the battlefront in long wars of attrition, the end was simply collapse. Yet even in these cases, the "flat conclusion of the war," as Southerner Edward A. Pollard puts it, was experienced as an unacceptable void.[22] The American South in 1865 and Germany in 1918 both clung to visions if not of ultimate victory then at least of a glorious defeat with flags flying. And both societies produced belated caricatures of *levées en masse* in the form of terrorist groups composed of discharged soldiers—the Ku Klux Klan and the Freikorps, respectively—who portrayed themselves as avengers of national honor.

Dreamland

Every society experiences defeat in its own way. But the varieties of response within vanquished nations—whether psychological, cultural, or political—conform to a recognizable set of patterns or archetypes that recur across time and national boundaries. A state of unreality—or dreamland—is invariably the first of these.

The deep and widespread depression caused by lost wars in the age of nationalism is as obvious as the joyous public celebrations of victorious ones. It is all the more surprising, then, how briefly the losing nation's depression tends to last before turning into a unique type of euphoria. The source of this transformation is usually an internal revolution following military collapse. The overthrow of the old regime and its subsequent scapegoating for the nation's defeat are experienced as a kind of victory. The more popular the revolt and the more charismatic the new leadership, the greater the triumph will seem. For a moment, the external enemy is no longer an adversary but something of an ally, with whose help the previous regime and now deposed system has been driven from power.[23] Seized by a mood of universal brotherhood, the masses look toward the future with confidence. "Beaming faces and joyous celebrations abound," recorded one Parisian in 1870. "Workers and national guardsmen arrive with ladders and pry the sculpted eagles and imperial crowns from the building facades. The cafés are bursting with people. From every corner, cries can be heard: Long live the republic! And at sundown, at the end of this lovely autumn day, the night life begins. Businesses and theaters are alive and humming; everywhere there is the same joy and gladness."[24]

Just as the declaration of the Third Republic in Paris on September 4, 1870, caused waves of elation to ripple through the assembled masses, allowing them to forget the two-day-old news of the French defeat at Sedan, the demonstration organized by the Bavarian socialist Kurt Eisner in Munich on November 7, 1918, served not to mourn Germany's imminent military collapse but to celebrate the overthrow of the monarchist regime. The mood of both gatherings was reminiscent of the carnivalesque festivities that historian Roger Caillois describes as typical of declarations of war. Even when, as in Berlin on November 9, 1918, the transfer of power takes place soberly and with minimal popular participation, the people are suffused, after their initial depression, with feelings of relief, liberation, and salvation that mirror their exhilaration at the beginning of war.[25] Their initial enthusiasm celebrates a departure from the regulation and discipline of normal society into the sacralized community of the warrior nation; similarly, the end of war is greeted as a comparably intense release from the constraints and privations of wartime. Contributing to the elation are the end of the mortal threat that oppressed the nation, the sense of triumph at having survived, and the humiliation of the former rulers, who will henceforth be held solely responsible for defeat. The outbursts of condemnation directed at Napoleon III's Second Empire after 1870 and Wilhelm II's *Kaiserreich* after 1918 are practically interchangeable. The old regime is accused of everything from materialism and corruption to laziness and selfishness and is blamed for the fact that, "believing in nothing more than money and pleasure, [the nation] lost sight of higher values."[26] Defeat thus becomes synonymous with liberation. The French bon mot "Praised be our defeats . . . they freed us from Napoleon" was resoundingly seconded in Germany in 1918 with regard to Wilhelm II, often by the very individuals who had been the loudest to exult at the beginning of the war. In the American South, too, foreign observers were surprised at the swift unanimity with which former slave owners condemned the old system as amoral and welcomed defeat as deliverance.

On the physical level, this sense of liberation was often expressed in what contemporaries described as a manic, even feverish epidemic of dancing. Most immediately, dance mania can be seen as part of a general explosion of sensuality and hedonism in response to the restrictions on pleasure and entertainment during wartime—a response shared by the victorious side. As the critic V. F. Calverton puts it, "Dance was an inevitable outgrowth of war-madness. . . . It was the mad, delirious dancing of men and women who had to seize upon something as a vicarious outlet for their crazed emotions."[27] A passage from Edmond de Goncourt's diary of 1870–71 suggests another significance of dancing for the loser: "France is dancing . . . as a form of revenge. It is dancing to forget."[28] In Germany, contemporary cultural-historical and medical observers drew connections between what they witnessed in 1918 and the St. Vitus dances and hopping processions that erupted in times of crisis during the late Middle Ages. Compulsive dancing, their analyses propose, was both a symptom of a hysterical disruption of motor coordination (the medical term is *chorea hysterica rhythmica*) resulting from a collective trauma and an unconscious therapeutic response to that condition.[29]

Yet if dancing is treated not as a physical compensation for the trauma of defeat but rather as an expression of triumph over the deposed, humiliated father-tyrant, it loses its pathological quality and takes its place within the long tradition of victory dances. What the waltz was to the Revolution of 1789 and the cancan (not to be confused with the dance popular in turn-of-the-century variety shows) was to the July Revolution of 1830, the so-called jazz dances were to the November Revolution in Berlin in 1918–19.[30]

The elation that follows the initial postdefeat depression thus signals a recovery from collective psychological breakdown, a recovery triggered by the overthrow of authority. In the wake of Germany's defeat in World War I, Ernst Troeltsch coined the term *dreamland* for this phenomenon, in which all blame is transferred to the deposed tyrant and the losing nation feels cathartically cleansed, freed of any responsibility or guilt.[31] In the wishful thinking of the dreamland state, nothing stands in the way of a return to the prewar status quo. The expectation in the American South after Lee's surrender at Appomattox was that the Southern states would resume their former place in the Union as equal partners. In France after Sedan, many believed that peace would be concluded with Bismarck without their country's having to give up an inch of territory. In Germany after November 11, 1918, the empire was expected to return to the relations and borders of August 1, 1914. In all these conceptions, the nation was represented as the mother who, having been duped, deceived, even defiled by the father-tyrant, was now, with the help of her sons, about to regain her freedom, innocence, and sovereignty. In turn, the former adversary was expected to honor this act of self-purification, since to revenge himself upon and punish a nation that was deceived by its leaders would be to commit an injustice on a par with that of the leaders themselves.[32]

The dreamland period typically lasts several weeks or even months. The incidence of civil unrest during this time (the Paris Commune, the Spartacist street battles in Berlin, the revolutionary councils and their suppression in Munich) is merely one of the many expressions of the eschatological state of anticipation and illusion. Meanwhile, the expectations vis-à-vis the victor remain undiminished. The unusually long duration of the dreamland condition in the American South—almost two years from Lee's surrender to the beginning of congressional Reconstruction—can be explained by the special situation of civil war, in which the external enemy is simultaneously a long-lost brother.

Awakening

"The victor has freed us from despotism, for which we are very grateful, but now it's time for him to go." Such is the prevailing sentiment within the dreamland state. Should the victorious nation turn out not to be content with this role—if it holds its defeated enemy liable for wartime damage and calls him to account, instead of treating him as an innocent victim—the mood shifts dramatically. The enmity that had been transformed into conciliation reemerges with all its former force or is even intensified by the feeling of having been doubly betrayed. In the dreamland state, memories of the real circumstances of defeat fade away, replaced by the losers' conviction that their nation laid down its arms of its own free will, in a kind of gentleman's agreement that placed trust in the chivalry of the enemy. The German myths of 1918 portraying Woodrow Wilson as the honest broker in whose hands Germany entrusted its future are the most striking example of this phenomenon, and there are corollaries in France and the American South after their defeats.[33]

The change in mood and the accusation of deceit or betrayal leveled against the external enemy are accompanied by an internal shift of a slightly different sort. Once the dreamland state has passed, the postwar revolution loses its aura of liberation and salvation. The revolutionaries find themselves gradually being cast in the role previously played by the deposed regime, whose counterrevolutionary representatives don't hesitate to take their revenge. Their best weapon is the accusation that the revolutionaries are putschists and mutineers who deserted the nation in its hour of greatest need, delivering it up, bound and helpless, to the merciless conqueror. In post-1918 Germany, the idea of the *Dolchstoss*, or "stab in the back," became the most successful counterrevolutionary myth of betrayal. In the American South, which did not experience an internal revolution, and the Third Republic, which legitimized itself through the *défense nationale*, no comparably drastic myths arose, but numerous accusations of betrayal were leveled at individual figures. The scapegoating of failed military leaders such as Confederate general James Longstreet and French marshal Achille-François Bazaine proved to be a relatively simple and effective mechanism for clearing the collective conscience, one that had few consequences except for the individuals concerned.

The absence of a stab-in-the-back legend in America after the Vietnam War shows that accusations of betrayal can grow only if the political and historical soil in which they are planted is fertile.[34] One important element is the role played by betrayal in the mythology of the nation. Nineteenth-century national legends were heavily based on medieval or pseudomedieval epics: the *Song of Roland* and the myth of Joan of Arc in France, the *Nibelungenlied* and Wagner's *Ring* in Germany, and the novels of Walter Scott in the American South. Taking up Hamilton James Eckenrode's appellation for the South, Walter Scottland, one could characterize nineteenth-century France in terms of its mythological disposition as Rolandland or Joan of Arcland and its German equivalent as Nibelungenland or Richard Wagnerland. Since nations shape, experience, and judge their wars, their defeats, and their heroes, traitors, and dissidents according to the models set out in their great epics, the connections between these fictional narratives and historical reality merit close attention.

Unworthy Victories

The military ethos envisions victory in heroic terms, as the subjugation of the enemy through superior martial skill and ability, mythologically exemplified by the hand-to-hand combat between Hector and Achilles. Although real war proceeds according to very different rules, as the Trojan horse and Paris's shot at Achilles's heel demonstrate, the distinction between civilized and barbaric warfare remains very much alive, especially in the losers' perennial claims that the victors cheated and that their victories were therefore illegitimate. The massacre of French knights in 1346 by English archers at Crécy, for example, is considered even today less a military defeat than chivalric martyrdom, in which the actual losers were the moral winners and vice versa. "With their emphasis on individual heroism, the French succumbed to the plebeian collective discipline of the English. . . . Our enemies were anonymous, mechanical, soulless assembly-line workers, devoid of any imagination, who were only victorious because of their greater numbers."[35] These sentiments from a French textbook account of the events at Crécy recur in the rhetoric of every defeated nation: the enemy owes its victory not to soldierly virtue and military acumen but to the deployment of masses of soldiers and matériel that crush one's own hero warriors by their sheer weight. "Make it a fair fight and we'd [have] whipped you all the way through," a Northern correspondent quoted an ex-Confederate soldier as saying after Lee's surrender. The post-1918 German equivalent goes: "Ten times outnumbered and twenty-seven times deceived."[36]

Along with the size of the opposing force, what most often comes in for pillory is the "unworthy" deployment of "unsoldierly" techniques and technology—everything from tanks, submarines, bombers, and mustard gas to economic blockades, propaganda, and psychological warfare. This accusation is inevitable, since every major war is ultimately decided by a technological innovation that the losing side either does not possess or, misjudging its effectiveness, fails to utilize. Thus, the defeated party can always declare the decisive factor to have been a violation of the rules, thereby nullifying the victory and depicting the winner as a cheater.[37]

Despite its pejorative, propagandistic intent, Werner Sombart's distinction between the (German) heroes and (English) shopkeepers of World War I contains a kernel of sociological insight into the divergent character of military-authoritarian and bourgeois-liberal societies. The derisive term *shopkeeper* already appeared in French anti-English propaganda during the Seven Years War and the Napoleonic campaigns and was a variation of the centuries-old stereotype of "perfidious Albion." In the semifeudal Confederacy, the Civil War was similarly viewed as a struggle between the heroic cavaliers and the mercantilist Yankees. And the French stereotype of the Prussian schoolmaster who emerged victorious at Sedan once again expressed the resentment of a military culture at unsportsmanlike behavior— in this case that of a likewise militaristic but technologically modernized culture. Given that wars between "military" and "bourgeois" nations often begin with glorious victories for the former, only to be decided after a prolonged battle of attrition by the material and economic superiority of the latter, the losing side's resentment at being cheated of ultimate triumph is not completely incomprehensible.[38]

It is a short step from the idea that victory achieved by unsoldierly means is illegitimate (or deceitful, swindled, stolen, and so on) and therefore invalid to an understanding of defeat as the pure, unsullied antithesis of false triumph. Christian concepts of victimhood and martyrdom coincide here with their classical counterparts. The more victory becomes a matter of winning in the sense of profiting, the more it becomes, from the perspective of the militarily oriented culture of the loser, the realm of tradesmen and merchants. Once material gain supplants the laurels of victory, the heroic loser is left with little more than the materially disinterested beau geste— the satisfaction of having fought bravely and honorably, if hopelessly, to the bitter end. The loser becomes a Leonidas, a Judah Maccabee, a Brutus who plays out the tragedy with his comrades by his side, in the face of certain death. In view of this sacrifice, the losing side attains a dignity in its own eyes that is as inaccessible to the victor in the age of profitable triumphs as the kingdom of heaven is to the rich man in the New Testament. The German saying after

1918, "*im Felde unbesiegt*," or "undefeated on the field of battle," was consolation and self-aggrandizement in one. In the myth of the "Lost Cause," the post-1865 American South celebrated its demise as both a heroic and a sacral event: "The war has purified and elevated our natures, taught us to respect ourselves, and has won for us the respect of foreign nations," wrote one prominent Southern commentator.[39] In a speech to the returning troops a few days after Sedan, Victor Hugo struck a similar tone: "You will always be the world's best soldiers. . . . The glory belongs to France."[40] The war memorial by Antonin Mercié that was erected in 1874 in Paris's Montholon Square bears the inscription "*Gloria victis*"—"Glory to the Conquered"—and the Weimar Republic's first president, Friedrich Ebert, would repeat much the same sentiment forty-five years later in a speech to the returning troops after Germany's defeat in World War I.[41]

From glory to justice. If the victors' triumph is seen as illegitimate profiteering and thus can stake no claim to glory or honor, defeat is not an outcome that must be acknowledged and accepted but an injustice to be rectified. In the wake of every forced capitulation, therefore, a new struggle begins, a kind of ethical and juridicial *levée en masse* in which the loser, casting himself as the personification of defiled purity, tries to score a "moral victory" against the winner. It makes no difference whether the victor attempts to justify his postwar punitive measures in moral and legal terms, as the Union did in 1865 and the Entente in 1918, or forgoes all such legalism, like Bismarck in 1871. The losers' propaganda will stop at nothing in pressing accusations of injustice and protestations of innocence.[42] If the vanquished make any acknowledgment of a failing of their own, it is only the sarcastic admission that they were perhaps too much like Rousseau's noble savage, punished by civilization for not joining in its hypocrisy. Conservative author Arthur Moeller van den Bruck wrote of German responsibility for the First World War that Germany's "congenital and cultivated naïveté" misled it into declaring war, with the result that "the peoples who actually started the war are exonerated, while we stand accused, . . . a guileless people whose only guilt resides in [our] innocence."[43]

Losers in Battle, Winners in Spirit

The fear of being overrun and destroyed by barbarian hordes is as old as the history of civilized culture itself. Images of desertification—of gardens ransacked by nomads and of decrepit palaces in which goatherds tend their flocks—have haunted the literature of decadence from antiquity to Edward Gibbon, Oswald Spengler, and Gottfried Benn. In reality, however, highly developed cultures do not usually perish when defeated. Instead, the victors are often assimilated into the vanquished civilization, as the Dorians were in Mycenae, the Macedonians in ancient Greece, the Germanic tribes in the Roman Empire, the Mongols in China, and the Arabs in Persia. Even if too weak to repulse the barbarian advances militarily, developed cultures possess sufficient seductive qualities and civilizing resources to absorb their conquerors. The vanquished nation's culture thus becomes a trophy in a dual sense: its strengths and capabilities are symbolically transferred to the conqueror, along with the material spoils of victory—a fate that, incidentally, befalls all losing elites in collapsing cultures as they are replaced by the *homines novi* who buy their castles and boxes at the opera and marry their daughters.[44]

The one great consolation for the defeated is their faith in their cultural and moral superiority over the newly empowered who have ousted them. At its most primitive, this conviction manifests itself in the opposition of the vanquished culture to victorious barbarism. The image of the Yankee in the American South, of the Prussian German in France in 1870, of the post-1918 Afro-French occupiers in the Rhineland—all conform to the negative stereotype of the "savage." With his hulking size, animalistic physiognomy, searing glare, coal-black beard, and weapon bared in his hand, the savage menaces defenseless women and children, who nonetheless lead him around by the nose thanks to their superior intelligence, courage, and wit.[45]

Probing deeper, we come upon another element in the mentality of the defeated—the conviction that the loser is, in terms of knowledge and insight, a step ahead of or, rather, a half-turn further on the wheel of fortune than the victor. The loser knows what the winner does not yet even begin to suspect: that the triumph won't last since the positions of victor and vanquished are in constant rotation. The loser thus casts himself as a figure of warning, whose claim to authority is that he speaks as yesterday's winner. "*Vae victoribus*" (Woe to the victors!), Ernest Renan and other French intellectuals warned Prussian Germany in 1870, recalling France's own hubris under Louis XIV and Napoleon, whose reign marked the beginnings of French decline. Likewise, the liberal Heinrich Mann spoke in November 1918 of the "curse of victory" in 1870–71, which had plunged Germany into the abyss, and warned the victorious Entente not to follow the same path. "You will find it more difficult," he wrote, "to overcome the consequences of your victory than we will to overcome those of our defeat."[46]

To see victory as a curse and defeat as moral purification and salvation is to combine the ancient idea of hubris with the Christian virtue of humility, catharsis with apocalypse. That such a concept should have its greatest resonance among the intelligentsia can be explained in part by the intellectual's classical training but also by his inherently ambivalent stance toward power. To see one's own father-ruler overpowered by another is invariably a source of satisfaction. Indeed, the sons' vision of liberating the mother-nation—a stage of the dreamland state—transforms the fathers' defeat into the sons' own victory.

At this point, all previous loyalties are annulled. Just as there are international affiliations of pacifists and occasional fraternization between enemy soldiers on the front lines, cross-border alliances of intellectuals arise after large-scale wars under the motto *Vae victori-bus*. Oddly enough, the phrase itself originated among the victors. Coined at the end of August 1870 by a German liberal, it was within days taken up by the French intelligentsia as a means of making sense of France's defeat.

The progenitor of the first of these alliances was Germaine de Staël. Her image of Germany as a land of thinkers and poets held sway among French intellectuals as the counterimage to imperialist Napoleonic France until Sedan. This idealized view revealed for the first time the susceptibility of intellectuals on the victorious side to the notion that victory threatens culture, whereas defeat might enhance it. A critical minority within the German intelligentsia after 1871 thought in much the same terms about France. Nietzsche was not alone in prophesying that France would only gain in culture while Germany, the land of thinkers and poets and now a great power, would decline.[47] Criticism of imperial Germany's power-bred arrogance, materialism, and hostility toward intellect and culture contrasted with the oft-noted respect for the mores, spiritual values, and cultural dignity of defeated France. A similar picture of the defeated was painted by the intelligentsia in the victorious American North. Disgusted by the vulgarity of the Gilded Age, writers like Henry James, Henry Adams, and Herman Melville cast the figure of the Southern gentleman as a moral hero in a deeply immoral world.[48] In slightly skewed form, the scenario was repeated after World War I. America's "Lost Generation" took refuge from the prevailing political intolerance, intellectual dessication, and commercial superficiality of their homeland not in the defeated capital of Berlin but in nominally victorious Paris. Nonetheless, since in their eyes the actual loser of the war was not just Germany but all of Europe, their choice followed the familiar pattern.[49]

The empathy felt for the vanquished by a minority of intellectuals within the conquerors' camp should not be confused with the appropriation by the victor of the losing side's cultural symbols, which is yet another aspect of the culture of defeat. The romantic plantation of the Old South, which, if indeed it ever existed, became extinct with the North's victory, was re-created in the 1880s by New York publicists and theater producers for Yankee literary and dramatic audiences. In Wilhelminian Germany, the image of the French was likewise appropriated, feminized from a threatening military power into the supplier of high fashion, luxury perfumes, and haute cuisine. The view of Germany in the United States, the two-time winner of world wars, suggests a third form of trophy taking. Postwar America holds two contradictory images of Germany. The first diminishes the once-threatening enemy into a peaceful junior partner and producer of high-quality beer. The second and deeper of the two tendencies echoes the wartime propaganda that portrayed Germany as the ultimate public enemy. Although present-day Germany is by no means the chief representative of evil for present-day Americans, the concept of ontological evil in the United States since 1945 bears distinctively German or, more precisely, Nazi features. This stereotype acts as a moral lightning rod, preventing the purity and innocence of America's own motives from being seriously called into question.

Revenge and Revanche

A few days after the atomic bomb was dropped in 1945, the rumor went around Hiroshima hospitals that Japan had exploded a similar weapon over one of America's major cities. A doctor who was present noted: "For the first time since Hiroshima . . . everyone became cheerful and bright. Those who were most seriously injured were the happiest. Jokes were made, and some began to sing the victory song."[50] That same summer, a group of Jewish former members of the Polish resistance, under the leadership of Abba Kovner, planned to poison the water supplies of several German cities until six million Germans had been killed. Twenty years later, the Israeli writer Hanoch Bartov wrote of the sense and purpose behind a similar, fictional act of reprisal: "We'll all go into one city and burn it, street by street, house by house, German by German. Why should it just be us remembering Auschwitz? Let them remember the one city that we'll destroy."[51]

The instinct for revenge is as elementary as thirst or sexual desire. It is also part of that larger behavioral complex of exchange that Marcel Mauss describes as a *fait social total*, or total social phenomenon.[52] According to Mauss, the ritual exchange of objects and actions is generally well-intentioned. Since every gift must be requited with a somewhat greater gift, however, the result is a never-ending spiral of exchange, a competition, like a test of strength or battle. Much like someone who fails to return a greeting, whoever ultimately receives more than he gives disrupts the equilibrium and becomes either an enemy or, if he acknowledges his weakness, the inferior in the social relation.[53] The idiom *to pay back* in the sense of requiting one favor with another—for example, a dinner invitation—can also mean "to take vengeance." Nietzsche's definition of gratitude as revenge is the most concise formulation of the insight that even a good deed or a gift represents an encroachment on the autonomy of the recipient, one that the recipient cannot leave unanswered.

If gifts and good deeds follow the law of unyielding reciprocity, one can imagine how much more stringently that law is enforced when it comes to injustice, pain, or violence. The *Iliad* and its surrounding myths form one long chain of revenge. Hera and Athena plot revenge against Paris. Menelaus calls for a war to recover Helen after her kidnapping. In retaliation for their desecration of his temple, Apollo visits a plague on the Greek army. To avenge the injustice done him by Agamemnon, Achilles provokes a military crisis by refusing to fight. By killing Hector, he avenges Patroclus.

The situation is much the same in the medieval epic. Ganelon, whose betrayal of the hero sets the *Song of Roland* in motion, is motivated by his desire to avenge his belittling demotion by Roland. The *Nibelungenlied* is the great epic of feminine vengeance: Brunhilde takes her revenge for Siegfried's infidelity; Kriemhild exacts hers for Hagen's murder of Siegfried. In Shakespeare, too, Richard, duke of Gloucester, declares in his very first scene that he is bent on bloodshed as retribution for his misshapen form, and vengeance is the core theme of *Hamlet*. The means and conditions for revenge within the modern centralized state, which claims a monopoly on justice and violence, can hardly be more vividly depicted than in the figure of the murderer-king Claudius, who merely looks on as a spectator while his surrogate is killed. Hamlet, on the other hand, exemplifies the corruption of revenge: his vengefulness begins to dissolve as he broods on it, and his melancholy itself may be seen as the neurotic reaction of one who is burning with vengeance but is no longer allowed to act on that impulse.

Beginning in the sixteenth century and parallel to the modern state's prohibition on private acts of vengeance, retribution was decisively formalized and ritualized. In military conflict between sovereign states, the motivations for revenge—restitution for an injustice, punishment for acts of violence—were codified into laws of "legitimate" warfare.[54] At the same time, war itself was rationalized, refined, made to obey rules, and, in Johan Huizinga's formulation, "played" like a game. Eighteenth-century warfare was a seasonal military contest conducted according to set rules, barely distinguishable from an exercise or a tournament, without any great concern for its largely peasant victims, but with an extraordinary degree of cultivated reserve among the officer caste. The central operative mechanism for this culture of war was *revanche*—which was more like redress than revenge. The universally acknowledged ideal of a balance of power proved to be an invisible guiding hand ensuring that no side was ever driven completely from the field of battle and that all parties would be around to take part in the next contest of strength.

Ironically, this culture of war was based on precisely the institution that the state had forbidden within the private sphere: the duel. Although persisting as an archaic relic, dueling had become so formalized and ritualized that it served not to perpetuate but to dissipate the emotional impulse toward revenge. The ideal of the modern duel was not the destruction of an enemy but a sporting encounter free of emotion. "The duel is a contest between men free from hate and passion for revenge," says François Billacois. "The duelists respect and have regard for each other, for the opponent's honor is the sine qua non of one's own."[55]

From its very beginnings, hand-to-hand combat contained something of this cathartic element, as we can observe in the indecisive encounters in the *Iliad* between Hector and Ajax or Diomedes and Glaucus, with their exchanges of gifts, armor, and professions of friendship. The warrior caste of the nineteenth century still lived by the French general Galliffet's words: "In order to be reconciled, we must fight again or, better still, fight together against a common enemy."[56] Victor Hugo writes of two hostile soldiers who fraternize as the best of friends after inflicting wounds on each other: "First they tried to kill each other, then each of the combatants proclaimed his willingness to die for his adversary."[57] The fact that such incidents occurred even in twentieth-century total warfare indicates a kind of anthropological continuity.

For such reconciliation to occur, however, the act of redress has to follow immediately, blow for blow, without any Hamlet-like postponement or reflection. Clausewitz characterizes the psychodynamics of score settling during battle as the "recapture of what has been lost." If the response is not immediate, the result is not catharsis but a psychodynamic block. Freud, who defines a successful (that is, spontaneous) act of revenge as the cathartic abreaction of a traumatic effect, categorizes such a block as hysterical neurosis.[58] Max Scheler calls the decision to wait for a later and more promising opportunity for revenge or retribution, in contrast to immediately striking back, "ressentiment," and Karen Horney's term *vindictiveness* applies to a similar notion.[59] Whatever one calls it, this pattern of behavior serves to create an imaginary (in clinical language, "neurotic-hallucinatory") fantasy world into which the traumatized ego—incapable of either countering the injury or accepting the loss—can retreat and live out its desires.

What neurosis is to the individual, the creation of myths is to the collective. Our three losers' myths—the Lost Cause, the dream of *revanche*, and *im Felde unbesiegt* (undefeated on the field of battle)—all deny that the nation has been defeated and postpone the settling of accounts (most explicitly in *revanche* and most obliquely in the Lost Cause) to an indefinite, messianic future.[60] Such myths (or, in the Freudian term, fantasies), arising from frustrated desires for revenge, are the psychological mechanisms for coming to terms with defeat. Moreover, they are not merely neurotic fictions of the imagination but also healthful protective shields or buffer zones—emotional fortresses—against a reality unbearable to the psyche. Their function can be compared to the coagulation of blood and formation of scabs necessary for wounds to heal, or to the convalescent world of the sanatorium, or lastly (Freud's analogy) to the "reservations" or "nature reserves" in the industrial landscape.[61]

Not all lost wars unleash the impulse toward *revanche*, only those where the losing side is defeated by a single enemy. Defeat at the hands of a coalition lacks the single object necessary for *revanche*. In that situation, the loser concludes that the greater the number of enemies, the greater the honor. "Our newly won honor," wrote Eugen Rosenstock of Germany in 1918, "is to have been vanquished by the entire world, so that we needn't acknowledge the power of any one people over us."[62] His words apply equally well to France after 1815. In both cases, the losing side did not call for *revanche* but demanded *revision* of the war's outcome, making that a central point of its postwar policies and propaganda.[63]

Where *revanche* is not an option—when defeat comes at the hands of a coalition—yet another possibility for psychological compensation presents itself. The losing side can define itself as the equal of the strongest member of the victorious coalition. The loser thereby degrades the other winners as mere hangers-on and scroungers for scraps at the main victor's table and claims the title of runner-up in the order of power, directly behind the leading opponent and ahead of all others. Post-1815 France liked to view itself as the primary power after Great Britain and Russia, one whose continental hegemony was not seriously challenged by "ancillary victors" like Prussia and Austria. Post-1918 Germany took this self-conception one step further, insisting that it had succeeded in subduing its European enemies before America intervened at the last minute to save them. The converse holds true for the junior partners of victorious coalitions. Should they be rewarded with less than what they see as their due, as was the case with Italy in 1919 at Versailles, they quickly come to view themselves as the losers among the winners. Such feelings also arose after 1815 when Prussia, at England's insistence, was denied its private *revanche* for Jena-Auerstedt and Tilsit and in 1918–19 when France was not allowed to indulge its long-standing desire for *revanche*, which included invading Germany, forcing a peace treaty in Berlin, and establishing the Rhine as the new Franco-German border.[64]

From Revanche *to Unconditional Surrender*

Revanche, with its overtones of a gentlemanly settling of accounts, has no place in the total warfare of mass democracy. In total war, military confrontations are fought no longer between mutually respectful warrior castes and ruling dynasties but between the unconstrained popular wills of opposing nations, which see the adversary as the incarnation of evil, an archenemy with whom there can be no common ground or compromise. The only option is to destroy or at least permanently incapacitate the enemy. In its insistence on irreconcilability, the total war of modernity is closer to the religious crusades of the sixteenth and seventeenth centuries and the annihilatory campaigns of antiquity, such as the Third Punic War, than it is to the national conflicts of the nineteenth century, its immediate predecessors, which still largely followed the rules of classic cabinet warfare.[65]

The modern legal term today for the total subjugation of the enemy is *unconditional surrender*. In contrast to classic surrender, which was a contractually negotiated, "honorable" laying down of arms by one warring party, unconditional surrender can only to a limited extent be considered an instrument of international law since it essentially liquidates the losing side as a legal entity. This contradiction dates back to the Civil War, when Lee's unconditional surrender at Appomattox in April 1865 had bearing not just for his army but for the entire Confederacy. Although almost a century would pass until the next unconditional surrenders—by Germany and Japan after the Second World War, which has been described as a "world civil war"—the American Civil War paved the way for total warfare driven by mass democracy and mass media.[66] With its explicit interactions between military strategy and journalistic agitation, the Civil War functioned, according to Eric L. McKitrick, "almost as an expanded political platform." McKitrick draws some remarkable conclusions about the psychology of triumph and subjugation in mass democracies: "The victor needs to be assured that his triumph has been invested with the fullest spiritual and ceremonial meaning. He must know that his expenditures have gone for something, that his objectives have been accomplished, and that the righteousness of his principles has been given its vindication. . . . He must have ritual proofs. The conquered enemy must be prepared to give symbolic satisfactions as well as physical surrender; he must . . . 'act out' his defeat."[67]

Should the conquered enemy, like the post-1865 South, not fulfill this "protocol of defeat," the victor will feel cheated of his triumph and react by imposing punitive measures. These, in turn, demand a counterreaction from the losing side, leading to a progressive hardening of the fronts, a kind of cold war.[68] McKitrick describes the ressentiment-free unconditional surrenders by Germany and Japan in 1945 as having lived up to the protocol of defeat. Here, however, he risks confusing cause with effect. The two societies in question were indeed free of ressentiment toward the victor, but not because they wanted to live up to their unconditional surrenders; rather, having been utterly destroyed both physically and morally, they were simply too exhausted to generate the energy needed for ressentiment. There are thus degrees of defeat and capitulation. As long as losing nations have an intact national identity at their command, they will stubbornly refuse to comply with the victor's demands for moral and spiritual surrender through demonstrations of regret, conversion, and willingness to be reeducated. The situation is different when, together with the physical properties of a nation, its spiritual and moral backbone has been broken. The losers in 1865, 1871, and even 1918 had not yet reached this nadir.

Renewal

After the initial shock has passed and defeat is seen no longer as a national catastrophe but as a kind of liberation and salvation, its forward-looking, almost missionary aspect comes to the fore. In the dreamland state, the loser describes the world from which defeat has freed him much like a convert recalling his former life of sin. In post-Sedan France, observers spoke of the "complete paralysis," the "forty years of torpor," and "the Chinese lethargy into which the empire had plunged us," declaring that it had taken Krupp-manufactured cannons to awaken the nation from decadence and stagnation.[69] William Gilmore Simms described the prewar corruption of the American South as a "scum" that could only be skimmed off by war and defeat.[70] In Germany, the collapse of the Wilhelminian empire was similarly greeted as an opportunity for national renewal.

The conception of war as a purifying and renewing force is the most important legacy granted to the defeated. Although the dreamland euphoria may not last any longer than the feelings of elation at war's outbreak, it does not vanish altogether. Instead, it becomes part of the ongoing, long-term interpretation of events. Alongside their perennial identification with the Passion of Christ, defeated nations look for connections with history to provide a point of orientation. Anchoring one's defeat within the tradition of history's great losers offers both meaning and consolation. For one thing, it is an honor to join the ranks of tragic-heroic forefathers. In addition, the lesson is quickly learned that defeat has its advantages. Naturally, only those past defeats that have led to periods of national renewal are invoked. In both German and French nineteenth-century historiography, Jena-Auerstedt became a symbol for the demise of Old Prussia and the birth of the new reformed state. After 1871, the Third Republic declared Sedan to be the Jena-Auerstedt of the Second Empire and justified its reforms with reference to Wilhelm von Humboldt, Friedrich von Stein, General Gerhard Johann Scharnhorst, and Friedrich Ludwig Jahn, the modernizers of Prussia. In Germany, November 1918 was compared to October 1806, and hopes were offered that the post-Jena sequence of reform and war of liberation would be repeated. In this way, France and Germany traded off the lead part in their duet between 1806 and 1918, with each side's cycle of damnation, purgatory, and rebirth alternately setting the tone. The opponent's latest victory was seen as the direct result of the defeat that had preceded it. The current loser was thus cast as the author of his enemy's victory, just as the current victor (and inevitable loser of the next round) would sire the other side's future victory.

If defeat is understood as a national crisis of infirmity and decadence from which the nation, having purged itself, emerges healthier and stronger than before, the question remains: What of the poisons that prompted the crisis in the first place? It is astonishing how easily the goals and agendas for which nations go to war are forgotten. In the post-1865 American South, no serious resistance was mounted to the abolition of slavery. No one in post-1871 France voiced any further desire to advance the Franco-German border to the Rhine or expressed any yearning for continental hegemony. Likewise, post-1918 Germany abandoned its "*Weltmacht*" aspirations and dismissed the construction of a naval fleet to rival England's as an unfortunate idiosyncrasy of Emperor Wilhelm II's.

While defeat is denied on *one* level of consciousness, it can at the same time result in extraordinary mental flexibility on another, a paradox that is explained by the vanquished nation's postwar embrace of a glorious past at the very moment when defeat draws the curtain on a collectively dreamt imperialist future. By rejecting the path that led to war and defeat as an error, a nation is able at the same time to declare the stretch of history before the mistaken detour to be more consonant with its spirit, destiny, and true character. Jeffersonian America, post-1789 France, the Germany of the anti-Napoleonic campaigns, and the Revolution of 1848—these legacies were, for the generations of 1865, 1871, and 1918, respectively, signposts from an untarnished past that pointed the way toward a harmonious future.[71]

This future promised not only internal renewal but a new role for the nation in the international community. It is a short step from understanding defeat as an act of purification, humility, and sacrifice—a crucifixion of sorts—to laying claim to spiritual and moral leadership in world affairs. The three loser nations discussed here took this step by transforming their philosophies of defeat into a moral bulwark for the protection of all humanity. To accept their own defeat as a verdict by the court of world history was one thing; to sit idly by while all humanity was threatened by future disaster was quite another. Who, they reasoned, was better equipped to act as moral standard-bearer against such evils than those who had only recently stared them in the face?

What the American South had to offer the world, along with its embracing the end of slavery, was the warning that the political equality of blacks must be resisted at all costs. "When [the South] defended Slavery by her arms," wrote one Southerner following the war, "she was single-handed, and encountered the antipathies of the whole world; now, when she asserts the ultimate supremacy of the white man, she has not lost her cause, but merely developed its higher significance, and in the new contest, she stands with a firm political alliance in the North . . . and with the sympathies of all generous and enlightened humanity upon her."[72] Swearing off its imperialist past, post-1871 France recommended itself as a bastion of humanity and civilization against the German *barbarie scientifique* that threatened the whole of the civilized world. Post-1918 Germany, having denounced its Wilhelminian mistake, offered its threefold services as a bulwark against the flood of Russian Bolshevism, a bastion against American commercialism, and a champion for the colonial world—in short, as the guide to a "third path" between capitalism and communism.

All three cultures aspired to the role of moral authority that the rest of the world—including the victors—would find indispensable. Only the losers, they argued, commanded such authority because only they had suffered through the Passion and emerged on the other side, beyond all considerations of earthly power. However, while the problem of moral force could be satisfactorily solved by this deft if quixotic twist, the question of how to regain *real* power was infinitely more difficult. As even the most impassioned defeat moralists had to acknowledge, the world of realities was determined by the victor.

Learning from the Victor

It is well known that the United States's intervention in 1917 transformed the Great War into a world crusade. What is less well known is the fact that the two men most responsible for this crusade both came from the South and had both experienced the demise of the Confederacy in childhood. Woodrow Wilson, whose name is forever connected with the introduction of moral considerations into international relations, was the first Southerner elected to the presidency since the Civil War. Walter Hines Page, before becoming Wilson's ambassador in London, had made a name for himself as a leading spokesman for the New South reform program. And it was Page who was the main driving force behind American intervention in World War I.

The careers of Wilson and Page help elucidate how losers learn from their conquerors. For the United States, intervention in 1917 on the side of the good (liberal-democratic) Entente against evil (militaristic) Germany recapitulated Abraham Lincoln's crusade against the South, which had sinned against both the North and humanity. Wilson's call for the abolition of the Central European military monarchy echoed the abolitionists' demand for the eradication of slavery.[73] Fifty years later, the opportunity arose to transfer the moral blight incurred by the South onto the contemporary world enemy Germany. By taking to the field of battle side by side with its former conqueror against the new enemy of humankind, the South could confirm its own long-coveted acceptance into the ranks of the victors.[74] This was the same mechanism that West Germany happily applied after the demise of Nazism, in its passionate identification with the West during the Cold War, and imposed even more happily on East Germany after 1989, this time itself gleaming with the shine of victory.

Losers imitate winners almost by reflex, as shown by the New South's emulation of the Yankee model, the reforms of the French army and educational system along Prussian-German lines, or the imitation of America by Germany after 1918 and 1945.[75] For decades, the New South, of which Wilson and Page were both fervent adherents, had been little more than a program of modernization and industrialization along Northern lines. Page's nickname at the time, the "Southern Yankee," derisively underscored his obsession with learning lessons from the victor, and figures similar to Page and Wilson emerged in France and Germany to set the tone after those countries' defeats.

Earlier examples of victor imitation abound. With Scotland's decisive eighteenth-century defeat in its long war of independence against England, the Scottish intelligentsia had no qualms about embracing the modernity represented by England. The result was the Scottish Enlightenment of David Hume and Adam Smith, as well as of the philosopher Dugald Stewart and the historians Adam Ferguson and William Robertson, who all, like the German idealist philosophers after 1806, subjected the new commercial order created by England to theoretical reflection.[76] France, whose bourgeoisie was perennially open to English influences and trends in its struggle against absolutism, experienced its two greatest waves of Anglomania after its defeats in the Seven Years War and at Waterloo.[77] And even as the French Republic conquered one part of Germany after another during the 1790s, German patriots and Francophobes like Ernst Moritz Arndt called on their nation to learn from the republican institutions and virtues of France.[78]

As these examples suggest, learning from the victor involves not just simple adoption or imitation but a complex, multivalent process of assimilation and cultural adaptation similar to what Thorstein Veblen describes in the context of technology and economics as "borrowing." The only superiority that "borrowing" societies grant their "creditors" is that of greater material progress and modernity, above all in technology and organization. The borrower is not interested in the soul, the spirit, or the cultural identity of the creditor nation. On the contrary, modernization along the lines set by the victor is, from the perspective of the borrower, nothing more than a useful means toward his own spiritual and cultural revitalization and regeneration. The goal of all borrowing is ultimately to bankrupt the creditor—to demonstrate that his technological, organizational, and economic innovations achieve their true purpose and attain absolute fulfillment only when adapted and enriched by the spirit and the culture of the loser. To invoke Karl Marx, one could almost say that the task of the downtrodden is to rescue innovation from its masters, delivering it from alienation.[79]

One last word on the choice of the three national defeats I treat in this book—the American Confederacy's in 1865, France's in 1870–71, and Germany's in 1918. The fifty years they span witnessed the final transition from the "civilized" pursuit of war and peace to the unsparing and unlimited warfare of the twentieth century. While this history of rebarbarization has been chronicled and reflected on exhaustively—there are entire libraries on each of the three wars in question—its psychological and cultural fallout remains largely unexplored.

THE AMERICAN SOUTH

The American Civil War squats in the middle of the nineteenth century like a monstrous irony. In Europe, the dominant powers had rationalized, even civilized warfare so that outcomes were reached quickly on precisely delimited battlefields, without great bloodshed—or even significant inconvenience—among civilian populations. Meanwhile, the United States, the nation that had been the embodiment of peaceful civic progress and republican reason, plunged into war with a bellicose fury that had not been seen since the Wars of Religion. It seemed incomprehensible that such a young, prosperous, and promising nation state could be determined to destroy itself so *prematurely.* Was this the work of an Old Testament God who, in disappointment or anger, had abandoned his people so soon after he had chosen them?

A few statistics suffice to illustrate the extent of the human and material destruction during the Civil War. The nation as a whole suffered 620,000 casualties, or 2 percent of its (white) population, more than in the two world wars and the Korean War combined. Add to that the destruction of territory and property: on the one hand, the systematic razing of cities, together with the burning of plantations and large stretches of agricultural land (the practice known as "Shermanizing"); on the other, the "disappropriation," in the form of the emancipation of slaves, of a capital resource whose estimated value was some four billion dollars.

It is clear from the statistics who the main loser was. The Confederacy bore the brunt of the wartime destruction. The 260,000 Southerners who fell in the war, out of a total white population of 5.5 million, represented a casualty rate of 5 percent, compared with 1.8 percent in the North. The South lost 20 percent of its white adult male population—an extraordinarily exact parallel to German casualties during World War II.[1] The long-term damage these losses inflicted on the South's social and economic fabric is evident in such poignant facts as that a fifth of Mississippi's first postwar state budget was devoted to the production of prosthetic limbs for those maimed in the fighting.[2]

Twentieth-century historiography has treated the American Civil War as the first example of total warfare and as a precursor to the two world wars. This view, while certainly true, obscures what is perhaps a more obvious comparison. Until 1861, the American experience of war was largely of the colonial variety. The military campaigns against Native Americans followed different rules from those governing a regular war between two armies. The goal of the Indian wars was not the destruction of the enemy's forces, but the destruction of the enemies themselves. The wars were as much a part of land clearing as the deforestation of primeval woodlands and the burning of the prairies. At the beginning of one such Indian campaign, General Philip Henry Sheridan issued an order to his subcommanders: "Let it be a campaign of annihilation, obliteration, and complete destruction."[3] Sheridan and his more famous colleague William T. Sherman would continue their scorched-earth policy during the Civil War. The only strategic component omitted when they transferred this practice from a colonial to an internal enemy (that is, one who belonged to their own civilization) was genocide.

A few years after the end of the Civil War, Sheridan was invited to meet Prussia's general staff during that country's war against France. He was astonished by the traditional tactics used by Prussian general Helmut von Moltke and recommended that the Prussians follow Sherman's and his own example: "The proper strategy consists in . . . causing the inhabitants so much suffering that they must long for peace, and force the government to demand it. The people must be left nothing but their eyes to weep with over the war."[4] Before embracing the practice of total warfare, however, most military commanders in the North had had to overcome ethical resistance similar to that of Moltke. The military high commander during the first phase of the Civil War, General George B. McClellan, was unwilling to draw the enemy civilian population into the fighting as a way of offsetting the South's military and strategic superiority. It was not until McClellan was replaced by Sherman and Ulysses S. Grant that the path was cleared for total warfare. As the side on whose territory the fighting was conducted, and that would therefore suffer most from total war, the South understandably rejected such practices. Nonetheless, it would be incorrect to say that the Confederacy refused to engage in total warfare just because it lacked the opportunity to carry it to the enemy. In the one instance when the South did operate in Northern territory, the campaign of Gettysburg, the Confederate army largely adhered to the rules of traditional warfare. The only exception was the destruction of Chambersburg, Pennsylvania, and even there Robert E. Lee authorized the burning of the town not to inaugurate a larger strategy but as an act of retribution for the Southern cities destroyed by the North. As the commander who carried out the action, General Jubal Early, stated: "I came to the conclusion that it was time to open the eyes of the North to [the barbarism of their methods], by an example in the way of retaliation."[5]

Exceptionalism

Military ethics was only one of many areas in which North and South differed. The separate identities of North and South date back to the establishment of the first British colonies in North America. The distinct geography and climate of the two regions gave rise to both economic and mythological dissimilarities. The prevailing image of the North, with its harsh winters and largely Puritan settlers, was that of the wilderness: the world after the fall from grace and Adam and Eve's expulsion from Eden. In contrast, the non-Puritan South with its friendlier climate became heir to the Elizabethan conception of the New World as a garden, an earthly paradise. Whereas New England Puritans devoted their lives to transforming the wilderness back into Eden through hard work, the purpose of life for the Virginians (as Northerners referred to all inhabitants of the South during the eighteenth century) was the epicurean enjoyment of the garden that Providence had bestowed on them.[6] The social and economic systems that evolved in the two regions, free wage labor in the North and slavery in the South, resulted from the interplay of climatological, ideological, and mythological differences. It is moot whether the South "opted for" slavery in order to maintain its epicurean lifestyle, while the North valorized hard work as the key to salvation, or whether these mentalities developed out of the existing economic systems. By the eighteenth century, the separate economic, social, and cultural identities of the two regions were well established.

Upper-class European visitors found that the "Americanism" first identified by Alexis de Tocqueville applied above all, perhaps even exclusively, to the North. The South appeared by comparison more European and aristocratic. After the Civil War, one liberal English publisher and detractor of the Confederacy, William Hepworth Dixon, summed up what generations of European travelers since the eighteenth century had perceived as the *cultural* superiority of the South over the North:

A tourist from the Old World—one of the idler classes—found himself much at home in these country mansions. The houses were well planned and built; the furniture was rich; the table and the wine were good; the books, the prints, the music, were such as he had known in Europe. . . . The South was made pleasant to its English guest; for the people felt that the English were of nearer kin to them than their Yankee brethren. A sunny sky, a smiling hostess, an idle life, and a luxurious couch, led him softly to forget the foundations on which that seducing fabric stood. In the Northern States such a lotus-eater would have found but little to his taste. The country-houses . . . were not so spacious and so splendid as in the South; the climate was much colder; and the delights of lounging were much less. He had nothing to do, and nobody had time to help him. The men being all intent on their affairs, they neither hunted, fished, nor danced; they talked of scarcely anything but their mills, their mines, their roads, their fisheries; they were always eager, hurried, and absorbed, as though the universe hung upon their arms, and they feared to let it fall. . . . In the . . . sunny Southern houses, with their long verandas, their pleasant lawns, no man was busy, no woman was in haste. Every one had time for wit, for compliment, for small talk.[7]

The hardworking, profit-obsessed, religious/moral-fundamentalist Yankee became the embodiment of New England, while the contemplative, cultivated gentleman—or "cavalier," as he would later be called—came to represent the South. As long as their respective regions functioned as a harmonious unit, the two types could co-exist without rancor. There is nary a hint of distrust or distaste in James Fenimore Cooper's 1828 observation "that in proportion to the population, there are more men who belong to what is termed the class of gentlemen, in the old southern States of America than in any other country of the world. . . . I do not know where to find gentlemen of better air or better breeding throughout, than most of those I have met in the southern Atlantic States."[8] The Puritan North did not resent the South for prizing the classics of antiquity above the King James Bible, nor did it object that the highest political offices in the land, from the presidency to the Senate to the Supreme Court, as well as the leadership of the military, were disproportionately occupied by Southerners trained in classical rhetoric.[9] As Southerner James D. B. DeBow wrote in 1851: "The Southern slave states of Greece and Rome had given to the world all the civilization, laws and government which antiquity offered. . . . The civilization of the world has come from the South as all history shows."[10] The South's conceit that it produced the Catos, Ciceros, and Scipios of the American republic and its insistence that its economic system was the extension of classical models attracted scant opposition as long as slavery was considered morally acceptable and as long as the South remained the superior within the national economy.

Beginning in 1830, however, the South was put on the defensive on both fronts. Under President Andrew Jackson, industrialization in the North took off at a furious pace, and the North soon outstripped the South economically. At the same time, slavery came in for increasing moral criticism. The South suffered a bout of collective panic after the bloody slave rebellion led by Nat Turner in 1831, and within a year open debates on the morality of slavery had become taboo. The South's suppression of all discussion put an end to its traditional role as the national seat of enlightenment.[11]

This double development upset the balance of economic and political power between the two regions, to the South's manifest disadvantage. The reaction there, as in other cases of historical decline, was varied. As cultural historian Rollin G. Osterweis puts it, the South was "slipping into the position of a minority people under attack."[12] Until 1830, the North had acted as an agent of the plantation in all its significant economic activities, including the slave trade, the transportation of tobacco and cotton to Europe, and credit and finance. It was therefore no wonder that the South felt abandoned and betrayed by the North's sudden moral and economic turnaround. In the decades before the Civil War, Southerners were full of resentment at the moral hypocrisy of former slave-trade profiteers in Boston and at the selective memory of the North in general as to the origins of its wealth. There was also a mood of elegiac pessimism comparable to that of Don Fabrizio in Giuseppe di Lampedusa's novel *The Leopard*, who sees in the new relations of power the inevitable end of his civilization. "We, who once swayed the councils of the Union, find our power gone, and our influence on the wane," mourned one member of Virginia's traditional elite in 1852. "As the other States accumulate the means of material greatness, and glide past us on the road to wealth and empire, we slight the warnings of statistics, and drive lazily along the fields of ancient customs." Hugh Swinton Legaré, an exemplary representative of the Southern politician-intellectual, remarked as early as 1832: "We are (I am quite sure) the *last* of the *race* of South Carolina. I see nothing before us but decay and downfall."[13] Cynics remarked: "We occupy virtually the same relation to the Yankee that the negroes do to us."[14]

Another reaction to the challenges suddenly posed by the North was evident in the yearning to secede. The roots of secession can be found in a new definition of slavery that began to gain currency among Southerners. Before 1830, slavery had been viewed in both the South and the North as a necessary evil. Within a few years, however, it had become nothing less than the basis of a new national doctrine, grounded in theology, philosophy, and sociology, of the Southern plantation system's superiority over the industral capitalism of the North.

Slavery as "Socialism"

"We have the wolf by the ears, and we can neither hold him nor safely let him go. Justice is in one scale, and self-preservation in the other."[15] Thomas Jefferson's words, spoken in the age of enlightenment and the rights of man, long epitomized the prevailing sentiment in the South toward the problem of slavery. Before the South broke off the slavery debate in 1830, quashing any further questioning of the system, the discussion was conducted there with an intensity that had no equivalent in the North. As historian C. Vann

Woodward points out, Southern critics of slavery "spoke against the effect on the master as well as on the slave; they exposed the harm done to the manners and morals of the South as well as its economy and society. Nor were the critics mere misfits and radicals. They included men of influence and standing—politicians, editors, professors, and clergymen. Antislavery thought appeared in respectable newspapers. . . . In the 1820s the slave states contained a great many more antislavery societies than the free states and furnished leadership for the movement in the country."[16]

Within a decade, however, all that had changed. Justifying slavery as its "peculiar institution," the South began its counterreformation against the antislavery agitation emerging in the North. The jesuitic cleverness applied to this task is fascinating even today. Strategically, the notion of the peculiar institution was a retreat into the offensive. Proslavery theoreticians depicted the system less as a positive good in its own right than as an alternative to unconstrained capitalist exploitation. For them, the antithesis of slavery was not freedom but wage labor. "We are all, North and South, engaged in the White Slave Trade," argued George Fitzhugh, "and he who succeeds best, is esteemed most respectable. It is far more cruel than the Black Slave Trade, because it exacts more of its slaves, and neither protects nor governs them." Attacking the industrial capitalists of the North, he continued: "You, with the command over labor which your capital gives you, are a slave owner—a master, without the obligations of a master. They who work for you, who create your income, are slaves, without the rights of slaves."[17] John C. Calhoun, the preeminent Southern statesman in the decades preceding the Civil War, defined slavery as a system in which the conflict between capital and labor was resolved by the slave owner's possessing both.[18]

Though by no means socialists themselves, politician-intellectuals like Calhoun and Fitzhugh were intimately familiar with the socialist literature of their day, and their arguments often resembled those of socialism. "Every plantation is an organized community," wrote Fitzhugh's contemporary William Grayson. He cited the ideas of the

French utopian socialist Charles Fourier, whose vision of the "phalanstery" perfectly described the plantation, "where all work, where each member gets subsistence and a home and the more industrious larger pay and profits to their own superior industry."[19] For Fitzhugh, the most widely read and radical proponent of this school, the ideas of slavery and socialism were interchangeable. "Slavery is a form, and the very best form of socialism," he writes in his *Sociology for the South* (1854), whereas in another passage he asserts, with a whiff of sarcasm, that socialism is "the new fashionable name for slavery."[20] Fitzhugh himself was introduced to Fourier's thought through the writings of Horace Greeley, and the phalanstery was a model Fitzhugh saw as a possible form of social order, lacking only a patriarchal leader. Of one of Greeley's projects, Fitzhugh remarked: "Socialism with such [a] despotic head, approaches very near to Southern slavery. Add a Virginian overseer to Mr. Greeley's Phalansteries, and Mr. Greeley and we would have little to quarrel about." In light of this affinity, Fitzhugh's explicitly stated goal of subjecting the white proletariat to slavery eerily anticipates the authoritarian socialism of the twentieth century.

As with every ideology, there was a kernel of truth to the idea of slavery as a positive good and a human right. Even visitors from Europe and the North who were dedicated opponents of slavery admitted as much. Michel Chevalier found the majority of slaves in the 1830s to be "less severely tasked, better fed, and better taken care of than most peasants in Europe. Their rapid increase attests their easy condition."[21] Charles Francis Adams Jr., a passionate abolitionist who became acquainted with the South firsthand as a soldier in the Union Army, confessed: "The conviction is forcing itself upon me that African slavery, as it existed in our slave states, was indeed a patriarchal institution under which the slaves were not, as a whole, unhappy, cruelly treated or overworked."[22]

It may seem ironic that, half a century after Jefferson wrote the Declaration of Independence, a number of fellow Southerners would declare slavery the system that best ensured the rights of man. But this new interpretation of an old institution was the logical outgrowth of the desire to formulate a specific historical mission for the American South. The sharpening of the language Southerners used to describe themselves and their Northern rivals after 1830 was one important aspect of this project. As the years passed, the nickname "Yankee" lost its affectionate connotations and increasingly came to evoke a gaunt, cold, greedy, miserly, and sanctimonious bigot. When the Yankee talked about God, Southerners believed, he meant Mammon; when he condemned slavery in the South as a mortal sin, he concealed both his own role in the slave trade and the Negroes' pariah status in his own neck of the woods. Indeed, in the South's understanding of the situation, the Yankee was the one actually responsible for the introduction of slavery to the colonies. It was he who, in his thirst for profits, had opened the slave trade in which the Southern farmer-planter was merely the innocent buyer, the dupe of the system. Mary Boykin Chestnut, for instance, wrote in her diary in 1861: "They say our crowning misdemeanor is to hold in slavery still those Africans they brought over here from Africa, or sold to us when they found to own them did not pay. They gradually slid them off down here, giving themselves years to get rid of them in a remunerative way."[23]

A precursor to the antisemitic bogeyman of the late nineteenth and early twentieth centuries, the Yankee was the Shylock from whose viselike clutches the South had to free itself in order to survive. The only means available was a war of independence like the one the colonies had waged against England a few generations before. And indeed the thesis of a second Revolutionary War provided the moral and legal framework for Southern secession. It became an article of faith allowing the South to band together in 1861 and eliciting an astonishing sympathy for the Confederacy in Europe, which was otherwise opposed to slavery.[24]

A Nation of Knights

The hardening of language between North and South in the years 1830–60 was also signaled by the replacement of the word *gentleman* by the term *cavalier* in the Southern vocabulary. This was nothing less than an act of linguistic secession. Whereas no one had any reservations about the positive character of the gentleman, with even the North acknowledging the South's superior capacity for producing this ideal type, the rise of the cavalier brought with it division and enmity. For Northerners, the cavalier was the direct descendant of the Spanish aristocrat, with all his negative attributes: arrogance, laziness, cruelty, and decadence. Moreover, the term made explicit reference to the civil war in seventeenth-century England. Just as the royalist Cavaliers had defended a higher culture against the attacks of the Puritan Roundheads, the cavalier South was now taking a stand against the Yankee Roundhead North.

According to this "invented tradition" that emerged in the prewar years, the colonies had been settled by two separate, incompatible groups, the North by Puritan Roundheads "squabbling, fighting, singing psalms, burning witches, and talking about liberty," the South by cavaliers, "persons belonging to the blood and race of the reigning family . . . directly descended from the Norman Barons of William the Conqueror, a race distinguished, in its earliest history, for its warlike and fearless character, a race, in all time since, renowned for its gallantry, its honor, its gentleness and its intellect."[25] Moreover, the North was not only puritanical and fanatic in its convictions but plebeian in its ancestry. Yankees, Roundheads, and Anglo-Saxons belonged to a single tribe, one that had never gotten over its defeat at Hastings in 1066 and that had developed the typical resentment of a subjugated people toward a superior race. By contrast, everyone in the South had aristocratic or even regal blood in his or her veins. Robert E. Lee, later to become the Confederacy's national hero, was depicted as the descendant of everyone from Robert the Bruce of Scotland to Lancelot Lee, a follower of William the

Conqueror. The family chronicles of humble farmers often contained such passages as "Hans Muller, a carpenter by trade and the son of Max Muller, who was the son of a Hamburg merchant and the daughter of a German emperor."[26] Even classical antiquity turned up in Southern family history. Before 1830, appreciation of Athens's and Rome's contribution to Southern culture was largely confined to the educated elite. But in the years that followed, direct family lineages were frequently "traced" back to the age of Pericles— a glorious early example of a civilization based on slavery—and brazenly announced to the world as proven fact.[27]

The South thus experienced the historical events of 1830–60 on two symbolic levels: as a repeat of the American rebellion against England and as a continuation of the seventeenth-century English civil war, with the South as the reincarnated Cavaliers and the North as the Roundheads. In addition, the South would discover a historical drama in which it could recognize its own cause even more clearly.

The Scottish Model

Scotland was the inspiration for romantic movements throughout Europe and North America in the late eighteenth century. The various national variants of romanticism chose among the corpus of material provided by James McPherson and his successors, adapting whatever seemed most suitable to their own purposes. For the American colonies and the young United States, Scotland served above all as a political and cultural role model. Scotland was the land of perpetual rebellion against England, a nation that defended itself valiantly against its mighty neighbor, forever coming out on the losing end and yet always demonstrating its virtue, its dignity, its moral strength, and its character. Scotland was the model of an anti-England that young America could emulate in its struggle to form itself into an independent nation. True to the dictum that nothing unites like a common enemy, Scotland's "protest history" and the idea of "greedy Egypt/England holding Israel/Scotland in bondage" were embraced across the Atlantic as a national cause.[28]

The South occupied a special place within this American-Scottish connection, both economically (since Glasgow—and not London—was the center of the eighteenth-century tobacco trade, the most important economic activity in the colonies) and in terms of immigration. With every unsuccessful rebellion, a wave of Scottish immigrants like William Faulkner's literary dynasty, the Compsons—poured into America, largely into the South, where the English-Puritan influence was weaker than in the North. According to recent research on the history of emigration, many people in the South were indeed of Scottish ancestry, if not the aristocratic one of myth.[29] If we replace the imaginary cavaliers of the house of Stuart with the masses of farmers and peasants who actually emigrated from Scotland, we get a more or less accurate picture of Southern heritage, as well as an appreciation for the Scotland-obsessed culture of the South. "The Scottish tradition . . . must have had a place in the 'cultural baggage' which the Scotch-Irish pioneer carried with him," Rollin Osterweis writes, "even if it were only in the form of fragmentary folk ballads and crude legends. . . . The tradition of the 'clan gathering about the chief,' accepting his leadership without question in times of stress, is familiar to every student of the history of Scotland. The Southern farmer displays an instinctive tendency to 'stand to his captain,' to look to his aristocratic neighbor for leadership, whenever the need arises."[30]

Other symbols of Scottish independence were adopted after 1861, such as the St. Andrew's Cross, appropriated for the war flag of the Confederacy, and the Highlanders' burning cross, which, in another transposition of literature into reality, became the chief symbol of the Ku Klux Klan, whose very name left no doubt as to which tradition was being invoked.[31] The history of unsuccessful Scottish rebellions—above all the final one, which was led by the twenty-year-old pretender Charles Edward and was put down at the battle of Culloden in 1745—was retold in countless tales and songs. Bonnie Prince Charlie and his "lost cause" became central to the folklore of the South, a figure who would rise up and intervene in times of national crisis.

Walter Scottland

The one person whose influence is acknowledged by virtually all historians of the antebellum South is Sir Walter Scott. "While the rest of America read Scott with enthusiasm," Osterweis records, "the South assimilated his works into [its] very being." W. J. Cash writes: "Scott was bodily taken over by the South and incorporated into the Southern people's vision of themselves." Edmund Wilson notes that Scott exercised an "intoxicating effect" on the South. And Mark Twain asserted in 1883 that the "Sir Walter disease" had left the South permanently incapable of apprehending reality: "Sir Walter had so large a hand in making Southern character, as it existed before the War, that he is in great measure responsible for the War."[32] Just as historians date the beginning of Southern separatism to 1830, so, too, do the advocates of the Walter Scottland thesis.[33] Before then, the South didn't respond to Scott's novels any differently from the North or the rest of the world. Only in subsequent decades did the South begin to internalize Scott's literature to the extent that, as Osterweis says, "instead of looking awkwardly for the days of knighthood . . . [it was] convinced that it [was] living in them."[34]

Scott, however, was a complex and varied author. Which of his novels was the South's favorite source? The immediate assumption will be that it was the chronicler of the Scottish lost-cause rebellions, the author of *Waverly*, whom the South selected as its new Virgil. *Waverly* would seem to be a parable for and an elegy to the lifestyle, the self-conception, and the historical situation of the South. In the story of the blue-blooded clan that takes to the battlefield against a materially superior, more efficient, but coldly mercantilist England, the South could hardly fail to recognize itself. The fact that the Scots were defeated could only cathartically confirm the South's sense of its own worth. *Waverly* was perfectly suited to be the national epic for the South, much as the *Song of Roland* and the *Nibelung-enlied* were for nineteenth-century France and Germany. Nothing seems to elevate a nation more than the demise of its heroes in hopeless struggle against a faceless mass of invaders, whether they go under the name of the English, the Saracens, or Etzel's Huns.

Yet it was not primarily Scott's lost-cause novels (*Rob Roy* and *Red Gauntlet*, along with *Waverly*) but rather his medieval romances, such as *Ivanhoe*, that fired the imagination of Southern readers. In contrast to *Waverly*, with its tragic, elegiac mood, *Ivanhoe* is boisterous, active, colorful, and vivid. Scott's fictional treatment of the Middle Ages, however, is not the sentimental and one-dimensional picture the Victorian public saw it as. It is full of ironic ruptures and develops the motif of a struggle between a venerable but obsolete past and a prosaic present. But these subtleties are obscured by the lavishly romantic medieval accoutrements, which were the exclusive interest of Southern readers. It is easy to see an escapist mechanism at work in this selective reading. And indeed, the implicit assumption of the Walter Scottland thesis is that the South withdrew into a mythical fortress of romantic chivalry free from all disturbing elements of reality, barricading itself against the outside world or—which amounts to the same thing—encountering it only as an Ivanhoe-Quixote.

But this interpretation overstates the importance of the cult of chivalry. Southerners may indeed have donned knightly garb with ridiculous frequency (contemporary accounts describe the South as a "fairyland where young men saw themselves as knights going to a tournament and girls were Queens of Love and Beauty rewarding them"); the reality, however, was more complex.[35] The South's simultaneous identification with the Scottish clans, the Stuart cavaliers, and the Lost Cause makes it impossible to ignore the concurrent elegiac mood. Although perhaps more subtle than the identification with chivalry, the South's preoccupation with images of defeat and demise was no less significant. How else can one account for the immediate emergence of the Lost Cause as the South's central myth after the collapse of the Confederacy? Myths are often kept in reserve, left to wait their turn, and the Lost Cause in all its continuations and variations is no exception. Historian Michael O'Brien concisely sums up the situation: "Certainly few cultures have been better prepared ideologically for the disaster of war. Ruins are vivid in Southern thought long before Columbia was reduced to ashes."[36]

The image of the South as Walter Scottland remains valid, but it is necessary to differentiate between two discrete versions of it. On the one hand, there was Ivanhoe Land, a world of passionate escapism and whistling in the dark, as naive as it was carefree. On the other, there was Waverly Land, an elegiac world of imminent decline and demise. It is hardly unique for the mood of a nation to be split in this way; indeed, tensions, ruptures, and doubts do not follow clear group or regional lines and are often present in a single individual. The remarkable thing about the mentality of the prewar South was that, despite the confusion and ambivalence created by the two contradictory moods, they conformed to clearly distinguishable regional borders. The cult of chivalry was concentrated in the Cotton Belt, the territories in the Deep South colonized after 1800 (Alabama and Mississippi), while the elegiac set the tone in the Old South (Virginia and the Carolinas). Significantly, these two regions also differed in their economic, social, and cultural structures. The picture of a stagnant South lagging behind the North is not sufficiently nuanced. It was not the entire economy of the South but rather only that of the Old South that turned sluggish after 1830. The new Cotton South, propelled by constantly rising prices for its staple product, experienced an economic boom comparable to that of the industrializing North. Moreover, in their attitudes toward technology and economics, the agrarian cotton barons were closer to the industrialists of the North than they were to their farmer colleagues in the Old South, who still managed their estates in eighteenth-century style. As recent studies have demonstrated, the cotton planters were a generation of entrepreneurs, so-called new men, who probably would have made their way equally well in the industrial centers of Pennsylvania, Ohio, and Illinois.[37] The single, all-decisive factor that distinguished them from their counterparts in the North was that even the most modern, dynamic, capitalist cotton planter was a slave owner, bound to a system that possessed regional—but not global—validity. The slave economy was like a reservation, allowed to exist only in a restricted and perpetually shrinking area, outside which the capital invested in slaves was no longer legal tender. Slavery yoked the entrepreneurs of the New South to the mugwumps of the Old South, ensuring that neither could avoid their joint destiny.*

If the Scottian cult of chivalry blossomed primarily in the economically vibrant New South, while finding noticeably less resonance in the Old, then the thesis of the escapist function of the cult obviously requires revision. The purpose behind all the medieval mimicry was not to suppress the reality of stagnation and to flee from social decline via romance but to dress up and decorate what was actually an ongoing process of economic modernization and expansion. Scott's knightly romanticism played a role in the South similar to that of Richard Wagner's Teutonic mythology in Prussian-led Germany. The "exceptional" path toward modernization taken by the South and by Prussian Germany is well summed up by Barrington Moore Jr.'s formulation: "a capitalist civilization . . . but hardly a bourgeois one."[38]

America's Sparta

When the South embarked on the Civil War in 1861, it seemed to have no hope of winning it. The material superiority of the North was breathtaking: it possessed five times the population and almost ten times the industrial production capacity for goods essential for

---

*The term *mugwump*, of Algonquian derivation, originally referred to dissident Northern Republicans in the 1880s. It has come to designate a type of conservative aristocrat present on both sides of the Mason-Dixon Line.

war, such as raw iron, firearms, munitions, textiles, and boots.[39] Nonetheless, after the first year of war, it was the South that appeared, at least in the eyes of the world, to be poised to triumph, controlling the action in the arena like a matador while the North plodded around like a clumsy bull. This image resulted from the South's spate of early military victories. Yet, before battles could be won, the necessary armies had to be recruited and outfitted. The South was faced with the dual task of raising its armies and constructing its industries from the ground up. Despite its agrarian past and its romantic-chivalric mentality, the South met these challenges, as Michael O'Brien puts it, "with remarkable thoroughness and little ideological discomfort."[40] How was this possible?

On closer examination, the Confederacy's achievement may not have been so surprising after all. In all likelihood, it was the "organic" product of the prewar South's characteristic combination of technological-economic modernity and feudal-romantic culture. Perhaps the sudden creation of large industrial complexes, including the second-largest munitions factory in the world, followed a fundamentally different pattern than the familiar process of liberal-capitalist industrialization. The thesis proposed by economic historian Raimondo Luraghi—that the South operated a system of wartime state socialism—may overstate the case somewhat: "No country," he writes, "from the Inca Empire to Soviet Russia has ever possessed a similar government-owned, or controlled, kind of economy."[41] But his thesis underscores the affinity with the "Prussian path" of successfully synthesizing old-school military values and industrialism.

The second aspect of the South's dual mobilization was its exploitation of its military potential. It was common knowledge in 1861 in both parts of the country that the South possessed a superior military culture and tradition and that the cavalier, true to his name, made for a better warrior than the Yankee. At the time, Virginia was known as the "Mother of Generals" in the United States. While the seven most prominent family dynasties in Massachusetts produced a total of nine army officers, twenty officers during the same period came from just two Virginian families (Lee and Randolph). According to other statistics, 80 percent of prewar Southern presidents came from a military background, whereas 80 percent of their colleagues from the North were "without military experience of any kind."[42] The bravado of the Southern cavalry during the Mexican War of 1848 remained relatively fresh in people's memories and had established the superiority—indeed infallibility—of Southern troops as a popular myth. The North's image of Southern military superiority was not unlike pre-1914 European appraisals of Prussian German militarism: a mixture of respect, ridicule, and moral outrage. Everyone assumed that slavery was the reason for Southern militarism: just as Sparta needed its military capabilities to suppress the Helots, the South depended on armed force to keep the slaves in their place. The permanent threat of rebellion did in fact ensure that military vigilance never lapsed. Moreover, the uprisings that periodically occurred produced a state of constant military alert, allowing for the lightning-quick mobilization that made such an impression on the surprised observers at the beginning of the war. The Confederacy's quasi-feudal social structure, in which the plantation owner, like the chief of a Scottish clan, was at the same time a regional military commander, completed the precisely calibrated and efficient military machine. The tournaments patterned after Scott's novels were also inspired by military concerns. Similar in popularity to sports such as rugby in England and football in the American North, they were a mixture of marksmanship contests, public festivals, and military maneuvers.[43]

The ultimate index of the South's superior military culture, however, was the large number of military academies and schools. The idea of a national military academy may have originated in the North with the founding of West Point in 1802, but in the following decades the South overtook the North.[44] Beginning in 1830, so many academies and schools were founded that soon every one of the Confederate states could boast of its own military academy, as well as numerous private institutions. As this trend coincided with the cult of chivalry, it supports the view that technological efficiency and romanticism went hand in hand. The mission of the military academies was, after all, to ground the romantic-chivalric fantasy in an efficient military professionalism.[45]

Nonetheless, the South's ability to compensate for material inferiority with superior military culture does not suffice to explain the early course of the war. Just as the German army in World War I was not truly "undefeated on the field of battle"—despite the popularity of that postwar myth—it is equally untrue that the commanders of the Confederacy were all military geniuses who were only defeated by the North's superior troop strength and weaponry. Despite the Confederacy's military standing, there was of course no shortage of mediocrity, incompetence, and unprofessionalism among its soldiers. On closer inspection, the South's military superiority appears less significant than imagined. In other words, it was the myth of the South's military genius that most influenced the outcome of the early battles. The myth was especially effective because it held sway not only in the South but in the North as well, especially among the officers corps of the Union army. As Michael C. C. Adams shows, a large number of officers came from the patrician class of New England, which rejected the speculative mercantilist spirit of the Jacksonian era and believed "that Northern manhood [had been] corrupted by money lust."[46] Northern patricians saw themselves as the last bastions of the old Republican culture. This mentality was nearly identical to that in the South, although it was not as all-consuming and it lacked comparable aesthetic symbols like that of the cavalier. Alienated from their own culture but incapable of creating an alternative, the military mugwumps of the North had little choice but to adopt the South as their role model and partake of its mythology. No Southerner could have been more flowery on the topic of innate Southern military genius as a certain Northern officer who described the soldiers he encountered in a Charleston garrison a year before the outbreak of the war as men "whose faces would help an artist to idealize a Lacedaemonian general, or a baron of the Middle Ages."[47]

The Confederacy's military victories in the early stages of the war led to a kind of folie à deux. The South felt confirmed in its chivalric romanticism, whereas the military leadership of the North lost what little self-regard it had possessed. Contemporaries blamed an "inferiority complex" and a "lack of confidence" within the Union army under General McClellan for its poor performance during the early part of the Civil War.[48] This phase ended with McClellan's dismissal and the appointment of Grant, Sherman, and Sheridan, all "new men," who felt no secret admiration for the soldierly virtues of the cavaliers or any particular alienation from the mercantile-industrial culture of the North. On the contrary, they readily adapted modern industrial methods to the conduct of war, an innovation that produced—among other things—the scorched-earth policy.

The Lost Cause

Defeated nations waste little time, after recovering from their initial shock, in finding scapegoats. The previous regime is held responsible both for leading the nation into the fateful misadventure of war and for directing it down a dead-end path long before the commencement of hostilities. Similarly, the policies and goals for which the old regime led the nation into war are often abandoned with few second thoughts. After Sedan, republican France no longer objected to a unified German nation, and after November 1918, Germany no longer contemplated achieving naval parity with England and trying to become a world power. In return, however, the victorious opponents are expected to honor the self-purification of the losing side, to renounce all punishment, and to agree to the reestablishment of the status quo ante. The outrage is thus all the greater when the winning side refuses to accept the distinction between the innocent nation and the guilty former leadership and insists that the loser pay a price, as happened after France's defeat in 1871 and Germany's in World War I.

The South reacted with the same sense of betrayal after Lee's surrender at Appomattox. With few exceptions, Southerners meekly renounced their claim to independence and the institution of slavery, for which they had fought so bitterly for four years. In turn, they expected the reinstatement of conditions as they were before the outbreak of hostilities. The incomprehension and outrage over being treated unfairly were therefore massive as soon it became clear that when the North spoke of "reconstruction" it did not mean the material rebuilding of the South but rather the cultural indoctrination, moral reeducation, and political subjugation of the vanquished. The South may have had no option but to give up on political independence, but like every other defeated nation, it drew a distinction between military defeat and moral victory. Under normal circumstances, nations continue to exist after their defeat and eventually return to the international arena, where they exploit such distinctions to serve the cause of *revanche* or redress. The South, by contrast, ceased to be a nation after the Civil War and transformed the distinction between failure on the battlefield and moral superiority into the central dogma of its new identity. In the mythologies of the vanquished, the Southern Lost Cause is unique in making sense not only of the defeat but of the entire nation itself. The South may have disappeared as a political entity but it lived on as a kind of national religion or community of faith for which the moment of defeat was as foundational and consecrating as the Crucifixion. "In the moment of death," writes Robert Penn Warren, "the Confederation entered upon its immortality."[49]

Edward A. Pollard—journalist, soldier, adventurer, and vigorous critic of the political and military leadership of the Confederacy during the war—published his version of Civil War history in 1866 under the title *The Lost Cause*.[50] The book was several things at once: a first attempt at chronicling the events of war; a settling of accounts with the old regime, which Pollard held exclusively responsible for the South's defeat; and an effort to make sense of that outcome. Pollard's insistent assertions in the book's final pages amount to the first formulation of the Lost Cause as a program for the conservation of national identity. The message was directed against the enemy's efforts, already apparent at the time, to "reconstruct" and "reeducate" that identity out of existence. Pollard's tome concludes:

> All that is left the South is "the war of ideas." She has thrown down the sword to take up the weapons of argument, not indeed under any banner of fanaticism, or to enforce a dogma, but simply to make the honorable conquest of reason and justice. . . . Defeat has not made "all our sacred things profane." The war has left the South its own memories, its own heroes, its own tears, its own dead. Under these traditions, sons will grow to manhood, and lessons sink deep that are learned from the lips of widowed mothers. It would be immeasurably the worst consequence of defeat in this war that the South should lose its moral and intellectual distinctiveness as a people, and cease to assert its well-known superiority in civilization. . . . That superiority the war has not conquered or lowered; and the South will do right to claim and to cherish it. . . . [The Civil War] did not decide negro suffrage; it did not decide State rights, . . . it did not decide the right of the people to show dignity in misfortune, and to maintain self-respect in the face of adversity. And these things which the war did not decide, the Southern people will still cling to, still claim, and still assert in them their rights and views. . . . It is not untimely or unreasonable to tell the South to cultivate her superiority as a people; to maintain her old schools of literature and scholarship; to assert, in the forms of her thought, and in the style of her manners, her peculiar civilization. . . . There may not be a political South. Yet there may be a social and intellectual South.[51]

To call Pollard the sole prophet of the Lost Cause would be incorrect. As a collective idea and an emotional necessity, the conviction was in the air that secession had been a noble but hopeless quest that Southerners had admirably insisted on pursuing. As such, the Lost Cause arose from that ambivalent consciousness of decline and cultural superiority that manifested itself in the South's identification with Scotland, Bonnie Prince Charlie, and the English Cavaliers. Nonetheless, it seems strange that a quest that was seen as spiritually triumphant should be termed "lost." Nations do not usually embrace defeat in their mythology. Indeed, they do everything in their power to deny it or to turn the tables by imagining the victor as the loser of the next round of warfare. What motivated the South to turn the negative connotation of the term *lost* into something positive by coupling it with *cause*?

One motivation has already been discussed. The South was a romantic culture inspired by its role model, Scotland, which represented nothing less than the nostalgic sublimation of lost independence. All romanticism involves an idealization of the past, and every past is in some sense "lost." A further explanation for the aura of the term is the centrality of Milton's *Paradise Lost* in American political rhetoric. As one scholar says of its rhetorical omnipresence around 1800, "Its transcendent personages and scenes could now evaluate any historical event, from attempts at political bribery in New York through the presidential activities of Washington. . . . Americans had turned Milton's epic into a measuring rod to read and assess political life of the times."[52] In the Civil War, the republic was for both sides a paradise fought over by the powers of light and darkness, God and Satan. The abolitionist Thaddeus Stevens wrote, for example, of the secession: "A rebellion only less guilty than that of the devilish angels was waged with fiendish cruelty against the best government on earth."[53] Pollard's Lost Cause can be understood as part of this tradition, as is confirmed by the title of his subsequent book, *The Lost Cause Regained* (1868), with its unmistakable echo of Milton's *Paradise Regained*. The South having traditionally defined itself as a "paradise on earth," in contrast to the "wilderness" of the North, the Lost Cause was not a military defeat but a lost paradise.

The Better Men

The losing side's conviction that its defeat is not the result of a fair fight was especially pronounced in the vanquished Confederacy. According to the self-conception that had crystallized in the years preceding the Civil War, the South's defeat by the mean-spirited, materialistic North was incomprehensible. After all, Southern superiority had been gloriously confirmed, even acknowledged by the enemy in the military victories at the beginning of the conflict. If the war had been ultimately lost, the reasons could not have been military. What the North had waged against the South was not war at all, several writers concluded, but a reprehensible perversion that compensated for the weakness of a mercantilist culture incapable of fighting a true soldierly war.

"Failing our men in the field, *this* is the way they must conquer!" wrote the diarist Emma Le Conte of the burning of Columbia, South Carolina, by Sherman's troops. The South as a whole saw the Union's scorched-earth policy and its practice of starving out the enemy with blockades in similar terms. "They cannot whip our soldiers," says a character in a novel by John Esten Cooke, "so they burn out and starve out our women and children."[54] For the South, the Union engaged in military encounters only when they could not be avoided and when the balance of forces, in accordance with its businesslike mercantilist calculations, was overwhelmingly in its favor: "Their armies scarcely ever ventured to fight," an editorialist averred, "without having two or three to one."[55] The reason found for this behavior was, along with the innate cowardice and lack of sportsmanship of the pinched Yankee soul, the fact that the Union army consisted in large measure of immigrants, the "trash of Europe."[56] This was an insult to the cavalier warriors comparable to the deployment of colonial troops by the Entente in World War I, which was viewed by Germans as a violation of the rules and an affront to and a betrayal of the West. The South thus chose to interpret decades of stagnant immigration as a positive, patriotic virtue. In the same vein, the Confederacy was seen to represent the true cause of the nation whereas the North, infiltrated by foreigners, played the role of the traitor.

In its search for historical analogies, the South also discovered the French *vendée*, the proroyalist peasant insurrection that lasted from 1793 to 1796 and was joined by members of the local nobility. As in the lost cause of Scotland against England, Southerners saw here the unfairness of a fight in which an aristocratic culture was overwhelmed by human masses and material advantage. "Both [the Confederacy and the *vendée*] gained prodigious victories," one observer noted. "Both exhibited miracles of courage and constancy, and both failed utterly and hopelessly."[57] Just as the aristocrats of the *vendée* were smothered by the masses during the French Revolution, the Southern cavaliers had been not defeated but suffocated by the sheer numbers of the Northern rabble. It was a battle of "bludgeon against rapier" and "of machinery against chivalry, in which the knight-errant was bound to be run over by the locomotive, if not overthrown by the windmill."[58]

The choice of words is worth noting. Southerners talked not of "defeat" but of "whipping." The axiom "We wore ourselves out whipping the enemy," for example, expressed their belief in their own military superiority.[59] At the same time, the Confederacy's ultimate defeat was also described as a "whipping": "Well," went a common saying, "you have conquered us. We are whipped."[60] The word apparently had a remarkable capacity for making the unthinkable acceptable, easing its sting and annulling its ultimate effect. "To whip" in the sense of "to defeat" had an undertone of contempt. It denoted not defeat in a battle between representatives of the same class or caste but rather the mass subjugation of the "peasant" by the "officer." Whipping also invariably called to mind the punishment of disobedient slaves. It was a ritual that the master swinging the whip and the slave at the receiving end experienced as a superficial enactment of punishment, one that went only skin deep. (Slaves may not have seen it in such a benign light.) In this way, the

South distanced itself psychologically from both its victories and its defeats at the hands of a contemptible enemy. When it triumphed over the North in battle, it was the punitive master. When it was on the receiving end, whipping was a mechanistic process, almost a piece of slapstick. It seemed a grand joke to compare one's own defeat with the lowliest form of punishment, the whipping of a slave. In short, "whipping" was the perfect mechanism to ironize and trivialize defeat.[61]

It is not immediately clear how such a belittling defensive reaction could be reconciled with the idea of defeat as spiritual and moral catharsis. Or how a degrading loss inflicted on "better men" by unworthy opponents could have any spiritual or moral value. But there are two fundamentally different types of defeat: the first results from a decisive battle, from the sudden recognition of one's own inferiority, which is followed by the loss of the will to fight, then flight, dissolution, capitulation, and subjugation by the opponent's armed forces. The second type of defeat involves no loss of the will to fight. The image of battling on to the last man, so that the end is not capitulation but extinction, plays a central role in the mythology of many cultures. In this scenario, defeat is seen as the highest form of exaltation. The Spartans at Thermopylae, Roland at Roncesvalles, and the Nibelungs in Attila's hall are classic examples of self-sacrificing national heroism. Even in recent history, there are devastating defeats that have become part of the national pantheon: the charge of the Light Brigade in England, the World War I battle near Langemarck for the Germans, the Paris Commune for the Communist International. The central instance of heroic sacrifice for the Southern Lost Cause was Pickett's charge at the battle of Gettysburg. Named for a commander, George E. Pickett, who in many ways resembled the stereotypical cavalier, this unsuccessful infantry offensive, which collapsed under withering Union artillery fire, served both to place the Confederacy in the tradition of grand defeats such as Thermopylae and to provide the kernel of a new myth that was all the South's own.[62]

Given the deeply rooted religious conviction that death is the pathway to a higher and purer state of being, the Lost Cause was far more than merely an emotional fortress into which the South retreated to lick its wounds. The significance of the Lost Cause, as even the enemy appreciated, went much deeper. The respect and admiration shown by William Hepworth Dixon, who celebrated the North's victory as a high point in human history, toward the noble figure cut by the South in defeat is a case in point. No Southerner could have summarized the attractions of the Lost Cause with greater sympathy:

> Men who can perish gloriously for their faith—however false that faith may be—will always seize the imagination, hold the affections, of a gallant race. Fighting for a weak and failing cause, these planters of Virginia, of Alabama, of Mississippi, rode into battle as they would have hurried to a feast; and many a man who wished them no profit in their raid and fray, could not help riding, as it were, in line with their foaming front, dashing with them into action, following their fiery course, with a flashing eye and a bounding pulse. Courage is electric. You caught the light from Jackson's sword, you flushed and panted after [Jeb] Stuart's plume. Their sin was not more striking than their valor. Loyal to their false gods, to their obsolete creed, they proved their personal honor by their deeds.[63]

The Scapegoat and the Saint

The simplest and most common means of national self-purification after defeat is to blame the old regime, exiling it to the figurative desert to wander as a forlorn outcast. If the scapegoating is not restricted to a leadership elite but encompasses a whole segment of the population, civil discord may follow, as it did in Germany after World War I. By contrast, the Lost Cause required few scapegoats, proof that, at least in this regard, the postbellum South was a relatively stable society. Although at war's end many Southerners blamed the Confederate leadership for their defeat, the victors' behavior gave rise to an increasing solidarity among the defeated. Before the Civil War, slavery had united the South and suppressed all dissent (or forced the dissenters to emigrate). After the war, it was the Lost Cause that answered the need for a common front against the victors during Reconstruction. Pledging fidelity to the Lost Cause—the South's new "peculiar institution"—was a surefire way of demonstrating membership in the community. Criticizing that community, on the other hand, automatically attracted all the rage directed at scapegoats.

During the Civil War, General James Longstreet was one of the Confederacy's most popular military commanders. Together with Robert E. Lee and Thomas J. "Stonewall" Jackson, he was part of a triumvirate representing the three cardinal military virtues: strategy (Lee), boldness (Jackson), and persistence (Longstreet).[64] At no point in the war did Longstreet come in for significant criticism, in contrast to Lee, under whose command Longstreet had served at the battle of Gettysburg and who was generally held responsible for the Confederacy's defeat there. Things changed, however, after the war, when Longstreet supported the Union's policies of reconstruction. The former war hero was transformed into a traitor to the Confederacy, and within a few years the historiography of the Lost Cause had succeeded in proving that the person mainly responsible for the Gettysburg fiasco was not Lee but Longstreet. The reassessment of Longstreet and Lee, which reached down to the smallest details, was one of the most impressive achievements of what has since been termed the "Lost Cause industry." Thus, Lee's ultimate emergence as the personification of the Lost Cause is worth scrutinizing in some depth.

What is noteworthy about Lee, according to some contemporaries, is how seldom he truly shone in battle. For Edward A. Pollard, the pre-Gettysburg Lee was "a general who had never fought a battle, who had a pious horror of guerrillas, and whose extreme tenderness of blood induced him to depend exclusively upon the resources of strategy to essay the achievement of victory without the cost of love."[65] Other commanders came far closer to the ideal of the cavalier warrior. James E. B. "Jeb" Stuart (known as the "Flower of the Cavaliers") and Stonewall Jackson were both, in contrast to the fifty-four-year-old Lee, young men at the beginning of the Civil War—reminiscent of Achilles and Alexander. Their deaths in battle as young men should have predestined them for the role of martyrs to the Lost Cause. Instead it was Lee, a peaceable man burdened by responsibility for Gettysburg, who won the favors of history. The argument that Lee's ascension was engineered by a pro-Lee cabal within the Lost Cause industry doesn't explain much since, without a majority consensus, hagiography is impossible.[66] Lee must have had a number of attributes that made him the ideal representative of the Lost Cause.

A hero in the strong, silent mold, Lee did not publish his war memoirs during his lifetime nor did he take part in the discussions surrounding the reasons for defeat and who deserved the blame. Whereas other former military commanders continually lost stature with their relentless self-justifications, Lee left the impression after his death in 1870 of having stood nobly above the fray. The only blot on his résumé, Gettysburg, was erased by the fact that his most persistent accuser, Longstreet, had disqualified himself with his subsequent "betrayal" of the South's cause and henceforth would be deemed the actual culprit. In biblical terms, Longstreet was Judas to Lee's Jesus. The obvious explanation for the choice of Lee as the incarnation of the Lost Cause is that the South was primarily honoring not the military hero but the martyr. His signing of the surrender at Appomattox was a consummate act of sacrifice, which he had undertaken as his nation's representative: "If Christ had his Gethsemane," historian Thomas Connelly writes, "Lee had his Appomattox."[67]

It is clear, then, why the South did not choose one of its youthful fallen heroes as its primary figure for identification. The only one who could play that role was a man who had experienced the full humiliation of defeat and still maintained his dignity. Lee's exaltation confirmed the South's venerable sense of its spiritual and cultural superiority. Moreover the concomitant cult, with its Christ analogies, allowed the South to embark on the path to rapprochement and reintegration with the nation as a whole. To cite a single example: in the early postwar years, Lee's support for secession was depicted as a spontaneous act of Confederate patriotism and his refusal of Lincoln's 1861 offer to assume supreme command of the Union army was compared to the temptation of Christ by Satan.[68] By the 1890s, however, his decision against the Union and for the South was depicted as the outcome of a painful process of soul-searching. The new Lee was no longer a fervent Southern patriot but rather, in his heart, a Union supporter who had decided, contrary to his own inclinations and common sense, to support his homeland's cause for reasons of loyalty and honor, although he knew from the start the quest was hopeless.[69] The myth of General Lee was thus the ultimate expression both of the Lost Cause and of the path back into the Union. It transformed the lost war into martyrdom, secession into tragedy, and national reunification into catharsis.

The Religion of the Lost Cause

Religions tend to see war as a battle between good and evil, with the enemy as the spawn of Satan and their own cause as that of God Almighty. The churches involved in the Civil War were no exception. Most, in fact, had taken sides long before war was declared. The three main Protestant churches in the antebellum South—the Methodists, the Presbyterians, and the Baptists—all seceded from the North in the 1840s, twenty years before the political institutions of the Confederacy did so, and remained separate long after national unity had been reestablished. (The Northern and Southern Methodist churches were reunited in 1939, their Presbyterian equivalents only in 1983. The Southern and Northern Baptist churches remain separate to this day.)[70]

In the prewar period, Southern churches had concentrated on justifying slavery as a God-given institution legitimated by the Bible, and during the war itself, they had functioned, in the words of one historian, as one of "the most effective morale-building agencies" of the Confederacy. After Appomattox, they discovered a new theater of activities in the "cold war" between the North and the Reconstruction South. Northern religious leaders took considerable pleasure in reciting to the South its litany of sins, encouraging it to repent and sending missionaries across the Mason-Dixon Line. In response, the three main Southern churches did everything in their power to repel these spiritual advances, casting themselves as the last defenders of the Southern soul in the face of persistent Northern efforts to corrupt it. Their role was comparable to that of the Catholic Church in Moorish Spain and Russian Poland or of the Orthodox Church in Ottoman Greece and Serbia. Nations that lose their state often take refuge in their church, with the result that nationalism and religion, secular and theological thought coalesce and become indistinguishable. In this vein, the South has been described as a "sacred society" and the Lost Cause as its "civic religion."[71]

The church's first and most important contribution to the Lost Cause was to explain the South's defeat. Its explanation included a comparison to the trials of Job, a perennial favorite among vanquished nations, according to which defeat and suffering are not evidence of abandonment by God but rather a sign of his special love. Theologians took to quoting Hebrews: "My son, despise not thou the chastening of the Lord, nor faint when thou art rebuked of him: For whom the Lord loveth he chasteneth, and scourgeth every son whom he receiveth" (12:5–6). If defeat was a sign of God's love, then the reverse also held true and the enemy's victory was a triumph for Satan. The aphorism "truth on the scaffold and wrong on the throne" echoed the secular concept of the "better men" who contrary to all reason were bested by the inferior masses.[72] Consolation could be derived from the idea that, as the example of Christ showed, defeat did not destroy but rather exalted the spirit. "His enemies could nail Christ to the cross," one preacher sermonized in 1897, "but they could not quench the ideals he embodied. His seemed to be a lost cause as the darkness fell on the great tragedy at Calvary, but out of what seemed Golgotha's irretrievable defeat has come the cause whose mission it is to save that which is lost."[73]

From Lost Cause to New Cause

Losers who have completed the first stage of reaction to defeat—surprise, dismay, disbelief, and the search for scapegoats—begin to examine their history for the deeper reasons behind their failure. Forced to admit that they took a wrong turn somewhere, they try to ascertain where they strayed from the true path. And this requires them to specify what was and is the proper destiny of their nation.

The South was not prepared to repent for the sin of slavery, as the North demanded. It was, however, willing to see slavery as a fateful misadventure. In so doing, Southerners took the new view that slavery, with its "narcotic influence" on the social body, had had equally deleterious effects on both masters and slaves that had hindered development and progress.[74] "The negro was a slave to [the master], and he was a slave to the situation," wrote one contemporary observer.

> He could not abandon it without disastrous results to himself, to the negro, to the state and the world. If ever man were impelled by an irresistible force, it was the Southern white man. What did it matter to him if the earth beneath his feet was loaded with all the minerals which contribute to the wealth, convenience or enjoyment of mankind, or that the stream running by his door had waterpower enough to turn a thousand wheels? He could not utilize them; he was bound hand and foot—bound to his slaves, bound to his plantation, bound to cotton, to his habits of life, to the exigencies of the situation.[75]

Speculation that the history of the South might have taken a different course if only the harmful effects of slavery had been recognized earlier inevitably led back to Thomas Jefferson and the period around 1800. At that time, the yeoman farmer was the ideal type for the entire nation, including the South. Seen from this vantage point, the South's going astray began with the onset of the cotton boom. Instead of slavery gradually dying out, as Jefferson and others had expected and hoped, it experienced a fateful upswing. Seduced by the gigantic profits promised by King Cotton, the South deviated from the correct path of yeomanry and set off on the treacherous road of a monoculture of cotton, the plantation system, and slavery. Such were the conclusions of the self-criticism undertaken after the collapse of the Confederacy. Having now been freed from the shackles of slavery, the South could begin anew at precisely that point where its proper development had broken off fifty years previously. Of course, no one seriously suggested a return to the conditions of the yeoman culture of 1800. Instead, the program for the future focused on the need for diversification rather than a single-crop economy, and that entailed industrialization.

The ideas and projects promising success after defeat are never really new; instead they merely recast prewar visions in a new light. The Southern concepts of diversification and industrialization were no exception to this rule. A minority of political economists had been trying since the 1840s to convince the public that, with its monolithic dependence on cotton, the South was in danger of becoming a colony of the North. "We purchase all our luxuries and necessaries from the North," wrote one antebellum journalist from Alabama. "Our slaves are clothed with Northern manufactured goods (and) work with Northern hoes, ploughs, and other implements. . . . The slaveholder dresses in Northern goods, rides in a Northern saddle . . . [and] reads Northern books. . . . In Northern vessels his products are carried to market . . . and on Northern-made paper, with a Northern pen, with Northern ink, he resolves and re-resolves in regard to his rights."[76] James D. B. DeBow, whose *Commercial*

Review of the South and West was the main mouthpiece for the critical minority, compared the South's dependence on the North to that of Ireland on England. "Action! ACTION!! ACTION!!!" he demanded, "not in the rhetoric of Congress, but in the busy hum of mechanism, and in the thrifty operations of the hammer and anvil."[77]

His calls to action, however, remained precisely that—rhetoric. Even in the sector of the Southern economy that seemed to lend itself most naturally to industrialization—the production of cotton textiles—no progress was made. At the beginning of the Civil War, 90 percent of all textile mills were located in the North. Given the great profits to be made from raw cotton, the impetus to industrialize and diversify was as slight for the nineteenth-century plantation owner as it is for the present-day oil sheiks of the Persian Gulf. Along with cotton's enormous profitability, anti-industrial prejudice, (the other face of the South's agrarian ideal) convinced those below the Mason-Dixon Line of their superiority to the North. Thus, DeBow's Cassandra-like warnings went unheeded, and the advocates of the one-crop economy with their hymns to cotton always had the last word. "Our Cotton is the most wonderful talisman. By its power we are transmuting whatever we choose into whatever we want," explained one cotton farmer, while James Henry Hammond opined in the Senate three years before the Civil War: "The slaveholding South is now the controlling power of the world. . . . No power on earth dares . . . to make war on cotton. Cotton is king."[78]

The Confederacy's defeat and the abolition of slavery finally seemed to create a situation in which industrialization could take off. DeBow energetically resumed his efforts where he had been forced to break them off in 1861, and others followed his lead. Daniel Harvey Hill, for example, devoted his periodical *The Land We Love* to reviving the old planks in the modernizers' platform: industrialization, diversification, expansion of the transportation network, and exploitation of natural resources. In addition, there was a new demand that no one before the war had dared to articulate explicitly. The aristocratic spirit of the "Old South"—the appellation caught on almost immediately after the Confederacy's defeat—had outlived its time, and a fundamental reorientation around mercantile pragmatism was required. Physical labor, which like almost every other kind of practical skill was beneath the dignity of the cavalier gentleman in the Old South, could no longer be denigrated or accepted only reluctantly; it had to be promoted as a virtue. The transition was not an easy one, as Hill, a former general, pointed out in the first issue of his newspaper, but there was no alternative:

> The pride which we might have felt in the glories of the past is rebuked by the thought that these glories have faded away. It is rebuked by the thought that they were purchased at the expense of the material prosperity of the country; for men of wealth and talents did not combine their fortunes, their energies, and their intellects to develop the immense resources of the land of their nativity. What factories did they erect? What mines did they dig? What foundries did they establish? What machine-shops did they build? What ships did they put afloat? Their minds and their hearts were engrossed in the struggle for national position and national honors. The yearning desire was ever for political supremacy, and never for domestic thrift and economy. . . . The old method of instruction was never wise; it is no worse than folly. . . . Is not a practical acquaintance with the ax, the plane, the saw, the anvil, the loom, the plow and the mattock, vastly more useful to an impoverished people than familiarity with the laws of nations and the science of government? . . . God is now honoring manual labor with us as he has never done before with any other nation. It is the high-born, the cultivated, the intelligent, the brave, the generous, who are now constrained to work with their own hands. Labor is thus associated in our mind with all that is honorable in birth, refined in manners, bright in intellect, manly in character and magnanimous in soul.[79]

The willingness to effect a fundamental reorientation, as proclaimed after 1865 by men like DeBow and Hill, did not last long. DeBow died in 1867. His periodical was continued for a year by his employees, then was sold, only to cease publication the following year. Hill continued publishing *The Land We Love* until 1869, before likewise throwing in the towel. He had already given up his program of radical cultural reorientation. The failure of this initiative, which had begun with such great conviction, raises the possibility that the South's brief infatuation with industrial capitalism had been nothing more than a "dreamland" episode, so common in cultures of defeat.

The Cold War of Reconstruction

When DeBow and Hill began publishing, they assumed that the only price the South would have to pay for its defeat would be the abolition of slavery and the renunciation of its claims to independence. Everything else, they believed, would be restored to its former place and the prodigal son would return home. This was how the South in general envisioned the aftermath of the war. As foreign observers noted, the word *union* became a kind of magic formula in the South during the months immediately following Appomattox: "a word of grace," wrote William Hepworth Dixon, "of sweetness, and of charm. . . . Disunion, a word so musical not thirty months ago, is now a ban, a stigma, a reproach." Dixon summarized the prevailing Southern sentiment in the summer of 1865: "We are all for the Union. The Union as it was, if we may have it so; our sole desire is to stand where we stood in '61 ."[80]

The assumption that, with the exception of slavery, everything would go back to the status quo ante also conformed to the policy officially pursued by Abraham Lincoln and, after Lincoln's assassination, Andrew Johnson. Both men had understood the primary purpose of the Civil War to be not the abolition of slavery but the preservation of national unity. Historian Kenneth Stampp says of Lincoln's interest in emancipation that "rarely has a man embraced his destiny with greater reluctance than he," but Johnson clearly went him one better: "I wish to God every head of a family in the United States had one slave to take the drudgery and menial service off the family."[81] Even after emancipation, neither Lincoln nor Johnson considered making the ex-slaves full citizens of the United States. Their plans, insofar as they were formulated, vacillated between deportation to Africa and a status that in the twentieth century became known as "stateless."[82] Far from being extreme, such opinions reflected prevailing sentiments throughout the North. As C. Vann Woodward notes, blacks only had the right to vote in five Northern and Midwestern states as of 1860, and as late as 1869, the New York state legislature voted down a proposed law that would have enfranchised them. It is one of the great ironies of the American antislavery movement that many of its most committed supporters were also opponents of legal equality for ex-slaves, indeed, dedicated racists.[83]

As for the reintegration of the South into the Union, Lincoln's and Johnson's plans fit nicely with the expectations of the losing side. The prevailing spirit was one of moderation and reconciliation. Only the most recalcitrant rebels were to be excluded from the common project of national rebuilding, while moderates on both sides of the Mason-Dixon Line would work side by side, like the Founding Fathers, to patch the nation back together. Since the expectations of the victors and the vanquished seemed nearly identical, the chance for a harmonious peace appeared great in the spring of 1865. But neither Lincoln nor Johnson took account of the hate and hysteria that four years of war had unleashed on both sides, and they failed to realize that such passions could not be eradicated with the stroke of a pen. Historians still speculate whether Lincoln, in contrast to the politically weak Johnson, could have used his authority to achieve his aims. In the days before Lincoln's assassination in April, however, Northern editorialists were already raising doubts that he was the right man to deal with the "cancer of wickedness" in the South, warning that more "misjudged leniency" would be unacceptable. Ralph Waldo Emerson clearly articulated this view in his diary a few days after the assassination: "The heroic deliverer could no longer serve us, . . . the rebellion touched its natural conclusion, and what remained to be done required new and uncommitted hands."[84]

The fact that the Union's leaders favored reconciliation while the public passionately thirsted for revenge and punishment seemed at first to open some room for Southern political maneuvering.[85] The mood was liable to alter at any time, however, and in short order the South began to overreach. Southern politicians relied too much on Johnson and did not give sufficient consideration to the power of public opinion in the North. In the six months following Lee's surrender, the South restored its political institutions so thoroughly that it gave the impression of believing that Appomattox, the secession, and the Civil War had never happened. And all of this transpired without the symbolic acts of penitence and subjugation that the North surely expected. The final straw came with the institution of the "black codes."[86] Enacted in late 1865 by the reconstituted state legislatures, the codes amounted to a de facto reversal of emancipation, restricting freedom of movement for ex-slaves and adopting a number of measures that served to retie them to their former masters.

As a result, over the next two years the promise of reconciliation began to unravel. In 1866, radical Republicans in Congress seized control of Reconstruction from the moderate "presidential Reconstructionists." Two years later, Johnson was impeached, while Congress took over numerous executive powers and refused to acknowledge the elected representatives from the South. Moreover, the state legislatures and governments that had been reconstituted under Johnson were dissolved, and the entire South was subjected to military occupation. Divided up into five military zones whose commanders possessed dictatorial powers, the South was transformed into occupied enemy territory. Reconstruction no longer sought to revive the South's prewar ideas and traditions but instead became synonymous with a complete overhaul and revision according to the alien conceptions of the North. The granting of civil liberties by

Congress to the former slaves was considered the most hostile of the enemy actions—and not without some justification, considering the North's previous ambivalence on this question. Again accusing the North of hypocrisy, the South charged the Yankees with treating blacks like pawns in a game whose sole aim was to humiliate the South.

It is no surprise, then, that the program of renewal and modernization put forward after Lee's surrender by DeBow and Hill died such a quick death. The policy of moderate presidential Reconstruction lasted almost two years, longer than the typical dreamland period, but it was a dreamland all the same. In the cold war of congressional Reconstruction that followed, appeals for modernization and industrialization programs garnered little public support, based as they were on the Northern model. It was as impossible for the South, in the throes of reacting to perceived Northern betrayal, to embrace an industrial Northern reorientation as it would have been for the United States as a whole to adopt a program of socialism during the McCarthy era. For the duration of congressional Reconstruction, the South circled its wagons, as it had in the decades preceding the Civil War. The Lost Cause ceased to be a peaceable feeling of nostalgia and became the ideology of white supremacy, indeed an instrument of repression. The private militias that started to form in 1867, among them the Ku Klux Klan, were essentially the violent arm of this movement. These groups saw themselves not as lynch mobs but as the descendants of Robin Hood and the Scottish clans and as defenders of the chivalric ideal. A passage from the Ku Klux Klan's charter reads: "This is an institution of Chivalry, Humanity, Mercy, and Patriotism, embodying in its genius and its principles all that is chivalric in conduct, noble in sentiment, generous in manhood, and patriotic in purpose."[87]

The cold war of Reconstruction went on for ten years. It ended not with victory by either side but with a compromise, or more accurately, a recognition that both sides actually shared the same aims. (The radical Republican ideologues in Congress, who had been the driving force behind this cold war, may ultimately have been its biggest losers since the Republican Party eventually lost its congressional majority.) The North of 1877 was no longer the North of 1867. The Gilded Age had begun, and the accumulation and enjoyment of wealth had replaced moralizing as the order of the day. In shocked reaction to the Paris Commune in 1871, the spirit of the age had turned conservative, and since the South had always been considered a bastion of conservatism, there was no longer any need to cordon it off. On the contrary, in the fight against social disorder and radicalism of every sort, the South was seen as a welcome ally. In 1877, Congress declared its mission in the South to have been achieved, and the last of the occupying troops and the accompanying political and administrative bureaucracy were withdrawn. The old Southern elites returned to their positions of power. The North's about-face was greeted in the South as the start of its own redemption. The political conditions that had prevailed before congressional Reconstruction were restored, although former slaves retained their constitutional rights, which could not be officially revoked. They could, however, be skirted with the methods of manipulation and repression that had been perfected since the end of the war. The result by the end of the century was a new set of black codes, imposed with the North's tacit blessing.

In 1877, the South found itself in a situation comparable to that of France in 1879 and Germany in 1924. After years of external cold war and internal instability, of crisis and the search for a new consensus, things had begun to settle down. This new phase signaled the actual end of the war and the beginning of a new era in Southern history.

The Idea of the New South

Reformers who fail to achieve their goals the first time around because the world is not yet ready for them are usually shunted off the stage of history. This fate befell DeBow and Hill not once but twice. Their second attempt to spread the gospel of Southern industrialization would most likely have foundered in any case given the unfavorable political climate, but it is also true that prophets, having predicted a catastrophe, are rarely rewarded afterward for their prescience. And ultimately DeBow and Hill were unable to coin a slogan that would move and excite their audience. No matter how eloquently and thoughtfully they articulated their ideas about renewing the South, they never hit on the seemingly simple formulation "New South." The reason was probably reluctance rather than lack of imagination. For prior to 1880, when the term acquired a near-universal resonance, "New South" had predominantly negative connotations below the Mason-Dixon Line. In the first year of the Civil War, the Union military administration that occupied the Sea Islands, off the coast of South Carolina, published a newspaper called the *New South*. As might be expected, the periodical found little favor with the native white population. With what one historian calls its "peremptory, hostile tone," it read like a broadside for the congressional Reconstruction to come.[88] There may have been other propagandistic uses of the term, and if so, that would explain why loyal Southerners did not take up what would have been seen as a Yankee idea. This is pure speculation, but another episode in the history of the New South sheds additional light on the problematic origins of the term.

In 1870, not long after the demise of DeBows's and Hill's publications and a full decade before the term *New South* came into general usage, an article was published bearing the title "The New South: What It Is Doing, and What It Wants." Its author, Edwin DeLeon, an ex-diplomat, was of the same generation as DeBow and Hill but had not weighed in on the questions of modernization and industrialization in the South before the war. This program was the same as DeBow's and Hill's; his rhetoric, however, was markedly different. Instead of criticizing the Old South and demanding reform, DeLeon painted a picture of a region already in the full swing of modernization, one "whose wants and wishes, ends and aims, plans and purposes, are as different from those of 1860, as though a century instead of a decade only divided the two."[89] Along with the rhetoric, there was another important difference. DeBow and Hill had published their articles in their own periodicals, which, having been written, edited, printed, and distributed in the South, were considered the mouthpieces of traditional separatism. DeLeon's article on the New South, by contrast, appeared in *Putnam's Magazine*, one of the largest Northern periodicals. It was therefore primarily addressing a Northern audience, which may account for DeLeon's demonstrative use of the term *New South*. The fact that the phrase does not occur in any of the articles on the topic that he published in the South would seem to argue for this hypothesis.[90] Edward A. Pollard, the advocate of the Lost Cause, also tailored his message to his audience. Two years after calling on the South to defend its traditions, he metamorphosed into a propagandist for a New South, albeit without calling it such. Significantly, however, he took care not to publish his reformist articles south of the Mason-Dixon Line, confining them to magazines that appeared in New York and Philadelphia.[91]

These men were transitional figures, forerunners and prophets who either found no honor in their own country (DeBow and Hill) or sought their audience elsewhere (DeLeon and Pollard). The change in political climate that accompanied the end of congressional Reconstruction in 1877 made the journalistic detour north unnecessary and for the first time attracted Southern interest in the New South. Astonishingly, portions of the North had been receptive to the New South program even while the punitive policies of Reconstruction were proceeding full steam ahead. These Northerners probably saw the South as part good and part evil—a division common in the propaganda techniques of the twentieth century, which typically designate the "good" half of the enemy nation as the "other" (as in "the other Germany" of World War II) and regard it as a potential ally. The tendency of the early New South propagandists to use the North as a model certainly made them ideal representatives of the "other" South in Northern eyes. In the end, these few, isolated voices sufficed to give the North a sense that its efforts had not been in vain and that the seeds sown during Reconstruction were now taking root.

It was largely thanks to the efforts of the generation of public figures who took the stage after 1880 that the slogan and vision of the New South was established in the South itself. Born in the 1850s, these men had no personal memories of the prewar secession movement and only childhood recollections of the war itself. Growing up during Reconstruction, they observed firsthand the omnipotence of the North. The conclusion they drew could not have been clearer. The return to the Union was not a defeat but a chance to rejoin the victorious nation. "The greatest blessing that ever befell us was the failure to establish a nationality," wrote journalist Robert Bingham.[92] Another member of the generation, Woodrow Wilson, used similar words: "*Because* I love the South, I rejoice in the failure of the Confederacy. . . . The perpetuation of slavery would, beyond all question, have wrecked our agricultural and commercial interests."[93] What allowed the young men of the 1880s to renounce the positions of their fathers so easily was precisely the fact that the positions were their fathers'. To distance oneself from one's father is often to affiliate oneself with one's grandfather, in this instance with the generation that had steered the course of the nation before it had split apart and that therefore could provide a model for the task of reunification. Thus, most post-Reconstruction Southern leaders went about their business not as political economists (like DeBow) or economic journalists but as descendants of the great statesmen-orators of the Old South. Their role was not to disseminate specialist knowledge but to sketch out the general direction of the economy and propose areas for expansion. Rhetoric played a central role. Just as the grandfathers had accomplished great political deeds with their oratorical skills, so the grandsons set out to achieve great economic results with theirs.[94]

In their view, the New South was less a distant goal than a more or less finished project. This conceit was hardly new; DeLeon and Pollard had advanced it earlier. But whereas those two men tempered their proposals with self-criticism, self-doubt, and a demand for public reeducation, the New South generation portrayed itself and the region as at the height of their powers. "In all lines of industry the advance is steady and continuous," editorialized the *Manufacturers Record*, a Southern economic magazine. "The old agricultural South has ceased to be. . . . From henceforth the South stands in the front rank . . . as the exponent of American progress. . . . It is in truth not 'the coming' but the existing 'El Dorado of American Adventure.' "[95] Nonetheless, for all the bluster, an uncertain, contrived tone seemed to underlie the optimism. The most prominent propagandist of the New South generation, Henry W. Grady, for instance, assured his readers: "We have sowed towns and cities in the place of theories and put business above politics. We have fallen in love with work."[96] Or, as the *Manufacturers Record* proudly announced, Virginia was no longer "the mother of presidents" but "the mother of millionaires." The South, it said, "has learned that 'time is money.' " The lead article in a Richmond newspaper declared: "The almighty dollar is fast becoming a power here, and he who commands the most money holds the strongest hand. We no longer condemn the filthy lucre."[97]

The New South promoters were less at ease, however, when they were pledging their loyalty to mercantile materialism than when they were boasting about the advantages of their homeland. These advantages were twofold: an inexhaustible supply of raw materials and a temperate climate. In addition to reaping its traditional agricultural bounty, the New South aimed to begin exploiting its abundant natural resources, which had been scandalously neglected by the plantation system. And the North could not hope to compete with the South's mild weather. "Why," Grady asked rhetorically, "remain to freeze, and starve, and struggle on the bleak prairies of the northwest when the garden spot of the world is waiting for people to take possession of it and enjoy it?"[98] No Northern capitalist or European immigrant, it was thought, could possibly resist the double lure of resources and climate. They would be drawn to the South as inevitably as bees to the flower. "The certain and steady shifting of the greatest industrial centers of the country from the North to the more favoured regions of the South," Grady wrote, would transform the South into the nation's wealthiest region.[99] "The Eldorado of the next half century is the South," Richard H. Edmonds, publisher of the *Manufacturers Record*, prophesied.[100] Such gestures of reconciliation scarcely concealed the fantasy of *revanche* that would turn the lost military war into a postwar economic victory. The image Grady chose to express that sentiment comes close to a Freudian slip: "From Virginia to Texas the woods are full of New England capitalists hunting investments, and you can hardly fire a gun without killing one."[101]

Revanche was only one subtext in the New South's vision of its attractiveness to the North. It is not hard to see in the South's depiction of itself as "mild," "charming," and "lush" the desire of the woman to be courted by the man. The North as the man of action, the South as the passionately courted belle—it was a pairing that conformed to the traditional gendering of the two regions in American mythology.[102] The most prominent mythological element in the self-conception of the industrial New South, however, was the old idea of paradise on earth. Already apparent in the South's praise for its mild climate, charming landscape, and inexhaustible natural resources, this idea was now extended into the unlikely realm of industrialization. Industry was depicted in words that evoked the plantation system, which had been described as a bucolic Arcadia and Garden of Eden. The South was not a gloomy manufacturing landscape like the Northern "wilderness" but rather, as Grady boasted, an industrial paradise, "resting in Divine assurance, within touch of field and mine and forest—not set amid costly farms from which competition has driven the farmer in despair, but amid cheap and sunny lands, rich with agriculture, to which neither season nor soil has set a limit—this system of industries is mounting to a splendor that shall dazzle and illuminate the world."[103] In contrast to the myth of the plantation, which had a powerful economy backing it up, this industrial Arcadia was almost entirely unreal, brought to life by nothing but the words of the propagandists of the 1880s.

FIFTEEN YEARS AFTER the end of the war, the impression made by the South on most foreign visitors was one of hopeless devastation. C. Vann Woodward's synopsis of contemporary travel reports runs as follows:

> Throughout the countryside and in the small towns travelers found the same grim poverty and dilapidation. Roads were in a "shocking condition," with "few bridges across the rivers, and almost none across the creeks." Railroads, "save for a few through lines operated by Northern capitalists," were "barely passable for trains running ten or fifteen miles an hour." In Alabama "the towns are lonesome and the stores empty of customers; hotels subsist on the patronage of drummers from Northern cities." Planters' homes were often abandoned and falling in ruins, and Negroes "live in the old cabins . . . or have built for themselves wretched huts." The picture was much the same in other states. "Everywhere the people show by their dress and manner of living that they are poor. Even the owners of large plantations wear coarse clothing, live on plainer fare than ordinary mechanics in the North, and are oppressed with debts."[104]

While the textile industry, a pet project of New South propaganda, began to gain a foothold in the 1880s, it was restricted to isolated regions. The total picture remained that of a "miserable landscape dotted only with a few rich enclaves."[105] Although absolute statistics showed the South making progress in industrialization, relative to the North, it was actually moving backward. Whereas in 1860 17.2 percent of national industrial production and 11.5 percent of national industrial capital came from the South, by 1904 the respective figures had declined to 15.3 and 11 percent. The discrepancy in standard of living was similar. Per capita income in the 1880s South was only a third of the national average.[106] Expectations of a wave of European immigrants who would provide a reservoir of cheap labor and so attract capital investments to the South also remained unfulfilled. New Jersey alone received twice the number of immigrants as the entire South during this period. Of the 250,000 immigrants who entered the United States in the two years following the war, a grand total of 3,000 settled in the South. And even then, not all remained. For example, a group of 213 settlers who had been recruited in the fall of 1865 for a plantation in Louisiana were clearly not happy there. "When the immigrants saw the dilapidated slave shacks and tasted the fatback and cornbread," one historian records, "they sat down and refused to work."[107]

The only economic reality to emerge at the end of the South's industrial apotheosis was that of an economic colony. In contrast to Henry Grady's surreal image of Northern capitalists wandering about the Southern forests like herds of deer, the South itself became the hunted game. Contrary to the expectation that Northern capital would flow into the South like a stream of milk and honey, the North withdrew capital gains as quickly as they were earned. Instead of becoming a new version of the North, much less achieving economic mastery, the South became the nineteenth-century equivalent of the Third World, condemned to the role of providing low-wage, low-tech labor and more controlled by and dependent on the North than ever before.[108]

Seldom in the history of economic modernization has the self-conception of a modernizing elite been so at odds with reality as in the New South. To some extent, the deafening proclamations of New South propagandists were an attempt to drown out the growing feelings of inferiority. Like other vanquished societies, the New South hoped to modernize by imitating the superior technological model of its former enemy—but preserving its cultural identity in the process and even establishing its superiority to that of the "uncultured" victors. Seen from this perspective, the New South program emerges as nothing other than the Lost Cause in modern dress or, conversely, a return to the Old South via the detour of modernization. The New South was "simply the Old South under new conditions," according to one version, or "the Old South asserting herself under a new dispensation," in another. In either case its mission was to "take up the unfinished work of the Old South so rudely interrupted by the shock of war."[109]

With these slogans, New South propagandists defended their program against attacks by traditional Lost Cause advocates, who accused them of selling out traditional values. It was the time-honored conflict between orthodox conservatives and those open to reconciliation and modernization—in the vernacular of the time, between the "mummies" of the Lost Cause and the "new men" who were seeking to preserve the Old South in the New.[110] Their contradictory aspirations suggest why the lush rhetoric of the New South was so radically divorced from its impoverished reality. The greatest obstacle to an economic boom turned out to be what has been described as a continuation of slavery by other means: the policies of racism, segregation, repression, and discrimination that continued well into the twentieth century. These policies were as integral a part of the New South program as the ideas of modernization and industrialization. Moreover, in contrast to such rhetorical chimeras, racist policies were a reality that scuttled all plans before they had a chance to succeed.

The New South thus reveals an astonishing affinity to that of the Old South. Just as the peculiar institution of slavery had driven the

Old South into isolation, the no less peculiar institution of racial discrimination condemned the New South's modernization attempts to failure. Nonetheless, the similarity conceals a more significant difference between the two societies. The prewar cotton barons were, within the context of slavery, highly modern agricultural industrialists who could measure up to the captains of industry in the North. The fact that they named their plantations after Walter Scott's heroes and took part in pseudomedieval tournaments in no way inhibited their ability to conduct business transactions. They knew how to keep the two worlds apart. Their sons, the New South propagandists, did not possess this ability. They were caught in a dilemma: slavery no longer being an option, they were able to accept and embrace liberal-industrial capitalism—with its egalitarian implications—only in rhetoric. Their position in a no-man's-land between Northern industrial capitalism and Prussian-style romantic-agrarian patriarchy prevented them from consistently pursuing either system. As a result, they hopelessly romanticized both the Old South that they were trying to restore and the industrial modernization that was to serve as the primary means to that end.

The Embrace

"It is with no ordinary pride and satisfaction that we thus record the completion of the task undertaken with the desire to enlighten our country concerning itself, and to spread before the nation the wonderful natural resources, the social condition, and the political complications of a region which needs but just, wise, and generous legislation, with responding good will and industry, to make it a garden of happiness and prosperity."[111]

These lines, written in 1874, flowed from the pen not of one of the New South propagandists but of the editor of *Scribner's Magazine*, which was based in New York. The occasion was a series of articles by *Scribner's* star reporter, Edward King, about conditions in the South during congressional Reconstruction. King had made his name a few years previously with his reports on the Paris Commune. Now he became the first Northern reporter to sketch out a new picture of the South, no longer depicting it as incorrigibly hostile to the Union and its values. King's South had been reeducated by its defeat and postwar sufferings, and its population was "as loyal to the idea of the Union today as are the citizens of New York."[112]

King was not alone in his depiction. Over the course of the next two years, during which many similar articles appeared, the North underwent a change of heart regarding the South. The policy of a strong punitive hand came to seem outmoded and obsolete: "Is it not time," one editorial asked, "to bring to an end the punishment of the innocent many for the crimes of the guilty few?" The commercial and conservative zeitgeist of the 1870s, rejecting the moralizing stance of congressional Reconstruction, was increasingly sympathetic to Southern viewpoints, particularly on the issue of white supremacy as the only means to prevent a feared "Africanization" of the country. It was the beginning of a national embrace, and the young men of the New South were the ideal figures to reach out to their former enemies. Too young to have been accessories to the crimes of slavery and secession, they were doubly likely to elicit warm feelings because they were admirers of the Northern model and because they gave their counterparts the sense of having won over the sons after defeating the fathers. The North proved all too eager to share in the fantasy of the New South's blossoming industrial landscapes. As a New York banker wrote of his journeys there: "It seemed to me that we traveled through a continuous and unbroken strain of what has been aptly termed the music of progress— the whir of the spindle, the buzz of the saw, the roar of the furnace, and the throb of the locomotive."[113]

Insofar as the former enemies were not sovereign states but two sides in a civil war, the postwar history of the South was destined to be one of reunification and reconciliation with the North. In this respect, the War of Secession (as the Civil War was also known) is comparable to the nineteenth-century European wars of national unification in Italy and Germany, which also feature a modern North (Piedmont and Prussia) compelling a traditionalist South (Naples and Austria) into a joint venture. The similarities do not stop there. In all three cases, the national unity that had been wrought by the sword was perceived to be complete only when the two sides joined to fight against a common external enemy. What the Franco-Prussian War of 1870–71 was for Germany and the 1911 Libyan war against the Ottoman Empire was for Italy, the Spanish-American War of 1898 was for the United States: an ordeal of fire that brought the nation together. It must be said that the Spanish-American War could only partially fulfill this function: the conflict did not last long enough to give rise to a mythology of sufficient depth. It was too short and too slight to qualify as a crusade; it lacked the gravity to take the mythological place occupied by the Civil War. Only World War I was able to accomplish that task, and then all the more thoroughly.

The First World War offered both sides in the Civil War the opportunity once and for all to transfer any lingering resentments to a common enemy. A comparison of the propaganda used during both conflicts reveals a similar psychology of demonizing the enemy, down to the very choice of words. Germany became what the North and the South had been for each other: the incarnation of evil. For the North, which considered itself the moral victor in both wars, the transference was easier than for the South, which had to grow accustomed to its new role. Nonetheless, thirty years of New South ideology had created enough identification with the former conqueror for the South to join the chorus calling for a crusade with full conviction, using much the same rhetoric as had been directed against it and its peculiar institution a half century earlier. To cite two examples, Randolph McKim, in his sermon "America Summoned to a Holy War," declared that Germany "must be beaten to its knees; it must be crushed, if civilization is to be saved—if the world is to be made safe for Democracy. . . . This conflict is indeed a Crusade. The greatest in history—the holiest. It is in the profound-est and truest sense a Holy War." And the *Baptist Standard* in April 1917 insisted: "This is not a war of conquest or of retaliation. It is a conflict between liberty and autocracy—between democracy and monarchism, a protest against the spirit of despotism and mil-itarism. . . . We hear the summons to a new crusade."[114] It is both an irony of history and a subject worthy of an extended psychohis-torical study that Woodrow Wilson, the man who led the United States in its moral crusade, was the first Southern president since the days of the secession.[115]

So what became of the Lost Cause? Did the South's shared vic-tory in World War I render it obsolete? On the surface, this would appear to be the case. "Dixie's cause triumphant is the South's 'lost cause' no more," ran a line from a poem composed to commemorate the year 1918.[116] Joining the ranks of the victors fulfilled the psy-chological demand for *revanche*, even though Germany—and not the North—was now the enemy. As a balm for wounded pride, the Lost Cause had fulfilled its mission by 1918 and might have been expected to disappear. But in the fifty years of its existence, the myth had developed a momentum of its own. Unlike the French desire for *revanche* after 1870 and Germany's stab-in-the-back legend of 1918–19, which both lost relevance after subsequent wars, the Lost Cause remained a piece of regional mythology, available to be tapped whenever the South felt out of step with the nation as a whole. It persists in varying degrees to the present day.

Its first renaissance in the twentieth century occurred ten years after World War I, as the failure of the New South became obvious. Far from acknowledging the South as a paradigm of modernization, most Northerners looked on the region with horror, disgust, or at best disdainful amusement, seeing it as the home of racial discrim-ination, lynchings, creationism, and other forms of barbarism. In response, twelve young Southern writers, including Allen Tate and Robert Penn Warren, banded together as the "Southern agrarians" and in 1930 published a manifesto entitled *I'll Take My Stand*. All twelve were rebels against their fathers' New South generation and defenders of the South against the rest of the country. As an intellectual offensive, their writings were nothing less than a second, "spiritual" secession.[117] *I'll Take My Stand* offered little more than a revised version of what antebellum Southern ideologues like George Fitzhugh had written. Once again, the South was depicted as an agricultural Arcadia and contrasted with the industrial hell of the North. But the timing of the publication, a year after the beginning of the Great Depression, could not have been more felicitous. The widespread suffering of that era—and the need for an alternative—undoubtedly accounts for the serious critical attention *I'll Take My Stand* attracted. Less significant was the work's reception by economists and social scientists who, like the authors themselves, were unable to see that the book was not an economic and political manifesto but a work of literature in disguise.[118]

Although they did not change Southern reality, the agrarians succeeded in transforming the Lost Cause into a new myth of the "other" America. Some historians have viewed this extended Lost Cause as a challenge to American capitalism comparable in its radicalism to Marxism. David M. Potter was the first historian to draw attention to this aspect of the agrarian ideals of the 1930s. But, he argued, "the real significance lay in the fact that it offered an alternative to Marxism. Here, in fact, was a way in which a man could renounce industrial capitalism and all its works without becoming a Marxist. This is perhaps why the agrarian ideal held so much attention for such a large number of social thinkers. It gave them a chance to express their dissent from the prevailing system without going outside the American tradition in order to do so."[119] The ideological development of Eugene Genovese, a leading historian of Southern slavery, from orthodox Marxist to "Southern conservative" serves as an ex post facto illustration of Potter's thesis. To complete the picture, one need only add what Genovese's wife, Elizabeth Fox-Genovese, says of today's Southern conservatives: "They are proudly and self-consciously heir to what may well be the most sustained critique of the excesses of capitalism that this country has known."[120]

The American South and the agrarian ideal of a "counter-America" offered both a criticism of the status quo and a preview of a better world. Depending on the prevailing mood, the rest of the nation has reacted to this challenge with either dreamy nostalgia or irritated hostility. For the nation as a whole, the South remains an exception usually viewed with simultaneous mistrust and nostalgia. Not coincidentally, the South in the twentieth century continued to share the German destiny of being periodically demonized by Northern moralists as the incarnation of evil.[121]

It may seem that we have exhausted the topic of the Lost Cause as the central myth of the South. Yet its significance for the rest of America merits a closer look. In particular, it is worth examining how Southern history made its way to the North and came to be accepted in the dual sense of "trophy taking": as the appropriation of the vanquished culture in the form of "booty" and as the tendency of intellectual elites to see their nation's triumph as a source of peril and to find in the loser's culture a positive counterexample. To the unified nation, the South and its Lost Cause constituted a trophy of both sorts.

The Nationalization of the Lost Cause

The folk wisdom that the Civil War resulted from the reading habits of the American people contains a kernel of truth. Just as Mark Twain identified Walter Scott as the cause of the South's ill-fated destiny, to this day schoolbooks contain the truism that Harriet Beecher Stowe's *Uncle Tom's Cabin* (1851) so excited moral outrage in the North as to make the Civil War inevitable. Undoubtedly, Scott's novels played a significant role in shaping the mentality of the South in the decades before the war. *Uncle Tom's Cabin* helped mobilize Northern public opinion against slavery. But literature also played a role after the war, in the reconciliation between the two sections of the nation. For the "plantation novels" that became all the rage in the 1880s and 1890s presupposed readers willing to embrace the reunited nation. It is ironic, then, that the plantation novel actually arose before the Civil War, in the very decades when the South was developing its cultural identity. Indeed, second only to the Walter Scott craze, the plantation novel was the most important literary vehicle for the idea of a discrete Southern culture. Without it there would have been no plantation mythology or myth of the cavalier, and without the myth of the cavalier there would have been no belief in Southern cultural separatism. In other words, Southern culture was as bound up with the plantation and its accompanying myths as the European aristocratic culture was with images of the castle and the court. The plantation was the counterpart to the Northern office and factory, the site not of working, calculating, and doing business but of enjoying life to its fullest in complete comfort. As a *locus amoenus*, it approximated the paradise on earth that the South had imagined itself to be since it was first settled.

The prewar plantation novel contains several recurrent elements. At the center, there is always a big white house with a Greek portico, an open staircase, an expansive veranda, the shady trees of an adjoining park, and the enchanting scent of magnolias. In the background, there are white fields of cotton where black slaves go about their work in choreographed harmony. The planter is always a cheerful, rather impractical elderly gentleman who devotes more time to his hobbies than to everyday affairs. Strangely enough, there is seldom a lady of the house, and when there is, she is usually a "dim figure, as though matrimony faded womanhood into rapid indistinctness."[122] All the more important, then, is the role played by the daughter. She is her father's beloved confidante and is frequently surrounded by eager young beaus. Usually she is described not as ravishingly beautiful but rather as highly attractive in her charm, wit, and grace.[123] The young master is an ancillary character compared with the daughter and is included more for reasons of family symmetry—

which is already disrupted by the absence of the mother—than for any compelling dramatic purpose. Among the slaves, the two most important figures are the old black butler, also a confidant of the planter, and the cheerful mammy. The rest of the slaves serve as a chorus, singing, dancing, and taking delight in life's small things, as innocent and carefree as children. It is a world "permeated with joy from top to bottom," much like that of the Central European operetta with its Hungarian princes and counts, servants, chambermaids, and gypsy musicians.[124]

In presenting readers with these idyllic visions, the prewar plantation novel merely conforms to the norm of nineteenth-century escapist literature.[125] What is remarkable is that it attracted such an enthusiastic readership in the North precisely at the moment when abolitionist sentiment was at its height. Apparently the soul of the North was divided in two. While one half condemned slavery as barbarism and demanded its abolition, the other enjoyed the beautiful illusion of a plantation Arcadia, "a sort of projection ground for its own dreams of a vanished golden time."[126] The plantation novel allowed Northern readers to withdraw for a few pleasant hours from their work ethic and discipline, to lose themselves in a lavish dream world, a society they would deem immoral as soon as they finished reading. This age-old conflict between the taming of the instincts and the desire for pleasure could not always be mediated by a simple switch of mental gears, as *Uncle Tom's Cabin* and other, more obscure antislavery novels of the 1850s clearly demonstrate. All are plantation novels—and not just in the sense that any work about slavery is necessarily set on a plantation. More to the point, they all follow the Arcadian paradigm, contrasting it with a satanic fall from grace. In *Uncle Tom's Cabin*, the genial but weak-willed planter is the Southerner St. Clare, whereas the evil slave master is the transplanted Yankee Legree. Historian W. R. Taylor describes the villainous Legree as an "anti-planter" and his mansion, which perverts the principles of the "good" plantation, as an "anti-home": "What we are given in a few pages is an evocative vision of the home become a factory, where everything, finally, is weighed in the balance scale of Legree's cotton house. Southerners, who almost universally objected to these scenes, never fully understood that Harriet Stowe had simply imported into the South the factory scenes which Southerners were fond of invoking as contrast to the paternalism of the plantation."[127] Thus, far from consistently embodying the evils of slavery, the plantation, even in abolitionist novels, continues to represent the idealized image of an intact agrarian-patriarchal society.

War and reconstruction only temporarily diminished the plantation novel's popularity. The example of John W. DeForest, for instance, shows how vital the tradition was and how easily it could be resurrected. DeForest, a New Englander, served as an officer in the Union army and in the administration of the occupying forces. He was thus not a man who could be accused of political sympathies with the South. In 1867, however, he published what was probably the first postwar plantation novel to be penned by a Northerner. *Miss Ravenel's Conversion from Secession to Loyalty* was written very much in the spirit of Reconstruction, "not unkind to the South in detail," as Paul H. Buck writes, but "altogether a triumph of Yankee virtue over Rebel frailty."[128] Having made his point, DeForest moved closer in his later novels to the prewar literary convention of the idyllic plantation. The shift can hardly be explained by opportunism since at this point there was little market in the North for plantation romanticism. What attracted DeForest, aside from nostalgic longings, was the picturesque quality of plantation life and the colorful cast of characters, both of which stood in stark contrast to the gray conformity of life in the North. He made this clear, not without an undertone of condescension, in a 1869 essay: "They [Southerners] are more simple than we, more provincial, more antique, more picturesque; they have fewer of the virtues of modern society, and more of the primitive, the natural virtues; they care less for wealth, art, learning, and the other delicacies of an urban civilization. . . . Cowed as we are by the Mrs. Grundy of democracy; moulded into tame similarity by a general education, remarkably uniform in degree and nature, we shall do well to study this peculiar people, which will soon lose its peculiarities; we shall do better to engraft upon ourselves its nobler qualities."[129] In the 1860s Albion W. Tourgée, another former Union army officer and occupation administrator who tried his hand at literature, foresaw a shift that would further enhance the plantation legend in the post-Reconstruction era. "Within thirty years after the war of rebellion," he wrote, "popular sympathy will be with those who upheld the Confederate cause rather than with those by whom it was overthrown; our popular heroes will be Confederate leaders; our fiction will be Southern in its prevailing types and distinctly Southern in its character."[130]

It was no accident that plantation romanticism became a national literary fashion at precisely the same time that the propaganda for the New South was being warmly received in both the South and the North. Nor was it mere coincidence that the authors of these novels, like the propagandists of the New South, were nearly all born in the 1850s. (At least one figure, Joel Chandler Harris, was a prominent member of both groups.)[131] C. Vann Woodward observes how intimately the two movements were connected: "The bitter mixture of recantation and heresy could never have been swallowed so readily had it not been dissolved in the syrup of romanticism."[132]

Postwar plantation literature (of which plays became an increasingly important part) retains most of the elements of its prewar predecessors. Its only significant innovation is to incorporate the Civil War and Reconstruction into the plot, enabling a clear contrast between the golden age of the past with the leaden reality of the present.[133] The plot was usually divided into three sections. The exposition depicts the idyll of the happy peacetime plantation. The outbreak of war and the dissolution of the community follows: the men go to the front; the women stay behind. A time of misery and danger commences. Marauding gangs and renegade Yankee soldiers overrun the plantation. But just as all seems lost, a young Yankee officer and gentleman appears, ready to protect the women from the terrible fate that awaits them. The young belle, initially distrustful of or even hostile toward the Yankee hero, discovers his good qualities one by one and falls in love with him. The plot concludes with a North-South wedding. In *Shenandoah*, the most frequently performed plantation drama of the time, no fewer than five couples get married at the end.[134]

The paradigm of symbolic reconciliation between the two regions of the reconstituted nation recurs again and again. As in the New South movement, both sides of the Mason-Dixon Line profit from the plantation-war-marriage trajectory. The South gets to retain the Lost Cause, and its unique cultural identity, symbolized by the plantation, is acknowledged by the North. At the same time, the spirit of the Old South is modernized by the infusion of energy and discipline embodied by the Yankee bridegroom—as it would not have been had the daughter married one of the Oblomovian planter's sons from her homeland. The Yankee bridegroom is the literary incarnation of the coveted Northern investor of New South propaganda. For his part, the Northerner, as new master, gains control over the plantation romance instead of being relegated, as before, to the role of passive reader. The plantation house, the belle, and the aristocratic lifestyle are cultural trophies with which the North can adorn itself without having to accept the unseemly connotations of any of these institutions. The nature of the trophy itself has been transformed: what once stood for power, substance, conviction, and religion becomes, in the hands of the victorious conqueror, mere ornament, decoration, plaything, and entertainment.

The situation in reality was much the same as in literature.[135] Yankee millionaires with economic interests in the South—such as Cornelius Vanderbilt, Henry M. Flagler, and Collis Huntington—inaugurated a series of aristocratic matches by marrying Southern belles, much as their sons would later marry the daughters of Europe's high aristocracy. Woodward's commentary is, as always, to the point: "For these aging buccaneers the South was a belated romance upon which they lavished endowments, investments, and the devotion of dotage."[136]

In this way, the plantation legend, taken over by the emerging culture industry, ceased to be exclusively a myth of the South. Instead, it became a part of the escapist dream factory that would ultimately appropriate all periods of human history and that would later be known as Hollywood. The Hollywood version of the plantation no longer articulated a distinct Southern self-conception and cultural identity but merely exploited it as raw material—"local color"—to provide the audience with entertainment, diversion, enchantment, romance, and melodrama. In other words, Southern culture was just as subject to Northern colonial exploitation as the Southern economy: both took their directives before and after the war from the cultural and financial center of New York. Like Henry Grady with his visions of the New South, novelists wrote their plantation romances primarily for a Northern audience. Thomas Nelson Page, the most successful exponent of the "plantation school," advised a young author who was having difficulty selling her novel: "It is the easiest thing in the world. Get a pretty girl and name her Jeanne, that name always takes! Make her fall in love with a Federal officer and your story will be printed at once!"[137]

The culture industry typically reworks mythological material so extensively, glossing over all genuine difference, that eventually distinctions between victor and vanquished vanish. When *Uncle Tom's Cabin* was staged during the 1880s, a number of changes were made in the text that illustrate this transformation. The first dramatic adaptation, written a year after the publication of the novel, retained the abolitionist elements of the original, as did all subsequent adaptations throughout the Civil War and Reconstruction. After the historic compromise of 1877, however, the text began to be "cleansed" of its political, abolitionist content, until what was once a polemical, politically charged drama criticizing slavery had become a piece of full-blown romantic plantation folklore. "The great plot over which so many tears were shed," Francis Pendleton Gaines writes, "became little more than a convenient thread on which were lavishly strung minstrel gems and rather sympathetic pictures."[138]

DID THE HAPPY ending of the plantation drama, with its North-South marriage, and the transformation of the plantation novel into kitsch indicate that the Lost Cause had finally been abandoned? Or was there still a place for it in the reunified nation? And if so, whose Lost Cause was it? Clearly, the Lost Cause remains part of Southern culture, but it has also, molelike, dug its way into the deepest layers of national mythology. Some concluding observations will suggest how it has.

Victory, like revolution, can devour its children, particularly those who expect more from it than what it actually delivers. The idealists who realize too late that violence can never achieve their goals are among history's most common losers in victory. This was the experience of Northern intellectuals, particularly from New England, after the Civil War. The outcome they had anticipated from victory over the South was the reconstitution of the old Jeffersonian republic. What they got instead was the Gilded Age, a society whose crass materialism outdid that of Bismarckian Germany and the French July monarchy. The ideals of intellectual New England, represented by men like Ralph Waldo Emerson, Henry James, and Henry Adams, became another Lost Cause, surpassing even that of the South in its existential intensity. The South was, after all, prepared for its fate. Three decades of stagnation and decline had psychologically attuned it to the possibility of defeat and had produced a fully developed lost-cause mythology that needed only a lost war to become operational. New England intellectuals, on the other hand, were caught by surprise, without any comparable mythological buttresses. Their philosophy, transcendentalism, which had arisen at the same time as the cult of chivalry in the South, was an attempt to create an up-to-date American version of humanism free of all mythologizing. But their effort was to be heavily punished, as Vernon L. Parrington realized in 1927: "In the world of Jay Cooke and Commodore Vanderbilt, the transcendental dream was as hopelessly a lost cause as the plantation dream; it was in an even worse plight, for it left no tragic memories to weave a romance about the fallen hopes."[139] What Parrington failed to see was the possibility that the disillusioned idealists of the North might borrow the South's mythology of defeat. Such borrowing, of course, did not take place openly and explicitly but rather partially and indirectly, like a shameful secret.

Within the American mythology of optimism, the South became a metaphor for dissatisfaction, self-doubt, and potential as well as for actual catastrophe. The economic crisis of the 1930s proved fertile ground for the Southern literary renaissance of William Faulkner, Robert Penn Warren, and Thomas Wolfe, among others, as the nation began to see its own destiny reflected in that of the Old South. Robert E. Lee became a national icon of heroic defeat, and Faulkner's Quentin Compson appeared no longer as a case study in pathology, as he had a few years earlier, but as a man of his times.[140] No fewer than eighty Civil War novels were published between 1930 and 1939, attracting a huge audience. The most successful of these, Margaret Mitchell's *Gone with the Wind*, became a national parable for America's fall from the heights of the 1920s into the depths of the Depression. The plantation Tara was America, with its own golden age, crisis, and ultimately—American optimism being indefatigable—reconstruction. As Woodward writes: "The experience of evil and the experience of tragedy are parts of the Southern heritage that are as difficult to reconcile with the American legend of innocence and social felicity as the experience of poverty and defeat are to reconcile with the legends of abundance and success."[141]

Woodward's thesis—that the experience of defeat and failure fundamentally distinguish the South from the rest of the nation—needs to be supplemented. The rest of the nation was in fact capable of *indirectly* comprehending the experience of defeat through the metaphor of the South. In an essay entitled "A Southern Critique of the Gilded Age," Woodward himself cites three examples of this very phenomenon. Herman Melville, Henry Adams, and Henry James were all among the losers in the victors' camp. In the prevailing climate after 1865, they all felt, in Adams's words, as lost as "the Indians or the buffalo who had been decimated by our ancestors."[142] None of these three men had been particularly interested in the South, let alone had sympathized with it. All had deplored slavery. Nonetheless, in their works they used Southerners as mouthpieces for criticizing their times and as representatives of the "other" America.[143] In all three cases, the heroes are former Confederate officers whose message differs starkly from that of the Yankee bridegrooms of plantation romance: not the optimistic belief in progress but a critique of a decadent civilization, not the elevation of the South of plantations and belles to the economic and ideological level of the North but the reverse—a profound questioning of the North's industrial and commercial triumph and a reminder that there were values other than that of the almighty dollar.

But more poetic than any literary representations of the Lost Cause was the personal lost cause of Ralph Waldo Emerson. The leading representative of transcendentalism had raised his voice as loudly as anyone in support of the crusade against slavery. After the Union victory, he fell silent. One reason was his premature senility at the age of sixty-two. For ten years, he existed in a condition of physical and mental decline, writing hardly anything, instead giving public readings of works by writers close to his heart. Among them was Henry Timrod, the unofficial poet laureate of the Confederacy, someone whom Emerson would have viewed with contempt before the war. One of the poems Emerson recited most frequently was Timrod's "Ode to the Confederate Dead." Literary historian Lewis P. Simpson surmises that Emerson recognized toward the end of his life that the South's defeat was also his own. He was no longer capable of articulating this insight, but in Timrod's lines he may have found the words to speak for him:

> Sleep sweetly in your humble graves,
>   Sleep, martyrs of a fallen cause;
> Though yet no marble column craves
>   The pilgrim here to pause.
>
> In seeds of laurel in the earth,
>   The garlands of your fame are sown;
> And, somewhere, waiting for its birth,
>   The shaft is in the stone.[144]

· 2 ·

FRANCE

In the long list of political and military leaders who, since the fall of the Roman republic, have taken their lives in the face of defeat, the case of Lucien-Anatole Prévost-Paradol is one of the least known yet most curious. At about one o'clock in the morning of July 20, 1870, Prévost-Paradol, the French ambassador in Washington, stood before his wardrobe mirror and shot himself in the heart. Just the day before, Napoleon III of France had declared his ill-advised war against Prussia, but the French humiliation was months in the future; indeed, the fighting had not even begun. Nonetheless, a diplomatic colleague's pointed remark that Prévost-Paradol was the first casualty of the Franco-Prussian War was right on the mark, but for other than the obvious reason.[1] It was not despondency over his government's future prospects that had made Prévost-Paradol decide to end it all; he was not a Napoleonic loyalist. Quite the contrary, since at the age of twenty-five, as an editorialist for the *Journal des débats*, he had been in the front ranks of the liberal opposition to Napoleon's Second Empire. When the regime began to liberalize in 1869, Prévost-Paradol must have thought he had achieved his goal, and he offered his services to his sovereign. But what should have been the crowning achievement of a successful political career—his appointment as ambassador—turned out to be fool's gold. Prévost-Paradol found himself, as another colleague, Charles Victor Cherbuliez, put it, "in the situation of a young man who marries a shrew for her money, only to discover the very next day that she has lost her entire fortune in a disastrous speculation."[2]

The tragic irony was that just two years earlier Prévost-Paradol had predicted the disastrous Prussian adventure with a clarity unmatched by his contemporaries. In his widely read and respected book *La France nouvelle* (1868), he described France and Prussian Germany as two trains speeding toward a head-on collision. "After various efforts at evasive action, the collision has become inevitable. . . . What rivers of blood and tears will flow when it takes place!" It made little difference that no one really wanted such a collision: "Human omnipotence and human foolishness will combine to ensure catastrophe." (Prévost-Paradol's term in the original is *holocauste*.)[3] Prévost-Paradol had little faith in France's prospects of prevailing since even a French victory would not eradicate Germany's nascent nationalism but only further fan its flames. A German victory, on the other hand, would signal the end of France as a leading power. The great nation would be reduced to the status of a middling European player, left to languish "in its own ruins with neither power nor honor."[4] As Prévost-Paradol saw it, the only way out of this dire situation was the creation of a greater imperial France through expansion in Africa, using Algeria as a base. "Eighty to one hundred million Frenchman on both sides of the Mediterranean would shore up France's long-term economic and cultural position in Europe."[5]

As prophetic as *La France nouvelle* may appear in the light of later events, Prévost-Paradol only summarized with special urgency and greater topicality a view that had been continually debated among the French intelligentsia since the 1840s. Many feared that the fall of Napoleon I marked the beginning of France's decline into a second-rate power doomed to lag behind the rest of the modern world and to suffer the pressures of the other great powers—England and America to the west, Germany and Russia to the east.[6] "Our role has been played out, at least in the short term; the future belongs to Prussia, America and Russia": in the two decades between 1840 and 1860, statements like this one, by Hippolyte Taine, were as common as the title *La décadence de la France* for the books and articles in which they appeared.[7]

The doom and gloom of this period may well have been a delayed reaction to the French collapse of 1814–15, which, far from being acknowledged as a national trauma, had rather been dismissed as the personal failure of Napoleon I. Stendhal, who was in Paris at the demise of the First Empire, recorded the indifference with which the nation reacted to the event: "It was all taken in stride, and the regime's representatives as well as ordinary citizens were only concerned with one thing: their personal interests." Of the Empress Josephine's departure from France, he wrote: "Nary a sign of popular sympathy. . . . People asked who it was that was traveling and shrugged when they were told."[8] The apathy can be explained as the result of general exhaustion with war itself, as Germany experienced at the end of World War I or Italy after the fall of Mussolini.[9] Perceived as the main obstacle to a quick peace settlement with the allied enemies, Napoleon was declared the chief culprit for the war and was duly sacrificed, to France's great relief. Thus the nation felt itself to have been untouched by defeat even though it had been vanquished and occupied by an external enemy for the first time in four hundred years. Along with the scapegoating of Napoleon, the relatively generous peace terms offered by the victors allowed France to maintain a sense of equanimity. Also important, however, was the fact that France had been defeated not by a single enemy but by a coalition, toward whose individual members the French nation could still feel as superior as Gulliver toward the Lilliputians.

This complacency—"*Nos gloires compensaient nos revers*" (Our triumphs make up for our setbacks)—was severely shaken during the

July monarchy.[10] One indication of the growing loss of confidence was the cult of Napoleon that arose at the same time as the debates over France's "decadence." The fact that Napoleon, barely one generation after his exile to St. Helena, was brought home to Paris, interred in Les Invalides, and enthroned as a new national hero indicated that the political establishment—which had staged the whole spectacle—was no longer sure of its own rule. Summoning the ghost of Bonaparte, as Marx described the phenomenon, was an attempt to slow or even reverse France's decline, and the Second Empire, inaugurated by Napoleon's nephew Louis, better known as Napoleon III, can only be understood as arising from this nostalgic source. Not surprisingly, therefore, Napoleon III's political and military activities never transcended the symbolic realm of operatic adventure; indeed, they gave concrete form to the discrepancy between grand gestures and great politics.

Such a discrepancy was clearly at work in 1866, when Prussia commenced the last phase of building a new German empire. It was obvious to even the most obtuse observers that France, which opposed German unification, would treat every step in that direction as a personal threat. Nonetheless, there was considerable amazement throughout Europe when, after Prussia's defeat of Austria at Königgrätz (known in France by the name of the neighboring village Sadowa), the cry *"Revanche pour Sadowa"* was heard on the streets of Paris. The uproar over Austria's drubbing was so loud, in fact, and so widespread that one might have been tempted to conclude that France itself had been vanquished. A government agent, gauging public sentiment, reported: "The irritation against Prussia is still very intense in my district and the feeling of the masses is that France must take her revenge." And another added: "We wish the emperor would take his revenge; I mention this wish, this familiar expression, because I hear it is on everyone's tongue today." The events that prompted this immense consternation had suddenly belied the conviction, held firmly since 1806, that the territory beyond the Rhine contained nothing more than a confederation of passive and powerless principalities. Empress Eugénie described to the Prussian ambassador her own awakening from this illusion: "The energy and rapidity of your movements," she wrote, had made clear "that with a nation like yours as a neighbor, we are in danger of seeing you in Paris one day unannounced. I will go to sleep French and wake up Prussian." French indignation persisted for four years, by which time the *revanchistes* were able simply to substitute "Sedan" for Sadowa. The imaginary defeat had become all too real.[11]

The Unfolding of Defeat

Although the Franco-Prussian War of 1870–71 was one of the shortest in modern history, it encompassed three distinct phases of military engagement. The first ran from the Second Empire's declaration of war on Prussia on July 19 until Napoleon III's surrender and capture at Sedan on September 2, 1870, which precipitated the fall of the imperial regime and the proclamation of the Third Republic two days later in Paris. The second phase began in October—after the provisional government's failed efforts to negotiate a lenient peace settlement along the lines of 1814 and the Prussian siege of Paris. Surrounded by Bismarck's troops, the republic mobilized the people in a *levée en masse* that lasted until January 28, 1871, when the provisional government gave up. Finally, in March 1871, following the acceptance of German terms for peace and the loss of Alsace-Lorraine, much of the population of Paris took up arms in what Marx termed "the French Civil War" and what has gone down in history as the Paris Commune uprising. It ended in May in such complete, murderous defeat that Prévost-Paradol's term *holocauste* may be applied with justice. While eighty thousand Frenchmen died in the war with Prussia, thirty thousand perished in the Commune— roughly one out of thirty Parisians was killed in the course of the uprising and its suppression.[12]

The phrase *l'année terrible*, much in use at the time and taken up by Victor Hugo to describe this cycle of war and defeat, was an obvious reference to the Reign of Terror of the 1790s. Indeed, on closer examination, the entire history around Sedan is shot through with French revolutionary mythology.[13] The 1840s revival of Bonapartism, which aimed at counteracting national decline, was followed in this period of crisis by the revitalized myth of the invincible Revolution. In this light, it was possible to see the German invasion of late summer and autumn 1870 as a repeat of 1792, when the Austro-Prussian invasion was halted at Valmy, a view that implied a belief in France's ultimate victory. Thus, even on September 1, 1870, one day before Sedan and the demise of Napoleon III's empire, reports of lost battles and German advances on Paris were depicted in the *Revue des deux mondes* not as a national emergency but as a welcome wake-up call for a nation spoiled by too many quick and easy victories. "These setbacks have awakened France," the paper editorialized, "and created an awareness of the growing danger just in the nick of time. Meanwhile we are experiencing something we haven't seen for ages: a people that, seeing the abyss before its eyes, reaches deep into itself, comes to its senses, musters its strength, and overcomes its surprise and inertia in order to confront a present danger." The same issue featured an article by Paul Leroy-Beaulieu, who had for years been advocating colonial expansion as the best means for reestablishing French power. Leroy-Beaulieu was full of confidence about the prospects for his plans: "After we have repelled the enemy and dictated a glorious peace on our own terms, the patriotic work will begin in earnest."[14]

The first days after Sedan showed just how thoroughly the catastrophic reality had been obscured by its translation into mythological terms. Hermann Grimm, a German commentator, later described the mood, with mild sarcasm, as the French gift for ignoring unpleasant facts: "A France vanquished by the Germans is in French eyes merely a demonic apparition; the hordes now laying

siege to Paris are mere ghosts."[15] The news of France's crushing
defeat produced an astonishing capacity among the citizenry to
invent an alternate, more comforting reality. Within hours, before
national malaise could set in, the revolutionary past was being reen-
acted. A Parisian mob disrupted the meeting of the *corps législatif*
on the afternoon of September 4 and joined republican delegates
under the leadership of Léon Gambetta in marching on the Hôtel
de Ville. There Gambetta assumed the role of Danton by proclaiming the republic. The crowds were not just following the models of
1789, 1792, 1830, and 1848; they had become the very reincarnation
of those earlier events. Or rather, the reenactment of revolution was
a triumph that erased the experience of defeat, or at least pushed it
to the back of people's minds. Once again, only Napoleon had been
defeated, not the nation, and the shame of Sedan disappeared with
him into a German prison.[16] The revolution, on the other hand, and
the republic it created were the guarantors of ultimate victory.[17] Of
that everyone was certain.

Confident in this conviction, the provisional government made
Bismarck a peace offer that refused all territorial changes and proposed a return to the status quo ante. Foreign Minister Jules Favre's
famous formulation "not an inch of our territory or a stone of our
fortresses" set the tone for the dispatch. When Bismarck insisted on
the transfer of Alsace-Lorraine and financial compensation roughly
equivalent to Napoleon's demand of Prussia sixty-three years earlier,
Favre burst into tears and exclaimed: "You want to destroy France!"[18]

The war that now began—the conflict's second phase—differed
from what had come before in being weighed down by the earlier
defeat. The new men at the helm had not wanted to take command
of a sinking ship; Gambetta had warned on the evening of September 3 that "in no case should the republic be held responsible" for
the French defeat at Sedan.[19] But he was in no position to resist the
push from the masses or the pull of revolutionary rituals. Indeed,
his decision to proclaim the republic just two days after Sedan had

as much to do with popular pressure as with the power of ritual. Perhaps the French situation after Sedan can best be compared to that of Germany after the battle of the Marne in August 1914: for both countries, the strategic failure was obvious, but the war was too "young" in the public mind to be concluded on the spot. The disparity between military strategy and popular psychology is, as we have seen, one consequence of the democratization of war in the age of nationalism. A war waged with everything at stake ("victory or death") tends to end only when one side has been utterly beaten down. And such an outcome takes time—twenty years in the case of the Napoleonic Wars, four years for both the American Civil War and World War I.

Sedan had thus shaken the French from their complacency without destroying their will to fight. What they had imagined would be a swift and easy victory now appeared to be a prolonged and perhaps treacherous undertaking. They continued to dwell in the realm of fantasy, only this time their fantasies swung to the opposite extreme. Instead of envisioning the conquest of Prussia as little more than a casual stroll to Berlin, people everywhere—and not just the hysterical Parisian press—prophesied the imminent demise of the French nation should it fail to beat back the Germans. For Ernest Renan, Bismarck's demands meant the *finis franciae*: "A weakened and humiliated France would be incapable of survival. The loss of Alsace and Lorraine would mean the end of France."[20]

The forces Gambetta assembled in September and October 1870 to mount a *défense nationale* were themselves a strange conglomeration of fantasy and reality. The soldiers were real enough, as were the losses they suffered at the hands of the Prussian army. Everything else, however, was a summoning of ghosts, a continuation of the revolutionary rituals begun on September 4 in Paris. The organizers of the *défense nationale* were convinced that the new Third Republic would follow the victorious course of the First Republic in 1792. But no victory was forthcoming. Instead, France suffered a second defeat, which this time could not be attributed to a deposed tyrant.

Only then did the revolutionary myth lose its power to mobilize and galvanize. As a result, the nation split into its two traditionally antagonistic parts: Paris and the provinces.

The Parisian War

The view that Paris *is* France is as old as the conflation of the nation with the monarchy, which ruled from the city. Paris's special status was evident as early as the fifteenth century in sobriquets like *"ville souveraine," "ville maîtresse," "chef de tout notre empire"* (Charles V), and *"la France de la France."* Recognizing Paris's secularized (or better still, urbanized) divine calling and anticipating the role the city would play in the Revolution of 1789, Montaigne opined: *"Je ne suis français que par cette grande cité."* If Paris owed its fame before Louis XIV's relocation to Versailles to the reflected glory of the monarchy, after the Revolution, it owed its power to no one but itself. The source of this power was the Parisian populace, or, to use the modern term, its urban masses. Uprooted, atomized, proletarianized, easily manipulated and seduced by demagogues, the Parisian masses may have seemed like a caricature of the Rousseauian ideal of direct democracy. But they were the people on site in that part of the nation where things happened, and thus they inherited the appellations *"ville souveraine"* and *"la France de la France."*

After Sedan, France would likely have agreed to Bismarck's offer of peace in exchange for Alsace-Lorraine if not for Paris, which was determined to carry on the fight. Indeed, September 4 was to be the last time the provinces would simply accept their marching orders from the capital. With the surrender of the provisional government on January 28, 1871, a rift that had begun years before widened into a chasm. For a half century after 1789, the Revolution had united the two groups who were its main beneficiaries: the working class and the bourgeoisie. The Parisian populace—that conglomeration of street life, literary myth, utopian aspiration, and demagoguery—had proved ever ready to do the bourgeoisie's bidding on the barricades, and every time it did, the reward was its recognition as the actual sovereign of the nation. In June 1848, however, when the people launched a working-class revolt and made their own political demands, what they got in return was repression, not recognition. In his role as populist emperor, Napoleon III was temporarily able to paper over the divisions and avoid civil war. But after his defeat at Sedan and the failure of the *défense nationale* to reestablish solidarity, the disunity of 1848 reemerged in full force, not only as class conflict but as an intrinsic part of the nation's life-or-death struggle against the external enemy. The rebellion of the Paris Commune, the third phase of the 1870–71 war, was thus not just the first great modern battle between social classes, as history has recorded it, and certainly not the harbinger of world revolution, as it was stylized in Communist mythology. Rather, the Paris Commune melded the entire history of revolutionary and class struggle into a single great phantasm that drew on the memories of heroism and sacrifice of the Parisian people, from the triumph of 1792 to the defeat of 1848. Only if seen in this light—as the culmination of a decades-old enmity—can the passion and the hatred with which the war was waged on both sides be properly understood; only from this perspective can one comprehend the quality of madness that seemed to grip Communards and government forces alike during the eight weeks of the uprising, a madness noted by those few contemporaries who managed to retain their impartial judgment.

There had been signs of the clash to come in the period preceding the Commune's declaration on March 28. Even during the prior four months of the *défense nationale*, the rampant mistrust that had marked the Reign of Terror was very much in evidence. Traitors were suspected everywhere. On October 30, 1870, the news of Marshal Bazaine's capitulation at Metz and rumors of peace negotiations led to the mob's occupation of the Hôtel de Ville. Following the provisional government's surrender, suspicions of treachery blossomed into full-fledged paranoia. The new government installed after

elections at the beginning of February was no longer the revolutionary republican body of September 4 but rather a conservative regime
of closet royalists. As soon became clear, the change in leadership
expressed not only the nation's war fatigue and desire for peace but
also the old provincial resentment against Paris. Signs began to
appear that, after concluding peace with the enemy, the government
would turn to its next task—enforcing discipline on the unpopular
capital. Adolphe Thiers, who in 1848 had advocated the bloody suppression of the proletarian revolt in Paris, was now the head of the
new government and summed up his political program as "the conclusion of peace and the subjugation of Paris."[21]

Thiers started with the *décapitalisation* of the capital, a neologism for transferring the National Assembly to Versailles.[22] Further
humiliations—half-symbolic, half-concrete—were to follow: a revocation of the moratorium on rent increases and debts that Napo-
lean III had instituted at the beginning of the war; a wage freeze
for the national guard; and finally a secret nighttime raid to remove
the cannons at Montmartre. This last act, carried out on March 18,
caused the simmering discontent to boil over; indeed, it is hard to
imagine a more symbolically laden incident. The cannons, paid for
partly by donations from private citizens, including Victor Hugo,
and regarded by the people as their own, were aimed not at the
government but at the German besiegers, who had staged a victory
parade into Paris two and a half weeks before, on March 1.[23] Thus,
when the Communards rose up, they saw their rebellion not as an
act of class warfare against the bourgeoisie but as an act of defense
of the nation against a foreign enemy, similar to that of 1792. Nor
did they intend to harm France—Paris had always considered itself
the soul of the nation—but only to overthrow the treacherous government and the National Assembly, which had stabbed the nation
in the back by capitulating.[24] As the National Assembly in Versailles
debated Bismarck's offer of peace, *décapitalisation*, and other measures aimed at Paris, the deputies from the capital warned of the

consequences. Gambetta proclaimed: "If we conclude such a humiliating peace, revolution will break out in Paris. . . . The unfortunates [in the assembly] fail to understand that what comes next will be worse than the war itself."[25] Louis Blanc, a deputy, listed the effects of *décapitalisation*: "Paris will be forced to create an independent government over which the National Assembly, convening outside the capital, will have no power. . . . Out of the still-glowing ashes of the war, a far more terrible civil conflict will be born."[26] Félix Pyat, a deputy and later a Communard, relayed the feelings of his Paris constituency even more bluntly: "There won't be enough dung on the streets of Paris to provide the deputies with the welcome they deserve."[27]

The tragedy—or lost cause—of the Commune did not reside in its continuing a militarily hopeless struggle down to the last man.[28] Had Paris, with the nation's blessing, made such a sacrifice, it would have entered into French mythology as a heroic city, a latter-day Thermopylae, universally admired or at least respected, as it had been before the armistice of January 28. The sole reason the Commune was damned as treacherous was that it was no longer in tune with prevailing national sentiment.

Heroic actions, even those that are considered misguided or morally dubious, usually command a measure of respect independent of ethical and pragmatic considerations. The draconian suppression of the Commune displayed none of this. After troops under Marshal MacMahon entered the city on May 21, retribution was swift and furious. Within a week, government forces cleared the last barricade and seized control. Communards by the hundreds were arrested and executed, and by the time Paris had been pacified, tens of thousands of its inhabitants had perished.

The ferocity of the campaign has traditionally been explained as a manifestation of bourgeois paranoia, which had been growing since 1848. This explanation, however, neglects those who actually carried out the massacre. If there was one institution whose self-confidence had been especially shaken by the defeat in the Franco-Prussian War, it was the army, which had failed to win a single battle; indeed, the army's only actions had been retreats. It had surrendered not once but twice and had been unable to prevent the siege of Paris or to break through the German troops encircling the city. And finally, it could only stand by and watch helplessly as the heroic *défense nationale* was mounted by civilians like Gambetta and the soon-to-be-legendary fighters of the *franc-tireurs*. It would be difficult to imagine a more thoroughly defeated, demoralized, and generally despised force than the French army after its final capitulation in January 1871. To add insult to injury, the newly elected National Assembly placed so little faith in the armed forces that it sued Germany for peace at any price and restricted the army's role to maintaining law and order among its own civilian population.

Particularly despondent were the members of the officer corps. Although the decision to end the *défense nationale*, which was taken by the National Assembly and the government and was backed by public opinion, spread the burden of humiliation over various shoulders, further action was necessary to revive the officers' sense of pride. Hence the fury they displayed in suppressing the Commune. Whereas the rank and file, according to various eyewitness accounts, went about their jobs with mechanical efficiency, the officers threw military ethics to the wind and did everything to ratchet up the level of violence. The higher the rank, the greater the brutality.[29] Their motivation, of which they themselves could hardly have been conscious, is fairly clear: the annihilation of the Communards enabled the officers to eradicate their own mark of shame. The Paris Commune—the living, breathing ideal of heroic resistance—was a profound irritant to the officers, who had proved unequal to the German challenge. Their humiliation sealed the Commune's fate and determined the way in which it was destroyed—not in a surgical, professional military operation but in a bloodbath, as the army sought to drown the memory of its defeat.

To some, this act of self-purification was a success. At the end of the week of bloodshed, Edmond de Goncourt wrote in his diary:

"Thus the army has won back its self-confidence. The blood of the Communards is the best proof of their fighting capacity."[30] Others were less convinced. The sarcasm with which Flaubert's lover, Louise Colet, described the victorious posturing of the army two weeks later was as arch as it was cutting: "Decked out from head to toe in medals, the officers celebrate themselves. Ovations, embraces, laurels. As though they had conquered Berlin."[31]

The rest of the nation reacted as the army did, if in less extreme fashion. As the rebellion's prospects dimmed, the initial applause and admiration for the Parisian spirit of resistance turned slowly to disaffection, then condemnation. This is abundantly clear from editorials in the liberal *Revue des deux mondes* of spring 1871. Early on, even the startling proclamation of the Commune as an independent government failed to provoke outrage; it was seen, at worst, as "the result of a gigantic misunderstanding." "During the siege," one editorialist wrote on April 1, 1871, "Paris had some justification for the idea that it was saving France. . . . In this patriotic role, illusory as it might have been, Paris showed qualities that impressed all of Europe. . . . Its battle was stubborn, brave, and righteous." Six weeks later, on May 15, a few days before the bloodbath, the tone was sharply accusatory: "Thanks to the behavior of Paris, we stand to lose all that we were about to regain and have become, on top of that, a laughingstock and an object of derision for the entire world." After the suppression of the rebellion, there was no room for compromise, understanding, or even pity—the Paris Commune was criminalized. The worst "criminals" were the fighters on the barricades, who had been glorified only a few months earlier. By June 1, the Commune was described as "the would-be tyranny of the scum of the earth," and the uprising was dubbed "the most despicable crime imaginable that one could perpetrate against the nation."

Major intellectuals, except for those who actively participated in the Commune, thought along similar lines. Normally polarized by political developments, they now joined in the near-unanimous chorus of condemnation. Edmond de Goncourt wrote: "Excellent. There were no overtures, no negotiations, no lazy compromises, just complete suppression with brute force. . . . This bloodletting of the rebellious part of the population will guard for years hence against any new uprisings." Emile Zola, who described the bloodbath as an instance of "uncompromising justice," foresaw an epidemic: "The bandits who while alive plundered the city and set it aflame will now infect it with their corpses." Last but not least, the positivist and archrepublican Emile Littré declared that the Communards were "guilty of the most appalling crime of all. They rebelled at the very moment our nation was lying defeated, bleeding, and defenseless at the feet of the victorious enemy."[32]

Excoriating the Paris Commune was the first attempt to forestall the emergence of a full-blown stab-in-the-back legend by blaming a marginalized part of the nation for defeat and collective shortcomings. This impulse was an extreme variation of the scapegoating of Napoleon that had occurred after Sedan. Condemnation, however, did not remain the last word, at least for the republican left. In years to come, the earlier conciliatory view—which held that the Commune was merely the product of "confusion" and "misunderstanding"—regained popularity. Eyewitnesses to the events, such as the young Georges Clemenceau, and more sovereign minds like Ernest Renan saw the Commune not as a criminal act of treason but rather as an instance of collective insanity.[33] As soon as *la folie de la défaite* was recognized as the catalyst for madness, the damnation of the Commune uprising as a crime against the nation subsided.[34] Indeed, it led to the Commune's rehabilitation. In contrast to the unheroic and opportunistic capitulation of the National Assembly and the government, the Commune was ultimately credited with the one true heroic and radical deed of the era.

That change of heart, however, took time. For years, the trauma would continue to divide the Third Republic: conservatives, who favored Realpolitik and the fulfillment of German demands, called their opponents, who resisted reconciliation, "Radicals," while these in turn derided their critics as "Opportunists." The Commune thus became a two-faced ghost haunting the Third Republic.[35] The Opportunists were beset by the nagging spirit of Banquo, who never ceased to remind them of the massacre during the week of bloodshed. The Radicals were hectored by Hamlet's father, who urged them to avenge the carnage and carry on the struggle against Germany. The side that would win the conflict would be the one best able to cast the other as traitor to the nation. There was, however, a case of betrayal on which both parties were of one mind.

The Scapegoat

In France, everyone who loses a battle is a traitor. This aperçu, attributed to Bismarck and consonant with a number of similar remarks by European contemporaries, refers primarily to the tradition, dating back to the First Republic, of holding generals responsible for lost battles and premature capitulations.[36] The offending officers were guillotined or, if they were clever, like the famous Revolution-era general Charles-François Dumouriez, sought exile with the enemy and thus transformed the accusation of treason into a self-fulfilling prophecy. The fate of Marshal Achille-François Bazaine would hardly be worth mentioning were it not for the purity of the traitorous impulse he was seen to embody.

Bazaine commanded the only army corps to remain intact after Sedan and survive the transition from empire to republic. At the end of October 1870, instead of leading it back to besieged Paris to assist the provisional government and the *défense nationale*, Bazaine allowed his army to be encircled by the Germans at the fortress of Metz and, following the example of his commander in chief, Napoleon III at Sedan, he surrendered. The reaction in Paris was even more furious than it had been to Napoleon's own capture and defeat. In the unmistakable tone of his Jacobin predecessors, Gambetta announced: "A general upon whom France was counting . . . has, in the nation's hour of greatest need, robbed it of more than a hundred thousand defenders. Bazaine is guilty of high treason."[37] Bazaine was never proven to have committed such a crime intentionally, either in the press campaign that commenced immediately or in the trial, which took place three years later. The impression he made then in the Hall of Justice at Versailles was of someone merely carrying out orders, who had been rendered mindless and incapable of acting in the absence of his commander in chief. Nonetheless, the military tribunal handed down a death sentence, which was commuted to life in prison. Bazaine miraculously succeeded in breaking out of jail and fleeing. He spent the rest of his life in Madrid, unmolested and in peace.

What made Bazaine's case a national cause célèbre was its usefulness to all sides concerned. His former colleague General MacMahon, loser of the battle of Sedan and later president of the Third Republic, prized Bazaine as a figure of darkness in contrast to whom he could appear bathed in light. The same held true for the army in general, including the officers who served on the military tribunal; all the contempt directed at them could easily be shifted onto the defendant's shoulders. The Bonapartists valued Bazaine because, in the hierarchy of crimes against the state, his treason overshadowed their own failure and incompetence. The monarchists, who from the start had opposed the wars of both the empire and the republic, hardly needed a scapegoat; nonetheless, they too welcomed Bazaine as an example of the decadence of their political opponents. Finally, public opinion supported this scapegoating, as evidenced by the immense popular success of an anonymously published book, in which an underling and personal enemy of Bazaine renewed the accusations of deliberate treason.

Seventy years later, the factors that had made Bazaine so ideal a scapegoat were summed up as follows: "It was a consolation to large numbers of French patriots to find that one man was responsible for the long roll of their defeats, as it was growing fashionable to blame Bazaine for MacMahon's disaster at Sedan as well as for his own campaign. This view, which left other military reputations unimpaired, was a welcome tonic to the self-respect of a defeated people. If it had all been Bazaine's fault, they had not really been defeated. . . . This simple ritual act preserved the nation's faith in its own invincibility."[38] There is no clearer evidence of this dynamic than Gambetta's comment on Bazaine's conviction: "With this, France has taken its first step on the road to honor, justice, and *revanche.*"[39]

"Prussia's Victory, France's Glory"

Of scarcely less consequence for the French psyche than the transition from foreign to civil war was a second shift: the conflict began as a war against *Prussia* but ended as a defeat by *Germany.* France had never felt very warmly toward Prussia. Ever since the publication of Mirabeau's scathing *De la monarchie prussienne sous Frédéric le Grand* in 1788, Prussia had been considered less a state, to say nothing of a nation, than a gigantic factory whose capacity for producing *hommes machines* may have been impressive but whose utter lack of soul and inability to bring forth *hommes libres* was thoroughly alienating.[40] Prussia's ignoble collapse and capitulation to Napoleon I in 1806—after a single lost battle—had shown how unreliable that factory could be and how inferior it was to the vital power of France.

This insight, so flattering to the French self-image, was reinforced in Germaine de Staël's *On Germany*, the work that, more than any other, shaped France's picture of Germany in the first half of the nineteenth century. De Staël's Germany was both the counterideal to Napoleon's authoritarian state and the counterimage to militaristic Prussia: the most peaceable nation on earth, a "people of dreamers" (Flaubert), the "country of the soul" (Edgar Quinet), the land of poets and thinkers, a tender, almost maidenly figure that was not only an alter ego but a potential lover—Renan referred to Germany as "my mistress"—in need of France's chivalric protection. This conception gained in popularity the more Prussia strove for hegemony over other German territories and became (in France's eyes) a "carnivorous force" bent on devouring the smaller states.[41]

The year of Königgrätz/Sadowa and Prussia's annexation of nearly the entire region north of the Main River—1866—marked the high point of France's notion of a threatening Prussian beast preying on the rest of Germany. The idea that the *terreur prussienne* (the title of an allegorical novel by Alexandre Dumas about Prussia's military occupation of Frankfurt) could become a *terreur allemande* would have seemed absurd to most Frenchmen at the beginning of the war in 1870. But that was precisely what happened in the months that followed. It was as if the good-hearted Schmucke of Balzac's *Cousin Pons* had suddenly acquired the rapacious allure of Rastignac at the end of *Père Goriot.* To make matters worse, France found itself on the losing end of a humiliatingly gendered role reversal. To have been unseated from its position as chivalric protector was bad enough. But to be cast in the role of defiled maiden must have seemed a particularly bitter instance of treachery, all the more galling since the former damsel in distress had suddenly metamorphosed into a murderous monster. Gretchen had become a Valkyrie, if not a Bismarck. The French trauma of 1870–71 cannot be understood without taking account of this erotic component.[42]

How deeply the injury ran is shown by the fact that the image of Prussia could not easily be transferred onto Germany. Since prior to 1866 France itself had never felt directly threatened by Prussia, the image of Prussia lacked the requisite aura of monstrosity to serve as a national enemy. An emotional leap was required to transform the caricature of Prussia into the nightmarish face of Germany. It was precisely France's former love for the land of poets and thinkers, now distorted into horror and deadly enmity, that provided the necessary stimulus. Practically overnight, Madame de Staël's Germanic Arcadia was reenvisioned as an evil empire of scientific barbarism threatening not just France but the whole of civilized humanity.

Along with this reversal, the image of England, France's traditional national enemy, was transposed wholesale onto its new arch-rival. Characteristics usually attributed to England—the stereotype of "perfidious Albion," in currency since the Hundred Years War, and the idea of the mercantilist modern-day Carthage, fashionable during the eighteenth century—were similar to the dismissive view of Prussia first articulated by Mirabeau.[43] English mercantilism and Prussian militarism were parallel scourges, both departing from French esprit in their "calculating coldness, heartlessness, methodicalness, lack of grace, fighting spirit and heroism." Mirabeau identified in Prussian soldiers a "coolheadedness, obedience, order, and discipline," in contrast to the French, who, in the strict sense, were "less than perfect soldiers" but "more animated, spontaneous, and courageous."[44] He left no doubt as to which type he preferred. Likewise, in the aftermath of defeat in the Seven Years War in 1763, there was no question among the French public that the moral victor was not England—"this restless people of accountants and egotists"—but France, thanks to its "reliably loyal national integrity and strength of character."[45]

Thus the Third Republic's tendency to transform military defeats into spiritual triumphs—widely noted by social historians—was not born at Sedan.[46] Moreover, what scholars have called the "art and greatness of demise" and the "pedagogy of failure" are not specifically French—they are evident as well in the American South and in Weimar Germany.[47] Still, the Third Republic displayed an extreme case of defeat hysteria and the question remains as to why. The answer, perhaps, is suggested by the example of Victor Hugo.

Hugo, the poet laureate of romantic and republican France since the 1840s, had three fundamental convictions, which he put forward with unflagging persistence. First, that humanity had found its ultimate expression in republican France. Second, that the cause of French republicanism was accordingly the highest cause of humanity itself. And third, that the unification of Europe could only be envisioned as an extension of the French republic. In 1842, during a period of expansionist enthusiasm in France, Hugo had demanded that the Rhine be set as the border with Germany, a move he advocated not in the name of his country but in the name of Europe and humanity. Against this backdrop, it is easy to predict his attitude toward the Franco-Prussian War and France's defeat and territorial amputation. As the leading poet of the republic of humanity, he more than anyone set the tone after Sedan and his writings of the period firmly established him as the choirmaster of France's oratorio of martyrdom.

"Like ancient Greece and Rome," he wrote, "France today is civilization and a threat to France is a threat to all. . . . Should the *unthinkable* transpire and France be defeated, it would be a sign of how far humanity has sunk." That was not all: "Saving Paris means more than saving France: it means saving the world. For Paris is the heart of humanity, its holy city, the capital of civilization." And: "The mutilation of France by Germany strikes at the core of all of Europe."[48]

All these statements were made in the immediate aftermath of France's defeat. Hugo's later comments, such as those offered at the Congress on World Peace in 1874, are of similar tenor: "Every slap in the face of France is a blow felt by all of humanity." And a year later: "The amputation of France is a disaster for all humanity, for France is not just France but the world, and all progress depends on France's remaining intact. Every province lost by France is a loss for humanity and for progress."[49] In contrast to the outrage that would greet the next German invasion of France almost half a century later, European public opinion did not take these lamentations any more seriously than it did the triumphalist effusions emanating from nationalist German intellectuals. The consensus ran with Thomas Carlyle, who in his famous letter to the *Times* of London on November 11, 1870, deemed French sentiment "delirious," "pitiable," and "miserable" on the one hand, and "blamable" and "contemptible" on the other.[50]

The great handicap of revisionist French propaganda after 1871 was that, unlike in the revolutionary era, there were no reserves of fighting spirit left to mobilize. The prevailing plaintive tone was an authentic expression of the nation's lack of aggression and energy. Moreover, Germany had not yet been perceived as the world's most dangerous barbarian, as it would be in 1914. Rather it was seen as a country that, having suffered two centuries of French hegemony and humiliation, had simply achieved a well-deserved *revanche* in the spirit of fair play. Carlyle was one of many to speak in such terms. German intellectuals, whose nationalism still had liberal-republican foundations, also characterized the Franco-Prussian War as a settling of accounts, not an act of wanton aggression. Beginning with David Friedrich Strauss's open letter to Ernest Renan in August 1870, a month before Sedan, one can chart the development of a German equivalent to the French republican summoning of "ghosts." Strauss, along with Theodor Mommsen, Hermann Schulze-Delitzsch, Georg Herwegh, and other intellectuals whose national hopes had been shattered in 1848, found redress for their domestic defeat in the *revanche* now exacted upon France.[51] To their mind, the shift in focus from an internal to an external enemy was logical since, after all, hadn't imperial France consistently blocked all efforts to achieve German national unity? Was it not true that Germany's fragmentation into multiple states was largely a consequence of French meddling?

It quickly became apparent that German historical arguments were better grounded in fact than Victor Hugo's pitiable wailing. Those among the French intelligentsia who had not succumbed to hysteria soon joined the discussion started by their German counterparts. Historians like Ernest Renan and Fustel de Coulanges who had studied at German universities were willing to abandon the indefensible position that France stood alone as the nation of humanity. Instead they took up a more promising vantage from which to launch a new offensive. The old idea of France as the active agent of world history was replaced by France as the object and victim of that history, not only in defeat but also—and this was the main departure from Hugo's worldview—in victory. Fustel de Coulanges compared past French triumphs and present Prussian-German successes, treating neither as glorious achievements or treacherous crimes but as mere turns of the wheel of fortune. In so doing, he made questions of blame and responsibility seem irrelevant. The French should appeal to the world not as a nation of defiled innocence, he argued, but rather as a nation that had fallen from the heights of power and therefore was well suited, indeed obliged, to warn the states now scaling those heights of the inevitable consequences. "Every nation that adopts military glory and power as its motto, as we once did, will make the mistakes we made."[52] Warning the victors of the perils of triumph was nothing new; it had often seemed, as in the American South, an effective means of transforming defeat into moral superiority.

Vae Victoribus

On September 15, 1870, two weeks after Sedan, Ernest Renan published a long essay on the German-French conflict and what was by then its incontrovertible outcome. In the final sentence, he reversed the famous warning *Vae victis*, or Woe to the vanquished: "Wise friends now say to Prussia, quietly, not as a threat but as an admonition: *Vae victoribus!*"[53]

Renan did not coin the phrase. It had been used two weeks earlier in a Parisian weekly, *L'illustration*, which in turn quoted an article published in the *Neue Freie Presse*, a Viennese daily, under the title "*Vae Victoribus.*" According to *L'illustration*, the admonition had been addressed to Prussia and read: "*Vae victoribus!* Victory is a poor adviser, and nations tend to slip on the blood they have shed. Rome under its Caesars did not suspect that its *Vae victis* would apply in equal measure to Rome itself. After every victory, there's a new tomorrow. Waterloo follows Austerlitz. And so, too, our cry: Victor, beware!"[54]

Austrian voices carried special weight in the Parisian press during those critical days. Ever since the defeat at Königgrätz/Sadowa in 1866, which France considered its own, Austria was regarded as a kind of partner in misfortune. Apparently Parisians did not know that the article had appeared simultaneously in the Berlin paper *Die*

Zukunft and that its author was one Jakob Venedey of Prussian-ruled Cologne. A old-school liberal and a delegate at the failed constitutional convention at the 1848 German National Assembly, Venedey had become a Francophile during long years of political exile in Paris. The question of victorious Prussia's treatment of defeated France, however, was not the focus of his article. Rather he primarily addressed an internal threat that, as one of the few forty-eighters not to be carried away by victory, he recognized all too clearly—namely, that military triumph would cripple the German democratic movement.

France, however, hoped to use the magic formula of *Vae victoribus* to sour the champagne of German victory. The fact that the incantation had been conceived by a German political émigré was only an ancillary bit of historical irony. What made the slogan effective was its basis in the ancient conception of the wheel of fortune, whose top and bottom switch with every half rotation—an image that fit quite well with the Christian dogma of "the last shall be the first." Maxims by Renan such as "Today's victors are tomorrow's losers" and "Defeat is the price for a past victory and the guarantor of a future one" cast the victor in a mute and passive role.[55] If the next rotation of the wheel was to make today's victor into tomorrow's loser, and today's loser into tomorrow's victor, then the "temporary victor" (as Reinhart Koselleck calls him) was like the rich man in the New Testament, more to be pitied than feared.[56]

On March 1, 1871, the day the National Assembly accepted German peace terms and ceded Alsace-Lorraine, Victor Hugo gave his last speech before resigning his seat in protest. No other document from the time reveals as clearly the intellectual and moral dynamics that transformed the idea of *Vae victoribus* into that of *revanche*. *Vae victoribus* dictated that the victor would be felled by history, with the vanquished merely in the role of passive onlooker, while *revanche* encouraged the losing side to take destiny into its own hands. The relationship of *revanche* to *Vae victoribus* was thus roughly that of Communist class struggle to the Marxist concept of historical inevitability (and as we will see, it led its adherents into a similar cognitive dissonance).

Hugo began his speech with an expression of sympathy for Germany: "We deeply regret its transformation from a people to an empire."[57] The culprit here was Prussian despotism, from which, he promised, France would eventually free herself, just as she had freed herself from English hegemony during the Hundred Years War. The necessary strength for the task would be drawn from hatred. Hugo was quick to add that he was talking about hatred of despotism, not nationalistic hatred, but given his long list of potential targets, it is doubtful that he really meant good old-fashioned hatred of tyranny. "From tomorrow onward," he said, "France will have but one thought: to gather her strength; instruct her children in righteous anger; forge cannons and citizens so that the people and the army will be one; enlist science in the service of war; learn from the Prussian model as Rome did from Carthage; construct defenses; modernize. In a word, the nation will once more become the mighty France of the spirit and the sword." The transcript of the proceedings indicates that the speech was interrupted here with applause and cries of "*Très bon, très bon.*" "One day," Hugo continued, "the nation will be ready, and its revenge will be terrible. First it will retake Lorraine, then Alsace. Will that be all? No, I repeat, no! Next—listen carefully—will come Trier, Mainz, Cologne, Koblenz. . . ." Here the transcript notes, "Cries from various sides: *Non! Non!*" At that point, Hugo explained that he envisioned not a war of national conquest but a war to free Germany from despotism. "My form of revenge is brotherhood!" he declared. "Let us form a single republic, . . . let us shake hands! For in the end, we will have done one another a great service: you have freed me from my emperor, and I will free you from yours."

The resourcefulness and spirit with which Hugo guided his speech through its rocky passages do not quite conceal the moments of turbulence. Put another way, Hugo's universalist soul seemed to be struggling against his nationalist one. The question remains whether those who protested *"Non! Non!"* were simply too impatient to wait for the conciliatory end of the passage or whether Hugo would have ended his speech differently without their interruption. Whatever the answer, the speech announced a turn of the tide from the "old" liberal-republican to the "new" chauvinistic, all-encompassing nationalism that took hold of France after the experience of 1870–71. Victor Hugo was the medium through which both ideologies spoke.

La Revanche

> If I have committed the mad blunder, in a grim century, of taking life for an epic, it is because I am a grandchild of defeat. Convinced materialist that I am, my epic idealism will compensate, until I die, for an affront and a shame which I never suffered, for the loss of two provinces which we got back a long time ago.
>
> —Jean-Paul Sartre, *The Words*

The rallying cry *"La revanche"* points to a phenomenon whose role in history is well known but whose true meaning remains obscure. There is widespread agreement that *revanche*—as a political religion, foundational myth, and integrating force—gave the Third Republic a cohesion without which the new state, born of defeat and rent by internal polarization, would hardly have survived its first months.[58] The fact that it did survive was quite an achievement, especially if one compares it with the similar but far less successful Weimar Republic in post–World War I Germany. At the same time, *revanche* has been dismissed as a collective delusion, an enormous "life lie" that held France in thrall from 1871 to 1914. These two readings of *revanche*—as integrating force and mass delusion—are not, however, mutually exclusive. Indeed, they play off each other in myriad ways.

Surprisingly, *revanche* has never itself been the subject of a historical study.[59] As a first step, one must go back long before 1870–71 and look at the etymology of the word, at the courtly concepts of honor that sustained *revanche*, and at the medieval myths and legends that were resuscitated in order to express competing types of *revanche* in the combative climate of the Third Republic.

Etymologically, *revanche* is not the same as vengeance, although the words share the same root. Unlike vengeance (or revenge), which, although prompted by an earlier action or offense, is not subject to a statute of limitations—think of *Macbeth* or *Forza del destino*—*revanche* must be exacted immediately after the offense is commited. If this connection is missed, an act of *revanche*, like that of offering thanks belatedly, no longer has any meaning.

In its most attenuated form, *revanche* may take on the sublimated meaning of *satisfaction*, or even the fully neutral one of *response* or *reply*. *Revanche*, then, is better understood as a gift and exchange ritual rather than as part of revenge, though all three—gift giving, expressions of gratitude, and revenge—as philosopher-psychologists like Emerson and Nietzsche recognized, are related.[60] But every shading of *revanche*—be it the brutality of revenge, the formality of athletic competitions, or the reflexivity of a return invitation—entails a reestablishment of the equilibrium disrupted by one of the parties concerned. Perhaps the purest sense of the term occurs in games and sports, where protocol requires that the winner offer the loser "satisfaction" (or redress) in the form of a rematch. Emile Littré's *Dictionnaire de la langue française* of 1878, which gives the basic meaning of the word as "an action that compensates for an earlier offense," makes no reference to *revanche* as a contemporary slogan. It does, however, provide a pair of definitions that refer to sports and may help to illustrate the psychology behind the concept: "a second match in which the loser seeks to balance the result of a first. To play for *revanche*. To offer *revanche*" and "every new game that the loser demands after a lost match."

In its double sense of revenge and the peaceful reestablishment of equilibrium, however, the French concept of *revanche* is unique among European languages. Other languages clearly distinguish between the two meanings. The words for violent, martial, bloody retaliation are *revenge* and *vengeance* (English), *Rache* and *Vergeltung* (German), and *vendetta* (Italian). For peaceful equalization, the words are *compensation, satisfaction, reparation, atonement* (English), *Genugtuung, Befriedigung, Zufriedenstellung* (German), and *soddisfazione* and *riparazione* (Italian). *Rivendicazione*, from the verb *vendicare* (to revenge), also falls into the category of peaceable settlements, meaning the successful enforcement of legal or property claims. In contrast to *revanche*, its etymological twin, *rivendicazione* does not contain the idea of *vendetta*.

French, of course, also has terms signifying an exclusively peaceful reestablishment of equilibrium: *satisfaction, réparation, compensation, conciliation, accommodation, arrangement*. These words, which evolved with the development of bourgeois society, essentially expressed the bourgeois understanding of law and order, an understanding based on nonviolent exchange. Their usage also signaled the emergence of a specifically bourgeois code of honor, or rather a split of the courtly code into two distinct forms. From then on, the bourgeois concept of honor as honesty and the chivalric one of honor as bravery coexisted in more or less separate spheres.

As these etymological facts suggest, the idea of *revanche* is rooted in a continuation—even a pathological exaggeration—of the chivalric code of honor. The story of how politically disempowered aristocrats in their gilded cage at Versailles—locus of the newly centralized monarchy—cultivated ornate forms of etiquette by which they lived and not infrequently died is too well known to bear repetition. Equally well known is the role played by the duel in this thicket of obligations, entitlements, ceremonies, and rivalries of honor. Since, however, there is a direct line leading from the duel to *revanche*, it is worth briefly dwelling on its history.

In both qualitative and quantitative terms, seventeenth-century

France was the leading dueling nation in Europe. Roughly ten thousand duelists were killed between 1589 and 1610 alone.[61] And nowhere was the threshold of offense lower and the demand for satisfaction or *revanche* more lightning quick. The French were ever at the ready to take up arms over "a somewhat too direct stare, a thoughtless brush of contact, a word spoken too loudly," or (in one case) even "a glass of lemonade," and the ritual of the duel—its choreography—was more strictly and artificially formalized in France than anywhere else.[62] A key moment in the evolution of the duel from a contest between individuals to an expression of broader *revanche* was the French aristocracy's final rebellion against the absolute authority of the crown, which lasted from 1648 to 1653. The defeat of the Fronde—as the rebellion was known—was the fundamental trauma of the First Estate and would preoccupy it for over a century: the aristocracy would long for *revanche* up until the Revolution. The dueling mania of the seventeenth century thus can be seen not only as a compensatory action on the part of a decommissioned warrior caste but also as a form of ritualized resistance to the central authority. Every duel represented not just a contest of individual wills but a defiance of the royal prohibition on dueling and, as such, a tiny act of *revanche*. As irrelevant and laughable as the points of honor involved in dueling might have appeared to (bourgeois) outsiders, they were a matter of existential seriousness to the participants. Personal honor was, in the words of Marshal Blaise de Monluc, literally the last and only thing that remained to the aristocracy after its defeat: "Our lives and our possessions belong to our kings. Our souls belong to God, but our honor is our own. My king can do nothing about my honor."[63]

The possibility for *revanche* on a grander scale opened up in the eighteenth century with the decline of the absolutist system. The nation's defeat at the hands of England in 1763 pushed French society farther in this direction and sped up the process. It was perhaps the first defeat of the modern sort, not a battle lost in royal cabinet warfare but a humiliation experienced by the whole nation. The crisis of confidence into which the ancien régime was plunged offered the aristocracy two ways to revive its fortunes. It could confront the crown as a power center untainted by defeat—or scandal—and it could approach the nation, this newly discovered source of political legitimacy, as the embodiment of moral authority.[64]

The situation of the aristocracy was thus not unlike that of the republicans in the fall of 1870. Just as the republicans took the cause of national honor into their own hands with the *défense nationale*, the post-1763 aristocracy assumed leadership of the demands for *revanche* against England.

To be precise, it was not the aristocracy as a whole that took on this role but rather the generation entering political life in the 1770s, enlightened aristocratic patriots like Mirabeau, Saint-Simon, Lafayette, and Ségur. These men felt a greater affinity with the generation of their great-grandfathers than with that of their fathers, and they preferred the serious business of American rebellion against England to the easy life of Versailles. Certainly they supported and even fought in the American struggle as a means of gaining *revanche* against England, but they saw that conflict and their own ambitions for a renewal of France as part of the same quest, namely, to restore the aristocracy to the leading role it had occupied before the fall of the Fronde. An intimation that they knew these two aims were connected—that *revanche* was being sought at a remove, approached via detours and sideshows—can be gleaned from a statement by Ségur, Lafayette's fellow fighter in America: "We had had enough of this long, lazy peace. We were burning to settle the scores for previous defeats, and so we hastened to support the American cause against England."[65] What was the French participation in the American rebellion if not a transatlantic projection (in the psychological sense) of the struggle against—or rather *revanche* for—despotism at home?

This interpretation is supported by the manner in which the young aristocrats began their great undertaking. Lafayette, Ségur, and Saint-Simon refused to place themselves in the service of their government in its official support for the Americans. They wanted their own private *revanche*. Pointedly demonstrating his sovereignty like a feudal lord of the Middle Ages, Lafayette equipped a frigate, the *Victoire*, at his own expense and set off to sea under cover of darkness and in direct disobedience of explicit orders from the king.

If the origins of *revanche* lie in the aristocratic tradition of the seventeenth and eighteenth centuries, then ironically, the Parisian street rabble of the 1870s—the most *revanche*-ready group in France—appears as the direct descendant and heir of the aristocratic code of honor. Though the connection is speculative, several points argue in its favor. Both the aristocracy and the masses were collective subjects who defined themselves against the monarchy, and in this their histories ran parallel. For a time, in the early days of the Revolution, the Versailles aristocracy in its satins and silks and the Parisian masses in their rags seemed to function as a pair of pliers, squeezing the monarchy from both sides. During this phase of the Revolution, the masses could perceive themselves as an equivalent of the aristocracy, their common interest being the restoration of the old relationship between lord and vassal that had been interrupted by absolutism. There was also a trickle-down effect of aristocratic forms of behavior and concepts of honor into the lower classes. "Paris is a person," Roland Mausnier says of this population, possessing "all the eminent qualities of the gentleman and cavalier."[66] With the reformist aristocracy's departure from the Revolution in 1790, the Parisian masses became the sole heir and bearer of this aristocratic inheritance, which was recast as the concept of national honor.

Although in the Third Republic *revanche* would function as a universally accepted slogan, there were at least two conflicting interpretations of the idea. They corresponded to the long-standing split between "the two Frances"—the red and the black, the liberal-republican and the royalist-Catholic. The two camps had been mortal enemies since the Reign of Terror in 1793 and would continue to polarize political life until the Dreyfus affair a century later. Indeed, far from having seized lasting power with the 1870 proclamation of the Third Republic, the republicans were defeated in the elections of February 8, 1871, and spent almost ten years in opposition to a government that was republican in name only—and in fact not even that. The *République des Ducs*, as historian Daniel Halévy called the new French state, had no constitution, and the head of state was called not the president of the republic but the chief of the executive power. Perhaps the most revealing aspect of the regime was that it was located in Versailles, not Paris.[67] The reason parliamentary democracy was not abolished altogether was only because the Bourbonist, Orléanist, and Bonapartist factions could not agree on a common pretender. Furthermore, none of these factions had an interest in burdening itself with the legacy and consequences of France's defeat. It was far more advantageous to take unpopular steps in the name of the republic and thereby discredit everything republican. That way, the monarchists and Bonapartists could step in at the crucial moment as the nation's unencumbered saviors.

During this interregnum—the period from 1871 to 1879, when the republic was established on more solid ground—the two Frances competed by blaming each other for the events of the *année terrible*. While the republicans regarded Sedan as a consequence of France's deviation from the path of republican virtue into Catholicism, royalism, and Bonapartism, the royalist-Catholic camp saw France's collapse as divine punishment for social secularization. In 1870–71, a second blow served only to widen the schism. The impact of the Paris Commune for bourgeois-liberal France was matched for the Catholic legitimists by the demise of papal world authority when Italy annexed Rome.

More significant than their antithetical explanations for defeat, however, were the two Frances' contrasting visions for the future. For Catholicism, reconciliation with God (*réparation*) through repentance was the first step out of the abyss and the precondition for the nation's salvation and reinstatement in the Almighty's good graces. Actual *revanche* would then be carried out through the *grand roi* sent by heaven.[68] The republican corollary was the moral and organizational reform (*régénération*) of the nation, which would then, as a *republica triumphans*, undertake *revanche*. Both sides looked to the German victor as a model: republicans to the Prussian schoolmaster, Catholics to the pious German loyal to God and master. "While France abandoned herself to boundless skepticism, the German people followed their hearts, devoting themselves to the family and spiritual values and honoring what was truly great."[69] So ran the central message of Blanc de Saint-Bonnet's *La legitimité*, one of the essential documents of political Catholicism. The problem of how one could extol a conqueror as a role model while simultaneously condemning him as a barbarian or a Protestant heathen was solved by both republicans and Catholics in similar fashion. Just as Victor Hugo's vision of a republican crusade of *revanche* against Germany culminated in the liberation of the true Germany from tyranny, Catholic *revanche* achieved its apotheosis in the hoped-for return of misled German Protestants to the bosom of the one true church.[70]

The Sacré-Coeur *and the Cult of the Wound*

The double disorientation in the fall of 1870—caused by national defeat and the events in Rome—led to an outbreak of religiosity in France, especially in western France, that attained almost medieval proportions. There were public prayers, processions, pilgrimages, and other acts of penance for the supposed sins that had caused God to punish France at Sedan, and penitents swore religious vows in the conviction that such displays of piety would soften God's heart and protect the imperiled French homeland from the German threat. A religious vow common in Lyon, Angers, and Nantes was the promise to erect a Church of the Sacred Heart, or Sacré-Coeur, if the city was spared. Raised to the level of a national vow, the construction of the Sacré-Coeur basilica on Montmartre became the preeminent symbol of Catholic France's attempt to come to terms with military defeat.

To call on the sacred heart in times of emergency and vow to ensure its favor had become common practice soon after the rise of the cult in the seventeenth century. The practice simplified the cult's original aim, which seems to have been to bring something of the personal, Protestant quality of the relationship between God and man into the Catholic confession: the *sacré-coeur* was the embodiment of Christ's love for mankind, the heart, pierced and bleeding, serving as the link between the son of God and man. But after 1789, or, more precisely, 1793, the sacred heart took on a specific significance. It continued to be invoked in emergencies; now, however, the emergency was neither an epidemic nor a natural catastrophe nor a war but the Jacobin republic itself. Ever since the peasant uprising in 1793 adopted the *sacré-coeur* for its banner, it had become the battle symbol for Catholic, antirepublican, and counterrevolutionary France.[71]

Just as Catholics elevated the *sacré-coeur*, republicans looked to a related symbol, the image of the open wound with blood streaming from it. But instead of embodying divine love, the blood symbolized for republicans the wounding of the republic by counterrevolution and was used to justify calls for revenge. Whether in the displaying of gravely injured citizen-soldiers or the laying out of the murdered Marat (his stab wound carefully touched up by Jacques-Louis David) in the convent, the message was the same: "In the name of the wounds that have been done to it, the republic demanded the Reign of Terror, and it got it." Or: "O you despicable kings, . . . culprits of these terrible mutilations, . . . this beloved blood, soaking the soil of freedom, cries out to heaven for justice. . . . We shall not hesitate to avenge it."[72] In the case of Marat, the republican usurpation of Christian symbolism explicitly appropriated the image of the *sacré-coeur*: Marat's heart was carried in a separate urn during the funeral procession. "Let Marat's blood be the spring of life for uncowed republicans," read one passage from the elegy, while another asked: "O heart of Jesus. O heart of Marat . . . *Sacré-Coeur*. . . . Can one compare even the love and works of Mother Mary's son with those of the *Ami du peuple* and his disciples on the holy mount of the Jacobins?"[73]

As the ghosts of the First Republic and the first *défense nationale* were being summoned in 1870–71, the cult of the wound also made its reappearance. Victor Hugo, addressing the National Assembly in Bordeaux, proclaimed: "Every one of us feels the nation's wound in his own heart." Several months earlier, he had told wounded soldiers in a Parisian military hospital: "You are looking at a jealous man. More than anything else in the world, I wish I had one of your wounds. I salute you, children of France and favorite sons of the republic, you who have been chosen to suffer for our homeland."[74]

In 1879, the truly republican Third Republic, no longer dominated by the monarchists, further developed the cult of the wound by transferring the metaphor from the heroes of the nation to the nation itself. The wound the nation was duty-bound to avenge was the loss of Alsace and Lorraine, which had been ripped from the national body, and the task and obligation facing France was to not let that wound heal. The nation, according to the revolutionary Louis-Auguste Blanqui, was to preserve its wound "intact and permanently . . . as a sign that we have remained true to our pain." In 1886, when after a brief period of apathy the idea of *revanche* regained its hold on the public imagination, Paul Déroulède, known as the poet of *revanche*, greeted its renaissance with words of praise for the general who would become its main proponent: "Some people believe the wounds in our flanks caused by the loss of Alsace-Lorraine have healed. You have reopened these wounds. You have deepened them. You have bored into them with glowing iron. You have caused them to bleed anew and prevented them from healing."[75] Since there was, in the physical sense, no immediate way to repair the injury, the only possible treatment consisted of keeping the wound open, letting the blood flow, a fount of revenge lust that would pulse through the nation until *revanche*, in the form of reannexation of the lost provinces, could be carried out.

The repossession of Alsace-Lorraine was at the very center of the republican conception of *revanche*. The two provinces were venerated, seen to embody the Revolution as no other part of the nation except Paris could ever hope to. Before 1789, Alsace had been merely a conquered territory, without a deeper connection to the nation. The Revolution had established such a connection and, in so doing, had won the hearts of the Alsatians. The fact that the French national anthem was composed in Alsace, that it "conquered" the nation from there, symbolically completed the unification process. And when the Alsatians solemnly protested against their forced return to the new German empire, their resistance was seen as poignant proof that they had become true Frenchmen.

By contrast, Alsace-Lorraine played no role whatsoever in the Catholic conception of *revanche*. The reinstallation of the pope as a political authority seemed far more important than regaining two provinces so closely associated with the archenemy, revolution. Moreover, Alsace had a large Protestant population. Nevertheless, it cannot be said that Catholicism lost the battle for the true interpretation of defeat—and, consequently, for political power in the Third Republic— solely because it failed to recognize the importance of Alsace-Lorraine. Nor can the republican resurgence after eight years in opposition be explained solely by its successfully linking the two provinces with the idea of *revanche*. In hindsight, the *République des Ducs* looks like the last gasp of royalism, which had been on the wane since 1793, while the republican victory seems to be the long overdue, definitive institutionalization of the democratic principle after multiple restorations and usurpations. And yet, the disempowered old regime continued for some time to retain command of the symbols it had created during its long rule. When it came to symbolism, the newcomers were left with little choice but to feed off their opponents until they could develop some powerful symbols of their own.

The republicans of 1870–71, however, were no longer the havenots and parasites of 1793. In the eighty years that had elapsed since the Revolution, they had in fact developed some effective political symbolism, as they proved on September 4 and in the months of the *défense nationale*. Nevertheless, the limits that had always restricted their aspirations quickly reemerged. Every republican seizure of power since 1792 had been launched from Paris, only to be reversed sooner or later by the provinces. With the last of these reversals, the electoral defeat in 1871, it became only too apparent that the next advance could not restrict itself to the capital but would have to encompass the whole nation. Since the provinces still largely lived in the spiritual and symbolic world of Catholicism, the first goal of any republican regime determined to stay in power had to be the occupation of that terrain. Several figures from the pantheon of national martyrs and saviors were thus put on display, as the wounded soldiers of the Revolution had been in their time, in order to enlist the nation as a whole in the republicans' interpretation of defeat, their vision of France's salvation, and their certainty of successful *revanche*.

Joan of Arc

In the four hundred years since her historic appearance as the savior of France, Joan of Arc had become a legend without an institutional and ideological home. The absolutist monarchy had no interest in reviving memories of a people's heroine to whom it owed its existence and survival. The church could scarcely adopt a figure it had burned as a heretic. Even for the eighteenth-century Enlightenment, Joan of Arc was, as a servant of church and king, at best an object of pity and scorn, or, in Voltaire's words, *la pauvre idiote* who had allowed herself to be used and ultimately destroyed by the ruling powers. A figure "betrayed by her king and burned by the church" was also hardly a suitable standard-bearer for the Revolution. While there were efforts in 1789 to position Joan as the precursor of the revolutionary Marianne, they were rarely more than halfhearted, as in 1792 in Orléans, where during the first *défense nationale* there was some debate as to whether to melt down the Joan of Arc statue for cannons. One faction of the revolutionary city council advocated doing just that, arguing that Joan had been an archroyalist. Opponents pleaded for the statue's preservation as a memorial to one who had defended the nation against an external enemy. The quarrel ended in a compromise: the statue would be melted down, but the cannon forged from the iron would bear the name "Pucelle d'Orléans."[76]

The revolutionary-republican interpretation and appropriation of Joan of Arc only came about a full generation later, in the romantic-liberal historiography of the 1830s and 1840s. The weak-willed tool and victim of crown and church became Jules Michelet's *fille du peuple*, the personification of a people beginning to awaken and take destiny into its own hands. This Joan of Arc was both a triumphant conqueror like Christ, driving the money changers from the temple, and a passionate martyr with Christian features once she had fallen into the hands of the enemy and the church. One wonders whether her association with the *sacré-coeur* in the final sentence of Michelet's history of Joan of Arc was conscious or unconscious: "Let us as Frenchmen constantly remind ourselves that our homeland was born from the heart of a woman, from her gentility, her tears, and the blood that she shed for us."[77] The double face of triumph and martyrdom predestined Joan to become the leading symbol for post-1871 *revanche*, itself an ambivalent mix of militant rhetoric and peaceful realism.[78] One commentator pointedly characterizes the mood of the time as "a bizarre conglomeration of *revanchiste* pacifism and faint-hearted aggression."[79]

The republicanism of the 1870s exploited the innate advantage of this fully formed, ready-to-use Joan of Arc in the struggle against the Catholic and pro-monarchist regime then in power. Slower to tap her symbolic potential, Catholicism was just beginning to discover her as a figure for its own purposes, trying to build on the romantic-republican image to develop a suitable picture of the Catholic *fille du peuple*. Just how unlikely Joan of Arc was as a potential savior figure within the Catholicism of the period is illustrated by the numerous accounts of visions by devout Catholics in the crisis autumn of 1870. Many reported seeing a virgin with a sword in her hand, leading the fight against Germany. In every case, however, the woman in question was not Joan but the Virgin Mary.[80]

As the republican patron saint of the nation, Joan of Arc made numerous appearances during the 1870s—in poems (the most famous of which was in the *Nouveaux chants du soldat* of Paul Déroulède), in plays (such as Jules Barbier's enormously popular *Jeanne d'Arc* in 1873), on monuments (Emmanuel Frémiet's 1874 statue in Paris of Joan on horseback), and, perhaps most significantly, in the collective psyche, where she had lived on since her death. "Prussians, when you enter this humble house: tremble!" wrote Jules Michelet in the guest book at Joan of Arc's childhood home in Domrémy in August 1872.[81] One can assume that the figure of an armored and armed *fille du peuple* occasioned similar expectations in the popular consciousness in the immediate wake of the *année terrible*.

Over time, the conflict between the two Frances was subsumed within the two factions' struggles to control the government. Indeed, once republicanism regained power, it lost interest in Joan of Arc. The fact that she had in the meantime been sanctified by Catholics ("*Johanna nostrum est*") was one reason for this neglect. More to the point, during the 1880s and 1890s the "republican republic," enjoying domestic stability, no longer wished to recall its birth in defeat. More optimistic legacies and symbols were the order of the day, ones better suited to national renewal and modernization. It was time to bring back Marianne, the divine feminine symbol of the republic, whose genealogy was unsullied by associations to crown and church.[82] During the republicans' eight-year-long march back to power, Marianne and her connotations of revolution had been kept discreetly in the background, relegated to second-class status behind Joan, who was deemed a more appropriate figure for national integration. The mistake of prematurely frightening off the provinces was not to be repeated. Significantly, the new Marianne of the 1880s was a much more reassuring figure. She had been transformed from the bare-breasted goddess of freedom storming over the barricades in Delacroix's painting, to a majestically enthroned Minerva, *republica triumphans* in the serene repose of *republica sedens*.

Representing France's triumphal rise from the ashes of defeat, Marianne nonetheless satisfied only some of the country's emotional needs. She lacked that other quality, the mixture of triumph and martyrdom that had made Joan of Arc so attractive. To renounce Joan's ambiguity for Marianne's clarity was to neglect the need for martyrs that every vanquished nation feels. Perhaps, though, the role previously played by Joan of Arc could be taken over by yet another figure.

Roland

The legend related by the *Song of Roland* contains all the classic elements of the heroicizing of defeat: a hopeless battle against a faceless overwhelming enemy (the Saracens); betrayal within one's own ranks (Ganelon); sacrifice for a superior cause that emerges triumphant in the end (Charlemagne's revenge and the victorious conclusion of his crusade against the Saracens of Saragossa); and above all, the figure of a martyr-hero (Roland). It is not surprising, then, that this epic, "whose existence only a few scholars even knew of before 1870," as one historian writes, "was transformed within a few years from a minor part of the collective unconscious to a national myth."[83] Its significance in the interpretation of defeat would ultimately become as great as that of the legend of Joan of Arc.

It was easy to read the story of Roland and his men's demise at Roncesvalles as an allegory for the events of 1870–71: Ganelon, the traitor responsible for Roland's fall, stood in for Marshal Bazaine, while the avenger Charlemagne served as the *grand roi* of political Catholicism.[84] "Here we have the story of a great defeat for France," wrote one contemporary interpreter, Léon Gautier, "out of which the nation emerged not only glorious but having fully settled old scores. What could be more topical today? Defeat may be all we see at the moment, but this nineteenth-century Roncesvalles does not lack for glory, and perhaps before we know it we will be celebrating a new Saragossa."[85] Gautier wrote these words in December 1870 in an introduction to the first translation of the *Song of Roland* into modern French. A medievalist, he was an outspoken adherent of political Catholicism who interpreted the epic poem as a glorification of prerevolutionary (royalist-Catholic) France—a fact no more surprising than the emerging Catholic interest in Joan of Arc. What is remarkable, however, is that even a dedicated republican like historian Ernest Lavisse, who in his textbooks later portrayed Roland as a modern *patriotic* hero, depicted him at this point as an exemplary Christian knight and martyr.[86] Of course, Lavisse may have adopted the Catholic view out of political expediency, but if not, one must conclude that with Roland, as opposed to Joan of Arc, the Catholic and republican perspectives were not mutually exclusive. The astonishing consistency in the image of Roland across ideological lines during the 1870s argues for this conclusion. Gautier's edition of the text was retained even after the republican educational reforms of the 1880s and was only slowly supplemented, but never replaced, by the "republican" translations of Edouard Roehrich (1885), Gaston Paris (1887), and Maurice Bouchor (1899).

What made Roland, unlike Joan of Arc, a figure that could remain above the fray of political rivalries?

Joan of Arc and Roland may have been closely related as figures of medieval Christianity, but they diverge dramatically in their narrative and symbolic implications. Joan of Arc's demise and martyrdom is merely an epilogue to the main drama, the rescue of France. Roland's defeat, on the other hand, *is* the main drama. The subsequent victory, Charlemagne's *revanche*, lies outside the time frame of Roland's heroism. Although important to readers during the years immediately following defeat as a model for *revanche* against Germany, Charlemagne's triumph was comfortably distanced from a present that had other, more immediate concerns on its mind. For the Third Republic, Roland was a conglomeration of Christ and Leonidas, the Spartan king who, betrayed, died fighting.[87] Roland's demise is also more a self-sacrifice than a defeat. Refusing all attempts at rescue, he dies at the end of the epic not in the heat of combat with the saber-wielding Saracens but on the empty field of battle, after the Saracens have taken flight. Roland's death thus comes on his own terms. Although "defeated for the greater good," as one translation from the period puts it, the hero retains, in the words of a later commentator, his "undefeated status."[88]

Defeat as a condition for salvation and triumph—Michelet had already identified this Christian association as the central message of the *Song of Roland*.[89] Just as the love—the blood—of Christ in the cult of the *sacré-coeur* redeems sinful humanity, Roland's self-sacrificial end releases the nation from the burden of reckoning with a real, worldly defeat. In the temple of *revanche*, Roland occupies a quiet, contemplative niche, while Joan of Arc occupies the main altar as the savior of the homeland. This explains the lack of conflict surrounding the Roland figure in the ideological and symbolic competition between Catholicism and republicanism: one seldom fights for possession of minor side chapels and altars. But as the story of the *revanche* concept shows, the side chapel may over time become a church of its own.

Spiritual and moral composure, which should have been but the first step on the road to *revanche*, came increasingly to take the place of *revanche* as the national trauma healed. The ambiguous result, embodied most clearly in the figure of Roland, was an understanding of *revanche* that renounced any real action and restricted itself to laments and complaint. In iconographic terms, this innovation was a "Pietà of *revanche*." The illustrations to Gautier's 1872 edition, in fact, present Roland's corpse unmistakably in the pose of the dead Christ. Which brings us back to the First Republic's cult of the wound. Roland, however, spoke to a much broader public than the fatally wounded Marat. Instead of embodying *either* revolutionary or Christian France, Roland became the heroic symbol of the nation as leader of all civilization. Under the banner of this ideologically neutral slogan, Catholics and republicans alike could make common cause against barbarian Germany and at the same time declare France's *revanche* to be the entire world's cause.

One of the first to read contemporary political meaning into the *Song of Roland* was the literary historian Charles Lenient in 1872. Contrasting the French epic and the *Nibelungenlied*—"two rival works engaged in a nonmilitary duel, the only kind possible for us at present"—Lenient concluded that the *Song of Roland* was the product of a humane civilization, while its German counterpart was the expression of a darkly violent archaism.[90] Although Lenient's perspective is hardly original, it serves as an early example of the Third Republic's transposition of the *revanche* impulse into the pose of cultural superiority. The line of French propaganda arguing for innate German barbarism, which continued until the First World War, echoed almost word for word Lenient's formulation that the *Nibelungenlied* "is essentially barbaric, as is German thought as a whole, even if today it dons the guise of science and modern civilization." Among the numerous oppositions Lenient draws in his study of the two epics are the following:

1. *The contrast between the heroes*: "Roland fights with an open visor. Siegfried kills his enemy from behind. He is the inventor of the art of killing without being killed."
2. *The Franks fight for the Occident*: "This is no local quarrel but rather a prologue to the great battle between the Occident and the Orient. . . . The eternal glory of France has been to fight for the cause of humanity."
3. *Roland's battle is not one of self-interest*: "Roland conquers the world with his virtue and his bravery. His heroism is in equal measure cosmopolitan, universal, and patriotic." In contrast, the *Nibelungenlied* knows no ideal other than "stealing from

one's neighbors." Even the only positive hero, Siegfried, is filled with this "national trait in all its naïve brutality and primitiveness."[91]

4. *Two incompatible forms of* revanche: The *Song of Roland* depicts "an orderly retribution, exacted [by Charlemagne] in the bright light of day and with full legal justification." The *Nibelungenlied*, in contrast, is ruled "not by any morality, but by a sword- and torch-wielding Valkyrie, raging like a Fury or a bloodthirsty bacchanalian."

It is clear, then, that the call for *revanche* was not what it claimed to be. None of the historical and legendary figures it enlisted to interpret defeat—especially not the Christian martyrs—symbolized a call for immediate retribution. On the contrary, they stood for spiritual triumph through heroic endurance. "The defeat of the nation is sublimated by the heroism of its *sons*," writes one historian, "and the nation's lost honor restored through the *glory of the vanquished*. . . . For battle is always an opportunity for acts of heroism, and every '*belle action*' is self-justifying, deriving its dignity from its moral beauty."[92] Tellingly, the Third Republic's interpretation of defeat is also referred to as "consolation literature," "pedagogy of failure," and "the art and greatness of demise." Over the years, a veritable pantheon was constructed for the lionization of lost battles. From Crécy to Agincourt, Waterloo to Reichshofen, so the message ran, the French had only ever been defeated by the crude might of mechanically drilled plebeians. It was a short step from here to the self-affirming and consoling formula "We're invincible, once we put our minds to it."[93]

But while the gap between *revanchiste* expectations and reality was partially bridged in mythology by images of heroic defeat, the rift in the public mind of the Third Republic remained wide. "France desires *revanche*, but it wants peace": this sentence, popular among European diplomats during the 1870s and 1880s, summed up the French dilemma.[94] The French public was not particularly discomfited by the contradiction, nor did it take steps to resolve it. As always in such situations, a process of ritualization soon transformed unrealistic expectations into a *citadelle sentimentale*, an emotional fortress. Arriving in Paris in 1881, the German writer Max Nordau recognized "a kind of belief in the Messiah," whose coming, however, no one expected to see within his or her lifetime.[95] This development was, of course, encouraged by the mythology of heroicized defeat popularized, above all, in school textbooks.

If the process of psychological stabilization in the Third Republic is pictured as a kind of caravan, attempting to leave its misfortune behind, then the pack of barking dogs that pursues it represents the naysayers—present in all political and religious movements—who seek to ensure that pure theory will never fall victim to impure practice.[96] In times of general contentment, their cries of warning and admonition fall on deaf ears or are absorbed by preexisting ritual. In times of crisis, however, they are able to mobilize passions, as if the repressed defeat were once more standing directly on the doorstep. Not every trauma become ritual has the potential for being reawakened, but *revanche* certainly did. Before examining the questions of when, how, and by whom it was reactivated, a few words are appropriate about the man who, more than anyone else, was responsible for planting the seeds of *revanche* in the French soul after 1870. Léon Gambetta would prove to be uniquely adept at combining rhetoric, ritual, and realism in the decades to come.

Gambetta, or the First Revanche

Even today Gambetta's exhortation to *revanche*—"Let us never speak of it, but think of it always"—has not lost its refined ambivalence.[97] Was this a veiled admission that *revanche* was an illusion? Or was it an appeal to the French not to lose their way in rhetoric so that they could fight for the cause more energetically? If political genius consists of maintaining ambiguous positions long enough for time to decide the issue, and even then avoiding all hard-and-fast stands,

Gambetta was undoubtedly the greatest genius of the early Third Republic. This does not mean he was an unscrupulous opportunist. As the organizer and *spiritus rector* of the militarily hopeless *défense nationale*, he was the most committed republican-Jacobin ideologue imaginable. His refusal to proclaim himself dictator after the lost election of February 1871 also appears as an act of almost Roman republican virtue.

Gambetta's political genius was to capture the predominant mood and make himself its chief spokesman; to retreat when, as in the capitulation of 1871, the nation's mood had moved too far from the original set of declared goals; to leave others to perform the thankless tasks associated with political bankruptcy; and all the while to prepare for his return to public life as heroic defender of the nation and martyred savior of its honor. Gambetta alone possessed the political and moral authority to define *revanche* since, as leader of the *défense nationale*, he had also created the notion. The *défense nationale*, in its refusal to acknowledge the defeat at Sedan and its attempt to reverse the consequences, was, after all, the first expression of *revanche*. And what could be more in the spirit of *revanche* than resolving to achieve—even if only in the indefinite future—the goals left unfulfilled by the *défense nationale*?

Still, despite Gambetta's ambiguous exhortation to think of *revanche* always, he probably considered it a hopeless, indeed dangerous illusion. "Only madmen can think of regaining Alsace-Lorraine," he said. And: "We have to keep our heads."[98] Yet such political realism hardly prevented him from speaking out in public with an incendiary passion to rival even that of Paul Déroulède, founder of the Ligue des patriotes and poet of *revanche*. The transcript of one of Gambetta's speeches on the subject of Alsace-Lorraine reads: "Ah! Noble provinces! Now as before a part of France that looks to the tricolor. . . . How they have suffered from their forced separation, but oh, how they took the nation with them in their hearts. [Here the transcript notes that Gambetta had "tears in his eyes."] Gentlemen, I can no longer speak . . ." The record concludes: "Exhausted, the speaker sinks back into his chair. Several people accompanying him begin to sob, shake his hand and withdraw silently."[99] This speech also illustrates, however, how carefully Gambetta avoided talking about *revanche* as a national mission. His theatrical performances were not calls to action but attempts to prompt a collective catharsis by enumerating the nation's woes. Some critics accused Gambetta of performing a comedy of *revanche*, and George Sand memorably averred that he was "nothing, nothing at all, nothing, I repeat."[100] But this accusation confuses tactics with strategy. The strategy remained what it had always been: to keep the newly born republic free of the taint of defeat.[101] During the *défense nationale*, the tactic had taken the form of military struggle. Militarily speaking, the continuation of the fight after Sedan may have been a hopeless, irresponsible "slaughter without purpose," as one general observed, but politically and psychologically it made perfect sense.[102] In September 1870, after a five-week blitzkrieg, the French public could not have accepted a sobering, not to say humiliating peace. Months of intense warfare after Sedan were required to transform the "demonic illusion" of "hordes" of German "ghosts" into a full-blown reality. Gambetta's great achievement was to understand this dynamic of the modern mass psyche and to put his knowledge to political use. It was of relatively little consequence whether the war was won or lost. The important thing was to not allow the republic to go down in history as having violently toppled the government and then shied away from fighting the Germans. As a symbolic gesture and a confirmation of authority, the continuation of the war—once again, regardless of the outcome—was the republic's most solid foundation and the best guarantee against any challenge to its legitimacy by a stab-in-the-back legend.

After the end of the *défense nationale*, *revanche* took over this function. As early as March 15, 1871, the *Revue des deux mondes* cautioned against actual revenge "while France's wounds are still bleeding. . . . Only when all the preparations have been made, will the moment for *revanche* arrive."[103] Gambetta's adoption of this line, after he had called on his people to fight heroically, down to the last man, exemplifies the entire political spectrum's realignment once the decision had been made to adopt a new course of action. Even romantics like Victor Hugo resigned themselves to waiting patiently for better times.[104]

But if actual revenge was to be postponed, the role played by *revanche* in the republican struggle against monarchism in the years 1871–79 was all the more intense, since, in the deep trauma of defeat during this period, it served as a slogan for both national salvation and the republican cause. Although *revanche* did not commit the republicans to any concrete action, it succeeded thoroughly in calling the other side's patriotism into question. In 1879, with the republicans' return to political power, the unity that had held as long as there had been a common enemy disintegrated. Along with the two Frances of monarchism and republicanism, there now appeared to be two republics, or, more precisely, two models of the republic: the liberal-bourgeois one of 1789 and the radical-Jacobin one of 1792. The Paris Commune had already shown how murderously extreme the conflicts between the two could be. In light of this history, it was almost preordained that the call for *revanche* would sooner or later undergo a transformation of meaning and function.

Boulanger, or the Second Revanche

The first years of the "republican republic" were lively, expansive, and self-confident, a series of respectable successes. Long-overdue reforms like the introduction of compulsory primary education were implemented within a few months. In its foreign policy, France emerged from the isolationism of the 1870s and became an active player, above all in the realm of colonial politics. At home, the Third Republic solidified its status with a number of symbolic measures: the declaration of July 14—Bastille Day—as the national holiday; the adoption of the "Marseillaise" as the national anthem; the return to Paris of the National Assembly from Versailles, where it had met since the time of the Commune; and finally, as a sign of its new self-assurance and readiness for reconciliation, amnesty toward the exiled Communards.

In the meantime, the traditional political factions regrouped. In place of the old tripartite right, left, and center, people now spoke of only two camps: the Opportunists, the liberal-bourgeois republicans who had assumed leadership in 1880, and the Radicals of the Jacobin opposition, who were immediately joined by the former Communards. The remnants of monarchism, which even in its heyday had consisted of three mutually hostile groups (the legitimist Bourbonists, the liberal Orléanists, and the populist Bonapartists), were divided between both sides.

In 1885, five years after its promising beginning, the Opportunists' republic found itself in crisis economically, politically, and morally.[105] France had slipped from being the second-leading industrial nation (behind Great Britain) to fourth place (after the United States and Germany). Following setbacks in its colonial policy, which the Radicals had always opposed as an indirect betrayal of Alsace-Lorraine, the government fell. Soon after the president of the republic, Jules Grévy, was forced to resign in the wake of a number of corruption scandals. For the Radical opposition, these events were just the first bubbles of discontent rising from the swamp of parliamentary mercantilism into which the Opportunists had transformed the republic. Each of the various factions within the opposition, moreover, had a score to settle with the Opportunists, and all would eventually join together under a banner of *revanche* that no longer had much connection with Gambetta's notion of the 1870s.

For the ex-Communard faction, men like Henri Rochefort and Félix Pyat, the time had come to avenge the massacre of May 1871. "Real *revanche* gives these loudmouths the shivers," scoffed the conservative newspaper *Correspondent*. "The only *revanche* they are interested in is internal: revenge against the men of Versailles, the bourgeoisie and the Opportunists."[106] In fact, they sought more than internal *revanche*, seeing the occasion as one for resuming the battle with Germany. The Germany they now opposed, however, was a different nation from the one beyond the Rhine. It was synonomous with the world of French high finance that had been implicated in all of France's major corruption scandals through men who typically bore German Jewish names like Rothschild, Reinach, and Fould. Anti-Germanism thus became antisemitism.

Antisemitism had been, since Proudhon's day, "one of the numerous holy sites of French socialism."[107] Reconceived by Edouard Drumont, the author in 1886 of *La France juive*, as a strategy of resistance against the Opportunist regime, antisemitism provided the inspiration for a faction within the opposition, as well as a convenient scapegoat image for various groups. The antisemites shared with the ex-Communards the conviction that Jewish-controlled France was in reality a France controlled by Germany through French Jewish middlemen. In this formulation, the idea of *revanche* could be turned inward without losing its patriotic force: *revanche* against Germany had to begin with a battle against this sinister Other France.

The third group aligned against the Opportunists was the Ligue des patriotes, the all-purpose movement founded by Paul Déroulède for everyone opposed to the Opportunists' tacit renunciation of *revanche*. Like the ex-Communards and the antisemites, the Ligue, which, incidentally, counted Gambetta among its members until his death in 1882, had its roots in the Jacobin left of republicanism. That all three groups—nationalists, antisemites, and leftists—coalesced within the space of a few years into a nonparliamentary, radical right can only be explained by the fact that this new right was very different from the conservative old right, namely what Zeev Sternhell calls a revolutionary right.

Just as remarkable as the odd mixture of factions that constituted the anti-Opportunist opposition was the figure who now emerged to lead it. "You will encounter the greatest theatrical genius of all time," a fellow officer said of General Georges-Ernest-Jean-Marie Boulanger, "a man whose smallest action appears to be of immense significance. Whether he is giving an order or receiving a wound, all the attention is focused on him. Assemble a hundred generals and he will be the only one to get noticed." These words were uttered in 1886, when Boulanger was named minister of war, and the Radicals responsible for his appointment chose him for precisely such attributes. Boulanger was intended to be a constant thorn in the side of the despised Opportunist regime, whose newly deposed leader, Jules Ferry, warned against this "shameless demagogue, gifted speaker, populist politician, and dangerous actor."[108]

Boulanger fulfilled all expectations with breathtaking energy and speed. Quickly setting up a press office within the Ministry of War, he transformed the public perception of the ministry and the army, if not the institutions themselves, within weeks and established himself as a charismatic national leader.[109] When Boulanger took up his post in January, a general atmosphere of disillusionment and pessimism prevailed in the wake of the government scandals. By the summer, the ministry was a place of stability and national self-confidence, buoyed by a feeling of having recaptured its proper place. The zenith came with a completely revamped celebration of Bastille Day in Paris. The festival, which since its adoption as the national holiday had been characterized by bourgeois moderation and the lack of an army presence, was staged by Boulanger as the sort of military pageant not seen since the days of Napoleon III. As a sign of resuscitated French military power, the army paraded down the streets of Longchamps, in the Bois de Boulogne, with Boulanger on horseback at its lead—"handsome, virile, republican"—while bringing up the rear, as if ashamed, were the ministers of state, the incarnation of the "laziness of the Opportunist government with its scandals, cowardice, and ballast of crisis."[110] For his masses of supporters, Boulanger was a savior whom one addressed in almost god-like fashion: "Save us from the abyss," wrote one admirer. "Lead our legions into glory. Guide our two sisters Alsace and Lorraine back home with your strong hand." For his detractors, Boulanger was a charlatan and an adventurer, exploiting the fact "that humiliated France longs for a prince, or at least a soldier, and that only the general who gives patriotism its *revanche* for Metz and Sedan has a chance of success."[111]

Nicknamed General Revanche shortly after his assumption of office, Boulanger seemed to many a new Gambetta who would restore the nation's self-confidence. In fact, though, he possessed only some of his predecessor's talent. He was able to create a rhetorical, symbolic reality and use it to conduct politics, but he lacked the ability to distinguish between the two, which had been an essential part of Gambetta's gift. The nationalist fever he whipped up, especially among the people of Paris, had little ultimate significance. Although German propaganda never ceased to condemn France's desire for *revanche* as warmongering, internal German evaluations seemed to take French belligerence far less seriously. The military attaché in Paris, for instance, dismissed Boulanger's military spectacles as "misuse of the armed forces for popular amusement" and the aggressive *revanchiste* pampleteering as "literary speculation trying to exploit the current 'patriotic excitement.'" Bismarck's son and assistant, Herbert, regarded "the Parisian insanity" as of "greater pathological than political interest."[112]

Indeed, despite the sudden flickering of *revanchiste* sentiment in 1886, the country's double psychology—"France desires *revanche*, but it wants peace"—dominant since 1871, persisted. A glance at the literature of the time reveals an abundance of poems, songs, ballads, odes, and manifestos, as well as journalistic articles and science fiction stories, that fantasize about military victory over Germany. The national indignation, wounded pride, and impassioned whining that had inspired Victor Hugo's patriotic arias still determined the basic mood. If there was anything new, it was a nascent inferiority complex vis-à-vis Germany, albeit one that was never acknowledged and was certainly not conscious. Immediately after

1870, people had been able to explain defeat as an accident that would soon be corrected. Fifteen years of French passivity and Germany's Bismarckian empire—which showed no signs of disappearing back down the hole whence it came and indeed was steadily developing into Europe's mightiest nation—had consigned France's sense of its own grandeur to an ever more distant past. In the presence of this overwhelmingly powerful neighbor, *revanche* increasingly lost its original meaning and developed undertones of a readiness to *defend* France against renewed attack. More telling than all the rhetoric of *revanche* was the construction of a line of new fortresses on France's eastern border.

The bluster of the *revanche* literature of 1886–87, thus, evokes the prey puffing itself up to scare off the predator. Nowhere is this clearer than in a pamphlet entitled "Homage to General Boulanger":

> Dare not lay a hand on our beautiful France,
> Tremble before you take up the fight.
> Hope in vain of emerging victorious.
> Dare not, Prussians, dare not.

And a poem dedicated to Boulanger:

> France wants no war
> But if necessary, it knows
> How to enforce respect for its borders
> Should the enemy threaten.
> When our general
> Gives the signal
> We are ready to follow.[113]

Perhaps the most notable thing about the role of *revanche* in Boulanger's career as a charismatic leader was that, following his dismissal after only one year in power, the rhetoric vanished as quickly as it had appeared. The antiparliamentary movement, or "Boulangism," that formed in response to the general's ouster had no use for external *revanche*, only for its internal application.[114] To borrow an image from Zeev Sternhell, the opposition that gathered around Boulanger had turned its sights from the blue line of the Vosges, the Alsace-Lorraine border, to the Bourbon Palace, where the National Assembly met, and the Elysée Palace, the president's residence.[115] In the process Boulanger himself, whom dismissal had made into a martyr, became, as one of his adherents remarked, "the best of all war machines," not for *revanche* against Germany but "for softening up the republic so it could be taken by storm."[116]

Barrès, or the Last Revanche

With Boulanger's flight from France and his suicide at the grave of his mistress in Brussels, the liberal republic emerged triumphant once more. Having learned from its opponents the importance of managing appearances, the republic promoted itself at the 1889 World's Fair, which marked the hundredth anniversary of the French Revolution. This revitalized republic was no longer the regime of Opportunism, feeling its way carefully and timidly out of defeat, but a force of vitality, symbolized by the architecture of Alexandre-Gustave Eiffel, whose tower rose above Paris like a ramp to the future. Along with such internal confirmation came the consolidation of gains made in foreign affairs. Bismarck, France's nemesis for twenty years, was nearing the end of his career, and a French alliance with Russia offered, for the first time, the possibility of a serious counterweight to Germany's superior military power. Moreover, after ten years the nation's controversial colonial policies were finally beginning to bear fruit. After Great Britain, France possessed the second-largest overseas empire, elevating it to the status of world power, while Germany, for all its might, was merely a European one.

After 1890, *revanche* seemed to have lost its force. "The group advocating *revanche* consists of persons of no influence," declared a report by the Russian embassy. "It is small and has little success with public opinion. We can even have doubts as to its very existence."[117] The idea of regaining Alsace-Lorraine became the object of pointed sarcasm within intellectual circles, most notoriously in the writer Rémy de Gourmont's pronouncement: "As for me, I wouldn't give the little finger of my right hand for those forgotten provinces. My hand needs it to rest on as I write. Nor would I give the little finger of my left hand: I need it to flick the ash from my cigarette."[118]

Nonetheless, *revanche* made one final appearance before slipping free entirely of its tether to the defeat of 1870–71. Maurice Barrès, writer and philosopher, belonged to a generation that had no personal experience of the collapse of the Second Empire—or had it only as children. Barrès began his literary career as a self-proclaimed aesthete and dandy, without any feelings of connection to the national trauma.[119] Nothing was more foreign to him than the moralizing political poetry of Paul Déroulède, for whom he once recommended "a proper textbook on the art of poetry, which would stop him from scribbling verse—now that would be an act of patriotism."[120] The cosmopolitan nature of culture was for Barrès self-evident: "We have spiritual fathers in all countries." France, he was convinced, could not afford to close itself off but had to remain open to all influences, especially the influence of German culture. "The civilized world is a grand museum . . . and the German hall has some of the best attractions."[121]

Yet Maurice Barrès, cosmopolitan aesthete and creator of a cult of egotism that flourished during the 1880s and 1890s, had by the time of the Dreyfus affair been transformed into a militant, reactionary, racist nationalist and remained one throughout the years leading up to the First World War. Although the story of his transformation belongs more properly to the epoch of fascism than to the recovery from the trauma of 1870–71, Barrès's trajectory is worth examining as the last manifestation of *revanche*.

To the young Barrès, Boulanger was a hero, a man of action

"who energetically opened the windows, threw out the idle chatterers, and let in the fresh air."[122] And Boulangism, with its attack on the establishment, was a new kind of politics, the very antithesis of business as usual, a course of pure and purifying action. Barrès was able to make the transition from aestheticism to this sort of politics so seamlessly because both aspired to purity. His form of nationalism was at once aesthetic and racist—qualities that are not necessarily contradictory.[123] At its origin was his outrage at the corruption of the liberal parliamentary system, and only in his search for the causes of that corruption did Barrès come to confront the national defeat of 1870. His discovery of how Germany rose from the ashes of defeat after 1806 was also of great significance. He was profoundly influenced by the writings of the German philosopher Johann Gottlieb Fichte, whose notion of a self-contained national community, or *Volk*, developed at a time when "Germany was merely the name of a French protectorate."[124] Eduard von Hartmann's psychology of the unconscious, to which Barrès owed the insight that "society is the soul of all," was another important ideological source, as were the works of Ernest Renan and Hippolyte Taine.[125]

At the center of Barrès's philosophy stood the purity of the nation, which was to be reattained through the eradication of internal enemies and "impure" elements. How little Germany initially figured as an opponent is clear from Barrès's remark that "more than just the Rhine" separated him from the enemy at home.[126] Then came the Dreyfus affair. A standard-bearer for the anti-Dreyfus cause, Barrès insisted on the captain's guilt even as the case against him began to unravel. With the revelation that much of the evidence against Dreyfus had been forged, Barrès experienced his second personal and political defeat (after the Boulanger adventure) within a decade. Perhaps even more significant was the ultimate triumph of the liberal regime in 1899, when a government came to power headed by the leftist republican René Waldeck-Rousseau and committed to a pacifist foreign policy. These setbacks may explain why Barrès decided to make peace with the republic and redirect the energies he had long applied to the internal struggle outward, to Germany.

Barrès's about-face was the inversion of an inversion. His desire for *revanche* had initially been turned by Boulangism and the anti-Dreyfus campaign against internal institutions, where it seemed to have greater prospects for success; it now swung around once more, since those institutions had proven unassailable. After 1900, Barrès's *revanchiste* writings came to resemble those of his predecessors from the 1870s, with one significant addition. Everything German was now not only barbaric, violent, predatory, uncultured, and without spirit but also disloyal, assimilated, imitative, servile, and lacking in character—attributes previously reserved by antisemites for Jews. In Barrès's telling, these traits had enabled the Germans to gain power. In contrast, everything French was cultivated, humane, and redolent of spiritual greatness. The same man who fifteen years earlier had made fun of the political poetry of Paul Déroulède and dismissed popular anti-German pamphlets as the "vain crowings of brainless traveling salesmen" now embraced Déroulède ("a hero in the tradition of Corneille, . . . my greatest ally") and portrayed the German characters in his novels in the style of the antisemitic caricatures from the Dreyfus era.[127] As Ernst Robert Curtius was the first to recognize, late Barrèsian nationalism was nothing other than a means of voicing the fear, already evident in Boulangist *revanche*, of being once more overpowered by Germany, as well as an attempt to ward off this looming coup de grâce. "The very title of Barrès's *revanche* novel *Les bastions de l'Est* speaks volumes," writes Curtius. "Nationalism is forever in search of bulwarks and protective walls against foreign invaders."[128]

From Revanche *to* Elan Vital

In his analysis of Barrèsian nationalism, Curtius lists its defining attributes as "a permanent sense of threat," "an intense concern with mustering one's dwindling strength," and "a strange nervous anxiety about foreign powers." But he also emphasizes what Barrèsian nationalism *was not*, namely, "the result of a thoroughgoing consciousness of one's own strength and a boundary-shattering drive toward expansion . . . [or] a self-assured, calm expression of superiority."[129] *Consciousness of strength, drive toward expansion, superiority*— there can be no doubt as to what Curtius, writing after 1918, is referring to. For a few years before World War I, European observers had perceived just such renewed self-confidence in France. A new generation—known as the Agathon generation after the nom de plume of two writers who announced the movement—knew of events like Sedan, the German invasion, and the Paris Commune only from history books.[130] To members of the Agathon generation, all born around 1890, Boulanger was merely a historical figure and the Dreyfus affair a quarrel among their parents. The technological achievement of the Eiffel Tower, in whose shadow they had grown up, impressed them far more than the historical legacy and cultural achievement of their predecessors, whom they generally despised as dilettantes. In their rebellion against the prevailing liberal-pacifist spirit of the post-Dreyfus years, they looked to Maurice Barrès and his fellow traveler Charles Maurras as their nationalistic schoolmasters, but in truth they were less interested in the elder Barrès's *revanche* novels than in the young Barrès's cult of egotism. And Maurras, founder of the aggressively nationalist *L'action française*, impressed them mainly with his contempt for bourgeois hypocrisy and sentimentality, as when he made fun of the "eternal and infinitely stupid *gloria victis*" of the older *revanche* elegists.[131]

The youth of the Agathon generation comprised, however, no more than several hundred or perhaps a thousand students from the Sorbonne and the *grandes écoles*. As disproportionate as their influence was—not unlike the intellectual New Left's in the 1960s—the spectrum of opinion was much broader. The importance of Barrès and Maurras in fact paled in comparison with that of Henri Bergson, with his doctrine of the élan vital, which emphasized contingency

and creativity. To the disaffected young, Bergson offered the revelation of a world in which all traditional borders had been forced
open. Julien Benda, critic and philosopher, referred to Bergsonianism
as "intellectual Boulangism," a characterization that was unjust to
Bergson's philosophy but accurately captured its enthusiastic contemporary reception. Revocation of boundaries, expansiveness, dyna-
mism, and the questioning of all established facts were the order of
the day throughout turn-of-the-century Europe, expressed in everything from imperialism to physics, medicine, psychology, technology,
industry, art, and literature.[132] In Paris, the movement reached
extraordinary intensity, coinciding as it did with the period of
vibrant national renewal. For the Agathon-Bergson generation,
France's colonial empire, created in a mere two decades, was not
what it had been for their fathers, a self-awarded consolation prize
for the loss of Alsace-Lorraine and an occasion for twinges of conscience over the betrayed ideals of 1789. The empire represented
France's new role as a world power and was considered a reservoir
of strength without which national regeneration would have been
impossible. The expectation articulated a decade earlier that "the
colonial movement should yield a new generation of Frenchmen,
bolder, more active, and more self-confident than their predecessors"
seemed to have been fulfilled.[133]

Along with the colonial project, sports played an important role
in the revitalization of France. The kindling of interest in sports was
a Europe-wide phenomenon, but only in France did it lead to the
development of a subgenre, technological sports, which immediately
took hold of the popular imagination. The new enthusiasm for bicycle races and automobile and airplane competitions may well have
been an artful metaphoric corrective to the slow pace of industrialization in France compared with the progress in England, Germany,
and the United States. The pilot and the race-car driver were hailed
as a new *homme machine*, a technological hero and superman, the
product of industrial and anthropological evolution. Significantly,

preoccupation with this type manifested itself less in the highly industrialized (that is, the Protestant, Anglo-Saxon, Germanic) world than in the Latin-Catholic one, which observed the Industrial Revolution from a distance.[134] Where the French, for example, venerated the propeller-driven airplane—a roaring machine, speed become form—and, with it, the lone pilot, the Germans were attracted to the dirigible, which was monumental, grave, and above all the province not of a single individual but of a team.

If the Eiffel Tower had been the emblem for the early period of France's restored self-confidence, after 1900 the airplane became the symbol of French revitalization in full swing, or, more precisely, of the country's return to the ranks of the nations able and willing to wage war. According to the journal *Agathon*, the masses saw the airplane as "a war machine."[135] The compensatory mechanism is unmistakable: to overcome its industrial and demographic inferiority to Germany, France fixated on the airplane, which embodied the superiority of quality over quantity. Fantasy war novels never tired of recounting how a handful of French flying men forced whole German armies into ignoble retreat.

Nonetheless, the myth of the airplane was more than merely a new remedy for the old inferiority complex. One novel element was the connection between war and sport, sublimated in and embodied by international competitions such as the Olympic Games, which were revived in Athens in 1896 thanks to a French initiative. In a kind of osmosis of meaning, war increasingly began to appear as a *sport pour le vrai*, a "match" played with live ammunition, the winning of which was a question more of technology, training, and endurance than of national sentiment. Traditional national enthusiasm, as the adherents of the war-as-sport perspective insisted, was hopelessly outmoded: it did not take into account the new facts and rules of technology, sport, élan vital, and imperialism. It failed to recognized that only the blue sky of aviation—and not the blue line of the Vosges—had the capacity to renew the nation.

The "new nationalism"—the bellicose chauvinism and imperialism of the years immediately preceding the First World War—was accompanied by renewed debate about Alsace-Lorraine.[136] This was not a flickering, however, of the old nationalism. The return of Alsace-Lorraine to public consciousness in 1911, after a long absence, had less to do with the provinces themselves than with the French-German confrontation then taking place in Morocco, a purely colonial matter. People were thinking not of Metz and Strasbourg but rather of the imperialist commitments at risk and the national prestige involved. There is no better evidence of the truly "provincial" significance of Alsace-Lorraine in this context than the fact that all the major Franco-German crises before 1914 took place not along the Rhine and not over the "lost provinces" but over colonial spheres of influence in Northern Africa.[137] Sedan and Alsace-Lorraine were little more than afterthoughts in a *revanche* that was now primarily concerned with redressing French humiliation in the colonial sphere.[138] France's belligerent response to German expansionism in the Morocco crisis of 1911 resembled the combative "*revanche pour Sadowa*" sentiment of 1866 more than any of the other *revanche* surges since 1870. The uncanny similarity obtains even in the number of years it took both events to lead to an actual outbreak of hostilities: four after 1866 and three after 1911. Forty years after Sedan, France was once again prestige-conscious and ready for war.

The Renewal

According to the law—or reflex—of learning from the victor, the model for French renewal was preprogrammed: it was the Prussian schoolmaster, or, more generally, the modern Prussian-German public educational system with all its expectations and results, such as literacy and professionalization of the masses; broad dissemination of the latest technology and training in technical skills, and a high degree of social organization and discipline. German soldiers' detailed knowledge of geography, to take but one example, had made a deep impression on the civilian population of France. "When they asked for directions," recalled one Frenchman, "the question was never 'Where does this road go?' but rather 'Isn't this the road to . . . ?' And they never got lost."[139] In contrast, the German side was astonished by the level of illiteracy among French prisoners of war—officers as well as soldiers.[140]

National renewal would obviously have to begin with the army. It was clear, however, that the military caste, which had thought of itself since the seventeenth century as the most accomplished in Europe, would bitterly resist being remade according to a foreign model. Its resistance explains the halfhearted military reform carried out in the early 1870s. Conscription ostensibly became universal in 1872—the common practice of "substitution," for example, was outlawed—but the law was so full of holes that the old professional army continued to exist de facto. The general staff, created along Prussian lines after 1874, served only as an adviser to the war minister, having no competence in drawing up plans and making decisions. These remained the responsibility of the Conseil supérieur de la guerre, a committee made up of retired generals whose activities, according to one participant, were "confused and never methodically directed" and often consisted of "interminable meetings where one discussed everything but the army."[141]

More important in the present context than the patchy results was the way in which the reformers justified their policies. Adopting the Prussian system, they argued, ultimately meant nothing more than continuing their own tradition by other means. Was not the Prussian army of 1870, they asked, also the product of reform, specifically reform implemented after the 1806 German defeat at Jena-Auerstedt and modeled on the example of then-victorious France? To adopt the Prussian system was thus to return to the original French one, which had been developed in Prussia while France had rested on its laurels and lost its advantage. Reform, argued Jules Lewal, a leading military theoretician of the 1870s, was "a matter not of imitating a foreign model, but of returning to original French doctrine."[142] From this perspective, the Prussian army seemed not so much a superior power as a kind of medium for the conservation and regeneration of French military excellence, which had been criminally neglected at home since 1815. To support their view, the reformers cited Prussian officers' statements noting their debt to French role models. During the days of Napoleon III, for example, the French military attaché in Berlin, Eugène Georges Stoffel, reported that Prussians readily admitted their debt to France: "Jena forced us to think things over and we learned our lesson."[143] The picture of Prussia as both a parasite feeding off French excellence and also an heir to it was not restricted to the military. Ludovic Drapeyron's remark that "Germany after 1815 needed only to continue on the path down which France had pointed it" clearly invokes the old loser rationale that the opponent's victory is undeserved because it is based on appropriated superiority.[144]

After 1871 the notion of Prussian-style military reform as a continuation of "French achievement" certainly served to sooth France's wounded self-confidence but that was a secondary motive.[145] The primary concern was to promote Prussia's path out of defeat as a model for France. According to Ernest Renan, the real cause of France's exhaustion, decadence, and ultimate defeat was the humanist universalism to which the nation had subscribed since 1789.[146] The Prussian example showed that this decline could be reversed by focusing one's energies inward. The Prussian model was ideal for imitation because, as the philosopher Elme Carlo had pointed out even earlier than Renan, German culture, too, had gotten stuck in the illusion of humanist cosmopolitanism before the defeat of 1806 had set it straight.[147]

Most military reformers after 1871 entertained similar ideas. General Louis Trochu, for example, having already staunchly advocated thorough military reform after Königgrätz/Sadowa, characterized his country's traditional *esprit guerrier* as inadequate to the demands of modern warfare and contrasted it with the more up-to-date Prussian military spirit, "a constant, effective, disciplined, and reliable force . . . itself capable of holding together the army in the nation's hour of need and preparing it spiritually and morally for *revanche*."[148] Just as France, to survive as a nation, would have to give up the ideal of saving humanity, so too the army would have to renounce its anachronistic warrior ethos. This was the lesson of Sedan, distilled to its essence, and it was embodied in a figure who, with Joan of Arc and Roland, completed the triumvirate of France's personifications of defeat.

Vercingetorix

The hero of the unsuccessful Gallic resistance to Roman conquest had a genealogy that differed from that of the two medieval martyr figures. While Roland and Joan of Arc were already legends in the collective imagination before 1871, the entire Gallic period had been relegated to the prehistory of French national memory. It was the post-1879 republican republic that rediscovered Vercingetorix and made him a symbol of Gallic France, that is, the France of the people, as opposed to the "Frank" France of kings and aristocrats. Vercingetorix was seen as the progenitor of a long line of revolutionaries fighting against seigneurial France, with the 1789 Revolution serving as "the high point of a long battle between Franks and Gauls and the successful *revanche* of the second against the first."[149]

More important than this class-specific interpretation, however, was that Vercingetorix embodied a more complex experience of defeat than had either Joan of Arc or Roland. While they essentially filled the role of martyr-heroes of an ultimately successful cause, Vercingetorix posed the question of defeat as historical necessity. Gaul, the answer ran, had to be vanquished by Rome, more civilized and thus superior, so that France could be born. The demise of the Gauls was the "creative defeat" and "cruel necessity" of modernization.[150] Or, in the language of the republican reformers, "The Gauls lacked the quality of discipline essential to national greatness. They were incapable of following orders and subordinating their personal and group interests to the greater good. . . . Rancor and anarchy destined the Gauls to fall prey to a better organized and more disciplined nation. Rome's victory over the Gauls, thus, was ultimately the triumph of civilization over barbarism."[151] The lesson of 1870–71 could not have been drawn with greater clarity in regard to discipline, the one quality that Prussia was traditionally thought to possess in abundance. Of course, no one went so far as to demand the Germanization of France; the country still felt morally and culturally superior to its conqueror. Instead, the challenge resided in the old and recurring tightrope walk: how to adopt the discipline, knowledge, technology, and organization of the victor without damaging the national soul, indeed while strengthening it for future conflicts.

Educational Reform and the Black Hussars of the Republic

"Education is the concern of everyone. Society must do everything in its power to encourage the development of reason among the people and give every citizen the instruction necessary for it."[152] As article 22 of the First Republic's 1793 constitution makes clear, the French people did not need the Prussian model to appreciate the importance of popular education. A state that considered reason the highest virtue was naturally committed to spreading it even to the nation's most remote corners. What was lacking, however, was a plan for disseminating knowledge in an organized way. In practice, article 22 was never taken as seriously as other basic rights and duties of citizens. Education was always defined merely as a concern and not an obligation, the reason perhaps being that it did not have a natural place in the triad of liberty, equality, and fraternity. Indeed, compulsory education seemed to contradict the human right to freedom. Ernest Renan saw the contradiction as one reason France lagged behind Prussian Germany in popular education.[153] Another was the comparatively low prestige of institutions for practical education—as opposed to the idea of reason—in a revolutionary republic that saw itself, despite its celebration of democratic egalitarianism, as a primarily heroic undertaking.[154] With every military victory, the sword seemed more decisive and commanded more respect, while the chalk and the schoolmaster's switch seemed ever more irrelevant and base.

Thus, the cause of compulsory public education gained momentum only after the Napoleonic defeats of 1812–15. The famous adage that the battle of Waterloo was won on the playing fields of Eton emphasized for the first time the superiority of nonmilitary thought, training, and organization over their military equivalents. The stereotype of the Prussian schoolmaster was essentially an updated version of the playing fields of Eton. Significantly, Victor Cousin, who planned sweeping school reforms during the 1830s and 1840s, had justified his campaign in terms of the battlefield: "Adopting the Prussian education system would be a greater triumph than the trophies of Austerlitz and Jena."[155]

In their long struggle against monarchist restorations and Bonapartist coups d'état, French republicans were motivated by a different sort of defeat to reevaluate all aspects of public education. After the failed Revolution of 1848, they recognized that any revolutionary action in Paris was bound to be more flash than substance as long as the masses outside Paris remained under the control of the established powers. One instrument of this control was the public school. Hence the attempt in 1848 by republican minister Hippolyte Carnot (whose father organized the *levée en masse* of 1792) to introduce compulsory education with a secular, republican syllabus. This project, like that of the entire Second Republic, fell apart: in 1850, one year before his coup d'état, Louis Bonaparte reconfirmed the traditional leading role of the church in education and even revoked Cousin's nascent reforms. After this setback, republicans placed free compulsory education at the center of their political platform. Biding their time on the political margins throughout the Second Empire, they laid the foundations for a "counterculture" in which popular education would become the republican substitute for religion.[156]

The most important association created to support this goal was the Ligue de l'enseignement. Both the time (autumn 1866) and the place (not Paris, but Alsace) of the Ligue's founding underscored its reliance on the German model. Not only was the shock of Prussian victory at Königgrätz/Sadowa still fresh, but France's easternmost province was also the most open to German ideas and culture. It was hardly coincidental that French military attaché Stoffel, who repeatedly warned of the threat posed by the Prussian synthesis of militarism and education, came from the Alsatian border region. Stoffel's reports from Berlin languished in ministerial desk drawers until 1871. After France's defeat, however, they were published and soon came to serve as the basis for discussions about military and school reform. One of Stoffel's rhetorical questions asks: "What general would think twice if asked to choose between two armies, each with a hundred thousand men, one composed of graduates of the Ecole polytechnique and the military academy at St. Cyr and the other of peasants?"[157]

The vigorous public educational reform that began in 1879 astonished international observers.[158] It proceeded on three levels, the first in terms of secular subject matter and content.[159] On the structural level, the republicans instituted obligatory teacher-training seminars (*écoles normales*) in all regions and "cleansed" the Conseil supérieur de l'instruction publique of all "confessional" (that is, Catholic) members, transforming it into a professional committee for planning and decision making on national educational policies.[160] Finally, on the symbolic level, the status of the teacher was redefined. The old schoolmaster, as Balzac depicted him in the figure of Père Fourchon in *The Peasants*, had traditionally occupied the lowest rung on the village social ladder. Often barely literate himself, the schoolteacher was a kind of seasonal laborer hired by the community after the autumn harvest and let go again in the spring, as well as a factotum

who filled in as gravedigger, village chronicler, surveyor, and sometimes cobbler and tailor—in short, more a pariah than a role model.
By the early 1880s, republican school reform and its attendant propaganda had transformed this pathetic figure into the shining *instituteur
républicain*. Like the commissar in post-1917 revolutionary Russia, the
instituteur républicain became the figurehead for the new regime.
"*Solide, virile, austère*"—these were the characteristics demanded of
teachers by Jules Simon, education minister of the provisional government, and the schoolteacher soon became known popularly, on
account of his standardized uniform, as the Black Hussar of the
Republic.[161] A similar spirit of virile austerity drove the reform of
higher education. The superficial elegance of the French *esprit* was
contrasted unfavorably with the scholarly seriousness of the German
Geist and found to be too flighty (that is, insufficiently "masculine").
As one reformer wrote, "French higher education exists only in order
to prepare a people of dilettantes and bon vivants, fluent conversa-
tionalists, salon thinkers, and elegant writers. Modern knowledge has
never even knocked on the door of our universities. . . . From this
stems the superficial spirit that spreads throughout French society
from top to bottom."[162]

It would be misleading to cite the Prussian model as the explanation for the militaristic associations of the hussar-teacher since
what was considered worthy of imitation in the Prussian model was
never its "militaristic" quality but rather its pedagogical excellence.
The image of the Black Hussar of the Republic can be better understood as another expression of anti-Catholic agitation: the teaching
profession functioned as a kind of Praetorian Guard in the republicans' fight against the Catholic monarchist camp. As with *revanche*,
where one said "Germany" but meant the domestic enemy, republican educational reform was also a combination of external and
internal considerations. The *instituteur républicain* played a double
role as standard-bearer of the nation's educational renewal and hussar
in the fight against the dark forces of church and crown attempting
to block that renewal.

The "school battalions" that appeared in the 1880s embodied the republican military ethos at its most extreme. Equipped with wooden rifles and trained by professional soldiers from the regional garrison, these squadrons of uniformed schoolchildren marched on Bastille Day and on other representative republican occasions, to the consternation of local priests, who protested against such calculated acts of provocation as the banging of drums and the singing of republican songs outside church services. Disavowed by contemporary critics as a "childish and dangerous" institution and seen by historians as a "game of military adventure" and a "military masquerade," the school battalions served for several years as a miniature band of propagandistic storm troopers.[163] Reaching their zenith during the years of Boulangism, they soon disappeared as quickly as they had risen, failing to become a permanent institution because participation was voluntary and their activity confined to traditional republican, urban strongholds. Another reason for their decline was the development of an institution that proved far more suitable for the militarization of the schools—and of society with them.

Gymnastique

As early as Rousseau's *Emile*, republican pedagogy insisted that the education of the child into a future citizen must address the body as well as the mind. The First Republic had included physical education along with intellectual pursuits in its catalog of citizens' rights and duties but had done little, aside from military training for the *levée en masse*, to put the idea into practice.[164] Nonetheless, its inclusion marked the beginning of a close connection between *gymnastique*, the military, and the nation that would continue throughout the nineteenth century. In Prussia, Friedrich Ludwig Jahn, following the French model, would systematically develop the idea of physical education into a movement that has been rightly termed the "mobilizing capacity" of the masses but that could perhaps be more accurately described as their "nationalizing capacity."[165] Patriotically inflected physical education, with its accompanying institution, the gymnastics club, or *Turnverein*, played an important role in the formation of national consciousness not only in Germany but in Central and Southern European national movements as well.[166] *Gymnastique* finally made its way back to France after 1871 as a pedagogical movement of national renewal patterned on Jahn's example and propagated by the Ligue de l'enseignement. Clubs with names like La Régénératrice, Le Réveil, La Patriote, France!, La Sentinelle, and La Revanche sprouted up all over the country, and by 1880 physical education had become a mandatory part of the school curriculum. One historian cites the human pyramids made by hundreds of gymnasts at the national competition in 1900 as a vivid expression of national unity, and he quotes a contemporary commentator: "The gymnastics clubs show how their members are united by the same discipline, by the same method, regardless of whether they come from north or south, east or west."[167] What the republic expected to gain from *gymnastique* was, in the words of Gambetta, "the education of schoolchildren who are physically fit and courageous. The teacher is to be supplemented by the *gymnaste* and the military man. Only thus will our children learn later in life as citizen soldiers to wield the sword, use the rifle, and endure long marches."[168]

By the 1890s, *gymnastique* as a mass movement was on the wane, as were Boulangism, the Ligue des patriotes, and the school battalions, and the slogan of *revanche* was giving way to the aim of colonial expansion. That all these developments occurred around the same time suggests they were related, as does the simultaneous rise in popularity of another form of physical activity.

Le Sport

If *gymnastique* was practiced not for its own sake but for strengthening and disciplining the nation, sports, which had arisen in England, were initially an entirely self-referential activity, *sport pour le sport*. A concept like fair play was absent in *gymnastique* because there was nothing to be played for. Sports, by contrast, were organized as competitions for records and victories and thus were a sublimated form of warfare—with set rules, to be sure, but also with winners and losers to be determined in hard-fought if playful fashion. Furthermore, just as *gymnastique* gave physical expression to old-style republican nationalism, sports seemed to give physical expression to social Darwinism and imperialism. The concurrent appearance of sports and imperialism and the frequency of sports terms in imperialist language are too conspicuous to be coincidental. The English provenance of both is also significant since by the 1890s Great Britain had become the preeminent role model for the colonial and imperial aspirations of nations across the Continent—aspirations that pushed old rivalries over national borders, including the conflict between France and Germany, into the background.

The fact that imperialism in Europe from 1890 to 1914 was in many ways a utopian ideology has been lost in the emphasis on the crimes committed in its name. Yet that's what it was: the imperialist vision of salvation was to resolve conflicts in Europe once and for all by projecting them abroad; formerly irreconcilable differences would be forgotten in the wide-open spaces of the non-European world. For the French and Germans, this meant that their two nations would no longer pursue the endlessly murderous struggle over the Rhine but would instead divide up the rest of the world in the English fashion, that is, with minimal military involvement, each erecting an Augustan empire without disturbing or being disturbed by its neighbor, who was engaged in similar activities. Should conflict arise, however, it would be settled not through martial bloodshed, as on the European battlefields of the past, but through peaceful, sporting, commercial competition. *Competition* (for territories and markets) was one of imperialism's central images. With the world understood as an arena or a racetrack, there was little room to imagine battles, victories, and defeats as anything other than sporting events. As one contemporary, illustrating what Norbert Elias calls the "sportification" of culture, put it, "Ultimately war is nothing other than a sporting contest, a match between two nations, indeed the one true sport."[169] Only against this backdrop can one understand the sporting élan with which the generation of 1914 marched into the First World War. Henri Desgrange, founder of the Tour de France, spoke of a "grand match" to be won or lost: "Our soldiers at the front, aren't they in a familiar situation, like those international meets in which men measure their strength against that of the opponent?"[170] Some, like the English captain who led a charge by kicking a soccer ball across the line, held to the idea of war as sport to the very end, when they went down in a hail of machine-gun fire. The Christmas 1914 soccer matches between English and German soldiers in the no-man's-land between the trenches belong to the same tradition.

It is no surprise, then, that the father of the modern Olympic revival subscribed to the view that the conflation of sports and war was a step forward for civilization. One year before the outbreak of World War I, Pierre de Coubertin wrote in the *Revue Olympique:* "The idea of a sporting war—the phrase is carefully considered— seems to be increasingly taking hold: a contest of weapons that is no less harsh but that leaves behind less hatred and bitterness. People are beginning to learn from sports how despicable hatred is without physical contest. . . . An army of sportsmen will be humane and fair during wartime and calm and collected thereafter."[171]

The enthusiasm for sports in Belle Epoque France has been explained as arising from "the inexactible *revanche*"—the result of France's military inferiority to Germany.[172] This does not mean that France simply transferred *revanche* from the battlefield to the sports field. On the contrary, France's sports efforts were never directed against Germany, and they were characterized not by a *revanchiste* fixation but rather by internationalism and universalism. Yet compensation often takes indirect forms. Just as post-1815 Saint-Simonism, with which France sought to overtake England in the Industrial Revolution, explicitly reinterpreted industrialization as a human ideal rather than a national ambition, so France appropriated the English idea of competitive sports, refashioning it as a celebration of humanity and brotherhood. The revival of the Olympic Games in 1896, in which Paris took a leading role, cast the *grande nation* not only as the true heir to the original cultural nation, Hellas, but also as the director of the entire international sports movement.

Internationalism and universalism also marked the athletic events held within France itself, above all those that were considered typically French. Until 1914, all the leading international automobile races and aviation competitions began and ended in Paris, and the Tour de France, named after a famous French children's book, soon became the most important event in international bicycle racing. The enthusiastic embrace of technology in these competitions touches on yet another compensatory function of sports in the Third Republic. As already observed, the French between 1890 and 1914 favored machine and motor sports rather than purely physical games. At the center of their fascination was not the athlete but the *homme machine*, energized and given wheels and wings by the motorized vehicle. This preference was not as immediately apparent with the bicyclist, who moved the machine with his muscles, as it was with automobile drivers and airplane pilots; on the other hand, the *vélo* (bicycle) most vividly represented a synthesis of man and machine, in which the two worked together, enhancing each other. The popularity of bicycles in 1890s France—truly a *vélomanie*—can perhaps therefore be understood as a collective longing for release from the physical laws of the real world. Like the airplane, the *petite machine ailée* (little winged machine) and the *fée bicyclette* (magic bicycle) became the means "of freeing oneself from the laws of gravity," in the words of novelist Maurice Leblanc, a *vélo* enthusiast and the creator of Arsène Lupin.[173] "Riding. Riding. Movement transported them into an indescribable state," he says of two of his characters. "They seemed to themselves to be supernatural beings equipped with new capabilities and unknown powers, birds flying high above the heavens who simultaneously touched the ground with their wings."[174]

Clearly the French enthusiasm for sports, while internationalist in tone, fulfilled a national function. As the premier event of international cycling, the Tour de France has been described as a "forum for the nation in which the characteristics of the race are put to a public test" and as a "three-week-long national epic that glorifies France and Frenchmen."[175] One could also call it the most successful form of compensation for the real *revanche* that was never able to get off the ground.[176]

The Path to Africa

Every nation has a mythology centered on the idea of two fronts. In France that mythology was based on two bodies of water on its borders: the Atlantic Ocean (including the English Channel) and the Rhine. Beyond both were spaces for potential exploration as well as sites of potential threat. In the late Middle Ages, modern France unified in the face of an English (Atlantic) threat, and it soon discovered a taste for overseas expansion. The result was two hundred years of competition against England in the New World, ending in 1763 after the Seven Years War with the closing of the Atlantic "frontier." It was not until 1870–71, when the "across the Rhine" option became not only unfeasible but distinctly dangerous, that the French gaze once more turned to distant lands. History, however, seldom repeats itself: this time, the French looked not across the Atlantic but over the Mediterranean.

The idea that the nation's future lay in Africa was not new. In 1830, French troops had occupied part of Algeria in a punitive expedition that lacked any advance planning or vision.[177] On an ideological level, the utopian socialists had long assigned Algeria a role comparable to that of the American West for the United States:

Fourier wanted to found the first of his phalansteries there, Proudhon envisioned an agrarian colony, and Etienne Cabet imagined a communist collective.[178] Later on, French expansionists planned giant technological projects, like irrigation of the Sahara and the construction of a trans-Saharan railroad line (modeled on the American Union Pacific). The railway was intended not only to join North and Equatorial Africa and connect both to Europe but also, in competition with the Anglo-American monopoly on the North Atlantic, to prepare for a "Latin" connection across the South Atlantic to South America. It is difficult to imagine a more fantastic *revanche* for the defeat of 1763 than the reconquest of the transatlantic world via the Mediterranean.[179]

The coherent concept of a greater France extending across the western Mediterranean to Africa was first formulated in the decadence debates during the Second Empire. Lucien Prévost-Paradol, for example, believed that for France to survive in the competition with other great powers, it had to achieve the territorial integration of Algeria. In that way, the French population would be tripled, and eighty to a hundred million Frenchmen, he thought, would be capable of matching the United States, England, Russia, and Prussia.[180] Henri Verne laid out a similar argument in 1869, a year before Sedan. Referring to France's dim prospects in Europe, he recommended concentrating all of the nation's energies on developing Algeria: "Once this beautiful country has been settled, cultivated, and made economically useful, we will have made a much more important contribution to regaining our hegemony than by annexing the Rhineland and Belgium, which could only be accomplished with a bloody and ruinous war."[181]

These and similar projects never really caught on, owing to a lack of public interest. Flaubert's entry in his *Dictionary of Accepted Ideas* reads: "Colonies (ours): upsetting to talk about." Particularly after Napoleon III's unhappy adventure in Mexico, where he tried to establish an empire, anticolonial sentiment grew to such an extent that even a successful endeavor like Francis Garnier's exploration of

Indochina and conquest of the Mekong region in the 1860s was greeted with "profound indifference," as a disappointed Garnier noted on his return.[182]

IN 1881, THE French military occupied Tunisia and declared it a protectorate. While Tunisia seemed to be a one-shot colonial acquisition much like Algeria fifty years earlier, it was, in fact, the opening move in a carefully considered and well-planned political campaign, one that demonstrated that republican France, after ten years of forced passivity, was once more testing itself in the fields of military action and foreign influence. The occupation also revealed where the future emphasis of such activities would lie.[183] With this act, the newly elected government of Jules Ferry clearly showed that, instead of rattling the old European cage locked by Bismarck, France was determined to kick open the door to Africa, upon which the country had so long fixed its eye.

There were two obstacles, however, to the transition from a European to an overseas orientation. One was the anticolonial tradition of republicanism, which remained committed to the ideas of equality and the universal brotherhood of man. The second was the lingering demand for *revanche* against Germany. How could a republican regime nullify both of these principles? Once again, Léon Gambetta, appointed premier in 1881, proved to be the great integrator, able to unite the moral demands of the Radicals with the pragmatism of the Opportunists. Just as the anti-Communist Richard Nixon may have been the only man capable of restoring diplomatic relations with China, so it was "only possible for the man of *revanche* to introduce republican patriots to the idea that France could go down the path of colonialism without burying its other hopes," as one historian puts it.[184] Just as Gambetta's *défense nationale* had been militarily pointless but of great stabilizing importance psychologically and mythologically, so colonialism now served to create a complementary myth of a glorious new national mission.

During the 1870s, while in the opposition, Gambetta had been an orthodox anticolonialist, ready to trade French possessions overseas for the return of Alsace-Lorraine. "Is it better to preserve France's faraway territories or her future generations?" he asked. "Let us confront this anguishing dilemma: the lives of French youth or portions of our colonies. Wouldn't it be better if we profited from the German taste for colonies?" The idea of exchanging colonies for Alsace-Lorraine, although rejected by some as a "*jeu d'imagination*"—an intellectual game—attracted many adherents. As early as 1871, at the negotiations over the treaty of Frankfurt, Adolphe Thiers supposedly offered Bismarck Indonesia in exchange for the two provinces. (The colony most often put on the table was Madagascar.)[185]

With the republican takeover of the government, Gambetta would make a complete about-face. The man who had once advocated a policy of *recueillement* (self-containment) as the only possible course now warned against the dangers of provincialization. "The most important thing for France right now is to break out of the narrow circle in which the timid of heart want to confine it. We must learn to take a deep breath, puff out our chest, and, most importantly, march forward." He continued: "France lies not just between the Atlantic and the Alps, the Vosges and the Mediterranean, but wherever there are French interests and wherever French industry and trade are active."[186]

That the father of the *défense nationale* and *revanche* had given his support to the colonial project was of great importance, but Gambetta's blessing did not spell the end of anticolonialist opposition. On the contrary. Anticolonialism had never been more than a vague sentiment; now its champions organized themselves into a determined force of resistance and, having learned a few propaganda skills from the colonial party, sought to reduce the debate to a single question: How would turning France's attention overseas serve to overcome defeat and regenerate the nation?

Three positions crystallized in the "great colonial controversy" that followed the action in Tunisia.[187] According to the first,

France's role in continental Europe was over and the "continental strategy" was a waste of energy; the future, in emulation of England, lay overseas. The leading advocate of this position, Paul Leroy-Beaulieu, even described French continental policy since Louis XIV as one gigantic mistake that only the path of colonialization could rectify. The loss of Alsace-Lorraine appeared from this perspective to be not only a necessary evil but almost a nod from destiny. "Colonial or continental policies—how can we hesitate for a minute?" Leroy-Beaulieu wrote. "Would not France today be immeasurably richer and more respected if it had pursued a determined colonial policy in the past two centuries? Canada, Louisiana, Mississippi, and the Pacific Coast as part of our possessions . . . could hardly be dismissed as contributions to France's prestige, its material and spiritual power. . . . What prevents us from recapturing this sort of position in the world? Nothing but the continental policy."[188]

The second position was that of the ruling Opportunists, who could not afford the political costs of openly renouncing Alsace-Lorraine. Thus, they depicted the turn overseas as a tactical detour directed toward the ultimate strategic goal of *revanche*. The Parisian daily *Le siècle* summed up the concept as keeping "one eye on Tunisia and one eye on the Vosges."[189] Responding to the accusation that the government was seeking to substitute a colonial empire for Alsace-Lorraine, which it had given up as lost, cabinet minister Paul Bert retorted: "A substitute is as unimaginable as a consolation. But if the colonies cannot serve as a replacement for the loss of Alsace-Lorraine, they could be a means of bolstering national energy so that when the time is ripe we can win back the two provinces. Colonialism must not be allowed to distract us from what is sacred to every Frenchman, nor should it be allowed to heal the wound that still bleeds. If anyone can prove to me that our colonial undertakings undermine either of these aims, I will be the first to say adieu to the colonies."[190]

Finally, the third position was one of complete rejection. Its advocates dismissed on all counts the upbeat message put forth by Gambetta, Ferry, and Bert. The colonial strategy would not strengthen the nation, lead to *revanche*, and restore Alsace-Lorraine but hopelessly postpone all those goals. Rejectionists voiced moral reservations as well: "How can we, as republicans, who know ourselves what it is the conquered suffer," asked one skeptic, "do the same thing to weaker peoples?" They also recalled Napoleon III's Mexican fiasco, alluded to an ominous political mistake ("an additional weakening of the nation, already ruined by defeat"), and often resorted to incendiary rhetoric: "The breach in the Vosges can never be filled with the desert sands of Africa and the mud of Asia."[191] For these radical opponents, colonial policy was not only a mistake but a crime: high treason. Colonialism's main representative, Jules Ferry, who was already known as Ferry the German for his conciliatory stance toward Bismarck, became the chief target of attack. "For a couple of dubious mines in Indochina, Ferry is pawning off to Germany our security, our dignity, and our hopes," editorialized *La justice*, the Radicals' main organ. The young Radical deputy Georges Clemenceau said in Parliament: "I see before me no ministers, only traitors." And Henri Rochefort, the nemesis of the Commune, opined: "Ferry has gotten the order from Bismarck to send fifty thousand men to Indochina." The goal of such an action, Rochefort alleged, was to disarm France so it could be easily handed over to its enemy.[192]

Clearly, then, nationalism and anticolonialism went hand in hand, and since nationalism was largely represented by the political left at the time, it could be combined with economic and social concerns as well. One major theme was the "gold and blood of the nation," which were being sucked up by high finance and invested in distant lands to maximize profit and manipulate the citizenry at home: "A successful colonial expedition," wrote one Radical sardonically, "is worth as much as a suppressed insurrection."[193] The journalist and Radical representative Charles Anne Laisant declared: "First, one distracts the people in this fashion from politics at home. . . . Second, one creates sinecures for civil servants under the pretext of opening up new markets. . . . And third, the bourgeoisie believes that a regular bloodletting among the people is the best form of political hygiene."[194]

It was no accident that the most implacable anticolonialism emanated from the Boulangist camp. Nor was the fact that the fall of the Ferry government (and the political rise of General *Revanche*) began with a colonial setback in Indochina. Since most of the corruption scandals had colonial roots, the soon-to-be universal catchphrase *"affairisme colonial"* (colonial flimflam) came to be seen as a pure redundancy. In the end, however, Boulangism and anticolonialism would go down together, defeated by the liberal republic and the appealing idea of France as an imperial power. Like all fundamental opposition to the republic, resistance to colonial expansion also ceased around 1890. A kind of role reversal had taken place: the national mission had been transposed from *revanche* to colonialism. The latter had always been cast as the servant to the former, but now brimming with newly won self-confidence, colonialism boldly announced itself as indispensable to the nation's revitalization. Instead of having to justify its every initiative as a means toward the ultimate end of *revanche*, colonialism had become legitimate on its own terms. Increasingly, to object that colonialism had failed to win back the lost provinces seemed tantamount to complaining that a runner had failed to catch up with the runner in front, when in fact he had just passed him. Not only had colonial expansion led France out of the narrow confines of Europe into the vast arena of the overseas world, it had also proved that "the glory of the tricolor, planted in distant soil" was just as worthy as the concept of honor entailed in *revanche*. Indeed, as colonialism's stature rose, the idea of *revanche* came more and more to be seen as antiquated and provincial.[195]

The various reconceptions of Algeria in this period reveal the shift in France's geographical and psychological focus away from Europe. Even while the Franco-Prussian War was still going on, Charles Lavigerie, who had been the bishop of Algeria since 1867 and a driving force behind France's overseas mission, had suggested to the provisional government that the potential flow of refugees from Alsace-Lorraine should be channeled toward North Africa. In 1871, he addressed the people concerned directly, offering them "*la France africaine*" as "a home no less French than the one you have lost. It awaits you, and its love is as great as your misfortune."[196] Although the number of immigrants who eventually moved to Algeria from Alsace-Lorraine was no greater than from any other part of France, the propagandistic, psychological, and ultimately mythological significance of Algeria as the promised land after the flight from Egypt was firmly established.[197] The author of the patriotic children's book *Le Tour de la France par deux enfants* even dedicated a novel to the topic of Algeria as the new Alsace-Lorraine. The novel, *Les enfants de Marcel*, which depicts an Alsatian family in its Algerian home, was quickly adopted as mandatory school reading. "Blessed land," says the old grandmother, "you have become almost as precious to me as the motherland. After so many trials and tribulations, my children owe you their safety, their happiness, and their health. When my time has come, I will take my final rest in your soil without regrets, my new Alsace."[198]

The second myth connected with Algeria was that of national regeneration, the idea that provided the underpinning for the entire program of colonial expansion. Because of its psychological and geographical proximity, Algeria would become the main forge in the production of myths for the whole colonial enterprise. The "desert sands of Africa," dismissed so disparagingly by the anticolonialists, began in the regeneration rhetoric of the 1890s to represent a place of preservation, renewal, discipline, and masculinization (*virilisation*).

The national institution that was changed most profoundly by regeneration through colonialism was the army. The colonial successes of the 1880s and 1890s restored its sense of honor, lost at Sedan and only pitifully regained by the victory over the Commune. The military had won back its prestige, both in its own eyes and in those of the public. This rehabilitation, however, was available only to that part of the armed forces which had actively participated in colonial battles. While the regular domestic army, condemned to inactivity at home in the face of a superior enemy, sleepwalked its way through regimental routine, the colonial army was able to relive the drama of Napoleonic conquest. Its élan ultimately gave birth to the *esprit de l'offensive* that the regular army, led by former colonial army officers like Gallieni, Mangin, Gouraud, and Joffre, would bring to the First World War in 1914.[199]

ANOTHER IMPORTANT CONCEIT in overcoming resistance to overseas expansion was the idea that French colonialism, or, as we can now safely say, imperialism, would spread civilization throughout the world. While not quite as compelling as the argument for national regeneration, the French notion of the "white man's burden" provided a significant counterweight to those on the home front who rejected colonialism and imperialism as the antithesis of fraternity and equality. At the same time, the civilizing mission revealed a peculiarity within French imperialism that distinguished it from its English, German, and Belgian counterparts. Even the earliest French forays into colonialism, in the seventeenth and eighteenth centuries, had been primarily concerned with the prestige of the state, in contrast to the commercial aims of the English and Dutch. The trauma of 1870–71 only heightened that tendency, as did the other major aspect of the French tradition, the liberation ideology inherited from the Revolution, which was transferred to the colonial movement. In the words of Eugène Etienne, one of the main colonial propagandists of the 1890s, French imperialism saw itself as a successor to the Revolution, the only difference being that it was no longer European peoples but the overseas oppressed who needed to be liberated: "Our goal was always one of liberation, and we have liberated them. For black Africans were the booty of Arab conquerors who robbed them and sold them into slavery."[200]

The Opportunists of the Third Republic invested the same missionary zeal in their program of universal compulsory education. As Raoul Girardet rightly points out, "the republic's colonialism, at least in the minds of its theoreticians, [was] inseparable from educational reform. More precisely, the former [was] the expansion and universalization of the latter."[201] The link between colonialism and educational policies gave rise to an utterly novel function for government: the production of cultural propaganda for foreign consumption. As we have seen, after great defeats nations tend to seek consolation in cultural rather than in political or military power. For the first time in history, a nation—the Third Republic—created an institution precisely for the purposes of exporting its cultural superiority. The Alliance française, founded in 1884 by leading colonial politicians, combined the goals and methods of mass education with the drive toward external expansion. Its cultural mission—or, as modern-day critics might say, its cultural imperialism—was directed not solely at the colonial world but also at the wider circles of the European–North American nations where France hoped to regain culturally the hegemony it had forfeited politically in 1871.[202]

FRANCE'S COLONIAL UNDERTAKING thus served to distance the nation—psychologically and spatially—from defeat, to provide compensation, to stimulate regeneration, and to forge a new national mission. But it also led to new conflicts and confrontations. The territory France was entering was not, after all, a Garden of Eden, new, pristine, unclaimed. Everywhere except Algeria, France bumped into its old colonial rival and archenemy, England. Bismarck's calculation that encouraging and supporting French colonialism would deflect desires for *revanche* onto England was entirely correct, right down to the level of rhetoric. In the 1890s, while the movement for *revanche* against Germany was at its ebb, the concept experienced a sudden renaissance in the colonial conflict with England. France's repeated retreats in Egypt provoked fears over "our colonial Sedan" and "Egypt, our Alsace-Lorraine with England." The near war over Fashoda in 1898 prompted many to lament "this defeat, which is almost as complete and humiliating as anything we have experienced in Europe," and to rue "a catastrophe along the lines of Alsace-Lorraine."[203]

The application of *revanche* rhetoric to colonial politics shows how quickly and thoroughly the colonial enterprise had become a pillar of the new national self-image, shedding its controversial origins. Indeed, colonialism even stoked the ambitions of an extreme nationalist and neo-*revanchiste* like Maurice Barrès: "I love Morocco because it provides us . . . with thirty or forty thousand excellent soldiers."[204] In the end, of course, the "Sedan" of Fashoda led not to a Franco-German alliance against England but to an Anglo-French entente cordiale against Germany, the results of which are well known. Less so is the story of the first French-German confrontation under these new circumstances. Perhaps the most critical type of crisis in the age of mass society results from the stirring up of emotions around a collective trauma from the past. The Moroccan crises of 1905 and 1911 produced such a situation in both France and Germany: all the events and phantasms since the summer of 1870 came flooding back—kaleidoscopically and overwhelmingly—and were reexperienced anew.

Like no other point on the map, Morocco became the place where the consequences of France's overseas reorientation for its relationship with Germany would be played out. For France, Morocco represented the last piece needed to complete its North African empire and confirm its national revival. For Germany, Morocco represented the model and touchstone for its goal of participating in the division of the colonial world, as well as a locus for fears that France would succeed there in exacting the *revanche* it could not realize along the Rhine.[205] No one in either France or Germany—or anywhere else—doubted the supremacy of the German empire on the European continent. Yet there was growing German skepticism as to whether

Bismarck's continental orientation had been the correct course of action or whether it had ruled out or even fatefully delayed the nation's entry into world politics. No less astute an observer than Max Weber considered Bismarck's colonial-imperialist reticence, especially his support for French overseas expansion, a serious mistake since it ceded to France a promising arena for the future. When Germany finally and belatedly jumped aboard the imperialist bandwagon, "the noise that resulted," Weber wrote, "was out of all proportion to our truly moderate demands" and put the expansionists "in a disadvantageous position at home."[206]

Weber was describing the classic fall from grace of victors who, believing their superiority to have been confirmed by history, continue along the tried and tested path. Meanwhile the vanquished, forced to reorient themselves, are quicker to spot new paths they can follow. "Morocco" was a paradigmatic historical reversal in this sense. Most immediately, it represented a local victory for France over Germany. The French navy had achieved a standoff with its German counterpart, and France got the better part of the agreement that settled the crisis, exchanging territory in the Congo for the far more valuable Morocco. More important, however, France had maneuvered Germany into a corner and concluded an alliance with England that would allow it, finally, to exact *revanche* for the Franco-Prussian War and regain Alsace-Lorraine. In 1866 and 1870, Napoleon III's Second Empire had, in contrast to Bismarck's Prussia and its sober Realpolitik, broadcast its demands with bombastic—yet hollow—rhetoric. During the Moroccan crisis of 1911, in turn, it was the German politicians who, with their equally melodramatic and empty talk of "a panther's leap to Agadir," fell into the trap of performing "bad theater atop a grandiose stage."[207]

· 3 ·

GERMANY

Ten years after the end of the First World War, a French marshal, an English minister, and a German historian reflected on how things might have turned out differently. Marshal Ferdinand Foch, former commander in chief of the Allied forces, was convinced that Germany, instead of capitulating, "could have held the line on the other side of the Rhine in November 1918."[1] Winston Churchill, then chancellor of the Exchequer, further developed this train of thought, speculating that it would have cost the Allies six months of heavy casualties to reach the Rhine. For Germany, he argued, that period of time would have been

sufficient for strong positions to be selected and prepared, and for the whole remaining resources of the nation to be marshaled in defense of its territory. But far more important than any military advantage was the effect which Germany, by admitting defeat and withdrawing completely from France and Belgium, would have produced upon the cohesion and driving power of the Allies. . . . Had Germany . . . stood with arms in her hands on the threshold of her own land ready to make a defeated peace, to cede territory, to make reparation; ready also if all negotiation were refused to defend herself to the utmost, and capable of inflicting two million casualties upon the invader, it seemed, and seems, almost certain that she would not have been put to the test.[2]

In the view of Weimar historian Arthur Rosenberg, the decisive date was August 8, 1918, that "black day" on which General Erich Ludendorff, faced with the Allies' Amiens offensive, realized that the absolute military triumph he had envisioned could not be achieved. At that moment, Rosenberg argues,

> the majority in the Reichstag should have relieved Ludendorff of command . . . and formed a parliamentary government. The bourgeois democratic revolution that followed in October could equally well have taken place in August. The new German government could then have stopped the Military High Command's ventures in the East, unilaterally canceled the Treaty of Brest-Litovsk, and recalled all German troops from the occupied eastern countries. An understanding and a political alliance with Soviet Russia would thus have been possible. During August and September, Germany might have initiated the transformation of Austria-Hungary into a working confederation of states, reached an understanding with Poland and turned Alsace-Lorraine into an autonomous state. Had Germany and Russia moved closer, the situation in the Balkans, Rumania, and Bulgaria would also have been altered. Finally, a strong political coalition composed of Germany, Russia, and Austria would have been in a much better position to wrest favorable peace terms from the Entente than Germany, isolated and defenseless, was later able to negotate at Versailles.[3]

These ex post facto speculations accurately reflect the thoughts running through the heads of those in power at the time. Everyone from Prince Max von Baden, the last imperial chancellor, to the military leaders of the Entente was convinced that the German situation was anything but hopeless. Responding to a query by Prime Minister Lloyd George, the British commander in chief, Douglas

Haig, suggested that the Germans were certainly capable of organizing a retreat to within their own borders and "holding that line if there should be any attempt to touch the *honour* of the German people."4 Among the French, the old dream of *revanche*, which saw French troops marching on Berlin, still held sway among some, but no one within the military leadership thought such a thing likely. The only leader to take a different view was the American general John J. Pershing. Like Philip Henry Sheridan, who in 1870 had advised the Prussians to wage total war against France, Pershing argued for the necessity of an unconditional German surrender since, without it, lasting victory was impossible. "Accepting the principle of a negotiated peace rather than a dictated peace," Pershing wrote, "the Allies would jeopardize the moral position they now hold and possibly lose the chance to actually secure world peace on terms that would insure its permanence."5

The German capitulation of 1918 was historically unique not only in its suddenness but also because no nation had ever laid down arms while its forces were still so deep within enemy territory. As late as summer 1918, Paris was under siege from German artillery less than sixty miles away and London was coming under zeppelin attack in what later became known as the first battle of Britain. In contrast, not a single bomb had fallen on Berlin, which was about six hundred miles from either front. According to all accepted military and historical wisdom, German-dominated territory was vast enough to absorb even major frontline defeats. The distances between Berlin and the battlelines were almost as great as those involved in colonial or expeditionary wars, which, when lost, rarely led to the colonizer's collapse. As the classic examples of Athens's Sicilian expedition in the Peloponnesian War and the Russo-Japanese War of 1905 show, dramatic defeats abroad are softened by the time and distance word of them has to travel before reaching the home front. In both Athens and Russia, it took a massive defeat on home territory—by Sparta and Germany, respectively—to bring about the final collapse.

When Germany's military leaders suddenly called for a cease-fire on October 4, they were naturally thinking not of capitulation but of a defensive strategy similar to the one Foch, Churchill, and Rosenberg later outlined. Ludendorff's actions were not the result of a nervous breakdown, as is often assumed; he was planning to launch a new attack with replenished strength, once the truce had expired. He had not calculated, however, that the Allies would easily figure out and thwart his plans, nor did he foresee that the mood in Germany would turn so decisively against resumption of hostilities. With unmatched purity, Ludendorff embodied two characteristics typical of the Wilhelminian power elite: organizational and technical brilliance coupled with an utter lack of political, social, or psychological acumen. His inability to compromise can only partly be explained by his military background, evident in his modification of Clausewitz's famous axiom: "The maxim 'War is foreign policy by other means' must be followed by the statement 'But all politics are only a means in the service of war.' "[6] Ludendorff's intransigence was equally the product of the education and socialization of his whole generation.

Heinrich Mann was one of the few who were not surprised by Germany's sudden collapse, confirming as it did his views on authoritarian Wilhelminian culture; defeat, he said, "came in the appropriate fashion, not as an act of self-defense but as the conclusion to the last in a series of misguided wars of aggression."[7] Mann's intuitive understanding was supported by the English social psychologist Wilfred Trotter in *Instincts of the Herd in Peace and War*. Although written during the war and thus hardly free of partisan overtones, the book remained an authoritative text for many years. Trotter explains the German collapse in terms of a presumably characteristic German psychological aggressiveness that, while capable of achieving overwhelming triumphs at the outset, was unable to adjust to setbacks. As Trotter puts it, "German morale proved throughout extremely sensitive to any suspension of the aggressive posture, and showed the unsuitability of its type in modern conditions by undergoing *at the mere threat of disaster* a disintegration so absolute that it must remain a classical and perfect example in the records of psychology."[8]

Mann's further remark that Germany's collapse "could have been a heroic saga had it not in fact been a pathology report" concisely sums up opinion not just in Germany but also in the enemy camp and in the neutral world.[9] All agreed on its lack of tragic-heroic greatness. Germany was neither Hector nor Achilles; at most, it resembled Paris, who, on finally being confronted by Menelaus, flees the battlefield with the help of his patron goddess, Aphrodite. National feelings of honor, which Douglas Haig had expected to provide the basis for tenacious resistance, proved—much to everyone's consternation—nonexistent. Frederick Maurice, the English general to whom the German right would later attribute the phrase *stab in the back*, commented: "There was no precedent for a great and powerful nation, which was fighting for its existence, surrendering while it still had the means to resist." His view was echoed by Churchill: "Such a spectacle appals mankind, and a knell rang in the ear of the victors, even in their hour of triumph." The English journalist George Young added: "It would have been better for Germany had it shown more courage and collapsed less completely last autumn. A few weeks' patient endurance under punishment in a losing fight would have gone far towards restoring it some measure of the sympathies of the civilized world." Henri Lichtenberger, writing with the ressentiment of the aggrieved party whose malefactor has withdrawn precisely at the moment when retribution was at hand, seconded these sentiments: "The Germans, in laying down arms before they experienced firsthand the suffering and destruction of an invasion, have withdrawn profitably from the bloody affair into which they have plunged the world."[10]

The action Lichtenberger characterized as profitable could also be seen as "inspired by clever calculation rather than heroic greatness," which is how the German military machine was viewed by the moralists of the day. The Austrian writer Richard von Schaukal, for example, saw the defeat not as a tragedy in the classical sense but as the banal result of miscalculation: "Ludendorff, the master tactician and all-too-clever intellect made a mistake in his reckoning. . . . [He] was an organizer and a tactician, a boss and a commander, but not, despite lording over a political system enthralled by militarism, a true leader. His only leadership qualities were those of a director of a large modern-day bank or corporation, an anonymous collective endeavor drained of all soul and become mechanical. Such an endeavor has no guiding idea at its core, just an externally defined goal. If it does not attain that goal, as a result of its own erroneous calculation it will inevitably fall apart."[11] The crassest confirmation of this characterization was provided by Ludendorff himself when, a few weeks after his sudden call for a cease-fire, he had another change of heart and tried to continue the war, arguing, with no apparent awareness of his inconsistency, that national honor demanded a prolongation of hostilities: "A nation which accepts humiliation, allowing conditions to be forced upon it that threaten its existence, without having fought to the uttermost, is doomed to destruction. If the same things happen to it after it has made every possible effort, it will survive."[12]

Ludendorff's shortcomings as a strategic and political realist were not, however, the only revelations during the weeks of collapse. The "pathology report" of the whole generation of Germany's wartime leadership was put on display. Born between 1853 and 1865, this generation was too young to have taken part in the 1870–71 Franco-Prussian War but old enough to have experienced the founding of the German empire as the most significant event of modern history. In short, it was a classic "postheroic" generation of inheritors: victors' sons, "epigones" and "literati," as Max Weber dubbed them, vacillating between the duty to preserve their fathers' achievements and the pressure to produce great deeds of their own and developing, in the process, their own unique forms of "infirmity."[13] The American historian George B. Forgie, who investigates the generational question in a psychological interpretation of Abraham Lincoln and his age, shows how seductive the idea of *destructive heroism* is for epigonal generations. Where there is no space left to build, the only option is to tear down. This option, of course, remains confined to the unconscious and is projected onto the enemy, whom the "good" son then challenges as the savior of the nation.[14] Just as Lincoln's generation saw its task in 1860 as rescuing the republic of 1776 from destruction by the South, thus saving the inheritance of the founding fathers, so the Wilhelminian generation in the 1890s saw its own historical mission as the expansion of its inheritance, the Bismarckian empire, into a *Weltmacht* against the opposition of the other great powers. The old enemy France seemed insignificant in this larger context. The obstacle to be overcome was England. The victory at Sedan, so the logic went, would remain incomplete as long as it was not supplemented by a German Trafalgar.

Heinrich von Treitschke, the historian who most embodied Germany's transformation from liberal secularism to aggressive imperialism, pointed a whole generation of students toward this bright future.[15] He spoke of Germany as a "young" nation, an image enthusiastically embraced by this generation. England, the "old" global power, was past its prime. A firm shove was all that was needed to topple the clay-footed colossus, in whose shadow another "young" nation, the United States, was already lurking as the next probable adversary. Although Treitschke himself saw the youthfulness of the German nation as a guarantee not of victory but of difficult trials to come ("The German empire," he wrote, "like the Prussian state before it, will not be spared its Seven Years War"), the generation of his disciples succumbed to a kind of denial or revision of reality that has been fittingly called "symbolic inflation."[16] The term refers to the grandiose theatrical representations of empire and nation common under Wilhelm II, productions whose persuasive power began to affect the judgment of those engaged in organizing them. The diagnosis usually made of the inner circles around the kaiser—"they had enclosed themselves in a world of symbols"—can be extended to the entire ruling elite.[17] Even as these elites were loudly proclaiming Bismarckian Realpolitik to be the guiding spirit of their global ambitions, they were essentially acting symbolically. The great gesture replaced the great deed, or rather the two merged into one. Realpolitik was no longer understood as action on the basis of a realistic calculation of one's strength as well as that of the enemy but instead as the drive toward complete subjugation of the enemy. For this generation, all that remained of Bismarck's and Helmut von Moltke's victories—the result of careful planning, organization, diplomacy, and Realpolitik in the old sense—was the image of triumph, of success that had to be equaled or, if possible, exceeded. A relatively minor example of Wilhelminian inflation of, indeed addiction to, symbols was the award to Hindenburg of the highest German military distinction after he launched the spring offensive of 1918 (soon revealed as a disaster). Prussian general Gerhard von Blücher had been awarded the same distinction after his victory at Waterloo. Still stranger was the bestowing of the "black eagle," which had been given to Moltke for his victory over the French in 1871, to his son shortly before World War I for having successfully participated in a military exercise.[18]

In many respects, the psychology of the Wilhelminian generation resembled that of the Bonapartists of the Second Empire. Both were heirs to and prisoners of a heroic past that they sought to emulate with gestures and rhetoric. Both used modern technology to develop a highly romanticized style of public presentation and both lost any sense of realistic political proportion in the process. The most important difference between the two was that the collapse of 1870 did not leave France in a free fall. France's safety net was its sense of national pride, which had developed over the course of two centuries of European hegemony. The vanquished Germans of 1918 lacked any comparable heritage. The memories of centuries of national inferiority, supposedly relegated to the past by the victory of 1870–71, by the founding of the empire, and by forty years of power politics, now reappeared like an unwelcome guest on Germany's doorstep.

The burden of the past helps explain the response to the news of German defeat. People reacted not with manly composure, as the heroic vision would have it, but with everything from bewilderment to literal paralysis and nervous breakdown. At the end of September, when Ludendorff informed his general staff of his impending call for a cease-fire, one participant at the meeting noted: "The effect of these words on the listeners was *indescribable*! As Ludendorff spoke, there were audible groans and sobs, and tears ran down the cheeks of many, indeed most of those present."[19] The party leaders on the War Committee in the Reichstag reacted similarly on being briefed by Ludendorff's aide. Eyewitnesses spoke of a "devastating impression" and "great despair," and one described Social Democratic leader Friedrich Ebert as "seized with sobbing."[20] Memoirs of the period continue in the same vein, recounting a "sudden plunge of the barometer," an "instant regression from the fanfares of victory to mournful graveside wailing," and a "dramatic transition from yesterday's fanfares of victory to horrified cries of '*Hannibal ante portas.*'" One contemporary lamented, "We thought we were the Romans when we were actually the Carthaginians," while another recalled "pain, shame, and desperation."[21]

These scenes bear comparison with those of the French collapse after Sedan in September 1870. In both instances, there was an initial moment of surprise and consternation. Almost immediately, however, the French began to follow the script from 1789, 1792, 1830, and 1848: the uprising in Paris, the overthrow of the monarchy, the proclamation of the republic, the naming of a provisional government, and the continuation of the nation's struggle against the external enemy. Under the slogans *défense nationale* and *levée en masse*, which called to mind the heroic, revolutionary past, defeat could be cataloged as the responsibility of the previous regime and a new chapter in history could begin. The absence of a revolutionary republican tradition in Germany made such a parade of events impossible. The overthrow of the regime was carried out not actively and confidently but passively. First, on October 6, there was a mutiny—or, as Hans von Hentig called it, a "strike"—by the army, which by this stage was little more than "a mechanically disciplined, rolling mob in uniform that had effectively decided to stop fighting and had concluded, as it were, an internal armistice of its own."[22] Second, the Social Democratic (SPD) opposition, which seemed predestined to assume power, showed a decided disinclination against any sort of revolution. Symptomatic of the German state of mind in the late fall of 1918 was the fact that hopes for salvation were pinned not to a leading national personality like Gambetta but rather to Woodrow Wilson and his Fourteen Points. Wilson was invested with the same unquestioning trust and obedience that had been withdrawn from Wilhelm II and Ludendorff only a few weeks before.

As World War I was nearing its end, a group of Germans had pondered a different approach, one that would never make it beyond the planning stage. This strategy conformed to both the Gambetta model and the scenarios discussed ten years later by Churchill, Foch, Rosenberg, and others—namely, retrenching Germany's forces along the Rhine and continuing the war. Walther Rathenau was the best-known advocate of a German *levée en masse*,[23] but he was certainly not the only one to voice support for a popular uprising against the foreign enemy. Max Weber thought in similar terms, as did the Hamburg banker Max Warburg, who wrote: "It seems strange to me that I, a civilian, have to encourage today's military—fight on!"[24] The most important figure in this movement was the last imperial chancellor, Prince Max von Baden, who from the very beginning had spoken out against unconditional surrender and for a negotiated peace: "No suing for peace," he wrote. "Instead, the clearest possible declaration of our war aims, which, while containing the greatest possible concessions to our enemies, must emphasize our absolute determination to fight to the death if they insist on dishonorable conditions of peace."[25]

Now, at the end of the Wilhelminian era, these men—who had been outmaneuvered for years by militarists insisting on "peace through victory"—suddenly seemed to have resurrected the spirit of Bismarck and Realpolitik. Prince Max's thoughts on how to deal with Wilson recall Gambetta's wartime proclamations: "Our answer to the president must be such that, if Wilson refuses, his refusal will serve as a call to the German people for a national uprising. . . . Let us assume that we make Wilson sufficient concessions . . . and let us further assume that Wilson is forced by Allied demands to reject our proposals; the following situation will arise. Our enemies will be forced to fight on, not for Wilson's just peace but for Foch's military prestige. The exposure of such truths—and they would be exposed by a Wilsonian refusal—would entail an enormous weakening of the enemies' will to fight."[26]

The idea that a *levée en masse* in late autumn 1918 would have turned the tide in favor of the Germans has been rejected by historians as hopeless illusion, in part because public support for the war had been strong from the start. As Golo Mann put it, "You couldn't transform what always was a people's war into a people's war."[27] Nonetheless, it would be shortsighted to dismiss the opponents of Ludendorff's abrupt cease-fire request as quixotic dreamers divorced from reality. The problem was an inability among all concerned to envision a *levée en masse* operating in truly popular fashion. Rathenau, for example, had distinguished himself as an organizational genius at the beginning of the war by securing Germany's supply of raw materials and in 1916 by drawing up the Hindenburg Program, which militarized the Germany economy. He made his calculations with deliberate care before he went public with his suggestion to continue the fight. The only thing he failed to take into account was the mood within the army and the populace itself. Neither the fighting spirit of German army divisions, which Prince Max was counting on, nor the tenacious popular nationalism, which Rathenau was hoping to muster, could be mobilized for prolonging the war. In the end, Ludendorff's sharpest critics and the Wilhelminian system's most clear-sighted opponents proved to be products of that very system. Brilliant experts, technicians, and managers though they were, they utterly lacked what one might call the democratic instinct. As long it was possible to mobilize, organize, rationalize, and discipline "from above," the system possessed an efficiency beyond compare. Wilhelm II's remark at the onset of the war that he now recognized not parties, only Germans, represented the high point of the system. But when such lofty pronouncements failed to deliver democratic reforms, the nationalistic enthusiasm of the masses dried up and all the regime's calls for popular mobilization following the military collapse were met with stolid rejection.[28]

The inability to envision a truly popular *levée en masse* was common to the entire generation of leaders, from Prince Max to Friedrich Ebert. When Ludendorff, after his second about-face, imagined that the SPD leadership could mobilize the masses at will—"Grab the people by the collar. Pull them up on their feet. Can't Herr Ebert do that?"—his conception of popular activism differed from that of Rathenau and Prince Max only in degree.[29] By the end of October 1918, the leading advocates of a national war of defense realized that it was too late. "The masses would likely have risen," Prince Max later concluded, "but not against the enemy. Instead, they would have attacked the war itself and the 'military oppressors' and 'monarchic aristocrats,' on whose behalf, in their opinion, it had been waged."[30]

Around the same time that the idea of the *levée en masse* was abandoned as an instrument of Realpolitik, several upper-level military and civilian leaders came up with a plan to *stage* the national collapse as a heroic demise. Their idea, debated within the military high command at the beginning of November 1918, was to have Wilhelm II sacrifice his life, not only to save the honor of the nation and the crown but also to give rise to a latter-day myth of Thermopylae. "A small special assault at a designated target," was contemplated, "in which the kaiser could give his life as a frontline hero, encouraging loyal subjects to follow his example."[31] Even years later, this final fantasy product of the Wilhelminian passion for the grand gesture would continue to excite imaginations. In a book popular in the 1920s, Ludwig Reiners speculated as to the effect such a German charge of the Light Brigade would have had: "It would have been a worthy end to the tragedy [of the First World War] if several hundred officers, together with the emperor, the field marshal, and their generals, had met their deaths at the vanguard of an assault on a foreign division." Even historian Johannes Ziekursch, no friend of Wilhelminian romanticism, rhapsodized: "The Germans would have interred the fallen kaiser, like the mythological hero Friedrich Barbarossa, in the Kyffhäuser Mountain. . . . They would have endured years of disgrace until the mountain opened up once more and the emperor returned to rebuild the old empire in all its previous glory."[32]

Better known and historically more significant than the so-called *Kaisertod* was the idea of a suicidal deployment of the German fleet. This was not merely the private fantasy of isolated individuals but an actual plan drafted by the naval high command. The fleet was Germany's one remaining military reserve in November 1918, having, with the lone exception of the battle of Jutland, never actively participated in the war. It was therefore not unreasonable to use the fleet for a final offensive of the kind envisioned by Prince Max and Rathenau. The navy's plan, however, was based not on such calculations but on a desire to preserve German military honor. As Admiral Adolf von Trotha put it at the beginning of October, "We are seized by the horror of shame . . . at the thought that the fleet could be delivered up to internal destruction without ever seeing battle." In contrast, even an engagement that was senseless from a military point of view would have carried major significance as a symbol and a signal. "If the fleet fights an honorable battle," von Trotha said, "even one leading to its own destruction, a new German fleet will be born of it, so long as our people do not fail entirely as a nation."[33]

In France, the national defense after Sedan had signified the rebirth of the nation—a baptism of fire and blood legitimating the opposition in its seizure of power, and a foundational myth of the republic, which had been born of defeat but had overcome this "birth defect" through the heroism of the *levée en masse*. In Germany, the situation was precisely the opposite: instead of a heroic deed by the new government, Germans were offered a symbolic act by an old regime trying to save face. And in the end, even this symbolic gesture was never actually made—what transpired was one of the most unheroic capitulations in military history. Instead of falling heroically at the vanguard of his troops, the emperor fled in the night across the Belgian-Dutch border, while Ludendorff, after being relieved of command, went to Sweden. The German navy did not set sail for one last battle but mutinied, thereby hastening the national collapse it was supposed to prevent. With few exceptions, those who had preached resistance to the last man yielded without struggle. Those officers who were prepared to defend the monarchy were prevented from doing so by indecision and panic in the central command. Most of the thousand volunteers who reported to defend Berlin against the revolution were simply sent home.[34]

The spectacle of rioting soldiers tearing the insignia from their officers' shoulders on the street and in broad daylight would become the enduring image of German defeat; the antithesis of heroic capitulation, it blatantly revealed the failure and impotence of the Wilhelminian military and governmental elites. And just as the French bourgeoisie of 1871 sought to project its own patriotic shortcomings onto the Paris Commune, the German elites of 1918 took "flight in hatred," particularly of the witnesses to their miserable debacle of a last fight.[35] Among those witnesses were men like Philipp Scheidemann, who mercilessly reminded them of their failings: "Two years ago," he railed in a speech before the Reichstag in 1920, "you cowards deserted us. . . . *You deserted us!*"[36]

Eventually this caste, in order to shift the blame from itself, would invent the legend of the Germany military's having been stabbed in the back. But another image of defeat came to the fore immediately after the German collapse—that is, before the stab-in-the-back legend took hold—and served temporarily to console the nation.

"Undefeated on the Field of Battle"

"No enemy has defeated you. Only when the enemy's superiority in numbers and resources became suffocating did you relinquish the fight." These were the words with which Friedrich Ebert, the first president of the Weimar Republic, greeted the troops returning from the front to Berlin on December 10, 1918.[37] The idea that, while Germany may not have won the war, it certainly hadn't lost it held sway throughout the political spectrum. "You do not return defeated and beaten. You have defended our homeland against a world of enemies," the revolutionary government in Baden declared on November 16, 1918. "Having gone to battle with the will to win, you return, suffocated by a previously unknown superior force, as the unquestioned victors from your field of battle," seconded Minister of War Heinrich von Scheuch on December 18. "We have won victories in all directions of the four winds. It's only the war we have lost" was the assessment of Lieutenant General Arnold Lequis on December 14.[38] "Now you return to a fatherland that has collapsed, you who have not been defeated. . . . I bid you welcome, German soldiers, the victors of yesterday, today, and tomorrow," Alwin Saenger wrote in *Die Glocke* on December 7.

The slogan *im Felde unbesiegt*, or "undefeated on the field of battle," was the German version of the universal loser trope that the vanquished side has not been bested in combat but rather "suffocated" by the sheer mass of the enemy. Theoretically, the phrase could have given rise to a formula for national consolation akin to the idea of *revanche* in France or the Lost Cause in the American South. Historians explain the fact that it did not by citing the split in Weimar Germany between the powerful antirepublican forces and the relatively weak republican center. The temptation on each side to blame the other for the collapse was too great. But such logic ignores the similar split between republicans and monarchists in the French Third Republic. Why in France did the opposing camps compete over who would advocate the most promising form of *revanche* while in Germany they competed only to assign blame?[39]

For a brief moment immediately after the capitulation, *im Felde unbesiegt* seemed to possess the mythic potential to unite the nation; it was the most lapidary and penetrating expression of those weeks and months in which the suddenly shattered expectations of victory had to be reconceived as defeat. The verbal equivalent of the *levée en masse* that never was, the slogan aimed at restoring the nation's lost honor. Therein lay its temporary strength and its long-term weakness. In the direct aftermath of national collapse, the *im Felde unbesiegt* idea stabilized Germany's collective identity, but after the full dimensions of the unheroic capitulation became known, the slogan was unable to bear the weight placed on it. In fact, it backfired. That Germany had lost the war without being defeated in a decisive battle could no longer be held up as a sign of heroic triumph. "Undefeated on the field of battle" could all too easily be reinterpreted as "capitulated without having put up a fight."

Consequently, the Weimar Republic lacked a "legitimizing foundational myth," as historian Detlev Peukert puts it. Instead of invoking a necessary "heroic or at least heroicizable act" comparable to the French Third Republic's *défense nationale*, the Weimar Republic faced the abyss of capitulation without a struggle.[40] Although the slogan *im Felde unbesiegt* had the same integrative effect for the Germans in their moment of defeat as the ideal of *Volksgemeinschaft*, or "folk community," had inspired at the beginning of the war, it also contained the mechanism of its own destruction. Referring as it did explicitly to the army, it begged the question of who, then, was responsible for the defeat. The leaders of the SPD, the ruling party, who tried to use the idea to win the loyalty of the army and prop up national morale, failed to see that the backlash—the inevitable matter of blame—would be directed at them. As it happened, blame was apportioned most aggressively by the very people who had had the biggest hand in the national collapse and who then had disappeared. Their accusations had all the force of shame, of lost self-respect, and the search for appropriate scapegoats onto which their guilt and humiliation could be projected. The legend they created for this purpose had little evidence to back it up but nonetheless came to exert a formidable hold on the German psyche.

"Stabbed in the Back"

The idea of an internal enemy lying in wait to overthrow the rule of law, an enemy against whom it was legitimate to employ any and all means of defense, was one of the political-psychological foundations of Wilhelminian culture. For many years, this enemy was the Social Democratic Party. Chiefly responsible for the demonization of the Social Democrats was Imperial Chancellor Otto von Bismarck, who proclaimed in 1878 that "we have here in Berlin sixty to a hundred thousand well-organized men, split up into cells, who openly advocate fighting against the current system. . . . They are like an enemy army living in our midst."[41] Later, in 1905, Wilhelm II fantasized about eliminating the Social Democrats in the event of a European war: "First we will neutralize the socialists, shooting them down and cutting off their heads in a bloodbath, if necessary, and then we will fight the war abroad. But not before and not a tempo."[42] When war came to pass in August 1914, Wilhelm did not in fact pursue this plan; he accepted the Social Democrats as part of the *Volksgemeinschaft*, though only after they paid the price of renouncing internationalism. It was a price that Social Democracy, until then a dissident movement languishing on the margins of society, proved all too willing to pay. The intoxicating sense of brotherhood Germans felt in the days before and immediately following the outbreak of hostilities became known as the "August experience."

It did not last long. Undermined by the strains of war, the *Volksgemeinschaft* soon lost its power to unite, and the old "civil war" mentality returned, the difference now being that the internal enemy was no longer just the Social Democratic movement but all those individuals who had criticized the aim of "peace through victory." Anyone who advocated peace through negotiation, as the SPD, the Center Party, and the Progressives did in their Reichstag resolution of 1917, could be accused of having ambushed Germany's fighting troops from the rear.[43]

An obvious predecessor of the stab-in-the-back legend, this image could even be invoked, at least implicitly, against the civilian population.[44] As Max Weber wrote in May 1918: "If the army fighting Germany's battles takes the position 'What *we* have conquered with our blood should remain German,' 'we' who have remained at home certainly have the right to say, 'Think for a moment whether that is politically expedient.' But if they insisted on their perspective, 'we' would have to hold our peace."[45] Weber was writing from the perspective of the stay-at-home civilian who saw himself as indebted to the frontline soldiers because he had not risked his own life. Ludendorff's reversal of Clausewitz's axiom is relevant here: there was no doubt as to the primacy of war over politics, the soldier over the politician, the battlefront over the home front. Some even accused themselves of *potentially* stabbing soldiers in the back; the Bavarian progressive Ernst Müller-Meiningen, for example, said on November 2, 1918, a few days before the outbreak of the revolution: "As long as the external front lines hold, we have a damned duty here at home. We would be shamed in the eyes of our children and grandchildren if we attacked the frontline soldiers from behind and stabbed them in the back."[46]

Thus, by the end of the war, a mentality susceptible to a stab-in-the-back myth was already in place across the political spectrum.

On the right, suspicions of revolutionary treachery were rife, and the search for traitors took on almost paranoid dimensions after the conservatives' own failure in November 1918. The liberal center did not immediately project onto others its sense that the home front had failed the battlefront but instead internalized these feelings. In other words, the right did what it had to do to clear itself of moral culpability and the center joined in the blaming, thus restoring its strained self-respect. Ultimately, the various factions agreed on the version that cleared everyone of blame: it was not the *home front* in its entirety that had stabbed the military in the back but rather the *revolution.* The parallels to the situation in Paris in 1871 are obvious. Just as in nineteenth-century France, the Germans' sense of their failings and cowardice were inverted into paranoid hatred for those who had behaved differently. In November 1918, the critic and publisher Count Harry Kessler quipped that "the revolution had seen only flying coattails—people were already fleeing before it happened" and characterized the stab-in-the-back legend as a phantasm that the representatives of the old regime "feared with all the pathological cowardice of the imagination and hid from in the houses and cellars of Jewish bankers."[47] Much the same could have been said of the Parisian bourgeoisie's exodus to Versailles.

The stab-in-the-back legend made its debut in public political discourse one year after the German defeat. In autumn 1919, in an interview before the committee investigating the causes for Germany's military collapse, Paul von Hindenburg quoted an alleged remark by an English general: "The German army was stabbed from behind."[48] In the memoirs Hindenburg published the following year, he used a different image. "Just as Siegfried fell to the treacherous spear of terrible Hagen, so did our exhausted front lines collapse. They tried in vain to draw new life from the dried-up wellspring of the home front."[49] The change in metaphor is significant even if Hindenburg, whom no one would accuse of sensitivity toward language, was unlikely to have been conscious of it. For him and his generation, raised on Nibelungen mythology—especially in its Wagnerian version—Hagen's killing of Siegfried with a spear was a more familiar image of traitorous murder than the dagger. The dagger was the classic instrument for conspiracy and calumny, less a weapon than a means of murder akin to the most insidious tactic, poison.[50] No less enduring was the association of women with both daggers and poison, although both were put to heroic use by such figures as the Roman Lucretia and the biblical Judith.

As these connotations suggest, the metaphor of the dagger was ambiguous, all the more so given the Wilhelminian exaltation of manliness. Thus, even as Hindenburg promoted a stab-in-the-back legend, he preferred to speak of Hagen's spear. The spear—the weapon of Achilles, Hector, and all other Homeric heroes—was the opposite of the dagger. But the traditional notion held that a spear in the back signified not only the treachery of the spear-thrower but the cowardice of the fleeing. How can this view be reconciled with Hindenburg's use of the image? The answer is that Hagen's spear was directed not at a fleeing coward but at an unsuspecting hero; Hagen was no hero but a traitor and a murderer. Hagen's spear was thus in reality a dagger in the back, and the German stab-in-the-back legend nothing other than a latter-day version of the *Nibelungenlied.*

The Wilhelminian Siegfried

"While we were assembled, L[udendorff] entered into our midst, his face filled with the deepest worry, pale, but with his head held high. A truly Germanic figure of a hero. I could not help thinking of Siegfried, mortally wounded in the back by Hagen's spear." This was how a member of the military high command described Ludendorff's announcement of his decision to ask for an armistice.[51]

Nibelungen mythology had played a central role in the rise of German nationalism in the nineteenth century. Rediscovered by eighteenth-century philologists, the *Nibelungenlied* began its career

as national myth in the era of the German wars of liberation from
Napoleon. For nationalists seeking German unification, Siegfried
united the traits of two other heroes of liberation from foreign
hegemony, Arminius and Friedrich Barbarossa. Until 1848, as long
as German nationalism remained liberal and republican, the image
of Siegfried was that of the rebel. As Friedrich Engels put it in 1840,
"We all feel the same thirst for great deeds, the same stubborn refusal
to accept what has come before, which drove Siegfried from his
father's fortress. Eternal rumination, a philistine fear of bold deeds,
is contrary to our entire soul—we want to break out into the wide
world."[52] After Germany's unification following the wars of 1864–
71, however, Siegfried became a symbol of an empire built on military victory and an honorary title for Germany's founding fathers.
There was Bismarck-Siegfried:

> The long hard battle is done.
> The foreign dragon lies cold
> And Bismarck-Siegfried returns home
> Rich with the Nibelungs' gold.[53]

By his side the kaiser, the "Sieg-Fried of the German people," an
epithet that played on the name's literal meaning, "victory-peace."[54]
As the Wilhelminian empire progressed, the *Nibelungenlied*—a complex, rather ambiguous story with various heroes—was increasingly
reinterpreted as an extended homage to Siegfried.

The most influential figure in this reinterpretation was, of course,
Richard Wagner. He began, like Engels, with the image of the rebellious republican and ended up after 1871 with the sanctified Siegfried, who heroically meets his demise doing battle against the world
of gold, greed, and betrayal. In Wagner's *Ring*, Hagen is no longer
the loyal vassal of Gunther and Brunhilde whose deed avenges the
insult to Brunhilde's honor by the loose-tongued Siegfried. Wagner's
Hagen, the son of *Rheingold* thief Alberich, is part of a dark (that

is, Semitic) underworld that contrasts with the bright light surrounding Siegfried.[55]

The post-Bismarck generation was steeped from childhood in this version of Siegfried and Hagen's metaphorical significance. Thanks to Wagner, Germany became Siegfriedland, just as the American South had become Walter Scottland and France Joan of Arcland. No one recognized Wagner's influence more instinctively or described it more accurately than Walther Rathenau. A few months before Germany's collapse, he spoke of his generation's "theatrically barbaric pomp of virtue." "There's always someone," he wrote, "be it Lohengrin, Walther, Siegfried, or Wotan, who can do everything and beat everyone, who rescues suffering virtue, punishes vice, and offers general salvation, forever striking a pompous pose to the sound of trumpet fanfares and with the help of lighting and theatrical effects. Today this sort of opera is mirrored in politics."[56]

The humiliation the "Siegfried generation" suffered in 1918 was a double, indeed triple shock. Instead of the assured victories of their fathers' and grandfathers' time, there was an unexpected collapse. Then, to make matters worse, came the more personal failure at the outbreak of revolution: the silent stealing away into the night instead of the heroically tragic final battle in Etzel's hall. Not to face the dragon like Siegfried but instead to vanish like Alberich under his cloak, only to reemerge and take up posts under a government ruled by the hated Social Democrats, whose ascendance was a third shock—such a serial loss of face must have hit the military and bureaucratic elites of Wilhelminian Germany harder than they admitted. Their later attempts to depict November 1918 as "the greatest of all revolutions" served, like the stab-in-the-back legend, to erase the memory of their own failure.[57]

That this legend was tailor-made to the needs of Wilhelminian elites is clear from its lack of resonance outside their circles. The resistance of the liberals and the left, the groups villainized by the myth, is easy to understand. The radical nationalist right, however, also refused to accept it as an explanation for Germany's defeat. For

Edgar Jung, one of the right's leading spokesmen, Germany's collapse was the result not of betrayal but of the masses' justifiable desertion of a system that had not merited a defense to the last drop of blood.[58] In a remarkable affinity with the revolutionary left, the radical nationalists of the 1920s viewed national collapse as a purifying event. For them, the Wilhelminian empire did not represent a golden era whose demise was to be mourned but a lamentable detour into the crassest materialism, the worst taste, the most vacuous pomp, the emptiest rhetoric, and the purest decadence. They had welcomed the war as an opportunity for national renewal, and they accepted defeat as a fire that would cleanse and purify the nation. They did not reject the Weimar Republic on principle because it had arisen from defeat but because it had not broken radically enough with the Wilhelminian empire, instead perpetuating the decadence under a new name. The nationalists' great model was Gambetta's French Republic, which had been born of heroic resistance. Hitler's speeches sometimes made this link explicit, but more often it was left unspoken, as in Jung's statement that "if the republican left in Germany had adopted the cause of German liberation and pursued it in all its consequences, the gigantic gap that opened up in 1918 would have closed long ago."[59]

For revolutionary nationalists, accordingly, Siegfried was seen as the embodiment of the despised Wilhelminian culture: a Germanic *"miles gloriosus,"* "the absolute antithesis of a chivalric and noble hero," someone who "breaks his word and then like a cowardly criminal transfers the blame to his wife." The nationalist backlash against the Wilhelminian Siegfried figure is exemplified by a 1924 treatise on the *Nibelungenlied* that characterizes him as "dapper" and "internally shallow" and says of his fateful effect on the nation: "The whole country has to pay up . . . with beautiful garments and valuable armor to cover the debt resulting from the frivolity and coarse manners of the young Siegfried." To kill such a man is not an act of treachery but a political necessity, and Hagen, who carries out the deed, is no traitor or mutineer but a Realpolitiker: "We need to understand that Hagen *had to* get rid of this violent, unreliable man because he recognized him as a permanent danger to the Burgundian people and state."[60] Nothing could be more antithetical to the Wilhelminian view than the radical nationalist argument for the *necessity* of a stab in the back. In this interpretation, Hagen is the frontline soldier who frees his country in its greatest hour of need from an incompetent and decadent leadership, and Hagen's only real transgression, his violation of Burgundian law, is simultaneously a heroism of a new sort.[61] Six years before Hitler ordered the murder of his own commanders in the Night of the Long Knives, Hagen was being valorized in one high school syllabus as a monumental figure whose "stature, piety, and beauty" were to be emphasized. "The class should consider the state of an empire," the syllabus read, "whose leadership does not hesitate to break petty bourgeois laws in the interest of the general good. For: 'My country, right or wrong!'"[62]

Contagion

Along with the images of the army undefeated on the field of battle and the dagger/spear in the back, a third idea was invoked to explain Germany's defeat: that of the physical exhaustion, dissipation, and gradual disappearance of fighting spirit. In 1933, the military historian Friedrich Altrichter wrote of the "decline of a shared military spirit," "the predominance of egotism," the "feeling of impotence," and the "bitter rage against everything to do with war and being a soldier."[63] Others identified three causes for the demoralization of Germany's fighting forces: *Unterwühlung* (being undermined), *Vergiftung* (being poisoned), and *Verseuchung* (being contaminated). While the first two metaphors were traditional, the image of infection and contamination was new.[64] It was used by the military leadership for the first time at the beginning of November 1918 to refer to the danger that revolution at home would spread to the soldiers at the front. Shortly before the armistice on November 11, Ludendorff's successor in the military high command, General Wilhelm Groener, considered measures normally used in quarantines against infectious diseases: the establishment of a cordon sanitaire between the front line and the home front, and the use of "inoculators" ("loyal and skilled officers to immunize the troops against the spirit of revolution").[65]

The differences between the metaphor of a dagger in the back and that of epidemic infection are immediately apparent. In the former, the victim is a fighting warrior; in the latter a vulnerable patient. The stab in the back is masculine and instantaneous, the epidemic feminine and insinuating. The dagger is external; the plague, even if it is externally transmitted, suggests weakness in the patient's internal constitution. But above all, by 1918 the dagger was an ancient metaphor, whereas infection via bacteria or viruses was thoroughly contemporary. Robert Koch had discovered the tuberculosis bacterium a mere generation before, while Paul Ehrlich's cure for syphilis, Salvarsan, was only a decade old. Moreover, Gustave Le Bon used the analogy of bacteria and the image of contagion in 1895 to describe the psychological processes typical of modern society. In his *Psychology of the Masses*, Le Bon wrote: "Among the masses, ideas, emotions, passions, and systems of belief are transmitted with the same infectious capacity as microbes." And: "The power of infection is such that not only certain opinions but specific emotional states can be transmitted from person to person."[66] Adolf Hitler, an avid reader of Le Bon, would come to see the Jews as a kind of microbe harmful to the German body politic, an epidemic that had "broken out" in November 1918. For Hitler, too, the metaphor of bacterial plague better expressed the reality of Weimar than the image of the dagger in the back. In Hitler's bacteriological view of the world, the dagger was a foreign element; he used it specifically to appeal to conservative listeners.

The bacteriological metaphor transformed the view of the

defeated German army from a collection of soldierly Siegfrieds stabbed in the back by Social Democratic Hagens into an easily infectible mass in Le Bon's sense—irrational, moody, feminine, hysterical. Accordingly, the prevailing view about the conduct of war was turned completely on its head. In classic theories of war, the destruction of soldiers is not an end in itself but a means of influencing the will of the enemy. If, however, there were another, more direct, less destructive way to capture the hearts and minds of the enemy, the use of great armies would become obsolete. The megabattles of the First World War had shown that even the drastic destruction of human life entailed in the strategy of bleeding the other side dry was not enough to subjugate a determined adversary. Attention now turned to an alternate method of influencing the other side's will.

The Discovery of Propaganda

Before 1914, the term *propaganda* rarely appeared in encyclopedias and dictionaries. When it did, it was used in reference to distant institutions and events that were foreign to the bourgeois spirit of the times, such as the Catholic Counterreformation in the seventeenth century or the revolutionary agitation of the French secret societies in the nineteenth. Nor was the term especially popular in its commercial sense, as a synonym for *advertisement*, a word that enjoyed far greater currency. By 1918, however, propaganda had become a thoroughly fashionable term. New editions of reference works devoted not occasional sentences but whole pages to the subject.[67] The general view was that propaganda was a child—indeed, *the* child—of the world war and that the conflict had actually been decided not by weapons but by words. Many believed that without propaganda to motivate one's own people and demoralize the enemy, modern mass warfare could not be conducted, much less won.

The victors and the vanquished agreed on this point, although they drew widely divergent conclusions from it. The victors, as always, equated military and moral superiority and tended to see the triumph of their propaganda as a confirmation of their system and their idea of truth, while the vanquished were confronted by a cognitive dissonance. On the one hand, the idea of having been subdued not by weapons but by propaganda supported the conceit of being undefeated on the field of battle. On the other hand, it was unsoldierly and weak to have been bested by mere words. The postwar German debate surrounding this dichotomy led to a striking reversal of the usual psychology of defeat. Instead of seeing themselves as heroes crushed by the enemy's far greater numbers, some Germans came to believe that defeat had resulted from their own weakness of will. Ludendorff, for example, attributed Germany's defeat not to the material superiority of its enemies but to their superior propaganda, equating propaganda with the desire to win. The Entente, with its "powerful will to destroy," its "strong national thinking and steel-hard desire," its "unshakable resolve to annihilate and triumph," had held a decisive advantage over Germany, which lacked an "iron will."[68] No one pursued this line of thought more vigorously than the most fanatical of all the stab-in-the-back advocates, the publisher of the *Süddeutsche Monatshefte*, Paul Cossmann, who in the July 1919 issue called Germany a "nation of wretches." The sense of malaise and embarrassment that the war had been lost as a result not of a heroic battle but of susceptibility to enemy propaganda was widespread.[69]

The dilemma was all the greater since in the eyes of Wilhelminian warrior *Kultur*, propaganda amounted to nothing more than despised Western cant: nice-sounding words, under cover of which English shopkeeper *Zivilisation* plied its trade. Finally, though, it was concluded that the time had come to learn the art of propaganda. Edgar Stern-Rubarth, considered the leading expert at the time, defined propaganda as "the weapon by which we were defeated, the weapon that has been left to us, the weapon that will help us rise once more."[70] The German fascination with propaganda in the 1920s followed the same reflexive desire to learn from the enemy evidenced both in the post-1865 New South program of the former Confederacy and in France's educational reforms after 1871; it entailed walking a fine line between imitative modernization and preservation of national identity. What helped German efforts to view the new orientation as *not* another capitulation was the idea—present in the American South and France as well—that the reforms had already been suggested at home before the war and had not been carried out only because of obtuse opposition from the old regime.

Before 1914, reflections on the relationship of public opinion, psychology, and politics had come largely from liberal imperialists like Friedrich Naumann, Max Weber, and Paul Rohrbach, who shared a dissatisfaction with the muscle flexing and saber rattling of German foreign policy. Characteristic of the ambivalence of the Wilhelminian generation, and not without irony, was the fact that even Imperial Chancellor Theobald von Bethmann-Hollweg, who was responsible for the diplomatic fiasco of the 1911 Morocco crisis, privately registered the publicity blunders of official policy. Two years after the standoff at Agadir, he wrote: "We are a young people and have perhaps too much naïve faith in the military, so that we underestimate the value of more subtle means of obtaining power and fail to grasp that what has been won through violence cannot be kept by violence."[71] (This insight did not, however, prevent him from justifying the German invasion of Belgium a year later, in August 1914, by referring to the treaty on Belgian neutrality as a "scrap of paper" or from freely admitting to the German breach of international law in the Reichstag and thus before the eyes of the entire world.) There was a clear understanding among liberal imperialists that the status of world power to which Germany aspired required not just demonstrations of military and economic might but also moral and ideological acumen. It was a fatal mistake in foreign policy and in the court of public opinion, they believed, to pursue a place in the sun solely by conquering territory and markets.

Like the established world powers England and France, Germany required a "universally appealing ideology," as Paul Rohrbach put it. Friedrich Naumann wrote: "We Germans must come up with something as our world-historical mission that no other people can achieve as well as we can, indeed, that will remain unachieved if we do not carry it out. We need a national calling in the great assembly of humanity so that we can pursue our independent path with purpose and passion."[72]

Prior to the war, Rohrbach was the most active advocate of what he termed "ethical imperialism." In his 1912 book *Der deutsche Gedanke* (*The German Way of Thinking*), he argued for "the essential moral core of Germanness as the determining force on current and future world events" and specified the mission of ethical imperialism as "the peaceful penetration of the non-German world with elements of our spiritual and material culture." Culture and power did not merely reinforce each other; as the example of England showed, a self-confident imperial culture was the prerequisite for global power.[73] The liberal imperialists perennially complained about Germany's ignorance and incompetence in this area. Rohrbach wrote of "our weak capability as a moral conqueror" and of a Prussian-German "abrasiveness" that elicited not admiration but alienation and mistrust in international public opinion.[74]

These isolated voices of the prewar era came together after the German defeat in a great chorus of national self-criticism. Even a figure as strongly identified with political saber rattling as former minister Karl Helfferich joined in. "It was not clever," he wrote, "to talk incessantly about the sword, thus enabling our foreign enemies to portray the most peaceful people and monarch on earth as being obsessed by war. In this way, we unintentionally promoted the myth of our warlike intentions and helped produce an international mood that provided the coalition against us with the necessary, mass-psychological underpinning."[75] Many others offered similar judgments. Sociologist Johann Plenge wrote: "Because in our so-called Realpolitik we failed to grasp the very real power of propaganda, suggestions from the politics of ideas were ruthlessly kicked aside by jackbooted tacticians." And Ernst Troeltsch added: "Vain pride in our honesty for admitting that *all* morality in politics is just a pretense and a smoke screen and that politics comes down to questions of power and interest . . . only confirms every hostile opinion."[76]

The limitations of German propaganda were everywhere apparent. The political theorist Paul Rühlmann had, as early as 1914, cited the example of France as evidence of the need for Germany to foster better public relations in its foreign affairs. After the war, he accused the German diplomatic corps of being divorced from reality and declared this disassociation symptomatic of the government as a whole. Career diplomats, he insisted, failed to grasp the "imponderables of the foreign popular soul" and thus also lacked the capacity to recognize and exploit the potential usefulness of such "imponderables" to Germany itself. "The bureaucratic apparatus," he wrote, "was not set up for that purpose. The German diplomatic missions had no means for registering what moved the masses: their ideals, virtues, and passions. Consequently, the officials were helpless when confronted with these things. They simply did not understand that the emotions, urges, and ideals of the foreign masses had to be an object of scrutiny."[77] On the domestic front, the situation was equally dismal. Ludendorff, while operating at a high level concerning the techniques and organization of propaganda, lacked any sensibility for the disposition of the mass psyche. Though he supported the use of propaganda as a means of war and was the driving force behind the creation of the film studio Ufa as a propaganda instrument, he was hopelessly incompetent at gauging the mood of the masses. Sociologist Ferdinand Tönnies remarked that Ludendorff and the military high command were "totally unfamiliar with public opinion" and had acted with "the zeal of clerics who preach that God-fearing faith is a prerequisite for salvation and believe that their zeal alone is enough to bring it about."[78]

This belated discovery of propaganda repeats the familiar German pattern of appropriating a foreign concept—one that was viewed simply as a means to an end—and subjecting it to an idealistic transformation that renders it into a kind of theology of salvation. The start of the process was the publication of *The German Way of Thinking*, which Rohrbach expected to have a transformative effect on the international battle of ideas. What he and others overlooked in their missionary zeal, however, was the fact that unfavorable images of Germany were not just the result of clumsy public relations. As Max Scheler showed in 1917 in a book on the origins of Germanophobia, anti-German public sentiment had concrete economic and political causes that could not be dismissed with soothing words.[79] The view of propaganda as simply a weapon that functioned and could be deployed like traditional military weapons was not restricted to Ludendorff, who saw it as analogous to gas grenades, submarines, or zeppelins, all of which, he believed, could be activated by the push of a button. Few Germans seemed to comprehend that propagandistic effects could not simply be produced on demand but were dependent on the prevailing mood of the target population. Moreover, in contrast to the United States, England, and France, pre-1914 Germany possessed neither a metropolitan mass press nor the sorts of engineers of mass psychology needed to run one.[80] If indeed the Entente's propaganda was superior, the advantage was due to the participation of journalists who had learned the art of mass manipulation from their work in tabloids and were supposedly unencumbered by traditional notions of military fairness. Yet in the English army, as well, at least at the beginning of the war, propaganda had to battle against military ethics, as is evident in General Herbert Plummer's justification of his refusal to distribute propaganda leaflets on the front lines: "No, that wouldn't be fair," he declared. "We have to defeat these boys on our own merits."[81] The superiority of English propaganda was thus not as great as postwar Germans believed. Nor were German efforts in this area really as insufficient as they were later portrayed.

It is true that by 1914 England—thanks to its global communications network and its control over transatlantic cables—enjoyed a monopoly on the news that enabled it to isolate Germany, cutting off its communications with the rest of the world. Nonetheless, German propaganda theorists concluded that it was not technological deficiencies that had decided the war but rather the strength of will, manipulative skill, and unscrupulousness of the Fleet Street entrepreneur and master propagandist Lord Northcliffe. However, this man of "near Napoleonic significance"—for Germans the demonic embodiment of English wartime propaganda—was only named chief of British propaganda operations in 1918, nearly four years after the hostilities had begun.[82] Moreover, in 1914, at the beginning of the war, he had disparaged English propaganda much as the Germans did their own after 1918, praising instead Germany's superior capacity for mass mobilization.[83] Which estimation was correct, the German one after 1918 or Northcliffe's of 1914?

When Northcliffe assumed his position in 1918, the military situation was beginning to change fundamentally. Although the German spring offensive in France was still to come, the Allies had received a significant morale boost with the arrival of American troops in the theater of war. Notwithstanding the belief shared by the Germans and Northcliffe that propaganda could completely transform reality, it now became clear that the success of propaganda depended on the general mood, which in turn depended on the strategic situation. "As long as the military situation is . . . unfavorable to the Entente, it will be difficult to construct out of it effective propaganda," noted Undersecretary of State Lord Robert Cecil. This sentiment was seconded by John Buchan, the author of *The Thirty-nine Steps*, who worked for the Ministry of Propaganda: "The most active propaganda cannot undo the effect of an enemy victory or explain away an Allied check."[84] In other words, English propaganda could only boast of as many—or as few—victories as the English army could. Likewise, Northcliffe's initial respect for German propaganda was prompted by the military superiority of German troops, just as the German postwar admiration for English propaganda, and their biting criticism of their own, was born of England's battlefield success.

Significantly, German self-castigation went so far that even the one undeniable German propaganda success—the destabilization of Russia, culminating in revolution and the victors' peace of Brest-Litovsk—was hardly ever mentioned. The similarities between that war of words and Northcliffe's propaganda campaign of 1918 against the Central Powers were striking. Both used the same methods for "breaking down" the opponent's morale (riling up national minorities, assurances of a generous peace settlement, calls for the overthrow of the present system), and both achieved success because the ground they were sowing was suitably fertile.[85] The reason for Germany's silence on its propaganda victory in Russia was not modesty but a sense that it could hardly style itself as the unsuspecting, innocent victim of Allied machinations if it had successfully used the same means. Even the stab-in-the-back legend might lose its unique heinousness through such an admission, since it was the Russian troops, if anyone, who had been stabbed in the back by a foreign-propaganda-induced revolution on their home front. (The destruction of Russian fighting morale paved the way for the revolution carried out by Lenin, who was sped into Russia by the German military high command, and the subsequent acceptance of the punitive peace treaty dictated at Brest-Litovsk.) The postwar German propaganda debate hinged on how Germany, having opened the Pandora's box of propaganda in the war against Russia, could best cast itself as the blameless victim of similar methods.[86]

In many respects, the flip side of the never-mentioned success in Russia was the oft-remembered national enthusiasm at the outbreak of war, the so-called August experience. Unlike Lord Northcliffe, as ever an admirer of German efficiency, the people themselves did not view the August experience as a product of propagandistic manipulation. On the contrary, it was the totally spontaneous and unexpected nature of the celebration that elevated it to the status of a national myth. While there were also outbreaks of war enthusiasm in England and France in August 1914, these were one-time occurrences, which, once they had subsided, were no longer recalled and never again emulated. The German August experience, on the other hand, became something of a national mantra, even after the everyday reality of war had diffused the initial enthusiasm. Recent social history has begun to question whether the emotional outpouring was indeed universal, suggesting that the middle classes (including the Social Democratic leadership) were the ones chiefly caught up in the idea of a "folk community." Nevertheless, the August experience represented a fundamental reconstitution of the national psyche, in which the Social Democratic opposition abruptly ceased to exist, or, more positively, was subsumed within the nation. The national integration of the masses had already taken place in England and France, a process completed in the 1890s with the creation of a new jingoistic mass culture. In the course of a few hours, the August experience enabled Germany to catch up with developments that had taken years in other European nations. Such a sudden explosion, of course, would also echo far longer.

One further reason for the intensity of the outburst in August was Germany's paranoid fear of being encircled. This anxiety differed from other national paranoias, such as the French fear during the years 1866–70, in that it was based on more than just Germany's central geopolitical location. On the one hand, the upper and middle classes were frightened of the "secret army" of Social Democracy; on the other, the lower classes felt entrapped within a state run by their oppressors. The sudden disappearance of this reciprocal fixation and its redirection outward gives insight into the particular force of the August experience. Forty-three years after Wilhelm I and Bismarck had proclaimed the German empire in the Hall of Mirrors at Versailles, August 1914 came to represent the actual founding moment of the nation. To call upon the unity of the nation in the form of folk community was henceforth identical with reviving the spirit of 1914. And this would become the main goal of all post-1918 German propaganda.

THE PROPAGANDA OF the Entente, which was of such great interest to the postwar debate in Germany, contained two very different strains. One was the Anglo-American propaganda of mass manipulation; the other had originated and been perfected in France. French propaganda was directed less at the masses than at the elite and focused primarily on culture, building on the influence France had exerted since the seventeenth century.[87] Supplemented after the French Revolution by the theology of liberty, equality, and fraternity, the elitist cultural propaganda of the nineteenth century essentially amounted to a declaration that "*La France, c'est l'humanité.*"

France's fall from the heights of European hegemony in 1870–71 had increased the importance given to cultural propaganda and cultural politics, evident both in the institutional initiatives of the Third Republic and in pronouncements by Wilhelminian politicians and publicists who looked enviously to the French example. Post-1918 German elites, however, were less interested in France's cultural propaganda than in its *moral* propaganda, which had been elevated to something of an art form after 1871. The transformation of France in world public opinion from the Bonapartist conqueror state it had been before the Franco-Prussian War into the republican martyr nation it became after its defeat could hardly have failed to appeal to a vanquished Germany. "A bid for sympathy always works," wrote Paul Rühlmann in promoting the French example. "France was highly skilled at playing the martyr: as the bearer of freedom, carrying the torch of liberty to all oppressed nations, it suffered for the good of all humanity."[88]

France's 1923 occupation of the Ruhr region, on the pretext that Berlin had fallen behind on its reparations payments, offered the first opportunity for Germany to develop a martyr propaganda of its own. In an exact reversal of the situation in 1914, Germany could now cast itself as the defenseless victim and France and Belgium as the brutal conquerors. The passive resistance staged by the Germans, complete with the invocation of Gandhi as a spiritual brother, became the first great success of German propaganda. Less spectacular but similar in effect was the conciliatory German reponse to Allied demands for reparations payments between 1919 and 1922. Under its new "fulfillment policy," Berlin renounced the "grumbling arrogance" with which the hawks within postwar German society had reacted to the demands of the victors, seeking instead to display understanding and cooperation.[89] Walther Rathenau, for example, conceived a plan to send a kind of Peace Corps of German workers to northern France to rebuild destroyed territory, a proposal that, as his biographer David Felix succeeds in showing, was never meant seriously but served the purpose of "demonstrating Germany's good will and willingness to contribute to an international project of fraternity."[90]

Nevertheless, the experience of the Third Republic had also shown the limits of martyr propaganda. While French cultural propaganda, under the catchphrase *pénétration pacifique,* had proved successful wherever it was tried, including Germany, the French obsession with Alsace-Lorraine had elicited more alienation than sympathy, prompting Gambetta's warning to think constantly but never speak of *revanche*. The punitive Treaty of Versailles, which ended World War I, determined the political emotions of Weimar, just as the loss of Alsace-Lorraine had those of the Third Republic. And in both cases, "the fantastical self-delusion of an entire people" (as Carlo Mierendorff termed the German Versailles syndrome) undermined all efforts to gain a sympathetic hearing; the creators of propaganda were so caught up in their own obsessions that they frequently lost touch with world public opinion.[91] Even a Realpolitician like Paul Rohrbach never considered that the vanquished might have to take the first step in winning the sympathies of others.

Quite the contrary, Rohrbach argued, "reconciliation can only come after our moral restoration. . . . In other words, it is incumbent on the hostile world, our enemies, and the neutral peoples to rethink the *question of guilt* before we can even think about practicing genuine politics."[92] Both the German stance of martyred innocence and the Allies' moral condemnation of Germany had their origins in the central clause of the Treaty of Versailles. Since the entire treaty was based on article 231, the "war guilt" clause, which declared Germany solely responsible for the conflict, the amendation or propagandistic nullification of that article was destined to be the main strategic goal of postwar German politics. Germany's fixation on its innocence and the injustice of Versailles, however, took on a tendentious tone similar to that of Germany's prewar foreign-policy pronouncements, the difference being that whereas the mighty Wilhelminian empire had demanded from the rest of the world a place in the sun, the government now insisted that the world acknowledge the injustice that had been done to poor Germany.

As the ideas of *revanche* and the Lost Cause have shown, martyr propaganda tends to be so obsessed with the bruised, defeated ego that little energy remains for more productive forms of regeneration. Emulating "successful" models of martyr and moral propaganda may help a society recover from an initial trauma, but it can also confine that society to a mental ghetto. At the point when the first acts of mourning have been concluded and possibilities for national recovery become evident, most nations reorient themselves toward a victorious model. For post-1918 Germany, Anglo-American propaganda and not its French equivalent served this function, since it had so effectively undermined the German will to victory and ushered in the Allied victory. Those defeated by propaganda, so the logic ran, must also be able to achieve victory by propaganda. Thus, although propaganda was also used to argue for Germany's peacefulness and innocence, the main priority was to master its use as a weapon in anticipation of a further round of armed conflict.

THE DISCUSSIONS OF the 1920s were unanimous in their conclusion that wartime German propaganda had not understood how to appeal to the masses, that it was highly academic and removed from reality—"professorial propaganda," as Johann Plenge put it— and that it would have to be recast along Anglo-American lines.[93] It was assumed that the Anglo-American intelligentsia had a natural gift for mass suggestion because they were part of the mass *Zivilisation* of which propaganda was a product. By contrast, the German spirit, or *Geist*, was predestined to fail because of its identification with elite *Kultur*, the antithesis of *Zivilisation*. Thus, consciously or unconsciously, the discussion in the 1920s centered on the question of whether and to what extent Germany could adopt English and American methods of mass manipulation without endangering its soul. Most of those who took part in the debates lacked the sociological insight and, more important, the personal readiness to accept, as a price for effective mass propaganda, a thoroughly democratic and commercial—or alternatively, a thoroughly totalitarian—society. From Ludendorff to Tönnies, the prevailing wisdom was that effective propaganda was an instrument, a kind of whirling fan that, if operated properly, could vent a certain opinion, conviction, or message out into the world. Perhaps the most concise image of this take on propaganda is Charlie Chaplin's Great Dictator, who directs the applause of the masses with a single hand gesture, turning it on and off like a radio.[94]

Whereas the bourgeois propaganda theorists handled their subject gingerly, ever wary of being burned, the National Socialists were untroubled by scruples such as the distinction between means and ends. The lessons learned from Gustave Le Bon about the role of "contagion" in mass psychology and the latest advertising techniques were not lost on men like Adolf Hitler, Joseph Goebbels, and Nazi propaganda expert Eugen Hadamovsky. Theodor Heuss, a politician critical of Hitler, remarked that the section on propaganda in *Mein Kampf* was "better and more precisely written" than anything else in the book: "Here we see a man who knows what he's talking about."[95] Several of Hitler's formulations could have been written for, or lifted from, any one of a number of contemporary textbooks on advertising psychology.[96] In its methods of mass manipulation and mobilization, National Socialism was thus "more American" than any of the other political movements. Hitler's public appearances—for instance, his airplane tour through Germany in 1932—have been described as "rituals of German hero worship staged with American know-how," and the success of Goebbels's Propaganda Ministry was in no small part due to its entertainment value.[97] As Ernest K. Bramsted points out, "There was a good deal of showmanship and of the American circus à la Barnum in Goebbels's techniques."[98]

The reasons for the success of Nazi propaganda are twofold. For one thing, Hitler and his men not only knew their subject but also identified with it far more personally than any of their bourgeois competitors. For them, the masses were not a foreign world that had to be painstakingly researched but the very element from which they themselves had come and within which they moved easily and comfortably.[99] The Nazis, moreover, brought the expectation that propaganda could completely remake reality back down to earth. To the old adage that even the best propaganda can achieve only what reality allows, National Socialism added the idea that reality and propaganda had to be coordinated, indeed melded together into a single, novel instrument of mass manipulation. Indeed, the two were often indistinguishable. Did the state-sponsored *"Kraft durch Freude"* (Strength through Joy) vacations, instituted in 1933, serve the purpose of relaxation or political integration? Was the Volkswagen merely a motor vehicle, or was it also a catalyst for folk community? Was state terror simply physical oppression, or was it a kind of propaganda of intimidation aimed at bringing the home front into line?

Nowhere was the Nazis' skill with propaganda more evident than in their ability to keep both public morale and food supplies steady, a problem that had stumped Germany's leaders during World War I.

During World War II, the Nazis knew their calls for steadfastness would succeed only with a people who had enough to eat. That was the simple, nonideological, but thoroughly Machiavellian lesson they had learned from the collapse of 1918. As Hitler put it, "A people can do without some material good, so long as it gets powerful ideals in return. However, these ideals must never be purchased at the cost of material well-being, or they could have disastrous consequences for a people."[100] Finally, the National Socialists "propagandized" a domain that during the First World War had been considered inhospitable to propaganda, the military, which ceased to be used exclusively as the ultimate instrument of physical violence, coercion, and destruction and became, for several years at least, the primary weapon of foreign-policy propaganda. The great insight was that the perception of military strength was just as important as the actual number of planes and tanks. The mere threat of deploying Germany's armed forces could be used to break the enemy's will.

As the success of Hitler's foreign-policy bluffing before 1938 demonstrated, such calculations paid off. The Führer did not require a fully armed German war machine to achieve his desired effect. In the arms buildup that commenced in 1936, the actual production of warplanes and tanks was significantly less impressive than the accompanying propaganda made it out to be. The Luftwaffe, in particular, functioned as an effective instrument of terror and propaganda. Most historians today agree that its role in intimidating the Western powers during the Sudeten crisis of 1938 was decisive. "Hitler's adroit manipulation of the threat of aerial warfare," Edward L. Homze writes, "helped Germany achieve its stunning victory over England and France." By the late 1930s, as historian Uri Bialer shows, British foreign policy was being dictated by fears that England could become a target for German air attacks. Bialer calls the Luftwaffe during this period "one of the most effective weapons of persuasion of the Third Reich."[101] (The fact that Goering and Goebbels, the heads of the new departments for the

Luftwaffe and for propaganda, respectively, were the two figures with the greatest cultural power in the regime perhaps appears in a new light in this context.) One might ask, if the pre-1939 German army—like the threat of the atomic bomb after 1945—was such an effective deterrent that it didn't actually have to be used, was it not then primarily propagandistic in function, much like food supplies and Gestapo terror?

For a remarkably long time, it was. Even in 1939, when Hitler's propagandistic and psychological hand had been played out and war had become a reality, the military continued to an astonishing extent to operate "propagandistically." The blitzkrieg was basically the military continuation of Hitler's strategy of bluffs and threats from the prewar years. With a relatively scant but highly concentrated and, above all, rapid deployment of forces, the Nazis proved able to terrify and traumatize the enemy so thoroughly that it capitulated before its reserves and resources had been exhausted. This strategy of surprise and terror departed radically from the strategy of exhaustion in World War I, which aimed at the methodical physical destruction of the opponent's forces. The blitzkrieg applied, as the military historian John Frederick Charles Fuller points out, "mobility as a psychological weapon, mobility not in order to kill, but to terrorize, confuse and deceive, to call forth despair, uncertainty and disorder behind enemy lines." Moreover: "The physical principle of destruction was replaced by the psychological principle of confusion. . . . The effect of the *blitzkrieg* . . . was directed not at the enemy's muscles but at his nerves."[102]

Historian Marc Bloch, who himself took part in the war, describes this phenomenon with singular insight. In his account of France's lightning-quick collapse in the spring of 1940, the Wehrmacht emerges as victorious no longer because of its greater potential for destruction but because of its ability to inflict paralyzing fear. The French will to fight had been destroyed not by bombs from German Stukas, Bloch writes, but by the horrific, barbaric, and utterly enervating noise that accompanied them. That noise was not an accidental by-product of dive-bombing raids, like the thunder of cannons, but was deliberately created by sirens, so-called Jericho trumpets, expressly built for that purpose.[103]

Ultimately, though, the military propaganda of terror depended, like every other type of propaganda, on the circumstances in which it was applied. Hence the failure of Hitler's attempt toward the end of the war to turn the tide with a surprise attack in the Ardennes. Just as the bombing of London with V rockets proved of limited effectiveness, the unexpected advances of German armored divisions achieved only a short-lived, strategically insignificant effect within the ranks of a clearly superior enemy that now believed in its certain victory.[104]

From Propaganda to Spiritual and Moral Revival

Propaganda fascinated its German adherents above all as an instrument of mass manipulation and as a psychotechnical miracle weapon. But another view of propaganda saw it not as an amoral tactic but rather as the charismatic effusion of a vital historical strength. As the example of Wilhelminian Germany seemed to demonstrate, a bankrupt system that lacked charisma and a vision for the future could not produce persuasive propaganda. A master of propaganda like Adolf Hitler did not hesitate to acknowledge the charismatic quality of his archenemy, Marxism, or to recognize a self-confident will at work even in mercantilist England and America. Thus, even before the propaganda-savvy Nazis assumed power, criticism of enemy propaganda as a cause of defeat became criticism of the German system for being unable to project itself effectively. Like all other losing nations, Germany began to search for the origins of the false path that had led it to the abyss.

There were numerous starting points. The most obvious ones were the mistakes made during the war, from the German violation

of Belgian neutrality and the decision to pursue unrestricted submarine warfare to the uncompromising demand for peace through
victory. The question of how such mistakes could have been made,
however, led back to the prewar era and beyond. Many postwar
observers dated the origins of the catastrophe back to the founding
of the empire, seizing anew on ideas that had been advanced forty
years earlier by Nietzsche, Burckhardt, Konstantin Frantz, and other
opponents of Bismarck. The gist of the argument was that with the
founding of the empire in 1871, Germany had renounced its former
universalistic spirit, embraced non-Germanic traits such as materialism, mercantilism, and imperialism, and thereby lost all sense of
proportion and spiritual substance. In short, Germany had lost its
soul. This verdict had little to do with ideologized left-right divisions.
Just as Heinrich Mann spoke in the fall of 1918 of a "pathology
report," the radical conservative Max Hildebert Boehm wrote of
imperial Germany's "inner instability and external excess." Walther
Rathenau, who was among the first to recognize the Wagner cult as
a culture of the ersatz and make-believe, characterized Wilhelminism
as "electric-journalistic Caesaro-papism." Carl Heinrich Becker,
orientalist, reformer, and later Prussian minister of culture, saw in
the empire's militarism a compensatory culture. Arthur Moeller van
den Bruck, a radical conservative who ridiculed the "brass-band sentimentality" and "family-album idiocy" of Wilhelminian Germany,
wrote in 1919 "that ever since 1871 we have been moving backward,
not forward. The Germany we love and can admire lies prior to
1871, quite a few years prior, in fact, and not afterward."[105]

If there was a brief consensus immediately after the shock of
defeat, it resided in the idea that collapse and revolution should be
welcomed as a flood that would wash away Wilhelminian frivolity.
The idea spanned the radical left, which was awaiting the outbreak
of world revolution, the liberal center, which longed for the introduction of Western-style parliamentary politics, and the extreme
right, which hoped for a rebirth of the nation.[106] The results disappointed everyone. Instead of revolution, there was mere "rioting

in the guards' absence," as Rathenau called it, and the moral bank-ruptcy of the system presided over by the majority socialists of the SPD, who did everything in their power to prevent revolution.[107] After half a century in the opposition and four years of wartime solidarity, the SPD was revealed to be an integral part of the system, whose preservation in republican form the party made its overriding task. At least that is how the SPD was seen by those who refused to acknowledge the Weimar Republic, born as it was of military defeat and aborted revolution. As historian Ludwig Dehio noted after 1945, the Weimar Republic more closely resembled the 1815 French res-toration than it did the French republics of 1792 and 1870 or rev-olutionary Russia of 1917.

World War as Educational War

Disgusted by the unheroic republic, radical nationalists as well as radical socialists were reduced to finding another object for identi-fication. In psychoanalytic terms, this process is called regression: a wish that cannot be fulfilled in reality is compensated for through withdrawal to an earlier state of fulfillment and happiness. The most recent such state for Germans existed in August 1914. The enthusi-asm then had less to do with the war itself than with the expectation that a show of national military strength would once and for all resolve the contradictions between the nation and democracy or the nation and socialism.[108] But since the war brought about everything but such a quick resolution and since the enthusiasm died out almost as quickly as it had flared up, the August experience ceded to a second, darker myth of wartime brotherhood.

The German *Fronterlebnis*, or experience of the front, turned the August experience on its head. Death and suffering in the trenches were in no way seductive, liberating, or utopian. The equality and fraternity of the battle lines in World War I were purely negative and destructive, and those who directly suffered the war's fury had no illusions to the contrary. Soldiers felt themselves to be a community forged by the destiny of having been used as cannon fodder. If they maintained any ideal of socialism, it was that of the classless business of living and dying in the trenches. From their perspective, the *Volksgemeinschaft* proclaimed from above and behind the front lines was just another Wilhelminian slogan. The front was a world unto itself, hemmed in on one side by the enemy, for whom the soldiers had a certain existential empathy, and on the other by the rulers at home, with whom they had nothing in common.

The decisive element and defining criterion of the front line was fire. By passing through it, the so-called generation of the front underwent its baptism, its salvation ritual, or, to use one of the most popular terms of nationalistic war literature, its "purification" of the illusions, deformities, and pieties of prewar society. For the frontline soldier and radical conservative writer Ernst Jünger, for instance, the experience of war was nearly indistinguishable from the experience of fire.[109] There were only two alternatives: to perish in the flames or emerge hardened by them. Both involved becoming one with the barrage of fire, or *Feuerwalze* (literally, "waltz of fire"), described by Jünger as that "towering wall of fire and steel [that is] the image of ourselves." Whoever had encountered and gone through the fire was "hardened by the glowing element" and had all his impurities "burned off."[110] Conversely, the image of *slag* symbolized the impure elements cast out by fire: "The relativism and indifference of the time of corruption before the war had been burned to slag," wrote one observer shortly before the Nazi assumption of power in 1933.[111]

The idea of a world-consuming fire, which is as old as the Apocalypse, was familiar in Germany from Wagner's *Die Walküre* and *Götterdämmerung*, and the fire rituals of the Nazi Party, including ceremonial bonfires and torchlight parades, represented another modulation of the fire metaphors of war rhetoric. Even liberal politicians like Rathenau spoke of a "world fire that transforms material in order to free the spirit."[112] Across the political spectrum, then, the "fire" of the world war was seen as a medium for forging a new type of man, the war itself as a "war of education," and defeat as an intrinsic part of this education.[113] Had imperial Germany won the war, it would have meant the triumph of an inauthentic and superficial materialism. The German word meaning "to win," as in "winning a war," *gewinnen*, is derived from *Gewinn*, the word for "profits." *Gewinn* was an inherently material, financial, or mercantile concept like the treasure of the Nibelungs, with its central role in German national mythology. Moeller van den Bruck's conviction that Germany's road to demise began with the "accursed riches"— the five billion francs in reparations exacted from France in 1871— cast German defeat as a necessary corrective.[114] The philosopher Hermann Keyserling wrote in November 1918:

> We are experiencing at this moment probably the most over-whelming manifestation in history of the eternal truth, formulated most potently by Christ, that those who momentarily wield temporal power are not the ones who possess the greatest historical might. It is not just as a defensive mechanism . . . that oppressed peoples . . . so quickly come to join in messianic missions. Just as the individual ascetic has to suffer to transcend his present condition, so the creative desire for new life can blossom only out of the oppression of the here and now. For this reason, people of the lowest classes very often adopt the most far-reaching and future-oriented beliefs. . . . If the general socio-economic conditions of humanity improve, we will have this primarily proletarian yearning to thank. Salvation in times of great upheaval usually comes from those who are weakened or who have suffered most. Only they can find within themselves the strength as well as the motivation for radical change.[115]

National Socialism

Having emerged from its trial by fire, the wartime generation was convinced that it had been called to lead the nation. Its mission consisted specifically of bringing the education received at the battlefront back to the home front, where people remained stubbornly ignorant. Rituals of return in primitive cultures traditionally require that warriors who have spilled blood undergo purification rituals before being allowed back into the community. In Germany, by contrast, the warriors were to carry the knowledge of fire back to the home front, which would then be purified as well.

Thus, the image of the *march* from the battlefront back to the capital occupied a central place in Fascist mythology, suggesting the reestablishment of unity in a nation that had been split into a home front and a battlefront during the war. (The immediate forerunner of this image—which happened to reverse Marx's quip about farce following tragedy—was Wilhelm II's plan in November 1918 to lead the army from the front and restore order at home.) Neither Italian Fascism nor German National Socialism can be understood without the idea of the march back home. Nor can their respective death cults be understood without reference to the fallen who were "left" or "remained behind" at the front. The surviving veterans from whose ranks came the earliest Fascists explicitly portrayed themselves as the advocates of their departed comrades.[116] This "tragic" identification with the dead was a primary difference between frontline soldiers—and the Fascist community that linked up with them—and Bolshevik revolutionaries, with whom there were otherwise numerous affinities.

For its part, the home front, from which the soldiers felt alienated after four years of war, had undergone its own transformation since 1914. Once the conflict had entered the phase of total war in 1916, the nation had ceased to be a mere spectator, if it ever had been one, and was drafted into the fight as an active participant. Even in the numbers of their dead—for example, the many victims of the Allied food blockade—the noncombatants bore comparison to their counterparts in the army. Just as the fighters could accuse civilians of not having put their lives directly at risk, the starving home front could counter that the frontline soldiers had at least been fed. Regardless of where it occurred, death was the result of the same war.

The nation's enlistment in the cause was described as *war social-ism*, a term coined in 1915 by the sociologist Johann Plenge. Plenge's neologism did not connote Marxist socialism; the only thing the two concepts had in common was their opposition to capitalism and liberalism. War socialism meant that the German economy was ruled no longer by the free market but by central planning. In other words, economic organization was subsumed within military organization, and both were now instruments of the state. Plenge could just as well have spoken of "war organization" as of "war socialism" since for him the two were identical: "Organization is socialism." The fact that he chose the word *socialism* and that it immediately resonated even among people for whom it had previously been taboo can be explained by the psychology of wartime solidarity. Once the Social Democratic movement had rejected class conflict in favor of national struggle and folk community, the right, in a symbolic reciprocal gesture, accepted and redefined "socialism." A socialism that could be agreed on by all yet could be understood in any number of ways was the perfect label for the *Volksgemeinschaft* proclaimed at the beginning of the war. The majority socialists saw in it a potential escape from the pariah status they had occupied for so many years. A nationally redefined socialism was also ideal for the nationalists and technocrats, who sought to replace the reviled Wilhelminian amalgamation of liberalism and feudalism with a strictly organized bureaucratic state.[117]

A creation of the war like *Volksgemeinschaft*, the idea of war socialism was actually strengthened by Germany's defeat. The slogan had become so closely associated with the experience of the war that it shed its left-wing connotations and took on a mythological life of its own. One sign of its new independent life was the adoption and reinterpretation of the Marxist concept of the proletariat, the bour-geoisie, class conflict, and the liberation of the world through the emancipation of the workers. Translated into the language of national socialism, post-Versailles Germany was the proletarianized nation, the West was the bourgeoisie, the struggle against the West amounted to an international, or more accurately, inter-national, class struggle; and victory over the West would achieve world liberation. This was the German version of the martyrdom and salvation on a global scale that post-1871 France had celebrated under the banner of "*civilisation.*"

The idea of Germany as the world's proletariat occupied a central place in the thought of conservative revolutionaries such as Moeller van den Bruck, Boehm, Edgar Jung, Jünger, Friedrich Hielscher, Oswald Spengler, the group affiliated with the journal *Die Tat*, and the National Bolshevists (Ernst Niekisch, Heinrich Laufenberg, and Fritz Wolffheim).[118] But it also exerted an influence on the basic mood and, at times, the strategy of the political and cultural center. Rathenau, for instance, wrote, "The signature of our future existence is this: we have practically nothing except our own labor," and the Weimar Republic's first foreign minister, Ulrich von Brockdorff-Rantzau, was prepared to continue the struggle against the "bourgeois" West in alliance with proletarian Russia, presumably because Germany had nothing to lose but its chains.[119] Of course, an alliance with Soviet Russia was for the postwar mind-set merely the latest, "regional" version of Prussian Germany's historical orientation toward Eastern Europe. Yet others proposed a global alliance with the colonized nations of the Far and Middle East—Egypt, Persia, India, Japan—which were about to throw off the Western yoke or, in Japan's case, had already done so. After all, Germany had aided *their* cause as well, these partisans argued, by sufficiently weakening the colonial powers so that liberation movements like Gandhi's could arise. It was a short leap to the idea that Germany had actually fought the war as the representative, indeed as the messiah, of the world's oppressed. Having now been relieved of its own colonial burden, Germany was on the same level as the colonies. And finally the Germans, like the colonial populations fighting for their independence, were a "young" people whom the old rulers of the West were trying to deny their rightful place in the sun. The German obsession with being encircled, which could be overcome only

through a preemptive encircling of the enemy (as in General Schlieffen's Cannae plan, patterned on Hannibal's defeat of the Romans in
216 B.C.), found expression after 1918 in the imagined alliance with
colonial peoples.[120] United under German leadership into the
greatest ring the world had ever known, the oppressed peoples of
the world would encircle the West in a global Cannae.

It was not only the colonial proletariat, however, that was to be
mobilized for Germany's cause but also the proletariat of the victorious nations themselves. If Germany developed its wartime socialism into a "profound, inspiring, well-armed (peacetime) socialism,"
the nationalists believed, it would be a signal to the working classes
in the Western nations.[121] In the form of such phantasms, Berlin
presented itself as the national socialist alternative to Moscow long
before the Nazis assumed political power in 1933.

August 1914 Revisited

The Weimar Republic is usually divided into three distinct periods—
revolution and inflation (1918–23), stability (1924–29), and economic crisis (1930–32)—but one can also view it as a continuum,
one protracted megacollapse stretching over fifteen years, only briefly
interrupted by a period of economic and cultural respite. Indeed,
from the perspective of 1930, the "stable" years of 1924–29 looked
like a pleasant but illusory aberration from the catastrophe now
returning with redoubled force. What military defeat and revolutionary upheaval had unleashed in 1918 the economic crisis set off
in the late 1920s: a slow-motion implosion of the system, "an
uncanny, incomprehensible, and ineluctable process of decay and
decomposition." In the conservative magazine *Die Tat*, a barometer
of the post-1930 crisis mentality, Ferdinand Fried described the
behavior of the economy with the same language that had been used
in reference to the army in November 1918: "The absolute dissolution of morale among German entrepreneurs . . . is shown by the
fact that *they are now deserting their posts.*"[122]

The reflexive understanding of the economic crisis as a resumption of the world war following a "truce" (namely, the period of stability) was common not just in Germany. The sense that the war had begun as a traditional military conflict but ended as a military-industrial quagmire tended to support that opinion. It was but a small step from the idea, popular in the 1920s, that future wars would only be fought on the level of economics to interpreting the Great Depression as a continuation of the Great War.

For many Germans, however, the repeat of the military collapse in the form of economic disaster was not necessarily to be mourned. The only people who were truly distressed by the demise of the liberal republic in the economic crisis were those who felt that the republic was Germany's best hope despite being born of defeat. Those on the right and the left who had expected something more after 1918 than a reconstitution of the old system under a republican banner welcomed its failure as a chance—on a now empty stage—to do what had then been neglected. The party that declared itself best suited to the task was of an entirely new sort, consisting at first almost exclusively of combat veterans and sporting both "national socialist" and "workers' party" in its name—a fact pointing toward the legacies from which its success was derived. The socialism of the *Volksgemeinschaft:* a product of the war. The worker: a further refinement of the frontline soldier, an archetype central to the so-called soldierly nationalism of Ernst Jünger and others. And finally, at the head of the National Socialist German Workers' Party, a man who promised to bring about the national renewal that should have taken place in 1918: the frontline soldier Adolf Hitler. Without these equivalences, the connection between war, defeat, national rebirth, and renewed war in Nazi mythology would remain as obscure as the true significance of the Nazi assumption of power in 1933 did for the majority of liberal commentators. Most observers perceived only accidental parallels between that event and the revolution of November 1918 rather than a direct connection. The Italian journalist Filipo Bojano, for instance, wrote that as in November 1918 "the petty bosses [of the Weimar Republic] simply handed over the keys and disappeared with their masters."[123]

The spring of 1933 was usually compared not to November 1918 but to August 1914, the memory of that summer filling the void left by the aborted revolution of 1918.[124] Both moments in the collective mind helped define the nation's soul in 1933. Or, put another way, the failed and now revived "national revolution" of 1918 was imbued, years after the fact, with the spirit of 1914.

Publisher Peter Suhrkamp succinctly captured the "spirit of 1933." A veteran and an anti-Nazi, Suhrkamp also experienced spring 1933 as a recapitulation of 1914, as the rebirth of the feeling that anything was possible, a second chance for a nation that suddenly seemed quite young, as though the millions of fallen soldiers had returned to the realm of the living to help in the rebuilding effort. "I was repeatedly struck by the similarity to my memories of the summer of 1914," he wrote.

> The similarity extended to the smallest details. Uniformed SA and SS men and regular army soldiers now marched alongside private citizens, some wearing medals. There were children and older women and servant girls, and between the marchers and the spectators standing on the sidewalks or perched on fences or trees or on the roofs of the electric streetcars there ran a current of unanimity and heartfelt openness. . . . At the center of it all were always young men in uniform—and men in uniform always seemed young. Great columns of young men in neatly pressed uniforms marching in lockstep and taut, disciplined faces dominated the scene. Cities, towns, and country roads . . . all were filled with the presence of the army. The astonishing thing, however, was that although the soldiers sang war songs they seemed not warlike but rather, at that moment, thoroughly peaceful. Not complacent or collegial or clubby, though; the impression was of earnest readiness. What we experienced was an active army filled with the determination, zeal, and excitement of our old forces in the field, but without the threat of war or even the prospect of war on the horizon. What we were witnessing was something that

made no rational sense and can scarcely be imagined: the military as an end in itself, as the fulfillment and satisfaction of a feeling for life. . . . Without the past war, such a pure military phenomenon would hardly have been possible. But what we saw did not necessarily require a war.[125]

Reeducation

Among the "unfriendly services" that, in Arnold Toynbee's phrase, Germany and France provided for each other in their regularly recurring conflicts were the educational reforms, modeled on the respective victor's systems, that were carried out after every defeat. Wilhelm von Humboldt's reforms after the Prussian defeat at Jena-Auerstedt in 1806 would have been unthinkable without the influence of Rousseau and the French Revolution. Likewise, vanquished France would use those same Prussian reforms two generations later as a model for its own intellectual and moral renewal. The French studied the University of Berlin with special care, seeing it as the foundry in which men like Johann Gottlieb Fichte, the philosopher and nationalist agitator much admired in post-1871 France, had forged the German *revanche* against Napoleon. In 1872, when a group of prominent republican professors and politicians decided to establish a private university for the education of future political leaders, the Ecole libre des sciences politiques, they explicitly cited Berlin as their inspiration.

The imitation came full circle in 1920 when two groups of intellectuals and politicians in Berlin sought to found a political academy, independent of the state and the university, along the lines of the Ecole libre. The first of these groups was the conservative Ring Association around Moeller van den Bruck; the second consisted of liberal reformers. Both groups agreed that since Bismarck Germany's elites had utterly failed in their political leadership; if they hadn't actually brought on the catastrophe, they had done little to prevent it. But the two groups differed radically on the new academy's goals, and so two institutions were founded instead of one. The conservatives set up the Politisches Kolleg, while the liberals established the Deutsche Hochschule für Politik. The former remained little more than a debating society comprising various working committees that convened in Moeller van den Bruck's June Club at 22 Motzstrasse. The latter became a generously funded public institute for teaching and research housed in Karl Friedrich Schinkel's Academy of Architecture.

Both organizations became gathering places. Opponents and detractors of the republic assembled at Motzstrasse, while the republican establishment and a talented younger generation that included Helmut James Moltke and Sebastian Haffner met at the Academy of Architecture. The Politisches Kolleg debated how parliamentarianism and the party system could be most quickly overthrown so the work of national renewal could progress. The Hochschule forged the political cadre that was to lead the parliamentary republic in the future. The Politisches Kolleg measured the success of its activities by how closely it approximated the Ecole libre as a school for nationalism and preparation for *revanche*. Its director, Martin Spahn, wrote:

> The Ecole was . . . the vestal temple in which the fire of serious and profound appreciation for the virtues of the nation was guarded from 1872 to 1918. . . . We Germans should look back on the last fifty years and be embarrassed at how the French after Sedan . . . reflected and conducted those rays of light that illuminated us in the days after our defeat in 1809 [sic]. . . . They reaped the rewards of their efforts in the years 1914–18 in the determination with which their entire people opposed us. We are now faced with the challenge not of retreating to the old guidelines of 1809 but of revising them in the light of French achievements over the last half century, indeed of taking them one farther.[126]

Within the Deutsche Hochschule für Politik, on the other hand, the hoped-for renewal was to be not just national but Europe-wide, indeed universal. "To become a point of crystallization for the intellectual and spiritual reconstruction of Germany—*a new Germany and therefore also a new Europe in one new spirit*" is how Ernst Jaeckh defined the task. Jaeckh, the Hochschule's first director, oriented his institute around the ideas of 1789, while the Politisches Kolleg clung to those of 1914.[127]

A number of other political and sociological institutes founded in the immediate postwar period followed this pattern of polarization, among them Johann Plenge's Academy for Governmental Studies in Münster, Leopold von Wiese's Institute for Social Research in Cologne, and, a few years later, the Frankfurt Institute for Social Research. All of them either arose entirely outside the universities or were only tenuously connected to them. When a formal affiliation was proposed, the suggestion was sometimes rejected by the traditional faculties as alien to the missions of their universities, but the newcomers themselves also raised objections: political education had no chance of making inroads into German universities whether it was conducted by Johann Plenge in the spirit of 1914, by Leopold von Wiese or Franz Oppenheimer in the Enlightenment tradition, or by a liberal centrist like the Prussian minister of culture Carl Heinrich Becker. An academic outsider even before the war, Becker entered the ministry in 1916 and became a key figure in the educational reform movement. As undersecretary of state and minister of culture, he directed Prussian educational policies both administratively and politically from 1919 to 1930. In a 1919 pamphlet, he enumerated the ways in which German universities had contributed to national decline and collapse: overspecialization ("We've produced ear, nose, and skin specialists but no doctors"); the depoliticization that went with it, which was in reality a form of subservience to the ruling powers; and the loss of the capacity for intellectual, moral, and political synthesis. "It was precisely their dedication to their specific disciplines," he wrote, "that was to have dire consequences for professors' abilities to function as good citizens."[128]

Becker did not trust the universities to regenerate themselves. He regarded the Deutsche Hochschule für Politik in Berlin, which he personally helped establish, and the institutes for sociology in Cologne and Frankfurt as "pacesetters and experimental laboratories" designed to bring reform to the universities at some later date.[129] Aside from those few enclaves, however, reformers were doubtful that significant and timely results could be achieved within academia, so they focused instead on what had been described before the war as "popular" education. A new kind of school, the *Volkshochschule*— similar to the American community college—was set up in many cities for the explicit purpose of teaching civic consciousness. In contrast, public secondary schools, which had been so central to the process of national renewal in the Third Republic, played only a subordinate role in the thinking of German educational reformers.[130]

Of all the educational institutions, the *Volkshochschule* was the one most influenced by the experience of war. The architects of the *Volkshochschule* deliberately distanced it from its prewar forerunners, bourgeois philanthropic institutions aimed at popularizing culture among the lower classes. The Weimar *Volkshochschule* did not see itself as a charitable institution, distributing crumbs of bourgeois cultural sustenance to the poor huddled masses, but as an arena where high and popular culture could meet on an equal footing. For Werner Picht and other educational reformers of the early Weimar Republic, the August experience had been the harbinger of revolution, whose completion had been prevented by four years of wartime deprivation as well as by the lack of "solidarity between the classes," incompetent leadership, and "overreliance on patriotic sentiment."[131] The task of the *Volkshochschule* was to reconstitute the *Volksgemeinschaft*, or folk community, through an education that would bridge the divisions between social classes. Without such a unifying cultural hand, it was felt, *folk community, revolution,* and *republic* would remain empty phrases.

The German *Volkshochschule* took its name from and was patterned after the Danish *Landvolkshochschule* of the nineteenth century, itself a product of national defeat by France in 1807 and by

Prussia in 1864. More immediately influential, however, were the two reform movements of the prewar years. What the alternative school and the youth movement had previously offered only to small elite groups was to be made available to the general public, just as earlier protests against traditional schools' emphases on rote learning and discipline were now carried to the national level. From the alternative schools pioneered by Gustav Wyneken, Rudolf Steiner, and Paul Geheeb, the *Volkshochschule* movement adopted the idea of the *Arbeitsgemeinschaft*, a working group of students and teachers learning from one another in positions of equality. The reformers even borrowed the term *Arbeitsgemeinschaft* for the title of their official journal, thus placing the concept at the very center of the movement— and indeed of the new folk community.

The missionary zeal that inspired the *Volkshochschule* movement proved no more durable than the enthusiasm for *Volksgemeinschaft* had been at the beginning of the war, an outcome that is hardly surprising given the intimate connection between the two. Such enthusiasm was characteristic of the rhapsodic, idealistic, and expressionistic mood of the German revolution, which spewed out ecstatic buzzwords like *spiritual turning point, unified spirit, new humanity, impetus toward community, world consciousness* that quickly became fashionable in the salons of the educated middle classes but had no lasting influence.[132] By 1923, the *Volkshochschule* had lost its aura as a source of national revival and of competition with the university, reverting to the role it had played before the war, namely, providing continuing education to ambitious members of the lower classes.

The post-1918 German educational reform can perhaps be best understand by comparison with its French equivalent. In France, defeat was attributed to the backwardness of schools as institutions for transmitting knowledge. Accordingly, the main goals of reform were literacy and universal compulsory education. In Germany, the culprit was not a deficit in knowledge but a deficit in civic spirit. Thus, while the target of French reform was the politically empowered but illiterate citizen, in Germany it was the educated—even overeducated—but politically disempowered underling, who carried the blame for Germany's faintheartedness in the war. The German educational system had taken a wrong path, becoming a "noisy factory of reason" and a "mill grinding the brain into a malleable pulp." As the reformer Ludwig Gurlitt complained as early as 1902, the German system brought forth "pedagogical products of fear: pale, frightened, oppressed young people with no self-confidence, who live timidly and hope only to do the bidding of their masters."[133] Here, too, the French-German relationship had come full circle: France had originally admired the example of the Prussian schoolmaster as necessary for national survival, only to see Germany, forty years later, deciding that the schoolmaster had degenerated into a "petty dictator," who needed to be remade in the image of the republican *instituteur*. It was the *instituteur*, after all, who had "charged" victorious France's cannons "with ideas."[134] German educational reform in the Weimar Republic failed to involve Germans as active, committed participants in the revival of the nation, but there was another sort of "civic education" whose effects would prove more significant. It was economic—and American.

Paths of Modernity: Americanism and Rationalization

At the end of the First World War, virtually everyone agreed that none of the nations that had begun the conflict and bled themselves dry on its battlefields could claim a resounding victory. The big winner was the lone non-European combatant, whose late entry into the fighting had ended the stalemate and effectively decided the war. In 1914, the United States was Europe's debtor. By 1918, the situation had been reversed. For three years, until entering the war itself, the neutral industrial giant had supplied the Entente with matériel, which was paid for with Europe's gold reserves and then promptly consumed on Europe's battlefields. American industrial might, which had impressed European observers—and elicited some unease—before 1914, had taken another huge leap forward.

While no one among the former enemies disputed who had actually won the war, there was far less agreement about who had truly lost it. The Entente, of course, saw Germany as the loser. In Germany, however, a variation of the stab-in-the-back legend emerged according to which, having signed the treaty of Brest-Litovsk with Russia in March 1918, Germany was destined to prevail over the rest of the exhausted Entente. Only America's sudden intervention, at the Allies' behest, had saved England and France from the coup de grâce of the spring invasion in 1918. Put simply, the Americans had stolen Germany's victory. If one ignored the fact that it was German policies that had provoked America's entry into the war, the psychology of stolen victory and a treacherous European stab in the back seemed plausible: German defeat was the result of the Entente's betrayal of Europe to the non-European power America.[135]

In the German view, America's entry into the war instantaneously converted Germany's European enemies into second-rate powers; since the Allies had ridden America's coattails to victory, Germany had not been subdued in and by Europe. France had not been taken seriously as a great power since 1871 and had been respected during the war merely as a kind of David bravely fighting a hopeless cause.[136] England, the only enemy Germany had fought with any bitterness or hatred, seemed to have been devalued in comparison with America just as, earlier, France had been in comparison with England. Italy hardly counted at all, and Russia was its own separate case. All that mattered after 1918 was that America was the actual winner and Germany the loser—but only in relation to America. As painful as the defeat had been, it allowed Germans to imagine themselves as the only European power, the only serious participant in a future European-American duel, and therefore the only legitimate mouthpiece for Europe in a transatlantic dialogue. In sharp contrast to its prewar assertions of power, Germans could thus derive from defeat a claim to a leading moral role in Europe. This aspiration is clearly evident in statements like "Germany may have lost the war militarily, politically, and economically. Germany's European enemies, however, did not fight for themselves and their part of the world but for the spread of the American economy. That was their victory" and "In defeating us, the New World has defeated all of Europe."[137]

Along with Germany's moral calling came its military and financial independence. In contrast to the Entente, it had conducted the war not on American credit but with its own resources. Even as it was sinking into hyperinflation in 1922, Germany could look on in satisfaction as America coolly presented its former allies with the bill for its services. "That is the worst form of defeat, one that is meted out by a brother in arms," remarked radical nationalist Hans von Hentig, not without a trace of Schadenfreude. "The German threat has been repulsed at the cost of American vassalage."[138]

Germans were not alone in drawing such conclusions; some of the French saw the situation similarly.[139] Even with reference to reparations, the issue on which Germany seemed to be most at the mercy of its enemies, Germany could place itself on a par with the United States as a historical subject, whereas the nations on the receiving end of reparations were mere objects. Were they not obliged to first extract from Germany what they owed Washington, even if they tried to conceal that fact from themselves with the optimistic slogan "Germany will pay"? Were not the nations of the Entente thus the victims of a new two-front war, this one financial? Or to put it metaphorically, were they not the chaff caught between the millstones of Germany and America?

Such fantasies were a transparent way of compensating for Germany's actual powerlessness, but they pinpointed the victors' frailties with the sharp eye of defeat. England, which had come through the war physically unscathed, had a comparatively easy time redefining itself in relation to America. The *mother* country of the former colonies could see itself without any great difficulty as the *paternal* authority over its traditionless, not very cultivated, but undeniably successful offspring. This possibility was not open to France, which had suffered significant physical damage as the actual locus of the fighting. Moreover, the war had scarcely lived up to the expectations of *revanche* that the French had nurtured for forty years. The idea of *revanche* implied subduing Germany in a one-on-one contest. France, however, had merely been part of a victorious coalition that owed its triumph to the Americans. The image with which France resolved its ideological desperation and redefined its relationship to America was that of the beloved, cherished for her own sake. The United States, in this logic, had not entered the war in 1917 out of national interest but because it had been so enamored of French universal human rights, the French Revolution, and French civilization. America was thus the young hero who had rescued Marianne from the German defilers. As America's beloved, France had no cause to see American help as an encroachment on its autonomy—on the contrary, Washington's intervention was a belatedly returned favor for France's having supported American independence in 1776: General Pershing was the American *revanche*, in the positive sense, for Lafayette. But the romance ended there. In *Les américains chez nous*, a popular play by Eugène Brieux staged in 1920, a group of firemen extinguish a blaze in a grand manor house and promptly move into the lord's living room, usurping his place.[140]

AMERICA'S EMERGENCE AS the new world power in 1918 did not come as a surprise to those who had been following global political developments since the turn of the century. Politically and militarily, America had already challenged European hegemony in 1898 with its lightning-quick victory over Spain. But as its relatively small volunteer army attested, the military was only an ancillary part of America's real power. Its position resembled that of Great Britain a century earlier. Both countries relied far less on their armed forces than on their capacity for economic and technological innovation.

Just as the English monopoly on industry proceeded from the first Industrial Revolution, the United States's world dominance after 1900 was based very much on the second.

In these years, the European image of America was rapidly transformed from one of Indians, woodsmen, primeval forests, and empty spaces that sheltered the outcasts of the Old World into a new iconography of skyscrapers, automobile traffic, slaughterhouses, refrigerators, gramophones, telephones, sewing machines, vacuum cleaners, and conveyor belts spewing out thousands of such products a day, even an hour, with millionaire entrepreneurs guiding and directing it all. While books like *The Leatherstocking Tales* and *Moby-Dick* were cherished for their nostalgic view of an old America, the industrial novels of Upton Sinclair exerted a far stronger influence over Europeans and were more widely read. Books and articles by European authors about the brand-new New World were also consumed voraciously, though their titles left no doubt about the perceived threat. (Typical examples included *American Energy, The American Challenge, American World Power, American Danger*, and *The American Future*.)[141] Finally, as the neologisms *Americanization* and *Americanism* began to enter daily speech, the word *America* ceased to refer simply to a place but increasingly took on negative connotations: materialistic, nouveau riche, uncultivated, tasteless, and lacking in proportion.[142]

European cultural critics barely scratched the surface of the new image of America, adding little to what Tocqueville had written nearly a century before. European economists, entrepreneurs, and engineers, however, made more progress toward identifying the methods they suspected had facilitated America's sudden leap to prominence. These methods, known collectively as "scientific management" or "Taylorism," grew out of a theory of industrial rationalization developed by Frederick W. Taylor. The fascination Taylor exerted is difficult to overestimate. To call him, as one historian does, the Darwin of work organization whose historic achievement was to "separate thought and work" is to sum up only half of his influence.[143] In fact, Taylor reconceived all aspects of the production process—work, machines, materials, and organization—as part of a production flow, or, as it soon became known, the assembly line. Once this transformation had been achieved, industrial efficiency and "productivity" grew beyond the wildest dreams of economists and technicians alike.

Europeans first became aware of the specter of American mass production around 1900, and the three leading European nations responded in very different fashion. England had the easiest time adjusting to the new economic power relations. The old English antipathies toward America had long since given way to solidarity with their Anglo-Saxon cousins against Germans, Latins, and Slavs. The idea of England as the brain and will—and America as the workbench—of this new alliance was seductive indeed. For France, preoccupied with the direct German threat, developments in America were of secondary importance. If anything, growing American power was viewed less as a challenge to France than as a force that could be harnessed for the struggle against Germany.[144] Not surprisingly, the titles of French books about Germany resembled the titles of German books about America: *German Force, The German Menace, The German Danger, German Imperialism, German Expansion.*[145] And ultimately France had no reason to fear America, given the high regard in which prominent Americans from Wall Street to Harvard Square held the French intellect, culture, and way of life and how little they thought of the new Germany.

German reactions to America's economic ascendency, by contrast, were a mixture of dismay and active interest. Germany's cultural arrogance was no greater or less than that of the English or French; indeed, according to the German idea of *Kultur,* all three Western powers represented mere *Zivilisation,* and any distinctions between the two sides of the Atlantic were merely ones of degree. Nonetheless, Germans felt a special bond with America, one that differed markedly from the conceptions maintained by the English and French. First, the percentage of the American population of German origin was second only to that of English descent, providing the demographic basis for the German fantasy, nurtured since the 1890s, of outmaneuvering the competitor England in the New World.[146] Second, there were numerous affinities from recent history: at almost the exact same moment that the Union fought the Civil War, Prussia had unified the German nation in its war against Austria.[147] Prussia had openly supported the North, unlike England and France, both of which sympathized with the South. Carl Schurz—an immigrant who became a distinguished Union general, statesman, and publisher in his adoptive homeland—was something of a German Lafayette. Third, the United States and Germany had made their entry into the elite circle of industrial nations, global traders, and world politics at roughly the same point in history. They were both "young, energetic firms," one contemporary wrote, "who still had to fight for their place" against the "two old trading companies [England and France], whose operations have gradually fallen behind the times."[148]

Germany's feelings of affinity were offset, as in any other fraternal relationship, by the drive to compete and distinguish itself. The competitive urge was expressed in the view that Taylor's work was essentially not American but German. In a 1914 essay, "German Lessons from America," Wichard von Moellendorff, a distinguished engineer, approvingly dubbed Taylorism "the militarism of production."[149] And while Germans saw the American skyscraper as a technological achievement, they thought that the form only achieved cultural perfection in their very own *Turmhaus* (tower house).[150] German pretentions thus differed from those in England and France in being focused not exclusively on high culture but also on what was most American about America. While England and France were wisely content to be the model for and the supplier of high and luxury culture (art, literature, fashion, and tradition), Germany presented itself as a brash challenger in the quintessentially American areas of technological and industrial culture. This could hardly fail to have consequences for German-American relations as well as for Germans' self-image. Starting around 1900, their self-perception oscillated between the two poles of "American technology" and "German culture" without ever yielding the desired synthesis, "German technological culture." Even before its manifest Americanization in the 1920s, Berlin had been considered the most American of European metropolises. The accelerated tempo of life there, its advanced electrical system, its urban rail network, and its pneumatic postal system, as well as other technological achievements, were only part of the story. What struck European visitors as American about "Parvenupolis" and "Prussian Chicago" was the absence of proportion, the tastelessness, and the "lack of style as a style."[151] Berlin boasted the first imitations of American popular culture on European soil, like the massive Rheingold restaurant, in whose half-neo-Gothic, half-Oriental main hall more than four thousand customers could dine simultaneously at rock-bottom prices. American visitors who found Paris and London alienatingly old-fashioned felt right at home in Berlin.[152]

Berlin's conspicuous Americanism—indeed the entire style of imperial Germany, which was perceived as scarcely less vulgar—was treated as an embarrassment by pre-1914 German cultural criticism. Still, few people would have seriously advocated rigid adherence to tradition or a return to the sleepy world condition that existed before the empire. Men like Max Weber, Walther Rathenau, Friedrich Naumann, and Paul Rohrbach saw no alternative to the path Germany had chosen toward becoming a modern industrial world power, though all suspected that the venerated German cultural soul was going to have to pay a price for it. A discussion thus began—and continues to this day—as to whether and how culture should be defended against technological and economic modernization or preserved through integration into such a process.[153]

AS LOUDLY AS the United States had announced itself to turn-of-the-century Europe, its tremors were still distant enough to be fully registered only by a relatively small group of specialists. Public

opinion and politics were still tuned exclusively to European fre-
quencies, and even places like Berlin were perceived by the rest of
Europe less as a transatlantic threat than as a more acute, specifically
German one. Until 1917, the American phenomenon was seen only
in outline, as if through a translucent veil. By 1918, however, the
veil had dropped and with it all concealment. America did not just
become visible in the 1920s; it positively swamped the European
viewing audience with a wave of products, investments, tourists,
fashion, jazz, flappers, and movies—all the exports of American mass
culture. Hardly had the European public awakened from the night-
mare of the Great War than it sought refuge in the American dream
factory. It seemed as if America was soaking up all the moral and
hedonistic energies unleashed by the war; whatever was left over was
absorbed by the socialist utopia of Russia.

The one arena that remained untouched by these changes was
foreign policy. Encouraged by the United States's withdrawal into
isolationism, Europe resumed control of its own affairs. A replay of
the prewar era followed, as attempts to integrate Germany into
Europe were met with Germany's attempts to control Europe. Ultimately, of course, the United States would reintervene on behalf of
Europe and against Germany. But in the meantime, Germany's relationship with the new economic giant across the Atlantic continued
to evolve in a number of unexpected ways.

The Elevation of the Economy

That the First World War had been not a familiar sort of military
conflict but something entirely new quickly became apparent to the
participants and was expressed in neologisms like *matériel battles* and
human matériel. From there, it was a short step to the realization
that wars were no longer being fought solely by the armed forces
but also by the nations that stood behind them. That, however, was
the extent of the insight. Military and political leaders lacked suffi-

cient capacity for abstraction to go one step further and see that warfare had become the reciprocal "consumption" of both sides' total resources, material and human. The art of military strategy, which was based entirely on mobility, had been made obsolete by the new industrial realities of the First World War.

After being locked in trench warfare in the autumn of 1914, military commanders on both sides sought to regain their freedom of movement. They attained it only in 1918, in the last phase of the war, through the tactical innovation of shock troops. The strength of shock troops lay not in mass but in speed and mobility, and their goal was not only to eradicate but to surprise and demoralize the enemy. Along with their mechanical equivalents, the tank and the warplane, shock troops could penetrate systems of defense that, designed to ward off massive frontal attacks, were as helpless against sudden rapid maneuvers as a factory is against an act of sabotage. In light of the subsequent history of the shock troops, the comparison with sabotage appears apt. Both forms in which the shock-troop concept lived on after 1918—as a synonym for troops of thugs within the Fascist movements and as part of Germany's blitzkrieg strategy at the beginning of World War II—were deliberate attempts to sabotage the workings of highly organized societies and their defensive systems.[154]

While the military may have taken until 1918 to understand the new quality of industrialized warfare and develop appropriate counterstrategies, the economy was much quicker to make the transition. In all the countries involved in the world war, but particularly in Germany, the civilian economy was coordinated with the military or indeed fully militarized. The mobilization of the German economy, which had been carried out in 1916 as part of the Hindenburg Program, did not just subordinate the civilian sector to the war effort but rather melded domestic production and the military. As the economy reoriented itself to meet military requirements, the army had to tailor its demands to conform to the specific capabilities of

German industrial plants. As historian Michael Geyer writes, "The Supreme Command began to approach operations in terms of 'tasks' and available 'resources.' . . . Battle plans were drawn up accordingly, stressing the capabilities of the assembled weaponry rather than specific principles of strategy. . . . Technical and instrumental rationality replaced the remnants of a holistic approach to the conduct of war. Operational planning and strategy became a matter of the management of arms."[155] "War socialism," as this phenomenon was called, was the economic equivalent of the *Volksgemeinschaft*; the entrepreneur and the warrior, who previously had little in common or were in fact enemies, merged into a new type of engineer and manager. For both sides there were costs in this merger, but for the military they were steeper. What the military lost in heroic stature, the economy gained as a reward for its role in the nation's defense.

War was the great furnace that forged the military and civilian economy into a single new whole, but it only heated up and hastened a fusion that had already begun. Frederick Taylor and his idea of scientific management had already captivated the imaginations of turn-of-the-century engineers and entrepreneurs. Now, largely unnoticed by the public, a new perspective opened on the future of the industrial system, one that would seriously compete with the Marxist idea of inevitable revolution. In essence, scientific management aimed to replace the industrial entrepreneur with the technocrat, or in Marxist terms, the owner with the manager. Taylor's prewar adherents had not gone that far, but they did see themselves as a third force between capital and labor, one superior to both in that it represented not class interests but the objectivity of technology itself. Since the state also understood itself as such a third force, an instant affinity developed with the Taylorists. Before the war, a number of thinkers had argued for making technology, like the military, an instrument of the state instead of leaving it in the control of capitalist entrepreneurs. Men like Thorstein Veblen and Charles Steinmetz in the United States and Walther Rathenau and Wichard von Moellendorff in Germany wanted to see technology and industry liberated from the commercial entrepreneur and handed over to engineers, managers, and planners. The world war had made this dream possible, if only for a short time. The question was, what would come next?

The Surrogate Army

At the end of World War I, the victorious nations treated the return to a peacetime economy as a matter of course that no one questioned—not even the organizers of the war effort, who were now out of a job. But in Germany the situation was entirely different. There the Treaty of Versailles was perceived not as a cessation but as a continuation of the conditions of wartime, which differed from the war itself only in the sense that the demilitarized German empire was now a passive object in international politics. But was Germany really powerless? Since the German war machine had relied in equal parts on the military and the economy, the removal of the military component still left the economic arm intact. And since the postwar goal of the Allies—to extract reparations—could be fulfilled only by expanding Germany's manufacturing base, its economic leaders were put in a position not unlike that of the military high command. For those German politicians who had always viewed the war as an essentially economic endeavor, there was no doubt that German economic might could now be directly brought to bear. Foreign Minister Gustav Stresemann, for instance, called the economy "the strongest basis of current German power" and advocated its strategic deployment "to determine foreign policy along the lines of the one area in which we are still a major force."[156] In so doing, Stresemann demonstrated greater insight into the possibilities for economic Realpolitik than the traditional politicians either on the German right or among the Allied victors.

Suffice it to say that the reparations, which were conceived as an act of retaliation, yielded results quite different from those expected by the statesmen of Versailles, who were ignorant of several key economic principles. John Maynard Keynes, in his *Economic Consequences of the Peace*, warned the Allied camp—to no effect—that reparation payments in a modern global economy represented a gift of dubious value to their recipients and a potential economic boon to their supplier. Among the nations involved in the First World War, Germany was alone in experiencing an economic upswing in 1919–21 rather than a demobilization recession. This achievement was registered abroad with surprise and envy.[157] Since the German mark was no less stable during the first three postwar years than any other currency and since no one anticipated the devaluation and hyperinflation that would commence in 1922, the general picture of Germany abroad was that of an economic superpower beyond all competition. However one views the subsequent fall and then free fall of the mark—as a carefully staged plan or a snowballing catastrophe—the behavior of German economic planners bore an uncanny resemblance to that of the military strategists during the war. Ludendorff had been called a "gambler" whose only strategy consisted of an all-or-nothing insistence on absolute victory.[158] So too German policies on inflation were described as a "casino gamble" in which "Germany's political and economic leadership placed all their bets on one card—that England and America would intervene to save the day and that France would ruin itself in its attempts to enforce its demands."[159]

During the war, the traditional military strategy of inflicting maximum damage on the enemy with a minimum of risk had been reversed: with no consideration for one's losses, war became a matter of bleeding the enemy dry. Just as Germany's military high command primed the blood pump at Verdun in 1916, so its postwar political leaders pumped out bank notes in the hope that the resulting economic destabilization would pose a threat to the Allies as well and force them to relent.[160] There was an undeniable measure of gamesmanship in this strategy. But that had also been true of that quintessential German military strategy the Schlieffen Plan, which advocated bold flanking maneuvers to attack the enemy from behind. The plan, named after a former army chief of the general staff, was theoretically unimpeachable but militarily equivalent to betting on a single card. Could it be that the culture that considered itself the most highly organized, rational, and disciplined in Europe had a secret weakness, an Achilles' heel or a Siegfried's back, for taking enormous gambles?

Gustav Stresemann—the man who presided over Germany's stabilization in the mid-1920s—regarded the economy from the start as a surrogate army to be mobilized in 1919 for the cold war over reparations. But monetary policy was only half of the arsenal. The other half was technology, and the technocrats who volunteered their services did so with an enthusiasm comparable to that of the willing soldiers of 1914. Such economic patriotism was a consequence of the new confidence perceptible among the technocratic intelligentsia since the turn of the century. Members of this new elite considered themselves uniquely capable not just of reducing the unproductive friction of class conflict and of raising productivity but also of remaking the whole of society. This self-conception had been bolstered by their vital role in conducting what Lloyd George trenchantly called an "engineers' war." Predictably, then, the technocrats, mirroring the military, rejected any responsibility for defeat and developed a stab-in-the-back legend of their own.[161] "Wherever the engineer took an active part in defending the fatherland," editorialized their trade magazine,

> tried and tested technological procedures were blocked by the military leadership. . . . The German engineer may not be able to claim that we would have won the war without this interference, but he can say that, had the military high command truly recognized the importance of technology and been willing to admit its ignorance in technological and economic affairs, it would have listened far more carefully to the engineers. Then, the engineers could have determined, independently and reliably, what feats technology was

capable of achieving. . . . We have lost militarily but we have not been technologically defeated, since the German military forced German technology to fight with one arm tied behind its back.[162]

The engineers' reference to the American army and "its utilization of specialists in the proper areas" as a brilliant counterexample was part of this worldview, which also saw the rediscovery of Frederick W. Taylor.[163]

The war had not interrupted the spread of scientific management in Germany. On the contrary, methods that had previously been applied at individual firms or in particular industries were extended to the nation as a whole. The state-issued decrees simplifying labor regulations led to the creation of the DIN system, which set uniform standards for all of Germany's industries. Industrial sites, transportation links, and the allocation of raw materials were centrally coordinated so that decisions were made no longer by individual entrepreneurs but by high-level state or state-controlled agencies called "war collectives," which were divided up according to industry and assigned to the corresponding departments of the Ministry of Economics. In fact, the Ministry of Economics itself was founded during the war; economic matters had previously been dealt with by a branch of the Ministry of the Interior.

The earliest and probably most significant of the offices within the new ministry was the Department of Raw Materials. Germany's prewar military and political leaders had not foreseen the possibility of an Allied blockade threatening the supply of raw materials to the German armaments industry. The department, whose founding in August 1914 is usually credited to Walther Rathenau, was in fact the brainchild of his former employee at the electrical firm AEG Wichard von Moellendorff. A devout adherent of Frederick Taylor and scientific management, which he called a "German export from America," Moellendorff had continued to play a leading role in building the wartime economy. It was he who drafted the Hindenburg Program in 1916 (in a form that called for far more direction from the state than the one actually adopted).[164] And it was he who, within the Ministry of Economics, began to examine the problem of how to run the economy after a peace treaty had been concluded.

The war gave a great boost to the technocrats' sense of themselves as leaders and organizers of the nation: Moellendorff and others like him rose to senior positions in the newly created ministries, offices, departments, and staffs of the war economy, where they were free to do as they pleased. Largely unconstrained by the military leadership, which was interested solely in receiving armament shipments in full and on time, the technocrats enjoyed the sort of organizational independence from capital they could only have dreamt of before the war.

It is no surprise, then, that the idea of a postwar return to dependence on the whims of entrepreneurs did not appeal to them and strengthened their desire to see the exigencies of war prevail in peacetime. This desire furthered their own interest, although they were the last to recognize that fact. Like Johann Plenge, they understood war socialism as the economic manifestation of the *Volksgemeinschaft*. And since the *Volksgemeinschaft* was imagined as not just a temporary truce between hostile classes but a lasting achievement of the nation, it followed that the fundamentally altered, "socialized" economy of wartime would continue on after the end of hostilities. During his tenure in the Ministry of Economics, Moellendorff developed a program for a "social economy"—in essence, the continuation of war socialism in peacetime. His plan, as Moellendorff never tired of repeating, was not socialism in the Marxist or Social Democratic sense ("socialism of class interest") but a national socialism of the sort advocated before 1914 by Friedrich Naumann and his disciple Paul Rohrbach, which, having been exalted by the August experience, was now embraced by the bourgeois middle class under various names—"German," "Prussian," or "military" socialism—as the only original, pure form. In this way, the technocratic engineers, organizers, and managers took the leadership role for a new middle class that was defined no longer economically but universalistically. And they were as exemplary in that role as the academic mandarins had been for the old middle class.

As he was developing his ideas, Moellendorff assumed that Germany would win World War I. Germany's defeat was for him one more reason to retain the wartime economy, or rather to extend it into a "social" one. Since peacetime did not bring a return to normality but instead a continuation of the struggle—an economic cold war aimed at winning the victory in the marketplace that had eluded Germany on the battlefield—the national economy could not be demobilized. On the contrary, it was all the more necessary that the economy fulfill its function as an "instrument of peaceful national liberation."[165] Moellendorff's definition of Taylorism as "the militarism of production" echoes that belief, as does his characterization of the social economy as a "new national vow of brotherhood." The idea that national solidarity and technological and economic optimization were mutually reinforcing was expressed by Moellendorff in 1919. The social economy, he said, was the "form of economy in which awareness of the nation's impoverishment following the lost war unites all individual economic actors in the firm commitment to *rebuild the nation as quickly as possible without wasting strength and resources.*"[166] The losses that needed to be addressed were reparations and the ceded territories, with their plentiful raw materials. Only the social economy could make up for these shortfalls since only it— like its predecessor, the wartime economy—was capable of applying Taylor's scientific management on a national scale, thereby decisively raising productivity. In other words, social economy and Taylorism were one and the same thing: socialized Taylorism and Taylorized socialism. Once profits were redirected from entrepreneurs to the nation, Taylorism was relieved of the stigma it bore before the war as a mere means for maximizing capitalist exploitation. Gustav Winter, the most widely read post-1918 popularizer of Taylorism, compared its potential to the achievements of the wartime economy: "Just as during the war we Germans extracted precious ammonia from the atmosphere, we will now manufacture the equivalent of billions [needed for reparations] out of thin air."[167] Since the term "equivalent of billions" was used from 1918 to 1923 almost exclusively in the context of reparations payments and currency devaluation—with the former assumed to have caused the latter—increases in productivity seemed to be the only effective means of offsetting inflation. Winter even demanded that Taylorism be written into law to guarantee that productivity would rise sufficiently to combat the effects of currency devaluation.[168]

The promotion of Taylorism as the national dogma of recovery and salvation was not an exclusively German phenomenon. In France and England, the critical year of 1917 saw similar proposals. These, however, disappeared immediately after the Allied victory.[169] Only in Italy and Russia, the two other nonwinners, did Taylorism exert a postwar influence comparable in duration and intensity to that in Germany—hence Mussolini's enthusiasm for America and Lenin's pronouncement on scientific management stating that the young Soviet republic had to "adopt at any price everything valuable that science and technology have achieved in this area."[170]

The First Shift: From Taylorism to Fordism

The concept of social economy may have been a salvation theology for the technocrats, but for the public at large it had little resonance. After Germany's collapse, the masses could no longer be won over for grand ideological projects, whether conceived as national or universal. Walther Rathenau learned this firsthand in October 1918 with his call for a popular uprising, as did the Spartacists in January 1919 with their attempted Communist revolution. The drive for a social economy according to the principles of Taylorism also failed to attract mass support because it was too reminiscent of calls for folk community, which had been discredited by four years of war, and brought back memories of wartime privation as well as the negative image of Taylor as the Dr.

Frankenstein of human labor. The "military aroma" of all planned economies blocked any enthusiasm for this one.[171]

It quickly became apparent that the idea of social economy never had much of a chance in the postwar economic reality. A few days after Germany's collapse, representatives of labor and business agreed on a compromise addressing both of their interests: higher wages and shorter working hours in return for the preservation of private property. Moreover, both agreed that the state should not interfere in economic affairs. With Moellendorff's departure in 1919 from the Ministry of Economics, the social economy disappeared from the political agenda and returned to the obscure circles of the technocratic intelligentsia, where the reasons for its failure were discussed with great passion and not a small amount of pathos until the hyperinflation of 1923 challenged its relevance even there.

In 1924, after the imposition of currency reform, the unfolding drama of Weimar Germany began a new act entitled "Stabilization." In it, the roles of the social economy and Taylorism—both unpopular with the audience—were scrapped, replaced by a new part that effectively promised to deliver everything the other two, despite their best attempts, had failed to do. This new character was named after the American engineer and auto manufacturer Henry Ford.

FRANZ WESTERMANN, A German engineer traveling through the United States in 1926, recorded his impressions of a memorable visit to Highland Park (Detroit) and River Rouge: "I have long gone through life with perceptive eyes, a thinking soul, and an open heart," he wrote, "enthusiastic about everything beautiful, be it nature, art, sport, or productivity. Nonetheless, my most powerful experience was a visit to the Ford works, that gigantic production facility . . . which not only impresses the eyes by its size and the manner of its technical construction, but whose living spirit is palpably present to such a degree that it simply draws people into its orbit."[172]

The change in German mentality between late 1923 and early 1924 could not have been more dramatic. Whereas Frederick Taylor had been known as a technological revolutionary since the turn of the century, the name of the man who had actually revolutionized the automobile industry remained obscure. In late 1922, almost a decade after assembly-line production of the Model T had begun, the *Berliner Illustrirte Zeitung* introduced Ford to its readership under the headline "Curiosities from America." He was described as a kind of charlatan: "A relatively uneducated man full of futile, harebrained ideas for world salvation," the article read, "a personality not . . . to be compared to the old capitalist barons Morgan, Vanderbilt, etc., . . . a 'loudmouth' who supposedly produces 2,000 of his automobiles a day."[173] In the technical journals, Henry Ford was not even the object of scorn. His name simply did not appear before 1924.

What happened next is history. The German edition of Ford's autobiography was published in November 1923, at the very moment the German mark was stabilized. The book became an overnight best-seller, and Ford himself in the following decades became the messiah of the new religion of mass production. Ford's message was twofold: exploitation, the moral and physical burden that had plagued industry since its inception, had to be removed; and the division of industrial life into two halves, production and consumption, work and leisure, had to be eradicated. Fordism transformed industry into a gigantic wish-fulfillment machine, with the conveyor belt uniting production and consumption, work and leisure into a single system of circulation. The workers who staffed it were to be paid well enough to become viable consumers, thereby permitting the manufacture of goods in yet greater numbers and at lower prices. This, in turn, would stimulate production, further increasing purchasing power, consumption, and hence production in an ascending spiral. *Service*, Ford's term for the entire process, was a system that united employee, entrepreneur, and consumer, supposedly rendering the concept of exploitation obsolete. It represented socialization without socialism—or "white socialism," as Fordism was also known.

German engineers and journalists saw Ford's factories not as halls of industry but as a natural attraction, a great river of production from which workers, like the fisherman and poet in Karl Marx's utopian vision of perfect socialism, could extract profit and amusement in equal measure. The engineer Friedrich von Gottl-Ottlilienfeld characterized the assembly-line worker as someone who, "when he looks up- or downstream from his post, receives a vivid impression of how his rationally limited role contributes to a mighty total work."[174] Metaphors of games, sports, and dances were as popular as comparisons to nature. "The workers walk alongside their work, often backwards," wrote one Ford admirer. "The impression is almost one of sports, like the 'legwork' of a boxer."[175]

The essence and the appeal of Fordism for the zeitgeist of the 1920s represented a "synthesis," that is, the opposite of everything that made Taylor both famous and notorious. Whereas Taylorism broke down "organic" labor into its smallest units and relentlessly reduced the worker to a cog in the machine, Fordism appeared to be the great unifier. The assembly line, as Gottl-Ottlilienfeld and others described it, had restored the old unity of labor, indeed raised it to a higher level. It remains one of the great psychological ironies of the stabilization period that Ford, who essentially just took Taylor's principles to their logical extension, became a canonical figure, while Taylor sank into obscurity. Even Taylor's adherents among the technocratic intelligentsia either fell into resigned silence—like Moellendorff—or renounced their allegiance and transferred their loyalties to the new star. As long as the infatuation lasted, those few critics who pointed out that Fordism was hardly more than Taylorism with a conveyor belt found no audience. One critic attributed Ford's success to the promises of contentment that accompanied the production and distribution process. According to him, Henry Ford's main innovation was "not a Detroit factory of cars, but a Detroit factory of souls."[176]

Fordian promises of contentment were, however, more than mere advertising; they were part of that novel phenomenon propaganda. Just as propaganda had been directed toward the war effort, it was now turned back on the economy, enriched by the psychological insights gained in the war. Hopes for salvation were shifted from the nation to the economy, which was now the provider of dream-fulfilling, labor-saving appliances—above all else, the Ford automobile. Since propaganda can only awaken in its audience thoughts that are already present in some form, the question arises: What was the source of the quasi-religious readiness and faith, so astonishing in hindsight, with which both the general public and small circles of technocrats in Germany embraced Fordism?

The Dance Floor of Inflation and the Girl Machine

Times of crisis often witness eruptions of dance fever. As the dance epidemics of the late Middle Ages make clear, a threat to one's existence can produce an obsessive enjoyment of life. Contemporary accounts of postwar Berlin repeatedly mention an ostensibly pathological "dance mania," "dance craze," and "dance epidemic." The French author of one article, entitled "Berlin Amuses Itself," noted with disbelief that even the invitation to a memorial service for the murdered Spartacist leader Karl Liebknecht stated that there would be dancing.[177] During the Spartacist uprising of 1919, Ernst Troeltsch thought it worth remarking that "the theaters are open as always and attracting their usual public, who dodge bullets along the way. . . . Wherever possible, people go *dancing.*"[178]

The dance phenomenon is usually explained as a cathartic release of drives that have been repressed during war. If so, the German dance mania represents part of a more general erotic explosion, including everything from prostitution to free love to new women's fashions that bared the leg and shoulders, as well as substitutes like gambling or taking drugs. Perhaps dancing's appeal can be explained by the fact that it occupied a middle position in the sliding scale of sexual sublimation. But the decisive reason for its popularity in Weimar Germany was its break with the past: the only feature the popular dances of Weimar shared with the prewar variety was the necessity for a partner. Otherwise postwar dance was emphatically an American import. Dances were no longer based on prescribed steps and precisely circumscribed movements of the legs, arms, and upper body. Instead, popular favorites like the jazz and the shimmy set the body stamping, swinging, and swaying to a new rhythm, transferring the center of motor activity from the legs to the hips, the waist, and the shoulders. From there, the movements took over the whole body and then the mind—a state experienced as a form of intoxication. People spoke of musical groups "getting you drunk without alcohol" and inducing a trancelike sensation. "It's a great feeling to abandon yourself to the rhythm, having turned off the rational mind and the will," one observer recalled, "as though after a night of staying awake you're finally allowed to fall asleep."[179]

There was no doubt that the "sleepless night" referred to the old regime. The political significance of the jazz and the shimmy was to eradicate "any hint of dignity, correct bearing, trimness, and starched collars." As one wag remarked, "If the kaiser had jazz-danced, none of this [war and defeat] would ever have happened."[180] Jazz dances were "the revolution, the expressionism, the Bolshevism of the ballroom."[181] Ever since the ascendance of the waltz after the French Revolution, new popular dance styles had been recognized as the symbolic lifting of old constraints, which were danced off, danced out, and danced to death. The ecstatic jazz dances of the 1920s were, as one contemporary observed, "a reaction against troops marching in straight lines, against the military itself. The fact that the rows of soldiers consisted exclusively of men dictated the response of couples doing jazz dances: man and woman, released from the straight line, moved in circles. The straight line was directed toward battle and death, the circle toward love and procreation."[182]

Weimar critic Siegfried Kracauer saw more than just eroticism in the jazz dances of the early postwar years. Jazz, by which Kracauer meant the music as much as the dancing, was "the present tense and nothing else. A present that had turned its back on the war and was concerned only with itself. . . . The feeling of life it exuded was one of unencumbered physicality. The fact that it affirmed the moment, had no tradition, and was without any consequence explains its ascendance. It was only fair that, since jazz had freed the world from the curse of time and consciousness, the world should deliver itself up to jazz unconsciously and without limitation."[183]

SIMILAR TRANSFORMATIVE DEVELOPMENTS were occurring in society at large. Emil Lederer, an economist and disciple of Max Weber's, described the economic equivalent of the erotic freedom immediately after the end of the war: "If consumers had up to this point restrained themselves somewhat, recalling the earlier value of money and saving what they could . . . so as to invest wisely after the happy conclusion to the war, consumer excess now knew no bounds."[184] These lines were written in 1920, as the devaluation of the mark was still proceeding at the tempo of a slow fox trot. Since inflation was accompanied by an economic upswing, full employment, and an availability of products unknown since 1914, its catastrophic potential went unrecognized. On the contrary, people perceived the movement of inflation as lively and stimulating, like a long flirtation with occasional, not unpleasant feelings of giddiness. Indeed, the years 1919–22 can be seen as an economic "dreamland" following the political one that lasted from November 1918 to May 1919. It was only after this cheerful swinging motion had turned into a free fall that people wakened to the trauma of hyperinflation.

The historian Jürgen von Kruedener points out that, in the public mind, the military collapse of 1918 and the complete devaluation of the German mark in 1923 blended into a single trauma of defeat and that the currency catastrophe was ultimately more responsible for the depth of the trauma than the military debacle.[185] In many ways, the economic buoyancy of 1919–21 was reminiscent of the military and political euphoria after the signing of the Brest-Litovsk treaty and before the beginning of the spring offensive of 1918. Both times, Germans were confronted with the spectacle of what they saw as reality—military victory, the blossoming economy—dissolving into thin air. The analogy can be taken still further since in neither case was the demise physically apparent, as it was on the battlefields of Flanders and northern France; rather, they both left German society eerily intact. With no perceptible ruins or physical wounds to make the trauma concrete, the German perception of reality itself became unbalanced. Vertigo became the dominant sensation of and metaphor for the period of hyperinflation. In 1921, Heinrich Mann, noting the profusion of fairgrounds and cheap cafés popping up in the center of Berlin, spoke of a "compulsive desire for vertiginous intoxication." In 1939, Sebastian Haffner, looking back on the hyperinflation of 1923, wrote: "An entire German generation had a spiritual organ removed: an organ that gives human beings constancy, balance, even gravity, and that expresses itself, depending on the individual, as conscience, reason, the wisdom of experience, fidelity to principles, morality, and piety. A whole generation back then learned, or at least thought it had learned, how to live without any ballast."[186]

Vertigo results from the loss of equilibrium. Affecting the body and the mind in equal measure, it makes the individual stagger and sway without direction or orientation, and leaves him or her incapable of maneuvering, passive. But the German word for vertigo, *Schwindel*, has a second, no less important meaning: swindle. People who discover that they have been swindled lose trust in the ground beneath their feet. The two great swindles in this sense were the call for an armistice in October 1918 and the hyperinflation of November 1923, and in both instances the confidence man was the state itself.[187] If this bastion of reliability and security could no longer be trusted, an abyss of amorality opened up, as was evident in the lyrics to a hit song during the period of hyperinflation: "We'll drink poor

Grandma out of her tiny house." The thesis that inflation was the source of the nihilism that led directly to National Socialism seems quite plausible here. Elias Canetti, for instance, writes:

> In its treatment of the Jews National Socialism repeated the process of inflation with great precision. First they were attacked as wicked and dangerous, as enemies; then they were more and more depreciated; then, there not being enough in Germany itself, those in the conquered territories were gathered in; and finally they were treated literally as vermin, to be destroyed with impunity by the million. The world is still horrified and shaken by the fact that the Germans could go so far; that they either participated in a crime of such magnitude, or connived at it, or ignored it. It might not have been possible to get them to do so if, a few years before, they had not been through an inflation during which the Mark fell to a billionth of its former value. It was this inflation, as a crowd experience, which they shifted on to the Jews.[188]

In the light of *Schwindel*'s dual meaning, German postwar dance mania takes on an added dimension. The dance craze may have served not only to discharge frustrated erotic desire but also to act out the vertigo that the various collapses had produced in society. The jazz and the shimmy reproduced this seemingly infinite dizziness, articulating and absorbing it in cultural form. The vertigo that seized society from 1919 to 1923 was simply "danced off" and "danced out," much as the stresses of revolutionary, inflationary Paris had been waltzed away in the 1790s.[189] The dance epidemic represented both pathology and therapy in one.[190]

Weimar Germany's embrace of an American-style economy after 1924 can thus be seen as a desire for stability after an exhilarating but perilous roller-coaster ride. Many historians of the Weimar Republic note that the stabilization of the currency in 1924 was accompanied by an equally abrupt turnaround in cultural mentality. Up until 1923, expressionism had set the aesthetic tone; as of 1924, the New Objectivity, which prided itself on clinical sobriety, assumed that role. A similar shift can be observed in dance fashions. The erotically charged dances for couples did not disappear—indeed their popularity increased—but they were no longer seen as a manifestation of the zeitgeist. Another dance genre took their place: the show dancing of "troops" of young female dancers, known in Germany as *Girls*. This genre was distinguished by the near-military discipline and precision of the *Girls*, who performed as a single rhythmic body, or, as they were often described by contemporaries, as a "dance machine." The military associations, which were already present in the *Girl* troops' historical predecessor, the variety or operetta revue, were now both underscored (with coordinated movements, costume uniforms, and boots) and ironically undercut (with an erotic minimum of clothing, and bare legs and shoulders). In this respect, the show dancing of the *Girl* troops—like the fox trot, the jazz, and the shimmy, represented a release from and a dancing off of the military order of the war years. At the same time, though, it also entailed a physical reimposition of discipline on a world that had fallen apart because of inflation. Inflation, after all, was often pictorially represented as a pernicious femininity, unloosed from all restraints, that stirred up and broke down patriarchal, ordered value relations in a "witches' dance" or "witches' Sabbath."[191]

Contemporary cultural critics, however, identified yet another aspect of the "girl machine." "From the *Girls*," wrote industrial psychologist Fritz Giese, "we learn the value of mass conformity, the idea of the elevated average, in contrast to exaggerated eccentricity, which perhaps individualizes the individual to an extent he cannot bear."[192] Giese, the author of the book *Girlkultur*, published in 1925, was among the most thoughtful adherents of Fordian standardization and mass production, and understood the psychological and cultural reeducation that those phenomena required.[193] For Giese, the appeal of the *Girl* troops, whose very name evoked America, was the same as that of the workers "dancing" along Ford's assembly lines. In contrast to their strained and cramped European colleagues, who followed an externally imposed regimen, the *Girls* moved to their own rhythms since their "collective soul spirit" (Giese's term) recognized no distinction between the individual, the collective, and technology. *Girls* were "dance machines who never lapsed into military drills or zombielike obedience. The guiding thought was not the compulsion to obey but the idea of technology as something automatically collective."[194]

Giese's assertion that the *Girl* performances were "not a show but a production" placed them on the same level as sports, in which effort and pleasure were united, in contrast to work, which lacked such unity (unless it had been Fordized).[195] The assembly line in Ford's factories appeared to many to be effortless, light, playful, dancelike, and athletic, and the entire facility resembled "a symphony, a bacchanal of work, an entirely closed whole, a single otherworldly machine."[196] During the period of stability and prosperity, the dancers in the "girl machine," Giese wrote, were seen to be engaged in "work as a sports achievement" similar to that taking place on the assembly lines.[197] They were the apotheosis of the Fordian promise of salvation. Looking back from the vantage point of the Depression, Siegfried Kracauer had a hallucinatory vision of dancing *Girls* as "the fleshly metaphor for a blossoming economy":

When they formed a line, moving up and down, they provided a glowing depiction of the advantages of the conveyor belt. When they stamped their feet in double time, it sounded like: "Business, business." When they kicked their legs with mathematical precision, they were joyously affirming the progress made by rationalization. And when they repeated the same moves without any break in their ranks, an uninterrupted line of automobiles could be seen gliding from the factories out into the world, and one became convinced that the happy days would never end. Their faces were rouged with an optimism that immediately cut off any opposition to the economic developments, and the squeals of delight that issued from them in carefully calculated intervals praised the glory of this sort of existence always anew.[198]

THE NUMBER OF neologisms created between 1924 and 1929 shows that the *Girl* phenomenon transcended dance and even Fordism. Linguistic creations like "girl culture," "girl idea," "girl problem," "girlification," and "girlism" point to an underlying philosophy or psychology of gender.[199] In the decade following the First World War, the stereotype of the emancipated single young woman became an icon of the international zeitgeist, with France boasting its *garçonne* and Italy its *ragazza*. The use of the English word for the German equivalent seems all the more baffling since women of this type in America were called "flappers," not "girls." The prototypical flapper was a slim woman of about twenty whose clothing deemphasized her feminine curves (no bust, no hips) while exposing her healthy-looking, sporty legs, arms, and shoulders. Her favored hairstyle and headgear was noticeably influenced by the military: short hair and helmetlike hats. Ironically, the original form of the flapper hat was not the flat helmet of the American and British infantry but the rounded one of the German army, which covered most of the head, including the back of the neck and the forehead, leaving only the face free.[200] In her relations with men, the flapper displayed simultaneously an "ostentatiously sexless camaraderie" and an unromantic sexuality.[201] The androgynous look of the flappers paraded the gender-equalizing role of the war as well as the subsequent leap into modern-day equality of the sexes.

The *Girl* style of the 1920s was a trend in fashion and behavior throughout the West, but only in Germany did it inspire theoretical interpretations. Were *Girlismus* and *Girlisierung* simply inadvertent self-parodies of the German obsession with theorizing, or do they point up an actual instance of German exceptionalism? The most obvious exceptional aspect of post-1918 German relations between the sexes was that the men were not returning from war as victors. The *Girl* phenomenon might thus be read as a gendered version of the stab-in-the-back legend, the aim of which was to enable men to save face. The androgyny of the *Girls* spared men the humiliating prospect of coming back to their women as losers. Nonetheless, losers they were, and while winners can dictate their will, losers must accommodate. German "girlism" of the 1920s was the result of such accommodation, reflecting a shift in power relations in favor of women. At the same time, the blow was softened for men, who could understand the phenomenon as American, not German—in other words, as springing from the victors. Like a consolation prize, the *Girl* took the place of the goddess of victory in the postwar German psyche.[202] In a way, the comfort offered by "girlism" was similar to the downsizing of Germany's prewar aspirations for a place in the sun to the more modest postwar wish to bask in the light of the radiant eye on the back of the American dollar bill. It also called to mind the modification, in the 1920s, of Germany's ambition to be a world power into the more humble longing to make Berlin into a world city.

The World City

German contains more constructions with the word *world* than any other European language.[203] Goethe wrote of "world literature" and Kant of "worldviews." Hegel's "world spirit," Schelling's "world soul," and Fichte's "world will" have become inextricably identified with their creators, while the progenitors of "world plan," "world circle," "world trade," "world transport," "world history," "men of the world," "world citizen," "world power," "world inferno," and even "world war" are lost to history. Goethe was already speaking of a "world city" during his visit to Rome in 1787. Since the beginning of the nineteenth century, "world city" had served to designate great metropolises such as London and Paris. In 1824, for example, the geographer Carl Ritter wrote of Paris: "A world city like this is the artificial product of history, the most artificial fruit that the earth brings forth, the most intricate image of the civilization of a people."[204]

The German usage of the word *world* (*Welt*) contained a certain ambivalence. On the one hand, it referred to the global world opened up in the sixteenth century, in whose conquest and division the old German empire had played no part. On the other hand, it called to mind medieval universalism, which Germany saw itself as embodying. This dual sense was the origin of the inferiority-superiority complex that would make itself particularly evident in relation to what would become the German capital. If a city was capable of embodying universalism, it was Rome or, perhaps for the post-1800 German intelligentsia, Weimar, but certainly not Berlin.

Before 1871, no one would have thought of comparing the Prussian royal residence and garrison site to cities like London or Paris. With the founding of the empire, however, the new capital suddenly found itself in the same company as those European metropolises. Moreover, the decision in 1890 to transform Germany into a world power gave the question of Berlin's status a new urgency, since a global power was unimaginable without a metropolis. Nevertheless, Berlin, as even Wilhelm II remarked in 1896 in connection with plans for a World's Fair there, simply could not compare with London or Paris in historical importance, cosmopolitanism, population, or grandeur. The only option for Germans was therefore to redefine "world city" so that their capital would fit the bill.

That is what they did in the two decades before World War I. A new understanding of the world city evolved whose dimensions and scope were no longer those of London and Paris but of New York and Chicago. Underlying this shift was the conviction that, while the classical European capitals were no doubt grand historical monuments, they were as useless in the modern global economy as gigantic open-air museums. Long before Le Corbusier, who spent the prewar years as an architect in Berlin and coined the phrase *living machine*, Berlin architects, city planners, and transportation managers developed the idea of the world city as a functional construct of the global economy. World cities were those into which the international traffic in goods and money flowed, and the younger and more dynamic they were the more "worldly" they could be considered.

With the Chicago World's Fair of 1893, the promoters of Berlin had a model to follow. Defined as "Chicago on the Spree" (Walther Rathenau, referring to the river that flows through the city), the "clearinghouse of the global German economy" (Martin Mächler), and the "main junction of world trade" (Georg Simmel), Berlin appeared to be a world city in its prime compared with London and Paris, which were of interest only to tourists.[205]

GERMANY'S DEFEAT IN 1918 did not sweep aside Berlin's aspirations but rather reaffirmed them, much as Waterloo validated nineteenth-century Paris as the undisputed mecca of European civilization. The world does not quickly forget a capital that once threatened it and, conversely, that capital develops a hypersensitive, almost paranoid need to promote its own image. This need was abundantly clear in the post-1918 development of Berlin as a technological, functionalist center. Urban planners relentlessly extended the city's reach, establishing, for example, Greater Berlin as the central administrative unit in 1919 and pushing through numerous suburban development and transportation projects during the 1920s. At the same time, the world city ceased to be an exclusively infrastructural idea and began to develop theatrical aspirations. Martin Wagner, the man responsible for city planning in the 1920s, demanded that Berlin's "leading character as a world city" be made visible in an "appearance befitting a world city." This transformation would not occur on its own, he hastened to add: "The world city of Berlin needs a director."[206] In 1929, Wagner declared that the first act in this urban drama would be the completion of Alexanderplatz as a "world city square." Its purpose, however, would be not so much to provide an architectural representation of Berlin's "cosmopolitan spirit" as to embody the city's role as "a crossroads for a whole transportation network."[207] Wagner's vision of Alexanderplatz at once distilled and monumentalized the notion of the world city as a global traffic junction.

Although no director appeared on the scene, there were a score of writers applying themselves to the task of depicting Berlin as a world city. They, too, saw its defining feature as international traffic; they were primarily fascinated, however, not by the carefully directed stream of automobiles and streetcars flowing through the urban machine but by the mass traffic jam, by chaos as the most advanced form of movement. The world city square for the cosmopolitan Berlin feuilleton was Potsdamerplatz, whose chaotic traffic figured in article after article. Even today, devotees of Potsdamerplatz remain convinced that it was, if not the busiest traffic circle in Europe, at least comparable to Piccadilly Circus and the place de l'Opéra, perhaps even to Times Square. Whatever the case, it isn't hard to recognize in the Potsdamerplatz articles of the 1920s the venerable literary trope of metropolitan chaos, which began in seventeenth-century travel reports from Paris and London and had never ceased to remind Germans of their embarrassing backwardness. Germany's pride in the chaos of Potsdamerplatz was a tentative expression of satisfaction at having finally arrived at the point where others had been for nearly two hundred years. The satirist Kurt Tucholsky summed up the new Berlin obsession in perceptively sarcastic fashion: "When you arrive in Berlin, people will come up to you and ask pleadingly: 'Don't you think our traffic is overwhelming?' "[208]

The Second Shift: From Fordism to Rationalization

Historically, the vanquished tend to find self-serving explanations for why following the victor's model is so crucial. In Fordized Germany, the rationale went: "Ford's methodology is nothing more than the reawakening of the Prussian German ethic of service and work."[209] The mere imitation of Fordism, however, was never going to compensate for the inferiority complex Germany bore after being defeated in World War I, in part by America's manifest technological and economic superiority. An intellectual foundation was required that contrasted America's material productivity with Germany's intellectual and cultural power. This was possible only by promoting an economic concept free of American associations.

In theory, Johann Plenge's concept of organization could have been revived for this purpose but, like Taylorism, it was "semantically overburdened," discredited by its link to Germany's defeat.[210] The concept of "rationalization" carried no such burden. In 1908, when Max Weber had used the term as an approximate synonym for "scientific management," it had attracted little interest. Taylor's teachings were enjoying such resonance among the technocratic intelligentsia that no one felt the need for alternatives.[211] It was only after Fordism had transformed the technology debate into a broad popular discussion (relegating Taylorism, as we have seen, to obscurity), that rationalization's time finally came. As social historian Mary Nolan points out, rationalization was attractive because it was a general concept that signified both everything and nothing and because it "could at one and the same time incorporate, transcend, and Germanize various versions of Americanism."[212] Rationalization became the idealistic sum of everything embodied *materially* by Fordism, just as liberty, equality, and fraternity represented for eighteenth-century France the idealistic culmination of the practical right to ply the trade of one's choice.

The definition put forward by the National Board for Economic Efficiency (*Reichskuratorium für Wirtschaftlichkeit*), the main administrative body responsible for rationalization, still resonates with the Fordian promise of happiness as an endless increase in production and pleasure: "Rationalization is the identification and application of all means offered by technology and planned organization for increasing economic competitiveness. Its main goal is an improvement of the standard of living by reductions in the price, increases in the availability, and improvements in the quality of consumer goods."[213] To foreign observers, however, the German rationalization movement of 1925–29 seemed a "popular cult," a "national effort," an "ardor of faith," and an example of "almost apostolic fervor that could be compared in fanatical intensity to nineteenth-century Saint-Simonism and twentieth-century Bolshevism."[214] German commentators dubbed rationalization the "evangelism of the technological-social services"; phrases such as "magic word," "formula for salvation," and "formula for the general good" were widely used.[215] The psychology underlying the term is illustrated by the managerial scientist Eugen Schmalenbach's explanation of its appeal: "After four years of war and five years of inflation—a full decade of economic chaos—the whole world longs for a return to a healthy and orderly economy. And once the feeling 'If only we had a stable, orderly, healthy economy' is present, then the desire for order fosters a certain receptiveness to the word that signifies that order. . . . The word best corresponding to this desire has become the word of salvation."[216]

The promise of salvation extended beyond the economy. Herbert Hinneberg, director of the National Board for Economic Efficiency, argued that rationalization was a "slogan that stands for everything needed to restore *balance*."[217] Economic stabilization was thus characterized as part of an all-encompassing renewal of culture, everyday life, and society. Rationalization contained something of all the ideas about modernization and happiness that were under discussion in the 1920s. Small wonder then that its economic and technological side receded into the background. With only a few exceptions, such as the mining, steel, and chemical industries, the rationalization of the German economy in the 1920s lagged far behind the rhetoric. Even though rationalization was being envisioned and sometimes even initiated in a variety of areas—from sexuality to city planning, from the household to the managerial office, and from public transportation to leisure activities—only 1 percent of industry was actually rationalized along Ford's and Taylor's lines.[218] Robert A. Brady, the author of an influential American study of the German rationalization movement published in 1933, described the tremendous expectations behind what he called the "New Enlightenment" movement: "Rationalized production was to be followed by rationalized distribution, and this by rationalized consumption. Rationalization was somehow to supply the 'efficiency' key to orderly social and individual life; subscription and adherence to its working codes would free the round of productive and leisure activities from lag, leak, and friction, from waste and from the gravamen of social maladjustment to personal contumely."[219]

Up to this point, rationalization's reception in Germany was an overblown response to what was in fact a rather prosaic economic and technological process. In the late 1920s, however, people in France, England, and even the United States also suddenly discarded the terms *Fordism* and *scientific management* in favor of *rationalization*. "This neologism, which has come to us from Germany," one French paper editorialized, "can be found not only in technical trade magazines but in the daily press. It is omnipresent."[220] In a book published the same year, the English economic theoretician L. Urwick declared rationalization "a revolution in world economic thinking." Another English economist had earlier concluded that it was "impossible to survey the international economic situation without being convinced that what has been accomplished in Germany will be attempted in every country where similar industrial problems have to be faced."[221] And earlier still, in 1927, a congress convened by the League of Nations to examine the state of the global economy had discussed rationalization as part of its official program and passed a resolution calling on governments, international economic organizations, and world public opinion to put principles of rationalization into practice.

How did the German rationalization movement gain its illustrious international reputation given its rather modest successes in the areas of management and technology? One reason was Germany's improved image in the wake of the Locarno Pact of 1925, which made possible its return to the European fold. Along with the scaled-down tension in foreign policy, there was a psychological and ideological relaxation of hostilities. To all appearances, the German turn toward rationalization amounted to a turn away from militarism. The replacement of the authoritarian *homo militaris* with the liberal *homo oeconomicus* seemed to signal Germany's acceptance of liberal Western values and, with it, the achievement of Wilson's wartime aims. While recognizing the German origins of the concept of rationalization, the victors of 1918 could see themselves as the fathers without whom the child would never have been born.

To make the picture even rosier, the child turned out to be a perfectly behaved little boy. The massive infrastructure renewal projects Germany undertook from 1925 to 1929 in the name of rationalization—from urban and traffic planning to social and health policies—made the country seem like a vast laboratory of modernism. Berlin, even more than Detroit, came to represent a gigantic, smoothly running Fordian machine, the ideal prized by all nations with a faith in modernity. Rationalization appeared to be without peer both as a method of modernization and as a means to generate the capital required, a technological-economic *perpetuum mobile* that promised not only to make the American dream come true in Europe but to Europeanize the dream itself. Suppressed from consciousness was the fact that these ends were achieved least through rationalization and most by dint of American credit, which flowed freely into the Old World during those years.

FROM 1929 TO 1932, as the world's economy collapsed, so did most of the salvation theologies that were based on prosperity. Rationalization, however, was able to survive by adapting to the new circumstances. Unlike rigid Fordism, the rationalization movement reacted promptly to the change in climate and redefined itself accordingly. "The logical and historically necessary product of rationalization trends," wrote Robert A. Brady, "seems to be economic and social *planning*."[222] It is not difficult to recognize here the recurrence of war socialism and the idea of the social economy, from which the rationalization movement had tried to distance itself during the years of prosperity.

The vanguard responsible for redefining rationalization as a form of economic planning consisted of none other than those who had aspired to a German economic empire in Central Europe during World War I. Calling no longer on the nation but on rationalization to advance their strategy, they had clearly grasped the tenor of the times—even if they could not resist the temptation to advance grand historical visions. Werner Daitz, for example, proclaimed: "Germany today provides the only opportunity for finishing the work of Napoleon I and Bismarck, which has perennially been blocked by English policies."[223] Daitz, who in World War II would play a role in formulating a "new European order," made this remark one year after the signing of the Locarno Pact. Significantly, Gustav Stresemann, the architect of Germany's rehabilitation at Locarno, was not only one of the most prominent political advocates of a German-dominated Central Europe during the war but also the person who had said in 1920 that the German economy would have to reconquer what the German army had lost.[224] These connections were evident to the other side, as well. A contemporary French study, for one, noted that Stresemann's foreign policies were nothing more than "a manifestation of rationalization," which would inevitably lead to a "continental European economic bloc" under German leadership.[225]

National Socialist Americanism

A few months before the Nazis came to power in 1933, Robert A. Brady referred to the "supreme paradox" of rationalization in Germany: that it could be carried out successfully not within the borders of the German empire alone but only on a European scale. "Yet it is precisely in the international sphere that rationalization has the least chance of successful application as long as European nationalism survives in its present form." Brady also identified similar problems within German society: "Rationalization will be retarded in Germany as long as national, political, social, and other barriers stand

in the way of technological and economic forces. . . . There are definite limits set to rationalization and economic planning so long as
Germany remains a house divided against itself—so long as Catholic
Bavaria is pitted against Protestant Prussia, the right against the left,
the industrialists against the agriculturists, the urban against the rural
districts, the cartels against consumers, the states against the Reich."[226]

To describe the nazification of German society and the imperialis-
tic foreign policy of the Third Reich as the necessary preconditions for
total rationalization may be as exaggerated at Canetti's explanation of
the Holocaust as an outgrowth of the spirit of inflation—but just as
illuminating. Recent historiography on the Third Reich, especially in
the subfield of modernization, has reached astonishing conclusions in
its study of these long-ignored affinities. While the Third Reich talked
a lot less than the Weimar Republic about rationalization, it put it far
more thoroughly into practice, indeed involving the main Weimar
agency for rationalization, the National Board for Economic Efficiency, in the process of "economizing" mass murder.[227]

A similarly perverse continuity persisted between the Weimar
Republic's images of America and those of the Third Reich. Although the fetish for archaic Teutonism would suggest that the Nazis
rejected and criminalized everything American, research shows that
they were some of Germany's most eager students of American
methods.[228] Hitler's vision of a continental European empire dominated by Germany was copied not from the British Empire, which
in his eyes had outlived its prime, but from the contiguous and state-
filled landmass of the United States. The extermination of the
Indian population influenced Hitler as profoundly as the Monroe
Doctrine, which codified America's hegemonic aspirations.[229] In
1941, as Germany seemed on the verge of realizing its own, similar
goals, the economics editor of the *Frankfurter Zeitung* announced
that the basis had now been created for a properly "American" production of "automobiles, tractors, refrigerators, bathtubs, and other
consumer goods."[230]

Another American achievement that elicited Hitler's enthusiastic applause was mass manipulation. American propaganda during the First World War, he wrote, had mobilized the populace "in truly ingenious fashion." The Führer diverged from other prominent Germans—Ludendorff, for example—in focusing not only on America's success but on the conditions and methods necessary to achieve it. These Hitler accepted without reservation. What made American-style treatment of the masses so "ingenious" was not so much explicit political propaganda as a continuous forging of consensus. As great as Hitler's and Goebbels's admiration was for America's wartime synthesis of propaganda and state repression, the more significant lesson lay elsewhere.[231] National Socialism learned from America how to secure people's allegiance materialistically and hedonistically, rather than ideologically. The years after 1933 witnessed an almost twentyfold increase in Coca-Cola consumption in Germany, the development of an affordable popular automobile patterned on the Model T, and the conception of "*Volk* radio, television, and washing machines." An institute for consumer market research was also founded in Nuremberg in 1935, the same place and time the racial laws were announced. In all these moves, the Nazis' goal was a politically directed consumerism whose inspiration Hitler openly acknowledged: "We resemble the Americans in that we have wants and desires."[232]

The Hollywood Paradigm

In the area of popular entertainment, as in other areas, the National Socialists brought about not so much a radical break as a modified continuation of the technologically and organizationally progressive tendencies of the 1920s. The Nazi-supervised German film industry avoided explicit political propaganda to a surprising degree, continuing instead to produce the escapist films popular before 1933. The new element was that the man in charge of the cultural-industrial complex was an intellectual with definite views about the fundamental difference between German and American cinema, and not always in favor of the former. Joseph Goebbels's remarks about American film entertainment in the 1930s closely resembled what had been said about it in the 1920s in liberal periodicals like the *Weltbühne*. From opposite vantage points, Goebbels and the liberal critics agreed that America's intellectual and general cultural level was as modest as its cinematographic achievements were impressive.[233] Likewise, they shared the belief that American cinema was an authentic expression of the mass age and that, in this, German cinema lagged pathetically behind. Just as liberal intellectuals saw the superiority of American film as residing in its "inner rhythm," its "expression through tempo and dynamic force," and the "élan of the whole affair," Goebbels praised Hollywood for having a firmer grasp on what he called the "modern world feeling." "How easy it is for the Americans to produce this stuff. One can only admire them," he commented after seeing *Mutiny on the Bounty*. Of *Gone With the Wind*, he noted: "This film should be seen more often. We should take it as an example." He also maintained few illusions about Germany's ability to compete with Hollywood in the postwar world market. "We would have a hard time . . . and perhaps even lose the competition."[234]

Volkswagen Community

After cinema, consumerism was the second main means of Nazi popular integration along American lines. The advent of mass car ownership clearly shows how this other dream factory operated. Before automobiles became widely affordable in Europe, they provoked sharp class antagonisms. The enmity encountered by motorists on country roads has been compared to the "centuries-old hatred of the common people for aristocratic horseman"; in this regard, car ownership recalled hunting privileges.[235] In urban areas, especially during times of crisis, the resentment was much the same. In 1930, an observer witnessed Berlin pedestrians who "out of spite walk as close as possible to the street so that the tires scrape their shoes. They stare through the car windows with burning eyes, eyes that say: 'Get out, you scoundrels, get out of your limousines. Your time is up.'"[236]

To be sure, the German automotive industry had made attempts prior to 1933 to exploit the untapped mass market for their products. These efforts, however, had been hampered by the traditionalist view that an automobile was and had to remain an essentially bourgeois phenomenon. The very term for the affordable automobile, *Kleinwagen* (small car), made it clear that any vehicle designed for the masses would be a distinct and separate product, of lesser worth than the vehicle owned by the bourgeoisie. But Hitler had something else in mind when he ordered Ferdinand Porsche to develop a car that would be, "above all on Sundays and holidays, a source of previously unknown joyous delight" to the masses. The Volkswagen was to be a four-wheeled vehicle powered by a four-stroke engine, with space for four passengers and a price not to exceed 1,000 Reichsmarks, "not much more than a middling motorcycle," as Hitler put it.[237]

The model for the Volkswagen was none other than Ford's Model T, although the ideological affinity between the antisemitic and antifinance industrialist Henry Ford and Hitler played a minor role, if any. The decisive factor in the development of the Volkswagen was the car's function as an instance of mass production: it was "service" and "a factory of souls" all in one.[238] As Hitler's "gift" to the masses, the "plan, will, and deed of the Führer," the wish-fulfillment machine that was the Volkswagen proved to be one of the most effective and long-lasting instruments of propaganda ever, tying the individual tightly to the system.[239]

The "Volkswagen community" was completed with the Führer's additional "gift" of the autobahn, which, too, has been characterized as an "engineered advertisement."[240] Accounts from the 1930s are striking for their fascination with the autobahn's totally unimpeded traffic flow, the result of two innovations, one technical (a hard, smooth road surface of concrete instead of gravel or construction blocks) and the other organizational (restriction of usage to motorized vehicles and the channeling of traffic in a single direction). The sensation of driving was of pleasurably yielding to and becoming one with the road. A recurring theme in descriptions of the autobahn is weightlessness, the association with flying. With its lack of oncoming traffic, the autobahn was less a road than a starting ramp that received vehicle and driver, accelerated them on their way, and, after a certain speed had been reached, lulled the driver into feeling that he no longer had to operate the vehicle—by looking, steering, shifting gears, or braking—but merely had to allow himself to be transported by it. Few have described this seductive "totalitarian" quality better than the critic and journalist Walter Dirks, hardly a Nazi sympathizer. In 1938, he wrote: "Once we are in our lane . . . we no longer seem to be active ourselves. . . . So passive are we, so much does the great curve of the road determine our state of mind that relations seem to be reversed. It is the road that is active, that moves quickly and smoothly, without friction or violence, toward us, inexorably sucking the vehicle into it. . . . It is as if our own bodies, safely ensconced in smooth metal capsules, were merely following the twists and turns of the road, feeling the contours of the landscape in one long, rapid glide."241

How vividly this recalls the descriptions of the euphoria for the *vélo* in turn-of-the-century France. Was there a connection between the two phenomena? Was the car merely a new variation of that instinct for motion that had previously taken the form of the *levée en masse*, *gymnastique*, exercise, and racing sports? And what of dance mania, the assembly-line utopia, and the girl machine, not to mention the traffic-filled world city square, the *arditi* of Italian Fascism, and the storm troopers of National Socialism? Perhaps the longing for, or more precisely the drive to reclaim, motion is so central to the psyche of the vanquished because they experienced their defeat as a sudden and deadly halt. Perhaps, too, reclaimed motion is a form of *revanche*. And much the same energy may be at work in those revolutionary groups that since the nineteenth century have been referred to not as parties but as *movements*.

Epilogue:
On Falling

Let us turn now to the last great defeat of the twentieth century, the collapse of the Soviet Union, which began in 1989 with the breach of the Berlin Wall and concluded two years later when the hammer and sickle was removed from the Kremlin. Russia and the East European nations subsequently experienced almost all of the phases of defeat, from the dreamland state with its hopes for salvation and desire to imitate the victors, to disillusionment, moral outrage, and retreat into the bastion of nationalism. Today, historians routinely make comparisons between the Soviet Union of 1991 and the German empire of 1918. Yet quite some time passed before contemporary observers recognized the demise of Communist Europe as the defeat that it was.

There are various reasons the historical turning point of 1989–91 was not immediately acknowledged as a downfall. That it was prompted by internal decay without an external catalyst certainly played a role, as did the suddenness and lack of violence of the Soviet regime's collapse. Then, too, after forty years, no one had expected a decisive outcome to the Cold War. The idea that the Cold War was not a genuine war had, over the course of almost half a century, become deeply embedded in people's minds; the conflict, they felt, was the avoidance of war, the prevention of World War III. In truth, though, the Cold War was the third phase of the global civil war (as historian Ernst Nolte called it) that had commenced in 1917. Because of the post-1945 threat of mutual atomic annihilation, however, the third phase differed from the earlier stages in that it was not waged by military means. The Cold War stood in the same relation to the "total wars" of 1861–1945 as eighteenth-century cabinet warfare did to the unleashed fury of seventeenth-century religious wars: it was a successful strategy of self-preservation adopted by military cultures that otherwise threatened to destroy themselves.

While the Cold War seemed to break radically with a long tradition of armed conflict between competing states, it was at the same time the logical extension of tendencies in warfare since the nineteenth century. Without exception, the total wars of the modern age were ultimately decided by economic rather than military factors. The military was always just the tip of the sword: the weapon's real heft resided in the industrial capacity of the societies involved. The decline of the art of military strategy in the twentieth century was fully in keeping with the transformation of warfare into a competition between destructive systems of production, or, to recall the image from the battle of Verdun, industrial blood pumps. Warfare became a phenomenon in which human and material resources were delivered for destruction to the battlefield until only the economically more robust side—the victor—remained standing.

In a refinement of the pattern, the Cold War skipped over the actual process of destruction on the battlefield, pitting economies against one another directly. Perhaps its most important innovation was the liberation of the economy from a subordinate role as supplier to the military and its promotion to a power in its own right with decision-making prerogatives. From the Marxist perspective, the economy had, of course, always played this role, if in a surreptitious, subterranean way. The West's victory in the Cold War was, however, the first to be achieved explicitly by the economy in its own name. Perhaps it is for this reason that the economy received a new nom de guerre: globalization. The casino-like euphoria of the 1990s betrayed clear signs of hubris or, more fittingly, smug satisfaction at having avenged free-market capitalism's worst defeat: the Great Depression and the economy's subsequent subjugation to Keynesian state regulation.

The growth in the economy's power and prestige after 1990 was not confined to its functional efficiency but came to touch areas of society previously monopolized by religion and nationalism. If people looked toward anything in the hope of salvation or in fear of damnation, it was increasingly the economy. Having lost faith in God, the nation, and utopian politics, they credited the economy with the power both to create paradise on earth and to destroy life as they knew it. In the West, the threat of collective extinction attached no longer to war—which had in any case become a long-distance media event—but rather to the economy, with its double threat of devastating the environment and wiping out jobs. In her book *The Economic Horror*, Viviane Forrester even referred to the unemployed as the "defeated."

ACCORDINGLY, ON SEPTEMBER 11, 2001, the attack on the Pentagon was greeted with considerably less panic than that on the World Trade Center—a fact that can of course be explained by the divergent scale of destruction. Compared with the apocalyptic ruins and the deaths of thousands in Manhattan, the hole ripped in the side of the Pentagon had an almost old-world quality, like damage done to a medieval castle. But the function and symbolic import of the two sites also shaped the public reaction. Despite the shock of the event, it could hardly have been inconceivable to Americans that the nation's military headquarters should have been a target for attack. The strike against the twin towers was far more traumatic. In its lifetime, the World Trade Center stood as an example of 1960s shoe-box architecture, impressive primarily for its astounding lack of fantasy and aesthetic worth. But with the towers' collapse, two other dimensions were made visible: the sheer violence of their physical mass, evident in the wreckage, and the extent of the hatred that had chosen them as symbols to be destroyed. September 11 contained something of the fall of Troy, the first of all defeats, with which we began this book. Only in 2001, it was not the destruction of the warriors' fortress that carried the symbolic power but the fall of the merchants' towers.

In every culture, height—and its architectural expression, the tower—stands for power, control, lordship, and mastery. These qualities are symbolically elevated, just as homo sapiens, the only creature that walks erect, rises above the rest of the animal world. Conversely, those who lack power are put down, subjugated, subordinated, and subjected to the power of others. On the rotating wheel of fortune of victory and defeat, the positions of above and below are always being exchanged. The winner rises up in the world, while the loser falls. All Western languages use the verb *to fall* to distinguish a heroic warrior's death from ordinary dying. And the monuments erected to those who have fallen in battle are an attempt to lift them back up; borne aloft by angels and eagles, the body of the mortally wounded warrior becomes a majestic gesture of reelevation.

While the notions of rise and decline summon up grand yet gradual movements up and down the scale of power, the fall evokes a sudden and drastic plunge. Edward Gibbon avails himself of precisely this distinction in the title of his *Decline and Fall of the Roman Empire*. The timeless fascination with falls from power explains why the dominant image of the end of the Soviet Union is not the stately lowering of the red flag with its hammer and sickle over the Kremlin in 1991 but the dramatic collapse of the Berlin Wall two years before. This predilection also explains why the enduring image of the end of the Vietnam War is not the 1973 photograph of the Americans and North Vietnamese signing the cease-fire but the grainy television pictures of the chaotic evacuation of the American embassy in Saigon two years later. In this case, too, there was a time lapse between the official historical event and the image by which it was remembered and transmitted. Surely, the hold that those apocalyptic final scenes from Saigon have over people derives in no small part from the starring role of the helicopter in this act, for that vehicle symbolized the Vietnam War much as the machine gun and the tank represented World Wars I and II, respectively. The helicopter had seemed the perfect weapon for a guerrilla war, a means of close mastery of events on the ground from above, but the images of a hectic rooftop evacuation ultimately made a mockery of any such American superiority.

AFTER THE AMERICAN withdrawal from Southeast Asia, there was some debate as to whether Vietnam had been a true defeat or simply the first war the United States had not won conclusively. Then in the late 1970s, the Iranian hostage crisis—along with a failed rescue attempt (by helicopter!) in the Iranian desert—pointed up the extent of America's post-Vietnam malaise. Nothing made the country's disorientation more evident than the welcome accorded to the embassy workers on their return in early 1980. Not freed in a daring commando operation but handed over by the enemy in an almost patronizing gesture, the returning hostages were nonetheless celebrated with a ticker-tape parade in New York, much like the victorious heroes of two world wars.

The Vietnam debate was never settled; rather, it was buried under the Reagan-era defense buildup, the double victories of the Cold War and the Gulf War, and the reestablishment of America's universally acknowledged military, commercial, and cultural hegemony over the rest of the world. But earthquakes and aerial bombardments often reveal what lies beneath—for instance, the ruins of earlier, fallen cities—and it is possible that the destruction of September 11 uncovered the suppressed remains of Vietnam.

Though some European pundits spoke of an American defeat in the immediate wake of the terrorist attacks, the wreckage of the twin towers and the damage to the Pentagon were no more a defeat than was the attack on Pearl Harbor in 1941. Unlike 1941, however, the attack on Manhattan was perpetrated not by a clearly defined territorial state with a regular army but by a shadowy adversary, impossible to combat directly with military means. The great crater where the World Trade Center once stood provides a most telling image for the state of the post–September 11 American psyche: a vacuum crying to be filled with an act of military revenge for which there is no addressee.

COMMENTATORS HAVE UNANIMOUSLY agreed that the terrorism of September 11 is a departure in that it operates with all the anonymous modernity of the system whose symbol it so aptly chose to attack: global capitalism. Furthermore, with their advanced grasp of modern technology, the engineer-terrorists managed—perhaps unintentionally—to achieve a mega-effect entirely on a scale with the gargantuan appetite of that economy.

It is true that the economic and technical environment of the West is as much the natural element of the new brand of terrorists as the rural populations of the Third World were for earlier guerrillas. The nation attacked, though, is still limited to a traditional response: to nominate another nation as a terrorist or rogue state so as to locate the specter of terrorism within a concrete territorial enemy, a target. Thus the United States responded by taking action against Afghanistan, much as thirty years earlier when, tired of fruitlessly battling the Vietcong guerrillas, the United States trained its sights on North Vietnam. Indeed, the Bush doctrine of preventive military strikes eerily resembles the anti-Communist domino theory, that earlier expression of the horror of falling. Could it be that the decades of relative American peacefulness and readiness to cooperate that followed the defeat in Vietnam were merely an interim period, akin to the Weimar Republic, with its pleasant illusion of a pacified Germany? Or, as with the French cries for *revanche* for Sadowa, that America's post–September 11 war fever is really a response to an earlier and unresolved defeat?

Notes

Introduction: On Being Defeated

1. Pre-Virgilian literary treatments of the Aeneas myth, by authors such as Naenius and Ennius, existed as early as the third century B.C. On the English adoption of the myth, see A. E. Parsons, "The Trojan Legend in England," *Modern Language Review* 24 (1929): 253–63.

2. Ernst Cassirer, *Philosophie der symbolischen Formen*, 2nd ed., vol. 2 (Oxford, 1954), pp. 49–50.

3. Carl Schmitt, *Ex captivitate salus* (Cologne, 1950), pp. 30–31, 27. I wish to thank Henning Ritter for drawing my attention to these citations.

4. Reinhart Koselleck, "Erfahrungswandel und Methodenwechsel: Eine historisch-anthropologische Skizze," *Historische Methode*, ed. Christian Meier and Jörn Rüsen (Munich, 1988), pp. 51–53, 60. While Koselleck speaks at the beginning of his essay of short-term victors, his term by the end is "temporary victors" (p. 60). In an imaginative consideration of the battle of Sedan on the occasion of its hundredth anniversary in 1970, J.-M. Domenach proposed celebrating defeats rather than victories: "Victories are often deceptive, but defeats are always instructive. If we had consecrated a day to the anniversary of Sedan rather than to that of November 11, we might have been able to avoid the debacle of May–June 1940, which was nearly a repetition of that of the summer of 1870" (cited in Aimée Dupuy, *"Sedan" et l'enseignement de la revanche* [Paris, 1975], p. 5). John Keegan advances the opposite position: the most insightful and objective history comes not from the

defeated but from the victors. As examples, he cites the nationalistically distorted historiographies of France after 1871 and Germany after 1918, contrasting them with the sovereign Anglo-American historiography after 1918 and 1945. The latter, according to Keegan, allows for an objectivity impossible for the deeply traumatized losing side (*The Face of Battle* [New York, 1976], p. 61).

5. Hémon said of La Rochefoucauld that he wrote "with the obstinate rancor which is the revenge of the vanquished. Revenge for dashed hopes and hurt pride with one blow; the revenge of the man of action who always observed more than he acted, and who, more than ever, in the impotence in which he was to act, sought consolation in the delicate joy of observing, in the bitter pleasure of remembering" (quoted in Wolf Lepenies, *Melancholy and Society* [Cambridge, Mass., 1992], p. 151). On the contribution of the Frondist memoirs to eighteenth-century political enlightenment, Orest Ranum writes: "The variety, the richness, indeed the complexity, ambiguity, honesty, and at the same time self-servingness of these memoirs written by both men and women have encouraged civic activism since the early eighteenth century" (*The Fronde: A French Revolution, 1648–1652* [New York, 1993], pp. 346–47).

6. Russell Jacoby, *The Dialectics of Defeat* (Cambridge, 1981). Something similar could be said of the revolutionary right in the period between the world wars, before it came to power. Renzo de Felice's distinction between "*fascismo movimento*" and "*fascismo regime*" approximates the distinction between Western and Soviet Marxism (Renzo de Felice and Michael A. Leeden, *Intervista sul fascismo* [Bari, 1997], pp. 29ff.). Western Marxism and *fascismo di movimento* shared an idealistic orientation that was unrealized, indeed betrayed, by their respective regimes.

7. Along with blows, Toynbee lists the stimuli of "hard countries," "new ground," "pressures," and "penalizations." See *A Study of History*, abridged ed., vol. 1 (New York, 1946), pp. 88–139.

8. See Heinrich von Stietencron and Jörg Rüpke, eds., *Töten im Krieg* (Freiburg, 1995), especially the essays by Rüpke on the Roman republic and Walter Burkert on the Greek polis. See also Burkert's seminal *Homo Necans* (Berlin, 1972).

9. Ernest Renan's famous sentence, recorded by Paul Déroulède, reads: "France is dying, young man—do not disturb her agony" (quoted in Zeev Sternhell, *Ni droite ni gauche* [Brussels, 1992], p. 287). In his consistent acceptance of the inevitable death of the nation after its military defeat, Renan is something of a lone figure. The normal reaction to defeat, even among social Darwinists, is to seek out alternative explanations for military weakness, including treason, poor prepara-

tion, or unconscientiousness within the army. The belief in the inevitable death of the nation in case of military defeat usually only applies *before* the inception of hostilities and functions as an appeal to the nation's fighting spirit. On the fourth anniversary of Sedan, León Gambetta posed this all-decisive social Darwinist question without reaching a satisfactory answer in relation to France: "Could it be true that for peoples, as for animal species, the struggle for existence and authority periodically brings about the disappearance of the weakest, most ignorant, most heedless, by means of armed aggression on the part of the most strong, most learned, most wise? Could it be that politics is only a branch of human physiology? Perhaps" (letter to Juliette Adam, Sept. 4, 1874, cited in Linda L. Clark, *Social Darwinism in France* [Tuscaloosa, 1984], p. 31).

10. Jakob Burckhardt, *Weltgeschichtliche Betrachtungen, Gesamtausgabe* 7 (Berlin, 1922), p. 124.

11. Letter to Friedrich von Preen, Sept. 27, 1870, *Briefe*, vol. 5 (Basel, 1963), p. III. Emphasis in the original.

12. On the celebratory character of declarations of war, see Roger Caillois, whose descriptions of the outbreak of hostilities cast them as an event or condition related to the phenomenon of the festival. According to Caillois, the affinities are as follows: (1) on both occasions, the normal boundaries and rules of the class order are suspended; (2) forces of hostility, destruction, and waste take over; (3) the participants believe themselves to be in a "holy period" utterly unlike times of normalcy; and (4) the prevailing zeitgeist becomes one of societal renewal and rejuvenation (*Der Mensch und das Heilige* [Munich, 1988], pp. 220ff.). From the vantage point of historical psychoanalysis, Lloyd de Mause describes the festival nature of declarations of war as a liberating blow, characterizing it as a collective reliving of the individual trauma of birth. Just as the fetus perceives birth as liberation from its confinement within the uterus, the outbreak of war is experienced as liberation from a situation increasingly perceived to be overwrought with tension (*Grundlagen der Psychohistorie*, ed. Aurel Ende [Frankfurt am Main, 1989], pp. 32ff.). The pre-1914 German paranoia about being hemmed in—the classic case of this mass-psychological phenomenon—was foreshadowed by similar psychological states in the pre-1861 American South (the feeling of being encircled by the North) and in pre-1870 France (the concern about being threatened from the west by England and America and from the east by Prussia and Germany).

13. The connotations attached to the term *trope* include the ideas of transformation, reversal, flight, exchange, and alteration. *Nike* is the result of all this for the victor, *hetta* the equivalent for the loser. The seminal

sources all agree that the will to fight, the morale among the troops, is the decisive factor in battle, more important than the relative numbers of forces. To cite Napoleon: "In war, morale conditions constitute three-quarters of the game: the relative balance of manpower accounts only for the remaining quarter" (correspondence cited in Helen Friend Langlais, *Morale* [Oslo, 1955], p. 4). This explains why, even in encounters between armies of widely unequal troop strength, such as the battle of Marathon in 490 B.C., the side with the lesser numbers but greater morale is often bound for victory. This is a simple explanation for the role of *fortunas*, or military fortune, in battle, which is recognized by all the leading theoretical and practical commentators.

14. Carl von Clausewitz, *On War*, trans. and ed. Michael Howard and Peter Paret (Princeton, 1976), p. 231.

15. Ibid., p. 255.

16. The phrase *en plein roman* comes from Raoul Frary, *Le péril national* (Paris, 1884), p. 188. Clausewitz stipulates that "panicked terror" never occurs in a well-trained army, only among civilians as a consequence of lost battles (*On War*, p. 273).

17. *On War*, p. 244.

18. Colmar von der Goltz, *Gambetta und seine Armeen* (Berlin, 1877), pp. 20, 231.

19. Protocol of a speech delivered on Sept. 12, 1923, in *Hitler: Sämtliche Aufzeichnungen, 1905–1924*, ed. Eberhard Jäckel and Axel Kuhn (Stuttgart, 1980), p. 1007. Emphasis in the original. J. P. T. Bury, who called my attention to this reference, incorrectly dates the speech ten years later than it actually took place. See Bury, *Gambetta and the National Defence* (New York, 1970), p. 279.

20. This view of the significance of the Ruhr War is confirmed by numerous contemporary figures. Prince Max von Baden, who as imperial chancellor organized the October 1918 surrender, greeted the Ruhr War in his pamphlet *Der Weckruf aus Westfalen* (1923) as a national moral awakening. It "restored to us the sovereign power of decision making . . . and gave us back our will" (Arthur Moeller van den Bruck, *Das 3. Reich*, 3rd ed. [Hamburg, 1931], p. ix). Martin Spahn, a political scientist and philosopher associated with the conservative counterrevolution: "Today's hours are related to those of August 1914. . . . Destiny is once again putting us to the test, giving us a second chance to show that we deserve to survive as a people" (*Um Rhein und Ruhr* [Berlin, 1923], p. 15). The nationalist pacifist Max Graf Montgelas: "Even if we are not to be granted success in our stuggle at its present stage, we have at least won back our *honor.*" (*Ursprung und Ziel des französischen Einbruchs ins Ruhrgebiet* [Berlin,

1923], p. 38). Emphasis in the original. Chancellor Rudolf Cuno: "The consciousness has been reawakened among the German people of the value of those most valuable national possessions, freedom and honor. This consciousness seemed to have been erased by the terrible collapse of Germany . . . within broad sectors of the populace" (*Der Kampf um die Ruhr* [Leipzig, 1923], p. 209). Eugen Rosenstock: "What we are witnessing in the Ruhr is a refounding of the empire as an act of global self-assertion before the eyes of the entire world" (*Hochland*, June 1923, p. 234).

In retrospect, from the perspective of 1930, Paul Wentzcke wrote: "After the military end of the Great War, the second stage of the struggle took place around its tragic core; even more so than the army previously on the front, the populace took responsibility this time for the outcome" (*Geschichte des Ruhrkampfes als Aufgabe und Erlebnis* [Düsseldorf, n.d. (ca. 1930)], p. 4). Walther Schotte, publisher of the *Preussische Jahrbücher*, accused the government "of bureaucratizing the politics of resistance," that is, repeating the mistakes of November 1918, instead of fostering the "revolutionary mentality" present among the masses (*Preussische Jahrbücher* 193 [1923]: 351). Communists drew comparisons with the Paris Commune: "Just as once the Parisian proletariat rose up against Bismarck and Thiers, their German comrades are resisting Cuno, Stinnes, and Poincaré" (Leonid A. Friedrich, *Warum Ruhr-Krieg? 10 Prozent oder die Nation* [Berlin, 1923], p. 43).

Foreign observers were impressed by the unanimous support for resistance in Germany. The English ambassador to Germany, Viscount D'Abernon, wrote: "Day by day, the consciousness is growing among all classes in Germany that one is neither required nor obliged to compromise. I cannot ever remember there being so little class hostility or enmity among political parties as today. . . . The entire country seems to have been melded into a single unit" (*Ein Botschafter in der Zeitenwende*, vol. 2 [Leipzig, 1929], pp. 188–89).

On the Ruhr War as a central myth among the revolutionary German right, see Ernst-Otto Schüddekopf, *Linke Leute von rechts: Die nationalrevolutionären Minderheiten und der Kommunismus in der Weimarer Republik* (Stuttgart, 1960), pp. 139–64. The fact that the Ruhr War concluded without any great laurels for Germany led the extreme right back to the psychology of the "stab in the back," which, as the *Weltbühne* already prophesied in April 1923, was taken up as legend immediately after the end of the passive resistance. In this case, it was the populace of the Ruhr region that played the role of the fighting front abandoned and betrayed by the government in Berlin.

See, for example, Edgar Jung, *Die Herrschaft der Minderwertigen* (Berlin, 1930), p. 329; *Deutsche Rundschau*, Dec. 1923, p. 226; Heinrich Tötter, *Warum wir den Ruhrkampf verloren* (Cologne, 1940), p. 106. On the opposite end of the political spectrum, Social Democrats and trade unions were also haunted by the specter of 1918. To avoid the accusation that they were complicit in national betrayal they formed a common force for defense of the home front with the nationalists and business sector (Jean-Claude Favez, *Le Reich devant l'occupation franco-belge de la Ruhr en 1923* [Geneva, 1969], pp. 129 ff.).

In an irony of history, the political rhetoric used to mobilize resistance to the Ruhr occupation echoed almost exactly the Belgian call for resistance to the German invasion of August 1914. The call from President Ebert and Chancellor Cuno read: "We object to [this] act of violence in the eyes of Europe and the entire world. We raise our voice in loud protest that a foreign power is here desecrating the holy right of the German people to its own territory, its right to existence" (Hans Pyszka, *Der Ruhrkrieg* [Munich, 1923], pp. 49–50).

21. Jäckel and Kuhn, p. 1011.
22. Edward A. Pollard, *The Lost Cause* (1866; rpt. New York, 1970), p. 726. Rathenau's call for a *levée en masse* in October 1918 recalled Jefferson Davis's equally futile attempt in the American South to continue the conflict as a guerrilla war after General Lee's surrender at Appomattox (Dan T. Carter, *When the War Was Over* [Baton Rogue, 1985], p. 23).
23. The idealism with which the leaders of Munich's Republic of Councils adopted France's attitude toward Germany represents the zenith of such fraternization with the former enemy. See Henning Köhler, *Novemberrevolution und Frankreich: Die französische Deutschlandpolitik, 1918–1919* (Düsseldorf, 1980), pp. 102–04, 271 ff.
24. André Bellesort, *Les intellectuels et l'avènement de la Troisième République* (Paris, 1931), p. 46. Bellesort is paraphrasing a description in La Gorce's *Histoire du Second Empire*.
25. There were a number of reasons for the muted reaction in Berlin. Whereas the politicians involved in the rebellions in Paris and Munich either belonged to or had close contact with bohemian circles, the revolution in Berlin took place among politicians and bureaucrats, with semibohemian figures like Karl Liebknecht and Rosa Luxemburg remaining outsiders, excluded from the official opposition. The genius loci of the sites of the demonstrations may also have played a role. In 1870, the Parisian masses assembled on the *via triumphalis* between the National Assembly and the Hôtel de Ville, which since 1792 had been the site of every occurrence of popular unrest. Likewise in 1918,

the Theresienwiese in Munich, the site of the annual Oktoberfest, embodied the connection between revolution and festival. The Lustgarten in Berlin had no such popular tradition as a place of revolutionary assembly.

26. Th. Bost, *Le réveil de la France* (Brussels, 1871), pp. 15–16, 48.

27. V. F. Calverton, *The Bankruptcy of Marriage* (1928; rpt. New York, 1972), pp. 16–17. The sex researcher Magnus Hirschfeld characterizes the dance craze in post-1919 Germany in similar terms (*Sittengeschichte des Weltkriegs* [Berlin, 1931], pp. 317, 359 ff.).

28. Quoted in G. A. Masson, "Philosophie des Foxtrott," *La revue mondiale*; rpt. in *Das Tagebuch* 1 (1920): 959.

29. See, for example, a Dr. W. Morgenthaler: "The German people were badly shaken from 1914 to 1918 by war and famine, and their capacity for resistance was weakened. When it became clear that the reward for the endless suffering and silent heroism of persistence was to be political collapse . . . they suffered a commensurate collective psychological breakdown. . . . This psychic ailment was followed by compulsive motor activity as drastic compensation for the tremendous stress. Having reached the nadir of its suffering, Germany suddenly began dancing like mad" ("Die alten Tanzepidemien und ihre Beziehung zur Gegenwart," *Blätter für Bernische Geschichte und Altertumskunde* 21 [1925]: 282). See also Dr. F. Schwarz, "Tanzwut: Medizinhistorische Studie zur Massenhysterie," *Hygiaia* 3 (1933): 200–05.

30. "The penetrating force of the waltz is directly related to the sociological repercussions of the French Revolution and to the sociohistorical restructuring of the nineteenth century" (Hugo Riemann, "Walzer," *Musiklexikon*, quoted in Rémy Hess, *La valse: Révolution du couple en Europe* [Paris, 1989], p. 97). A sign was affixed to the Bastille, which was stormed on July 14, 1789, setting off the French Revolution: *"Ici on danse"* (p. 104). Of the eruption of the cancan in 1830 in Paris, David Price writes: "It seems too much of a coincidence that the cancan appeared in the same year as the revolution of 1830 and it seems fair to say that there are links between the cancan and the *carmagnole* of 1789, in so far as each was stimulated by the general upheavals in society and an urge to demonstrate *liberté*" (*Cancan!* [London, 1998], p. 26).

31. Troeltsch describes the months between the cease-fire and surrender in November 1918 and the announcement of the conditions for peace negotiated at Versailles as the "dreamland of the cease-fire period," since during that time the wildest delusions about the postwar order were maintained (*Spektator-Briefe* [Tübingen, 1924]).

The elation of the losers can perhaps be best understood when compared with that of the victors. What is remarkable is the relatively short duration of the victors' elation. It is spontaneous and momentary, lasting hardly longer than the parades, fireworks, and confetti, and is followed by sobriety and a return to the pedestrian everyday order, which as before the war is determined by the fathers' generation. There is hardly a more desultory spectacle in the world than that of youth returning home victorious from war and marching by the grandstands packed with parents, before returning to the office or the factory. In 1942, the English historian E. L. Woodward summed up this phenomenon after World War I with the sentence: "The men who came back from the war have counted for less, perhaps, in the political life of their country than any generation during the last two or three centuries" (quoted in Robert Wohl, *The Generation of 1914* [Cambridge, 1979], p. 112). The concept of a "Lost Generation" in the victorious nations of World War I applies beyond the literary realm it was originally intended to characterize. The opposite side of the coin in the defeated nation was the "Front generation." Its members, too, returned to a society and a home front ruled by their fathers. Nonetheless, the fathers were soon deposed and humiliated so that they no longer possessed any authority. Even when those fathers were not part of the antebellum regime and thus might have represented a new start, as was true in Germany with the pre-1918 Social Democratic Party leadership, their sons saw the world as a "fatherless society" (to use Paul Federn's term) in which the older generation appeared solely as losers and objects of ridicule. The loser-fathers were far less likely than their victorious and therefore unimpeachable counterparts to inspire the feeling among their progeny of having been the "victim of a dirty trick played by the older generation" (Wohl, *Generation of 1914*, p. 100). This appraisal is supported by a comparison of the social politics in post-1918 Germany on the one hand and France, England, and the United States on the other. While the victorious-father regimes were often allowed to forget the promises made during wartime or to shunt them on to a symbolic level, the humiliated loser fathers had little option other than to make real concessions, such as the 1918 Stinnes-Legien Agreement on employment and wages in Germany. The central Fascist and National Socialist myth of the long march of the former frontline soldiers to positions of power in the homeland was understood by its participants as nothing more than the belated overthrow of the loser-father regime by wartime youth.

32. There are various indices of a feminizing process in the psychology, rhetoric, and iconography of loser cultures, although they can be mentioned only briefly here. One example is the Queen Luise cult in post-

1806 Prussia, which France seems to have imitated after 1870 (*Revue des deux mondes*, Jan. 1, 1872, pp. 222ff.). There are the numerous sightings of the Virgin Mary reported in France in the fall and winter of 1870–71 and in the years following. The image of the "defiled nation" was popular above all among the revolutionary right in post-1918 Germany. See Friedrich Wilhelm Heinz, *Die Nation greift an: Geschichte und Kritik des soldatischen Nationalismus* (Berlin, 1933), p. 10. Heroic figures were portrayed less often as powerful and masculine than as sentimental, feminine, and romantic. In post-1871 France, Joan of Arc experienced her great renaissance, Roland bore the features of the suffering Jesus, and in general the image of the martyred savior increasingly replaced that of the active warrior hero. In the American South, portraits of General Lee reveal a similar sensitive softness, which accorded well with the contemporaneous cult of the Southern lady. No comparable phenomenon existed in post-1918 Germany. Perhaps, however, the predominant death cult can be understood as a sublimated form of the mother-nation cult. The hero's death, understood as a kind of immortality, represents another version of the son's reunion with his mother, which, according to C. G. Jung, signifies immortality (*Wandlungen und Symbole der Libido*, part 3, sect. 5).

33. On the Wilson myths, see Peter Berg, *Deutschland und Amerika, 1918–1929* (Lübeck, 1963), pp. 9–47, and Ernst Frankel, "Das Deutschland-Weltbild," *Jahrbuch für Amerika-Studien* 5 (1960): 66–120. A good example of corollary psychology in the American South is expressed by Edward Pollard: "It was this peculiar trust in the generosity of the North . . . that brought the Southern Confederacy to such a sudden and almost abrupt conclusion of the war" (*Lost Cause*, p. 50). In France, no such legends were constructed, in part because the war was divided into two parts—Napoleon III's war against Prussia and the *défense nationale*—each with its own surrender. Nonetheless, the projection of hopes and expectations of mild treatment onto certain leading personalities in the enemy camp was common to all three losing societies. What Wilson was for Germany, Lincoln's successor, Andrew Johnson, was for the American South. French hopes for a peace settlement like that between Prussia and Austria in 1866 were pinned to Bismarck up until a few days before his post-Sedan meeting with Thiers and Favre in Ferrières. Only after German demands for the annexation of Alsace-Lorraine were made known did Bismarck become a "monster."

34. On post-Vietnam reactions, see Jeffrey P. Kimball, "The Stab-in-the-Back Legend and the Vietnam War," *Armed Forces and Society* 14

(1987–88): 433–57. The rhetoric documented by Kimball across the ranks of the American military leadership, including President Richard Nixon, is quite similar to that among right-wing Germans during the Weimar Republic. The reason the Vietnam War did not polarize the nation or lead to civil war is, of course, that it did not entail national collapse and was not followed by a humiliation like that of the Versailles treaty. On the other hand, the German-American comparison raises the question of whether the stab-in-the-back legend was a uniquely German phenomenon, as most historians argue, or whether, during a more serious crisis, it might not have a similar effect in the United States.

35. Claude Billard and Pierre Guibert, *Histoire mythologique des français* (Paris, 1976), p. 174.

36. Quoted in Whitelaw Reid, *After the War: A Tour of the Southern States, 1865–1866* (Cincinnati, 1866), p. 310. The German equivalent is from Arthur Moeller van den Bruck, quoted in E. Günther Gründel, *Die Sendung der jungen Generation* (Munich, 1933), p. 395.

37. This is the same ethos—quality workmanship versus mass production—that artisans were simultaneously and with a similar lack of success promoting as an argument against industry. The sociologist Sebald Rudolf Steinmetz compared Germany's defeat in World War I with the "destruction of a hard-working small business by the overwhelming power of a giant trust company" (*Soziologie des Krieges* [Leipzig, 1929], p. 373).

38. The Confederacy and Germany in the two world wars provide examples of initial military successes, followed by defeats in wars of attrition. In conjunction with the Civil War, Michael C. C. Adams shows that the aura surrounding military nations can cause a kind of inferiority complex among civilian-bourgeois ones. This inferiority complex has a definite impact on the conduct of war and may indeed lead to tactical inferiority (*Our Masters the Rebels: A Speculation on Union Military Failure in the East, 1861–1865* [Cambridge, 1978]). Total war directed not only at the enemy's army but at its civilian population is a necessary innovation of bourgeois culture, the only means for overcoming the tactical superiority of a military culture. The initial reactions in the South to General Sheridan's and General Sherman's scorched-earth policies were disbelief and moral incomprehension. This military-ethical dichotomy recurred in twentieth-century air warfare. Whereas the Luftwaffe in National Socialist Germany was deployed (albeit for military and ideological and not humanitarian reasons) as a tactical instrument, the Western democracies used their air forces for the saturation bombing of civilian populations.

39. George Fitzhugh in *DeBow's Review*, n.s., 1 (1866): 76.
40. Victor Hugo, *Choses vues* (Paris, 1972), p. 84.
41. If one considers those who fall in battle on the victorious side as losers among winners, an idea for which there is strong anthropological and psychological support, the cult surrounding their heroic deaths takes on a similar significance. Glory and honor become the reward and compensation for exclusion from the victors' enjoyment of triumph. Wartime casualties are honored as heroes, victims, and martyrs—that is, for those very qualities that obtain generally among the losing side.
42. There are differences in the quality of offensive and defensive propaganda. The American South and Germany, which had to defend themselves against moral and judicial condemnation from the victors, tended to argue more defensively. France, which was spared such accusations in 1871, could afford to be more aggressive. Corresponding differences in the organization of propaganda resulted. The American South and Germany created special institutions for the dissemination of propaganda to protest their innocence: the Southern Historical Society and its series of publications and the *Kriegsschuld-Referat* in the German Foreign Office, which coordinated a multitude of organizations and publications. Activities in France required no such state coordination and planning.
43. Arthur Moeller van den Bruck, *Das Recht der jungen Völker* (Berlin, 1932), pp. 107–08.
44. In magical thinking, the transference of strength is not without its dangers, since what is transferred may include the evil sentiments of the enemy—his desire for revenge, his curse. Special rituals of purification and sacrifice are thus required to protect oneself against contamination. Warrior societies in the transition to pacified culture often develop a mythology of decadence according to which the "softening" of the old warrior values (as a result of the adoption of the luxuries of the losers) represents the losers' covert revenge on their conquerors. German romantic-reactionary cultural criticism up to Thomas Mann's *Reflections of a Non-Political Man* treats Western (that is, French) civilization as one of decay and dissolution. The softening elements of civilization (as opposed to German *Kultur*) are constantly equated with feminization and enfeeblement and are thus treated as the covert means of revenge (poison, seduction, defamation) utilized by those condemned to the role of treacherous weakness. The symbolism of iron versus gold (which arose in Germany during the war of "national liberation" of 1812) occupies a central position in this complex of ideas. Also worth noting is the tendency to speak of a *swamp* of decadence in contrast to heroism on the *field* of battle. Swamps and gold

go together, as do battlefields and iron. The battlefield, like the desert and the steppes from which the conquering barbarians emerge, is an open space.

45. On children and women as heroes, see Marieluise Christadler, "Zur nationalpädagogischen Funktion kollektiver Mythen in Frankreich," *Nationale Mythen und Symbole in der 2. Hälfte des 19. Jahrhunderts*, ed. Jürgen Link and Wulf Wülfing (Stuttgart, 1991), pp. 206ff. One must distinguish between the dehumanizing propaganda practiced during war by all sides and the postwar propaganda of the defeated. This is sometimes difficult, owing to the similarities in iconography, but such a distinction is essential for understanding the underlying collective psyche. The question arises, for instance, whether the side that most fears its military inferiority (for example, France during the first phase of World War I) is more assiduous in dehumanizing the enemy than the more self-assured opponent. If so, this would explain the relative lack of German dehumanization propaganda vis-à-vis the French in the First World War.

46. Heinrich Mann, "Kaiserreich und Republik," *Macht und Mensch* (Munich, 1919), p. 181. In another passage, Mann expresses the hope that France, enlightened by its defeat in 1870–71, will be wise enough to avoid such hubris: "Our fervent wish . . . is that the moral serious-ness that this nation achieved fifty years ago in defeat will outlive its greatest threat, today's victory" ("Sinn und Idee der Revolution: Ansprache im Politischen Rat geistiger Arbeiter," *Macht und Mensch*, pp. 161–62).

47. On the extinction of German culture, see Friedrich Nietzsche, *Unzeit-gemässe Betrachtungen, Werke in drei Bänden*, ed. Karl Schlechta, vol. 1 (Munich, 1982), p. 137. On the spiritual-cultural improvement of the defeated in contrast to the simultaneous decline of victorious Germany, see Nietzsche, *Götzendämmerung*, sec. 4, *Werke*, vol. 2, pp. 985–86.

In 1880, Bruno Bauer observed: "The last ten years have devoured [Germany's] cultural products as thoroughly as Saturn his offspring." On a painting of A. de Neuville: "The victors stand ashamed and downcast before the example of strength that its conquered enemy has developed in his spiritual battle with defeat" (*Zur Orientierung über die Bismarck-Ära* [Chemnitz, 1880], pp. 131, 141). Heinrich Sybel, a nationalist hardly plagued by self-doubt, merely recom-mended that Germany learn from France's negative example: "Above all, we should learn to recognize the causes for the demise of a pow-erful empire. We are now at our height—for that very reason, we have good cause, if we are not vain fools, for self-evaluation. We should be on guard against the beginnings of those false tendencies and ambitions that infected once-proud France and caused her collapse" (*Was wir von Frankreich lernen können* [Bonn, 1872], p. 3). Otto Röse commented in 1884: "It would be foolish not to recognize that our enemy has gained from its defeat an artistic advantage, a more splendid and powerful capacity for expression than we Germans, despite our great victories, currently possess" (*Bilder aus Paris* [Berlin, 1884], p. xi).

48. Friedrich Schönemann speculated in 1921 that the Civil War disrupted the Emersonian transcendentalist movement, out of which a "different" American culture—that is, one free of commercialism and materialism—could have developed (*Amerikakunde* [Bremen, 1921], p. 29). Walt Whitman was another of the Northern "loser intellectuals." A few years after the victory of the North, in which he had invested great hopes, he wrote: "It is as if we were somehow being endow'd with a vast and thoroughly appointed body and then left with little or no soul" (quoted in Charles A. Beard and Mary Beard, *The Rise of American Civilization*, vol. 2 [New York, 1930], p. 436).

49. Interestingly, the Lost Generation recapitulated the education in exile of the German hero in Romain Rolland's novel *Jean-Christophe*, who flees the negative developments in his victorious homeland and discovers true German culture in Paris. Another literary hero who breaks with his victorious homeland (England) and allies himself with the losing camp (the Scottish clans) is of course Walter Scott's Waverly. In his wartime diaries, Rolland quotes a young Japanese about the great cultural influence exercised on Japanese intellectuals after Russia's defeat in 1905: "Defeated Russia conquered Japan with its literature and philosophy. Tolstoy had Japanese disciples. Turgenev inspired an art-for-art's-sake movement. Even Arzybaschev (Sanin) had a greater effect in Japan than in Europe. But no one who has adopted and disseminated Russian ideas in Japan occupies an official position" (*Das Gewissen Europas*, vol. 3 [East Berlin, 1983], p. 488).

50. Quoted in R. J. B. Bosworth, *Explaining Auschwitz and Hiroshima: History Writing and the Second World War, 1945–1990* (London, 1994), pp. 167–68.

51. Tom Segev, *The Seventh Million: The Israelis and the Holocaust* (New York, 1993), p. 147. On Abba Kovner's plan, see pp. 140 ff.

52. Marcel Mauss, *Essai sur le don*, in *Sociologie et anthropologie*.

53. "The potlatch should be described as a war," writes Claude Lefort in the tradition of Mauss, illustrating his point with the fact that the language of the Tlingit tribe uses one word for both the potlatch and the war dance. Battle and the exchange of gifts are "men's struggles

for mutual recognition," so that "men have no choice but to fight or to give" (*Les temps modernes* 6, no. 3 [1950]: 1415, 1416).

54. Emmerich von Vattel lists three justifications for legitimate warfare: "to recover what belongs, or is due to us"; "to provide for our future safety by punishing the aggressor or offender"; and "to defend ourselves, or to protect ourselves from injury, by repelling unjust violence" (*Law of Nations*, book 3, ch. 3, sec. 28). The archetype of legitimate war is the Greek campaign against the Persians since it was motivated by the "desire of avenging the injuries that the Greeks had so often suffered" (sec. 31).

55. François Billacois, *Le duel dans la société française des 16è–17è siècles: Essai de psychosociologie historique* (Paris, 1986), pp. 358–60. Billacois illustrates his arguments with copious citations from contemporaries. For example, Giovanni di Legnano: "[The duelist] does not intend to destroy but to win, which he can do without the elimination of his opponent." Mutio: "Be careful to take up arms not in hatred or in the spirit of vengeance but instead as an instrument to serve the justice of his eternal majesty." Anton Maria Salvini: "Not only should a knight not approach [the duel] with hatred, but indeed he should do so with the desire of being of service to his opponent, while at the same time mindful of, or rather ministering to, his own honor. . . . He should act neither in anger nor inflamed by hostility or hatred but spurred on by reason alone." Vendramin: "The more we take our opponent for a man of honor and valor, the higher our own reputation and honor will rise."

56. Recorded by Bernhard von Bülow, cited in Walter Frank, *Nationalismus und Demokratie im Frankreich der Dritten Republik* (Hamburg, 1933), p. 635.

57. Victor Hugo, *Choses vues*, p. 120.

58. See Sigmund Freud, *Standard Edition of the Complete Works of Sigmund Freud*, vol. 2 (London, 1955), p. 8.

59. Max Scheler, *Das Ressentiment im Aufbau der Moralen: Vom Umsturz der Werte, Gesammelte Werke*, vol. 3 (Bern, 1972). For Scheler, vengeance always contains the seed of ressentiment, since it "does not coincide with the impulse to return a blow or defend oneself" but postpones the response. "This self-restriction, however, which results from the forward-looking consideration that one would incur harm from an immediate reaction, entails an accompanying feeling of 'inability' or 'impotence' " (p. 39). As a result, in Scheler's view, revenge and hatred are intimately connected. Both are ressentiments of the weak, especially women. See also Karen Horney, "The Value of Vindictiveness," *American Journal of Psychoanalysis* 8 (1948): 3–12.

60. As we shall see, because the South ceased to exist as a nation after its defeat, the myth of the Lost Cause involved a heroization of defeat and ruled out any real possibility for revenge. Nonetheless, the idea of nemesis obtained even there. "[Southerners] well know that in due time, they, although powerless themselves, will be avenged through the same disorganizing heresies under which they now suffer, and through the anarchy and woes which they will bring upon the North" (R. L. Dabney, *A Defence of Virginia and, through Her, of the South, in Recent and Pending Contests against the Sectional Party* (New York, 1867), p. 356.

61. Sigmund Freud, *Standard Edition*, vol. 16 (London, 1963), p. 372. To understand the mentality of myths of revenge, it is necessary to recall what Freud writes about "imaginary wish-fulfillments": "There is no doubt that dwelling upon imaginary wish-fulfillments brings satisfaction with it, although it does not interfere with a knowledge that what is concerned is not real. Thus in the activity of phantasy human beings continue to enjoy the freedom from external compulsion which they have long since renounced in reality" (*Introductory Lectures on Psychoanalysis*, trans. James Strachey [New York, 1966], pp. 372). Unlike individual fantasy, collective-national fantasy is not subjectively conscious of the discrepancy but nevertheless behaves realistically in that it strives not to cross the borders of reality. Like German demands for reunification after 1949, the French *revanche* slogans after 1871 were anything but a call for real action.

62. Eugen Rosenstock, *Hochland*, June 1923, p. 230.

63. In France, the thought of *revanche* seldom occurred between 1815 and 1870, although each of the successive regimes aimed at revising the political map drawn up in 1815, that is, setting the Rhine as the French border with Germany. On the bipartisan policies of revising the Treaty of Versailles in Germany, see Ulrich Heinemann, *Die verdrängte Niederlage* (Göttingen, 1983).

64. In conjunction with French contingency plans in fall 1918 to reject Germany's proposal of an immediate cease-fire and to start a final offensive under exclusively French auspices, that is, outside the Entente, Guy Pedroncini cites military planners: "The honor of delivering the decisive blow should be reserved for the French army. . . . We want the 1919 battle to bring us a decisive victory in the war" (*Pétain, général en chef, 1917–1918* [Paris, 1974], p. 423).

65. The nineteenth century witnessed the functional transformation of *revanche* from gentlemen's agreement to national propaganda weapon. (It says something about this transition that the moment when the idea of *revanche* lost its traditional meaning was also the moment when

the word was adopted as France's main post-1871 slogan. Following Hegel, one might describe this coincidence as the flight of the owl toward its own twilight.) The individual steps in the escalation and transformation of the concept can best be illustrated with instances of Franco-German *revanche* after 1871. Even the first of these, the proclamation of the German empire in the Hall of Mirrors in Versailles, was no longer *revanche* in the sense of reestablishing equilibrium but rather revenge by Germany for two centuries of French hostility and annexation. Freed from the specifically military context and transferred to the national level, the revenge continued with the signings of the peace treaty of 1919, again in the Hall of Mirrors, and of the cease-fire of 1940 in the historic railway car at Compiègne, which had to be specially retrieved from a museum. Instead of aiming at mere redress, each of these symbolic acts sought to trump, indeed, eradicate the previous victory of the enemy. In line with such symbolic spatial significance, one might even speak of a "trophyizing" of *revanche*. Consistent with this transformation, the Compiègne railway car was brought to Berlin in 1940 after the signing of the cease-fire and publicly exhibited. Gambetta's remark, made on the occasion of a visit to Bismarck's castle in Friedrichsruh, where he saw the desk at which the peace treaty of 1871 was signed, can also be understood in this sense: "I will not be completely happy until that little table is in my house" (quoted in Daniel Amson, *Gambetta ou le rêve brisé* [Paris, 1994], p. 369).

66. The unsuccessful argument of General Pershing for just such a conclusion to the First World War shows how far the traditional European culture of war and diplomacy still was from engaging with the changing reality. Pershing's English colleagues in particular refused to follow his suggested course of action. A further quarter of a century and the Second World War were required for the idea of unconditional surrender to be fully accepted. The significance of this change is signaled by the adoption of the American "surrender" instead of the British "capitulation." Surrender stemmed not from the vocabulary of warfare and international law but from the vocabulary of civil and property law. It signified the transference of property title to the purchaser, that is, the actual handing over of the object in question. An army that capitulates in the traditional sense lays down its arms but retains its status as a legal entity. An army that surrenders is subjugated *in toto* to the authority of the victor.

67. Eric L. McKitrick, *Andrew Johnson and Reconstruction* (Chicago, 1960), p. 24. McKitrick writes also of the "very intimate relationship . . . between battles and elections," asserting that "military campaigns had

to be 'ratified,' in effect, at the polls" (p. 25). The same, of course, was true of the civil wars attending the French Revolution in the 1790s, but the political agitation was restricted to Paris, whereas the American Civil War encompassed the entire Union.

68. Ibid., pp. 23–24.

69. Ibid., p. 27. ("complete paralysis" and "forty years of torpor"); *Revue des deux mondes*, Feb. 1, 1871, p. 568 ("Chinese lethargy . . ."); Elme Marie Caro, *Revue des deux mondes*, Feb. 1, 1871, p. 256 ("Krupp-manufactured cannons"). The topos of "Chinese lethargy" was common in contemporary newspapers and magazines (see, for example, the articles by Paul Janet and Albert Sorel in *Revue des deux mondes*, Nov. 15, 1872, and Apr. 1, 1873). A nice characterization of the political stagnation is provided by Empress Eugénie's bon mot that Napoleon III's regime couldn't sneeze without permission from the opposition (Annette Horvath-Peterson, *Victor Duruy and French Education: Liberal Reform in the Second Empire* [Baton Rouge, 1984], p. 284).

70. William R. Taylor, *Cavalier and Yankee: The Old South and American National Character* (1961; rpt. New York, 1993), p. 284. Another image was that of the purifying, productive fire: "It was providence placing the idle ore in flame and forge. God said, 'Go up and die,' but already the South has learned that the summons to death was a summons to life . . . and so, lying down on the rugged summit of her defeat and despair, the South is awakening to an inheritance that eclipses her past" ("Confederate Veteran," quoted in Richard M. Weaver, *The Southern Tradition at Bay* [New Rochelle, 1968], p. 353).

71. From the perspective of psychological history, it is no accident that it is the epoch of the grandfathers that the intellectual interpreters of defeat promote in contrast to the shortcomings and detours of the fathers. The generation of the grandfathers always serves the sons as a point of reference, allowing them to establish an identity independent of their fathers. And no type of father is more particularly suited to the role of negative example than the one who squandered the grandfather's inheritance and thus put the son in the position of having to recover it in heroic fashion or, when this is impossible, of restoring the nation's morale and honor. On the psychohistory of relations between generations, see George B. Forgie, *Patricide in the House Divided: A Psychological Interpretation of Lincoln and His Age* (New York, 1979). Naturally, competing ideological and political camps choose different pasts to invoke within internal political conflicts. In the Third Republic, the ancien régime and its restoration were the main points of orientation for the royalists, while the First Republic

fulfilled the same function for the republicans. The corollary in Weimar Germany was Bismarck versus the Revolution of 1848. The common factor, however, is a return to a "healthy" past before the nation took a wrong turn.

72. Edward A. Pollard, *The Lost Cause Regained* (1868; rpt. New York, 1970), p. 155.

73. See Anthony Gaughan, "Woodrow Wilson and the Legacy of the Civil War," *Civil War History* 43 (1997): 225–42.

74. It was only with the *union sacrée* of the United States's entry into World War I that the persistent reservations in the South toward the Union disappeared. World War I thus served the same function in the United States as the Franco-Prussian War, which healed the trauma of intra-German conflict in the 1866 Austro-Prussian War, did in Germany.

75. It makes no difference that the origin of all these reform and modernization efforts lay in their respective prewar periods. The all-decisive and irrefutable argument that allowed reformers to prevail was that the nation would not have been defeated in war if it had heeded their earlier advice.

76. Reinhart Koselleck writes of the conjunction between the Scottish Enlightenment and the historicist-idealist school in Germany: "Being defeated is apparently an inexhaustible wellspring of intellectual progress. Historical transformations gnaw at the defeated. Insofar as they survive, they have automatically learned the ultimate lesson of all history: that things often turn out very differently than intended by the parties concerned" ("Erfahrungswandel," p. 60). Along with reflections on the reasons for one's failure (that is, modernity), an equally consequential contribution made by the defeated is the romanticization of the past into a kind of lost paradise. Here we must distinguish between two complementary strains in the philosophy of defeat: enlightened reflection on the modernity of the victors and romanticization of the past that was lost in defeat. Scotland offers a perfect example of how these schools coincide. The romanticism of McPherson, Hogg, and Walter Scott existed alongside its antithesis, the Edinburgh and Glasgow Enlightenment. The international resonance and success of the romantic movement were, however, if anything, greater for its appeal to a mass audience. "Ossian" in the waning eighteenth century and Walter Scott in the nineteenth can be characterized as the first literary industries serving the world market of mass taste, arising together with and in the immediate wake of industrial mass production along the Manchester model. The symbiotic, mutually reinforcing nature of Scottish Enlightenment and Scottish romanticism meant that while

Adam Smith provided the theoretical underpinning for the Industrial Revolution, McPherson and Walter Scott produced the complementary world of romantic-escapist entertainment, a precursor of Hollywood. See Murray G. H. Pittock, *The Invention of Scotland: The Stuart Myth and the Scottish Identity from 1638 to the Present* (London, 1991), pp. 72ff.

77. Josephine Grieder, *Anglomania in France, 1740–1789* (Geneva, 1985).

78. Michael Jeismann, *Das Vaterland der Feinde: Studien zum nationalen Feindbegriff und Selbstverständnis in Deutschland und Frankreich, 1792–1918* (Stuttgart, 1992), pp. 80, 75, 93–94.

79. After the present book was completed, my old classmate Werner Sollors told me about Georges Devereux's term "antagonistic acculturation," defined as "the new means . . . adopted in order to support existing goals, sometimes even for the specific purpose of resisting the compulsory adoption of the goals of the lending group. . . . Means are adopted and the goals pertaining to them are rejected. . . . The borrowing of means is frequently understood only for the ultimate purpose of turning the tables on the lender" (Georges Devereux and Edwin M. Loeb, "Antagonistic Acculturation," *American Sociological Review* 8 [1943]: 133–47).

1: The American South

1. Norbert Finzsch and Jürgen Martschukat, eds., *Different Restorations: Reconstruction and "Wiederaufbau" in the United States and Germany, 1865—1945—1989* (Providence, 1996), pp. 316–17.

2. Eric Foner, *Reconstruction: America's Unfinished Revolution, 1863–1877* (New York, 1988), p. 125.

3. Quoted in Russell F. Weighley, *The American Way of War* (New York, 1973), p. 153.

4. Quoted in Michael Howard, *The Franco-Prussian War* (New York, 1961), p. 380.

5. Quoted in Mark Grimsley, *The Hard Hand of War: Union Military Policy toward Southern Civilians, 1861–1865* (New York, 1995), p. 167.

6. On the Puritan concept of wilderness, see Roderick Nash, *Wilderness and the American Mind* (New Haven, 1967), pp. 26–40. On the Elizabethan-Renaissance iconography of Virginia as a Garden of Eden, see Raimondo Luraghi, *The Rise and Fall of the Plantation South* (New York, 1978), pp. 27, 31; Henry Nash Smith, *Virgin Land: The American West as Symbol and Myth* (1950; rpt. Cambridge, 1970), pp. 145ff. For a comparison of the two visions, see Leo Marx, *The Machine in the*

Garden: Technology and the Pastoral Ideal in America (London, 1972), p. 43.

7. William Hepworth Dixon, *New America* (Philadelphia, 1867), pp. 461–63.

8. Quoted in William R. Taylor, *Cavalier and Yankee: The Old South and American National Character* (1961; rpt. New York, 1993), p. 97.

9. C. Vann Woodward, *Origins of the New South, 1877–1913* (1951; rpt. Baton Rouge, 1995), pp. 456–57.

10. Quoted in Edwin A. Miles, "The Old South and the Classical World," *South Carolina Historical Review* 48 (1971): 258, 263.

11. As Rollin G. Osterweis points out, the South's "intellectual blockade" against the North put an end to its traditional role as the national seat of enlightenment (*Romanticism and Nationalism in the Old South* [New Haven, 1949], p. 21).

12. Ibid., p. 11. The economic experience of the post-1830 South was not unlike that of sixteenth-century Central Europe. Both regions came out on the losing end of an epochal and global transformation of the world economy. Just as Central Europe was marginalized by the opening of overseas trade routes, the South was robbed by industrial development in the North of its leading role in agrarian industry. Throughout the first third of the nineteenth century, plantation products were the economic locomotive of the United States. That was where capital accumulation first took place, and without it the industrial takeoff of the North would have been impossible (see Douglass C. North, *The Economic Growth of the United States, 1790–1860* [New York, 1966], pp. 66ff). Raimondo Luraghi describes the global economic context of the South's decline, in all its "tragic" dimensions, as the demise of "seigneurial" culture in the European overseas colonies, which gradually lost its economic foundation to rising industrial capitalism (*Rise and Fall*). The feeling of abandonment and betrayal among those who are left sitting atop outmoded economic structures—while all around others are denouncing and attacking the older order—is common in history. England, which during its mercantilist-colonialist phase had engaged in the slave trade with unreserved energy, began to fight against slavery with much the same vigor after becoming an industrial society (David Brion Davis, *Slavery and Human Progress* [New York, 1984], pp. 127ff.). The drama is being replayed today in the warnings of the First World to the industrially developing Third World about preserving the environment. It goes without saying that the warnings, criticisms, and denunciations emanate from a moralistic minority that distances itself from the voraciously capitalist past of its own culture.

13. Both quoted in Taylor, *Cavalier and Yankee*, pp. 55, 57–58. Emphasis in original.
14. Quoted in Luraghi, *Rise and Fall*, p. 81.
15. Quoted in Osterweis, *Romanticism*, p. 20. Henry Clay would employ the same metaphor of the scales decades later, before the actual outbreak of hostilities, when the polarization had reached an advanced stage: "You Northerners are looking on in safety and security while the conflagration . . . is raging in the slave States. . . . In the one scale, then, we behold sentiment, sentiment alone; in the other, property, the social fabric, life, and all that makes life desirable and happy" (Barrington Moore, *Social Origins of Dictatorship and Democracy* [Boston, 1967], p. 122).
16. C. Vann Woodward, "The Irony of Southern History," *The Burden of Southern History*, rev. 3rd ed. (Baton Rouge, 1993), p. 198.
17. Quoted in C. Vann Woodward, *American Counterpoint: Slavery and Racism in the North-South Dialogue* (Boston, n.d. [1971]), p. 123.
18. Richard Hofstadter, *The American Political Tradition* (1948; rpt. New York, 1973), pp. 67–91.
19. Fitzhugh is quoted in Edmund Wilson, *Patriotic Gore* (New York, 1962), p. 345. Grayson in Eugene D. Genovese, *The Slaveholders' Dilemma* (Columbia, 1992), p. 71. Michael O'Brien, a leading representative of contemporary Southern intellectual history, grants the proslavery theoreticians that "their vision of the plantation . . . was as utopian as that of the phalanstery of Fourier" (*Rethinking the South* [Athens, Ga., 1993], p. 44).
20. "Slavery is . . ." quoted in Richard M. Weaver, *The Southern Tradition at Bay* (New Rochelle, 1968), p. 89. "The new fashionable name . . ." quoted in Woodward, *American Counterpoint*, p. 119. Woodward mentions that Fitzhugh used the same source material on the condition of the English industrial proletariat that Marx would use ten years later as the basis for the first chapter of *Das Kapital*. Describing Fitzhugh's anticapitalism, Woodward writes: "The ferocity of Fitzhugh's indictment of the capitalist economy . . . is equaled only by the severity of the socialist attack" (p. 125). In this context, it is worth noting that Eugene D. Genovese, the historian of the plantation economy and its social forms, began his career as an orthodox Marxist, only to become a committed conservative and antisocialist. His interest in Fitzhugh, indeed his open sympathy for this "conservative revolutionary," has remained so constant over the years that it could be attributed to both an authoritarian-socialist affinity and a romantic anticapitalism. Recently, Genovese has connected the collapse of Soviet-dominated real-existing socialism back

to the fall of the Confederacy, one similarity being the disillusionment of the intelligentsia. "The fall of the Confederacy drowned the hopes of Southern conservatives for the construction of a viable noncapitalist order, much as the disintegration of the Soviet Union—all pretenses and wishful thinking aside—has drowned the hopes of socialists. The critique of capitalism has led Southern conservatives to the impasse in which the Left now finds itself" (*The Southern Tradition* [Cambridge, 1994], p. 37).

21. Michel Chevalier, *Society, Manners, and Politics in the United States* (Ithaca, 1969), p. 153.

22. Quoted in Luraghi, *Rise and Fall*, p. 73.

23. Quoted in Sharon E. Hannum, "Confederate Cavaliers" (Ph.D. diss., Rice University, 1965), p. 54.

24. European public opinion was doubly divided about the American Civil War. Liberals condemned the South on account of slavery whereas conservatives sympathized with what they considered to be the South's feudal-aristocratic cause. Within the liberal camp, however, there was considerable sympathy for the South's cause when it was understood as a war for national liberation similar to those in Italy, Poland, and Hungary. Napoleon III supported the Confederacy not only for economic and political reasons but also for sentimental ones. Even Prévost-Paradol, a political supporter of the Union, found the aspirations of the South thoroughly comprehensible: "Let us suppose that we had received our slaves from our fathers at the same time we had received our fields, . . . that we had become slave owners in this great republic by a free contract and without argument. . . . Let us be just. . . . We would leave our homes armed, resolved to do everything to safeguard our security" (quoted in Serge Gavronsky, *The French Liberal Opposition and the American Civil War* [New York, 1968], p. 77). The German historian Heinrich Treitschke recorded among the Prussian officer corps, contrary to the official government line, "a certain sympathy for the slave barons of the South since they displayed such clear superiority in matters military" (*Politik* [Leipzig, 1898], vol. 2, p. 249).

25. *Southern Literary Messenger* 30 (1860): 404, 407.

26. On Robert E. Lee, see Thomas L. Connelly, *The Marble Man: Robert E. Lee and His Image in American Society* (Baton Rouge, 1977), p. 102. The Hans Muller family tree is cited in W. J. Cash, *The Mind of the South* (1941; rpt. New York, 1991), p. 64.

27. Edwin A. Miles, "The Old South and the Classical World," *North Carolina Historical Review* [1971]: 264–65. On the post-1830 reinterpretation of the cavalier-Yankee dichotomy into racial antagonism, see

Drew Gilpin Faust, *Confederate Nationalism: Ideology and Identity in the Civil War South* (Baton Rouge, 1988), pp. 10–11.

28. Murray G. H. Pittock, *The Invention of Scotland: The Stuart Myth and the Scottish Identity, 1638 to the Present* (London, 1991), pp. 5, 67.

29. See Grady McWhiney, *Cracker Culture: Celtic Ways in the Old South* (Tuscaloosa, 1988). According to McWhiney, the settlers in the South around 1800 came overwhelmingly from the periphery of England (Wales, Ireland, and Scotland) and were of entirely different social, cultural, and confessional stock than the English-Puritan middle class of the North. "Crackers" were lower-class, maintained archaic clan structures, had little use for the Protestant work ethic, acted on emotion, valued comfort and hospitality, and possessed an easily wounded sense of honor. In short, they represented all those qualities normally attributed to the cavalier. Thus the conclusion can be drawn in reverse, supporting W. J. Cash's thesis that an originally plebeian class had elevated itself to the status of an American aristocracy.

30. Osterweis, *Romanticism*, p. 19.

31. While the author had assumed this happening during the Reconstruction period, Harry L. Watson points out a later date and a more twisted story: "KKK cross-burning originated as a literary flourish of Thomas Dixon in his 1905 novel *The Clansman*. He borrowed it from the novels of Sir Walter Scott (who had described cross-burning as a signaling device used by the clans of medieval Scotland) and erroneously attributed it to the Reconstruction Klan. When the KKK was reinvented in 1915 in the wake of *The Birth of a Nation*, the famous movie version of the Dixon novel, cross-burning was accepted as part of the package because everybody involved had seen it in the movies. And so this bit of bogus folklore made it into vicious real life" (personal correspondence).

32. This oft-cited passage comes from Twain's *Life on the Mississippi* (1883). It is surprising, in light of the date of publication, that cultural historians have taken for granted that Twain was exclusively attacking the South. In the 1880s, it was the *North* that saw medieval chivalry again become fashionable, and this contemporary trend must have been more what Twain had in mind than the past one of the South. A few years after the publication of *Life on the Mississippi*, Twain satirized in *A Connecticut Yankee at King Arthur's Court* what he considered the unbearable foolishness of romanticism. Given that in the South the romantic disease Twain described had disappeared almost a generation before, whereas an outbreak was in full force in the North, it is tempting to conclude that his tongue lashing of the South was

actually directed at the North. See also Cash, *Mind of the South*, p. 65; Wilson, *Patriotic Gore*, p. 444; and John Fraser, *America and the Patterns of Chivalry* (Cambridge, 1982), p. 52. On Walter Scott's role in the South, there are no recent studies. The standard sources are still those from the 1930s and 1940s, on which Osterweis, too, relies. Along with Eckenrode, they are Grace Warren Landrum, "Sir Walter Scott and His Literary Revivals in the Old South," *American Literature* 2 (Mar. 1930–Jan. 1931): 256–77; Landrum, "Notes on the Reading of the Old South," *American Literature* 3 (1931): 60–71; and G. Harrison Orians, "Walter Scott, Mark Twain, and the Civil War," *South Atlantic Quarterly* 40 (1941): 342–59.

33. Hamilton James Eckenrode coined the term *Walter Scottland* to describe the South after its self-transformation ("Sir Walter Scott and the South," *North American Review* 206 [1917]).

34. Osterweis, *Romanticism*, p. 41.

35. Hamilton J. Eckenrode, *Jefferson Davis* (1923; rpt. Freeport, 1971), p. 11.

36. O'Brien, *Rethinking the South*, p. 51.

37. The standard regional study is J. Mills Thornton III, *Politics and Power in a Slave Society: Alabama, 1800–1860* (Baton Rouge, 1978).

38. Barrington Moore Jr., *Social Origins of Dictatorship and Democracy* (Boston, 1967), p. 121. Moore describes "capitalist-but-not-bourgeois" societies like the American South and Junker-dominated Prussia as "catonistic." In an attempt to get around an age-old question—whether a slave-based economy that produces for a global capitalist market is capitalist or feudal—Moore answers "both." This is the current consensus among historians. One horizon-expanding achievement of this discussion, initiated by Marxist historians, has been a comparison of the plantation system and the Prussian landed aristocracy in terms of their economic, social, and ideological structures. Shearer Davis Bowman's *Masters and Lords: Mid-19th-Century U.S. Planters and Prussian Junkers* (New York, 1993) provides a comprehensive survey and draws attention to the changing significance of the Marxian idea of a "Prussian path" into modernity. Whereas the phrase originally, in Lenin's usage, designated the transformation of feudal estates into capitalist-organized agrarian concerns, it now refers to capitalist modernization within authoritarian-patriarchal societies like Prussia and Japan, in contrast to the liberal-democratic model.

39. As of 1860, the North was producing 97 percent of all cannons and firearms, 93 percent of all raw iron, 94 percent of all textiles, and 90 percent of the shoes in the United States (James M. McPherson, *Battle Cry of Freedom: The Civil War Era* [New York, 1988], p. 318).

40. Michael O'Brien, "The Nineteenth-Century American South," *Historical Journal* 24 (1981): 755.

41. Raimondo Luraghi, "The Civil War and the Modernization of American Society," *Civil War History* 18 (1972): 246. See also the statistics on the rise of the munitions industry (p. 244).

42. Marcus Cunliffe, *Soldiers and Civilians: The Martial Spirit in America* (Boston, 1968), p. 338. A further indicator of the superior military tradition in the South was the fact that responsibility for both the War Department and the army rested overwhelmingly in Southern hands. (Jefferson Davis, later the Confederate president, was for many years secretary of the War Department.) Of the four commanding generals in the United States, three were from the South, as was the leading military theoretician in prewar America, Denis H. Mahan, father of the author of *The Influence of Sea-Power upon History*.

43. Unlike those in *Ivanhoe*, Southern tournaments featured not dueling but contests of skill (Esther J. Crooks and Ruth W. Crooks, *The Ring Tournament in the United States* [Richmond, 1936]).

44. It is worth remembering that the picture of the South as the military citadel of the United States was unknown at the time of the Revolutionary War. New England played the leading role as both the site of the main battles and the origin of major military players. See Cunliffe, *Soldiers and Civilians*, p. 350. An important question for further investigation would be when and why the North relinquished its military aura to the South.

45. On the founding of military academies, see John Hope Franklin, *The Militant South, 1800–1861* (Cambridge, 1956), pp. 146–70.

46. Michael C. C. Adams, *Our Masters the Rebels: A Speculation on Union Military Failure in the East, 1861–1865* (Cambridge, 1978), p. 39.

47. Ibid., p. 31. The esteem in which the military culture of the South was held by the Northern military leadership did not, of course, remain a secret to the Union's political leadership, as General McClellan's ultimate dismissal attests. In the decisive phase of the war, as politicians began to search for explanations for the South's early military victories, even West Point came in for criticism. The military academy was described as a breeding ground for traitors, and some demanded that the institution be abolished. One senator even suggested that the Union's epitaph, if the North was defeated, should read: "Died of West Point pro-slaveryism" (p. 374).

48. Ibid., p. viii.

49. Robert Penn Warren, *The Legacy of the Civil War* (Cambridge, 1983), p. 15.

50. On Pollard, see Jack P. Maddox, *The Reconstruction of Edward A.*

Pollard (Chapel Hill, 1974). During the war, Pollard had criticized the Southern leaders for their defensive strategy. To use a phrase from World War I, Pollard was a proponent of "peace through victory." Moreover, anticipating something like the Morgenthau plan for defeated Nazi Germany, Pollard suggested that the industrial system of the North, after it was defeated, should be completely destroyed so the South would never again have to fear a capitalist-industrial threat. At the same time, the South was to expand its area of influence through a slavery-based empire including the Caribbean and parts of Central America. In the immediate aftermath of Lee's surrender, Pollard was one of the few who wanted to continue the struggle with guerrilla warfare. The idea of the Lost Cause seems to have enabled him personally to jettison this sort of extremism. He spent the rest of his short life as a political moderate. Pollard died in 1872 at the age of forty.

51. Pollard, *Lost Cause*, pp. 750–52.
52. George F. Sensabaugh, *Milton in Early America* (Princeton, 1964), p. 264.
53. Kenneth Stampp, *The Era of Reconstruction, 1865–1877* (New York, 1966), p. 91.
54. *Hilt to Hilt* by John Esten Cooke. Le Conte is quoted in Hannum, "Confederate Cavaliers," p. 73.
55. *Southern Review*, July 1869, quoted in Susan Speare Durant, "The Gently Furled Banner: The Development of the Myth of the Lost Cause, 1865–1900" (Ph.D. diss., University of North Carolina, 1972), p. 130.
56. John S. Blackburn and William Naylor McDonald, "Southern School History of the United States of America" (1870), quoted in Durant, "Gently Furled Banner," p. 131.
57. The quotation is from the periodical *The Land We Love*, Sept. 1868, p. 447.
58. "Bludgeon against rapier" is John Esten Cooke's characterization, quoted in Lloyd Arthur Hunter, "The Sacred South: Postwar Confederates and the Sacralization of Southern Culture" (Ph.D. diss., St. Louis University, 1978), p. 248. "Machinery against chivalry" is from Edward McCrady Jr., "Address before the Virginia Division of the Army of Northern Virginia" (1886), quoted in Durant, "Gently Furled Banner," p. 370. The use of modern military technology was not, of course, considered "unmilitary" in the South. On the contrary, the South was perceived to have led the North in the realm of military technological innovation. The publisher of *The Land We Love* maintained that all major military inventions were discovered in the South

and then copied and mass-produced in the North. "The Southern mind is eminently ingenious and suggestive, while the Northern mind takes up the hints thrown out, appropriates and improves them" (*The Land We Love*, June 1866, p. 90). The same conviction was common in post-1871 France with reference to Germany.

59. Quoted in Durant, "Gently Furled Banner," p. ii.

60. The phrase is Union general J. W. Turner's version of a saying common in the South. Quoted in Michael Perman, *Reunion without Compromise: The South and Reconstruction, 1865–1868* (Cambridge, 1973), p. 29.

61. General Turner commented on the sentiment "We are whipped" with the following words: "I think if a man of generous soul felt deep mortification he would keep quiet on the subject. I have always thought that [Southerners'] feeling of mortification was more superficial than otherwise" (quoted in Perman, *Reunion*, p. 29). The frivolity or irony inherent in the term *whipping* is apparent in the record of a conversation between a Northern judge and an ex-senator from North Carolina. After the senator made a remark to the effect that his home state accepted the whipping, the exchange ensued: " 'Then they really feel themselves whipped?' 'Yes, you've subjugated us at last,' with a smile which showed that the politician thought it not the worst kind of joke, after all" (p. 29).

62. "He looked like a cross between a Cavalier dandy and a riverboat gambler. He affected the romantic style of Sir Walter Scott's heroes and was eager to win everlasting glory at Gettysburg" (McPherson, *Battle Cry of Freedom*, p. 662).

63. Dixon, *New America*, pp. 492–93.

64. Thomas L. Connelly and Barbara L. Bellows, *God and General Longstreet* (Baton Rouge, 1982), p. 36.

65. Quoted in Connelly, *Marble Man*, p. 17.

66. Along with Connelly's *Marble Man* and *God and General Longstreet*, see his "The Image and the General: Robert E. Lee in American Historiography," *Civil War History* 19 (1973): 50–64.

67. Connelly, *Marble Man*, p. 95.

68. Ibid.

69. This account follows Thomas L. Connelly's "Virginia argument" in attributing Lee's *national* stature to the fact that he came from Virginia. In the South's rhetoric, Virginia was used metonymically for the entire region to portray the South as the seat of the nation's soul and the victim of a tragic conflict (*God and General Longstreet*, pp. 39ff.). Two divergent regions—the "aristocratic" Old South and the dynamic,

nouveau riche Cotton Belt—had crystallized in the three decades prior to the Civil War. The South's postdefeat "rediscovery" of Virginia's leading role in the birth of the nation was accompanied by Virginia's own desire to distance itself from those usually held responsible for secession. (The corollary here would be the attitude among the southern German states, above all Bavaria, toward Prussia in November 1918.) What had begun as an argument for Virginia, however, was taken over and adopted by the rest of the South once it had become clear that there was indeed a considerable amount of sentimental-romantic sympathy for Virginia in the North.

70. Daniel W. Stowell, *Rebuilding Zion: The Religious Reconstruction of the South, 1863–1877* (New York, 1998), pp. 175 ff.

71. A "sacred society" is defined by the sociologist Howard Becker as "one that elicits from or imparts to its members, by means of association, an unwillingness and/or liability to respond to the culturally new as the new is defined by those members in terms of the society's existing culture." Its antithesis, "secular society," "endows its members with a high degree of readiness and capacity to change" (quoted in Samuel S. Hill, *Southern Churches in Crisis* [New York, 1967], p. 67). The definitions were originally contained in Becker's essay "Sacred and Secular Societies," *Social Forces* 28 (1950): 363 ff. Lloyd Arthur Hunter suggests the term *cultural religion* for the Lost Cause (*Sacred South*, p. 42). Coined by Fritz Stern in reference to the culturally pessimistic German intelligentsia during the Wilhelminian era, the term is in fact the first step toward a fruitful comparison of the two cultures. "Rebuffed in actuality and turned inwards by their beliefs, the German elite tended to become estranged from reality and disdainful of it. It lost the power to deal with practical matters in practical terms" (Stern, *The Politics of Cultural Despair* [Berkeley, 1974], p. xxv). Charles Reagan Wilson describes the Lost Cause as a "civil religion" distinguishing the South from the rest of the United States. He takes his definition of "civil religion" from Robert N. Bellah, Sidney E. Mead, and Will Herberg (Wilson, *Baptized in Blood: The Religion of the Lost Cause* [Athens, Ga., 1980], pp. 12–14).

A famous passage from William Faulkner's *Intruder in the Dust* illustrates the extent to which the Lost Cause was a sacred one and gives insight into the psychology of its believers. "For every Southern boy fourteen years old, not once but whenever he wants it, there is the instant when it's still not yet two o'clock in the afternoon in 1863, the brigades are still in position behind the rail fence, the guns are laid and ready in the woods and the furled flags are already loosened to break out and Pickett himself with his long oiled ringlets and his hat in one hand and probably his sword in the other looking up the hill waiting for Longstreet to give the word and it's all in the balance, it hasn't happened yet, it hasn't even begun yet but there is still time for it not to begin" (quoted in Douglas T. Miller, "Faulkner and the Civil War: Myth and Reality," *American Quarterly* 15 [1963]: 201).

72. A passage from an 1894 sermon reads: "I do not forget . . . that a Nero wielded the scepter of empire and a Paul was beheaded; that a Herod was crowned and a Christ was crucified. . . . Instead of accepting the defeat of the South as a divine verdict against her, I regard it as but another instance of 'truth on the scaffold and wrong on the throne' " (quoted in Hunter, *Sacred South*, p. 265). On theological explanations for defeat, see Wilson, *Baptized in Blood*, pp. 58 ff. On the Job argument in particular, see pp. 72 ff.

73. Sermon by James I. Vance, quoted in Wilson, *Baptized in Blood*, p. 75.

74. "Narcotic influence," coined by Walter Hines Page, is quoted in John Milton Cooper Jr., *Walter Hines Page: The Southerner as American* (Chapel Hill, 1977), p. xxi.

75. *Manufacturers Record*, July 9, 1887, quoted in Paul M. Gaston, *The New South Creed: A Study in Southern Mythmaking* (1970; rpt. Baton Rouge, 1976), pp. 57–58.

76. Quoted in McPherson, *Battle Cry of Freedom*, pp. 92–93.

77. Ibid., p. 93.

78. Ibid., p. 100. On the genesis of the antagonism between the pro-industrial North and the anti-industrial South, see Norris W. Preyer, "Why Did Industrialization Lag in the Old South?" *Georgia Historical Review* 55 (1971): 378–96. According to Preyer, the development of artisanry and early industry in the North and South around 1800 was basically comparable and, if anything, somewhat more advanced in the South. A half century later, the balance had tilted radically in favor of the North. Along with the traditional explanation that the cotton boom prevented further industrial development in the South, Preyer draws attention to an anti-industrial mentality common to both North and South. Both regions viewed the Manchester model as evil and sought to hinder it with every means at their disposal. Northern industrialization was understood as something altogether different from its English equivalent. The factories of Lowell, Massachusetts, were seen as stations of orderliness, morality, and hygiene, a kind of extension of Sunday school. In other words, factories were as much the holy counterimage to satanic industrialization for Northerners as plantations were for Southerners.

79. *The Land We Love*, May 1866, pp. 8–10.

80. Dixon, *New America*, pp. 474–75.

81. Stampp, *Era of Reconstruction*, pp. 44, 56.

82. Eric Foner, *Reconstruction: America's Unfinished Revolution, 1863–1877* (New York, 1988), p. 6.

83. Tocqueville himself noted early on that "the prejudice of race appears to be stronger in the states that have abolished slavery than in those where it still exists" (quoted in C. Vann Woodward, "The Antislavery Myth," *American Scholar* 31 [1961]: 316).

84. All quotations appear in Paul H. Buck, *The Road to Reunion, 1865–1900* (Boston, 1937), pp. 11–12.

85. Eric L. McKitrick distinguishes between two phases of postwar sentiment in the North. He characterizes the first as a "wait-and-see" attitude, in keeping with the North's expectation that the South would show visible signs ("rituals") of subjugation and regret. Only after this did not happen did the mood shift to one demanding punitive measures (*Andrew Johnson and Reconstruction* [Chicago, 1960], pp. 15 ff.). McKitrick is primarily referring to popular opinion as distinguished from opinions expressed in the media.

86. The black codes were "a melange of paternalism and repression" (Dan T. Carter, *When the War Was Over: The Failure of Self-Reconstruction in the South, 1865–1867* [Baton Rouge, 1985], p. 217). Considering the chaos prevailing in the postwar South, the black codes can also be seen as an attempt to reestablish order. In the months prior to the passage of this legislation, the occupying Union army had taken similar, often harsher disciplinary and discriminatory measures against blacks. See Carter, *When the War*, pp. 180 ff.

87. Quoted in Stampp, *Era of Reconstruction*, p. 200.

88. Gaston, *New South Creed*, pp. 18 ff. This study remains the classic on the intellectual history, mentality, and ideology of the New South.

89. Ibid., p. 32.

90. Of the four articles by DeLeon that Gaston lists in his bibliography, two were published in Northern magazines, two in the South. "The New South" was the title of an article in *Harper's New Monthly Magazine* (1874). The titles of the articles that were published in the South were "Ruin and Reconstruction of the Southern States" and "The Southern States since the War" (Gaston, *New South Creed*, p. 289).

91. Pollard's revision of his views took place in his book *The Lost Cause Regained* (1868). He published numerous other articles on the necessity of modernizing the South, using the North as a model, between 1870 and his death in 1872. See Jack P. Maddex Jr., "Pollard's 'The Lost Cause Regained': A Mask for Southern Accommodation," *Journal of Southern History* 40 (1974): 610 off.

92. Gaston, *New South Creed*, p. 91.

93. Quoted in John S. Ezell, "Woodrow Wilson as Southerner," *Civil War History* 15 (1969): 163. Emphasis in original.

94. Such figures were not, of course, aware that when they said "economy" they meant politics. Politicians' politics were disdained: "Politics won't increase the number of factories in a town. Politics won't build stores and houses. Politics won't attract investors; on the contrary, it often creates such oppressive laws for the benefit of its adherents that capital is kept away. Politics seldom increases a man's business in a legitimate way" (Richard H. Edmonds, quoted in Gaston, *New South Creed*, p. 109). What was meant by "politics" was "bad for business" politics, just as "business" was code for business-friendly politics.

95. Quoted in Gaston, *New South Creed*, p. 196. The *Manufacturers Record*, published in Baltimore, was more a propaganda organ than a source of information. C. Vann Woodward observes that the publisher, Richard H. Edmonds, "employed statistics for hortatory purposes, with something of the orator's license" (*Origins of the New South*, p. 145).

96. Quoted in Woodward, *American Counterpoint*, pp. 42–43. Grady was born in 1850 in Atlanta and died at the age of thirty-nine. His role as a figurehead for the New South was due primarily to his oratorical skills and secondarily to his journalistic activity as the publisher of the *Atlanta Constitution*. His youth and charisma seem to have had a kind of Alcibiades effect on his audience.

97. Ibid., p. 43. "Mother of millionaires" is quoted in Gaston, *New South Creed*, p. 79.

98. Gaston, *New South Creed*, p. 76.

99. Ibid., p. 78.

100. Ibid., p. 72.

101. Ibid.

102. As with all stereotypes, contradictions abound. The mirror image of the South as "mild," "lovely," "sensual," and "charming" was the masculine, aggressive, martial self-conception of Southern male culture, epitomized by its rigid codes of honor. This feverish masculinity can be seen as overcompensation for the feminine side. The self-stylized Southern knight defined himself as both defender and vassal of feminine cultural refinement. The ideal, of course, was a synthesis of both characteristics in the image of the "tender-hearted hero." General George Burgwyn Anderson was characterized at his funeral as "a soft, gentle, refined, winning, and almost womanly spirit" (Durant, "Gently Furled Banner," p. 204). William Gilmore Simms, the most prominent author of plantation novels in the prewar period, was not alone in seeing *Hamlet* as "a kind of parable for the South." Southern literature

was, as William R. Taylor argues, full of such "weak and sensitive heroes" (*Cavalier and Yankee*, pp. 293–96). The heroines were another matter entirely. The Southern belle was a female anti-Hamlet, a driving force, and, as Kathryn Lee Seidel stresses, a figure who owed her influence not to beauty but to a combination of charisma, energy, grace, and intellect (*The Southern Belle in the American Novel* [Tampa, 1985], p. 3). After the war, however, the active young heroine became a passive object to be married. Seidel discusses this shift in a chapter tellingly entitled "The Belle as the Fallen South" (pp. 127–29).

103. Henry W. Grady, *The New South and Other Addresses* (1904; rpt. New York, 1969), pp. 95–96.

104. Woodward, *Origins of the New South*, p. 108.

105. Foner, *Reconstruction*, p. 597.

106. Woodward, *Origins of the New South*, pp. 140, 111.

107. Carter, *When the War*, p. 171. On the thwarted expectations for an influx of immigrant labor and capital investment, see Woodward, *Origins of the New South*, p. 299. In this respect, as in so many others, the New South period resembled the two initial post–Civil War years.

108. On the South as "colonial economy," see Woodward, *Origins of the New South*, pp. 291 ff.

109. Richard H. Edmonds, quoted in Gaston, *New South Creed*, pp. 164–65.

110. The term *mummies* was coined by Walter Hines Page, one of the few critical minds in the New South movement.

111. *Scribner's Magazine*, Dec. 1874, quoted in Gaston, *New South Creed*, p. 39.

112. Buck, *Road to Reunion*, p. 131.

113. Frederick Taylor, quoted in Buck, *Road to Reunion*, p. 191.

114. Quoted in Wilson, *Baptized in Blood*, pp. 172, 173–74. Naturally the old antagonisms did not completely disappear in the crusade rhetoric. They lived on in the form of puns such as "German–Sherman" (p. 224).

115. An intriguing question is whether that segment of the loser elite that is bent on adopting not only the "technical" and "material" methods but also the idealistic-moral content of the victorious model is trying to be more Catholic than the pope. A comparison between Woodrow Wilson's and Theodore Roosevelt's attitudes toward U.S. entry into World War I suffices to illustrate the point. Long before Wilson, Roosevelt was a passionate interventionist; his rationale, however, was not moralistic but military and strategic. A psychohistorical interpretation of Wilsonian moralism might argue that Wilson was trying to compensate for the "moral defeat" of his father's generation by playing the

role of the "abolitionist" against the Central Powers. In any case, for Wilson the Civil War and World War I possessed a similar moral status and were intimately connected. "The Civil War was a war to save one country," he remarked. "The Great War is a war to save the world" (Anthony Gaughan, "Woodrow Wilson and the Legacy of the Civil War," *Civil War History* 43 [1997]: 241). Consistent with this attitude, Wilson saw his idea for a League of Nations as the extension of the American Union. Just as the Union soldiers had given their lives in the Civil War "in order that America be united, these men [the soldiers of World War I] have given their lives in order that the world might be united." Lincoln was Wilson's undisputed role model, and his influence was so great that, for example, after his stroke Wilson received visitors in Lincoln's bed.

116. "The Cause Triumphant," *Confederate Veteran*, Mar. 1918, quoted in Wilson, *Baptized in Blood*, p. 174.

117. The phrase *spiritual Secession* was coined by Donald Davidson (Daniel Aaron, *The Unwritten War* [New York, 1973], p. 291). *I'll Take My Stand: The South and the Agrarian Tradition* (New York, 1930) has been reprinted repeatedly since 1962.

118. "Out of this philosophy laced with selective facts and ancestral legend," writes Daniel Aaron of the agrarians, "came simplistic history, but out of simplistic history came fruitful myth" (*Unwritten War*, p. 293). In his review of *I'll Take My Stand*, Edmund Wilson recognized an authenticity and "warmth" in Southern life that the North lacked (*New Republic*, July 29, 1931; reprinted in Wilson, *The American Earthquake* [New York, 1958], pp. 330ff.). The most prominent authors in the group were, in addition to Tate and Warren, John Crowe Ransom, Donald Davidson, Stark Young, and Andrew Nelson Lytle. See Paul K. Conkin, *The Southern Agrarians* (Knoxville, 1988).

119. David M. Potter, "The Enigma of the South," *Yale Review* 51 (Oct. 1961): 148–49.

120. Elizabeth Fox-Genovese, "The Anxiety of History: The Southern Confrontation with Modernity," *Southern Cultures* 1 (1993): 66.

121. It is no accident that the term *exceptionalism* (*Sonderweg*), most often used in conjunction with pre-Nazi Germany, is here applied to the development of the South after 1830. The exceptional development undergone by the South and Germany is the same insofar as both societies belonged to the modern West yet rejected the ideas of 1789—democracy, equality, and progress—in favor of a romantic-aristocratic ideal of culture. In Germany, the rejection is reflected in the distinction between *Kultur* (positive) and *Zivilisation* (negative); in the South it is the idea of agrarian patriarchy as distinguished from Northern liberal

democracy. Similar, too, are the resulting forms of class hegemony—for example, the latifundia produce goods according to capitalist principles for the world market yet maintain an aristocratic-feudal culture and ideology. The ideal of a patriarchal *Gemeinschaft,* or community, was defined in both cases through a rejection of *Gesellschaft,* or society, which was deemed atomizing and inhuman. In this vein, David M. Potter characterizes the secession as a "conservative revolt" (*The South and the Sectional Conflict* [Baton Rouge, 1968], p. 293). What Germany was for Western Europe, the South was for the United States. Both conceived of themselves, to return to Werner Sombart's antithesis, as *heroic* versus *shopkeeper* cultures. This explains the contempt maintained for the ideological "cant" of the enemy and the high estimation of one's own "openness," which from the enemy perspective is nothing more than pure barbarism. Whether we are speaking of the German violation of Belgian neutrality in 1914, which was freely admitted by Chancellor Bethmann-Hollweg, or the comparison between slavery and free wage labor—the former as "an open system of undisguised force, the other . . . a system of disguised fraud," in the words of Francis Pickens (quoted in Carter, *When the War*, p. 130)—masculine plain talk was considered morally superior to the enemy's hypocrisy.

122. Francis Pendleton Gaines, *The Southern Plantation: A Study in the Development and the Accuracy of a Tradition* (1924; rpt. Gloucester, 1962), p. 16.

123. Seidel, *Southern Belle*, pp. 5 ff.

124. Gaines, *Southern Plantation*, p. 23.

125. The equation of "escapist" literature in the North and the South fails to take into account the fundamentally divergent social structures and mentalities in the two societies. Elizabeth Fox-Genovese draws attention to the danger of measuring prewar Southern literature according to Northern standards—for example, by expecting the hero to be internally tormented when such behavior would have violated Southern social and cultural norms. "The southern hero owes his identity to his identification with society, rather than his struggles against it" ("Anxiety of History," p. 76). The insistence on evaluating Southern literature according to Southern norms and not those of the West European or Northern hero is evocative of Henry Adams's oft-cited phrase that the Southerner is "simple beyond analysis." W. J. Cash develops this line of thinking even further: "From first to last . . . he did not . . . think; he felt; and discharging his feelings immediately, he developed no need or desire for intellectual culture in its own right—none, at least, powerful enough to drive him past his taboos to its actual achievement" (*Mind of the South*, p. 99).

126. Ibid., p. 62.

127. Taylor, *Cavalier and Yankee*, p. 310.

128. Buck, *Road to Reunion*, p. 229.

129. John W. DeForest, "Chivalrous and Semi-Chivalrous Southrons," *Harper's New Monthly Magazine*, Jan.–Feb. 1869, p. 192.

130. Tourgée cites this passage in his 1888 essay "The South as a Field for Fiction" (*Forum* 6 [1888]: 405), claiming that it was published "more than twenty years ago." No record of its publication can be found in either of the Tourgée biographies, Otto H. Olsen, *Carpetbagger's Crusade: The Life of Albion Winegar Tourgée* (Baltimore, 1965), or Theodore L. Gross, *Albion W. Tourgée* (New York, 1963). In the 1888 essay, Tourgée develops the motif of the heroicized loser even further:

> Our literature has become not only Southern in type, but distinctly Confederate in sympathy. The Federal or Union soldier is not exactly depreciated, but subordinated; the Northern type is not decried, but the Southern is preferred. . . . In sincerity of passion and aspiration, as well as in the woefulness and humiliation that attended its downfall, the history of the Confederacy stands preeminent in human epochs. Everything about it was on a grand scale. Everything was real and sincere. The soldier fought in defense of his home, in vindication of what he deemed his right. There was a proud assumption of superiority, a regal contempt of their foe, which, like Hector's boastfulness, added wonderfully to the pathos of the result. Then, too, a civilization fell with it—a civilization full of wonderful contrasts, horrible beyond the power of imagination to conceive its injustice, cruelty, and barbarous debasement of a subject race, yet exquisitely charming in its assumption of pastoral purity and immaculate excellence (pp. 405, 411–12).

131. Harris, who alongside Thomas Nelson Page was the leading exponent of the "plantation school" in the 1880s and 1890s, worked with Grady on his newspaper, the *Atlanta Constitution*, and was a public supporter of the New South program. Paul H. Buck notes the parallels between New South propaganda and plantation romanticism: the novelists of the 1880s, he writes, "set about to exploit the raw materials of fiction with much the same spirit that others of the same generation sought wealth in the undeveloped resources of the South" (*Road to Reunion*, p. 197).

132. Woodward, *Origins of the New South*, p. 158. The history of this quotation is a story all its own. Kenneth S. Lynn mistakenly attributes it to Henry James (*Mark Twain and Southwestern Humor* [Boston, 1959],

p. 231), and Daniel Aaron repeats the error in *The Unwritten War* (p. 245).

133. Several of the prewar novels also thematize the intrusion of the Revolutionary War on the plantation idyll. The difference is that the outbreak of the Civil War signals the end, in literature as well as in reality, of plantation culture.

134. Buck, *Road to Reunion*, p. 233; Osterweis, *Myth*, pp. 102ff.

135. Trophies are often those possessions that made the vanquished enemy powerful, particularly his weaponry. John W. DeForest identifies the connection between power and literature in the necessary disempowerment of the enemy that precedes his transformation into literature. The South, he writes, "had been too positively and authoritatively a political power to get fair treatment in literature." With the eradication of this power, the qualities that made the South an ideal literary subject are suddenly visible. The loser becomes an object not of aggression or criticism but of collectors' interest, since "his day is passing; in another generation his material will be gone; the 'chivalrous Southron' will be as dead as the slavery that created him. . . . It would be good both for him and for us if we should perseveringly attempt to put up with his oddities and handle him as a pet" ("Chivalrous," p. 347).

136. *Origins of the New South*, p. 148. On the role of the ideal of chivalry in the Gilded Age of the North, see John Fraser, *America and the Patterns of Chivalry* (New York, 1982): "Northern society increasingly made itself over in the light of aristocratic European and Southern patterns, partly as a defense against immigrant groups like the Irish and the Jews, partly to sustain the morale of the wealthy against the working class in general, partly because the older rich wished to preserve distinctions between themselves and the newer rich" (p. 26). In the late 1890s, with the rise of progressivism as a reaction to robber-baron capitalism, the ideal of chivalry was once more reinterpreted, with Theodore Roosevelt's trustbusters becoming the fearless knights laying siege to the fortresses of Capital.

137. Quoted in Wilson, *Patriotic Gore*, p. 606.

138. Gaines, *Southern Plantation*, p. 114. Examples of similar "cleansing" in both the North and the South could be cited endlessly. A memorable one is the sanitized image of Robert E. Lee as national hero. Southern historians edited out all recorded statements by Lee that were critical of the North, and their Northern colleagues refrained from calling Lee's patriotism into question.

139. Vernon L. Parrington, *The Romantic Revolution in America, 1800–1860*, vol. 2 of *Main Currents in American Thought* (1927; rpt. New York, 1987), p. 474.

140. On Lee, see Connelly, *Marble Man*, pp. 134ff., as well as Connelly and Bellows, *God and General Longstreet*, p. 109 (which lists thirteen biographies of Lee published in the 1930s alone) and pp. 127ff. on the Depression-era interest in the Lost Cause. "Never before had the entire nation been so close to the southern experience" (p. 130). An initial Lee renaissance had taken place between the turn of the century and 1914. Two biographies, whose authors (Charles Francis Adams Jr. and Gamaliel Bradford) belonged to the Lost Generation of the Gilded Age, presented Lee as a cross between a loser-hero and a nationalist—a more or less exact reflection of the authors' own status (see Connelly, *Man of Marble*, pp. 116ff.). Theodore Roosevelt's imperialist nationalism, coupled with the social philosophy of progressivism, took up the cause of idealism in reaction to the materialism of the Gilded Age, providing a signal of hope and a point of assembly for the disenchanted idealists of the older generation.

141. C. Vann Woodward, *The Burden of Southern History* (1960; rpt. Baton Rouge, 1993), p. 21.

142. Ibid., p. 117. In Henry Adams, one finds a characteristically off-the-cuff admission of his greater sympathy with the South in one respect. The following quotation comes from the passage cited above, in which Adams describes Robert E. Lee's son somewhat superciliously as "simple beyond analysis." Writing as always in the third person, Adams concludes his observation with the words: "Roony Lee had changed little from the Virginian of a century before; but Adams himself was a good deal nearer the type of his great-grandfather than to that of a railway superintendant. He was little more fit than the Virginians to deal with the future America which showed no fancy for the past" (*The Education of Henry Adams* [Boston, 1916], p. 59).

143. Henry Adams's novel *Democracy* appeared anonymously in 1880, Henry James's *The Bostonians* in 1886. Herman Melville's *Claret* was not a novel, but rather a "philosophical poem."

144. Lewis P. Simpson, *Mind and the American Civil War: A Meditation on Lost Causes* (Baton Rouge, 1989), p. 92.

2: France

1. Pierre Guiral, *Prévost-Paradol: Pensée et action d'un libéral sous le Second Empire* (Paris, 1955). The formulation *"la première victime de la guerre du Rhin"* is that of the embassy attaché Charles-Adolphe Chambruns (p. 714). On the circumstances of Paradol's suicide, see pp. 720–23.

2. Quoted in Guiral, *Prévost-Paradol*, p. 715. The remark was published under Cherbuliez's pen name, G. Valbert, in the *Revue des deux mondes*, May 1, 1894.
3. *La France nouvelle* (Paris, 1868), p. 388.
4. Ibid., pp. 381–83.
5. Ibid., pp. 418–19.
6. See Konrad W. Swart, *The Sense of Decadence in Nineteenth-Century France* (The Hague, 1964).
7. Hippolyte Taine, *Correspondence*, vol. 2, p. 332; quoted in Eduard Wechssler, *Die Franzosen und wir* (Jena, 1915), p. 11.
8. Stendhal, letter to Pauline, *Correspondence*, vol. 4 (Paris, 1934), p. 282; *Journal*, vol. 5 (Paris, 1937), p. 236 (this entry contains Stendhal's secondhand account of his friend Louis Crozet's description). Napoleon's commissars reported similar lethargy at the end of December 1815. See G. de Berthier de Sauvigny, *La restauration* (Paris, 1955), pp. 15 ff.
9. It is tempting to compare the businesslike manner in which Napoleon was deposed in 1814 by the *corps législatif*, whose members he had himself appointed in better days, with Mussolini's removal 129 years later by the Grand Fascist Council after the Allied landing in Sicily.
10. *La nouvelle revue* 65 (1890), p. 178.
11. "The irritation . . ." quoted in Lynn M. Case, *French Opinion on War and Diplomacy during the Second Empire* (Philadelphia, 1954), p. 226. "We wish . . ." quoted in André Armengaud, *L'Opinion publique en France et la crise nationale allemande en 1866* (Paris, 1962), p. 88. Representative of the mood within the press is the *Gazette de France* of Aug. 31, 1866: "After the invasions of 1814 and 1815, nothing has been more tragic for France than the events in Germany of 1866" (Armengaud, *L'opinion publique*, p. 80). Emile Ollivier, who was to inaugurate the war against Prussia four years later, spoke in 1866 of an *année fatale*, prefiguring the *année terrible* (Armengaud, *L'opinion publique*, p. 2). "The energy . . ." quoted in Hermann Oncken, *Die Rheinpolitik Kaiser Napoleons III von 1863 bis 1870 und der Ursprung des Krieges von 1870–71* (Berlin, 1926), p. 330. Königgrätz/Sadowa also anticipated the French defeat of 1870–71 in that, as of 1866, a comprehensive discussion of state, educational, and military reforms commenced. This discussion came to nothing, however, probably because it wasn't yet motivated by a dramatic defeat.
12. By contrast one out of every 450 Frenchmen died in the war against Prussia.
13. Naturally, there was also a historical and mythological legacy on the German side: the devastation of the Rhineland-Palatinate, the destruc-

tion of the Heidelberg castle, Jena-Auerstedt, the peace of Tilsit, and the annexation of Alsace-Lorraine. German *revanche* for two centuries of humiliation by the French, however, was a matter divorced from military events, which were determined by Bismarck and Moltke's purely pragmatic strategy, whereas mythology and strategy melded into one in France.

14. *Revue des deux mondes*, Sept. 1, 1870, pp. 181–82.
15. Hermann Grimm, "Voltaire und Frankreich," *Preussische Jahrbücher* 27 (1871): 2.
16. Also vanishing without a trace were any memories that public opinion, including that of the opposition, had enthusiastically supported the declaration of war and every military move by the regime. A recent study compares the national consensus in July 1870 with the *union sacrée* of August 1914 (Jean-Jacques Becker and Stephane Audoin-Rouzeau, *La France, la nation, la guerre, 1850–1920* [Paris, 1995], pp. 66 ff.). The only linguistic indication that the national enthusiasm of September 4 was any less intense than that before World War I was, as Michael Jeismann shows, the replacement of the terms *la nation* and *la France* with the more personal *nous*. See Jeismann, *Das Vaterland der Feinde: Studien zum nationalen Feindbegriff und Selbstverständnis in Deutschland und Frankreich, 1792–1918* (Stuttgart, 1992), pp. 174 ff.
17. In New York in 1981, I witnessed a similar phenomenon in which rituals of triumph served to obscure an actual humiliation. The release of the American hostages after their months-long imprisonment in Tehran was celebrated with the traditional ticker-tape parade with which victorious armies and heroes of air and space travel are welcomed back to the United States. No one seemed to notice that there was no victory to celebrate—at most a fortunate, and hardly heroic, escape.
18. Michael Howard, *The Franco-Prussian War* (n.p., 1969), p. 232. A. J. P. Taylor calls the treaty of Frankurt of May 1871 "a victor's peace on the Napoleonic model," observing that the five billion francs demanded as reparation was "a sum exactly proportioned to the indemnity which Napoleon I had imposed on Prussia in 1807" (*The New Cambridge Modern History* [Cambridge, 1957–79], vol. 11, p. 543).
19. Quoted in Jean-Pierre Azéma and Michel Winock, *La 3è République* (Paris, 1976), p. 44.
20. *Revue des deux mondes*, Sept. 15, 1870.
21. Quoted in Azéma and Winock, *3è République*, p. 59. In Theodore Zeldin's fascinating if undocumented portrait, Thiers emerges as the embodiment of bourgeois *revanche* for 1848. His carefully planned strategy was first, in March 1871, to abandon Paris to its own devices,

before turning it over to the military for a "final solution" (not Zeldin's term), in order to break the revolutionary backbone once and for all (*History of French Passions*, vol. 1 [Oxford, 1993], pp. 735 ff.).

22. In the face of German occupation, the newly elected National Assembly had convened in nonoccupied Bordeaux. In the short term, it planned to use the city as a temporary exile. However, the decision to relocate the government to Versailles—Fontainebleau was also considered—was intended to be permanent.

23. Victor Hugo donated the proceeds from all performances of his theatrical works during the occupation to the fund. One of the cannons that this money financed was named after him (Victor Hugo, *Choses vues* [Paris, 1972], pp. 106 ff.).

24. On the revival of the spirit of 1792, E. Malcolm Carroll writes: "The fall of the Empire had been followed immediately by the organization of numerous radical clubs where orators nightly renewed the memories of 1792" (*French Public Opinion and Foreign Affairs, 1870–1914* [1931; rpt. Hamden, 1964], p. 38).

25. Quoted in Daniel Amson, *Gambetta, ou le rêve brisé* (Paris, 1994), p. 223.

26. Quoted in Azéma and Winock, *3è République*, p. 58.

27. Quoted in André Bellesort, *Les intellectuels et l'avènement de la 3è République* (Paris, 1931), p. 16.

28. The comparison between the Commune uprising and the American Civil War is made by Jean T. Joughin, *The Paris Commune in French Politics: The History of the Amnesty of 1880*, 2 vols. (Baltimore, 1955): "Just as the Confederacy represented an obsolescent concept of the relationship between the state and the federal government, so the Paris Commune had an antique view of the role of the municipality vis-à-vis the national government. Both 'lost causes' were victims of the swing toward concentration of political power at the top" (vol. 1, p. 14).

29. Most of the victims were not claimed by the actual fighting, nor were they killed in "spontaneous" massacres. They were executed by "war tribunals," which usually consisted of the commanding generals. A not atypical case was the execution of the Republican deputy Millière, who did not participate in the uprising but was brought before General de Cissey during de Cissey's midday meal and summarily shot "between the pear and the cheese." For this and other examples, see Robert Tombs, *The War against Paris, 1871* (Cambridge, 1981), pp. 179 ff.

30. Edmond de Goncourt and Jules de Goncourt, *Journal*, vol. 2 (Paris, 1956), p. 453. Edmond had criticized the January capitulation as degrading, asking how a French hand could have signed the treaty (p. 386).

31. Quoted in Nicole Priollaud, ed., *1871: La Commune de Paris* (Paris, 1983), p. 110.

32. Littré quoted in Priollaud, *1871*, p. 181. Zola quoted on p. 75. For Goncourt, see *Journal*, p. 386.

33. Clemenceau: "It was one of those extraordinary nervous outbursts, so frequent in the Middle Ages, which still occur amongst masses of human beings under the stress of some primeval emotion" (quoted in Roger L. Williams, *The French Revolution of 1870–71* [New York, 1969], p. 114). Renan: "The biggest factor is the terrible chill running down the spine of an impressionable population unprepared for the embarrassment of Prussian invasion [the victory parade of the German army on March 1], one that has been stirred up by chimeras and impossible promises, gorged on arms and munitions, and nourished by the six months of inactivity it has had to endure. From that moment on, the population of Paris went crazy" (letter of July 17, 1871, *Correspondence*, vol. 10 of *Oeuvres complètes* [Paris, 1961], p. 571).

34. The *"folie,"* added Juliette Adam, the grande dame of *revanche*, was one she understood (*Mes angoisses et mes luttes, 1871–1873*, vol. 5 of *Souvenirs* [Paris, 1907], p. 123).

35. "Confused and short-lived though it was, the experiences of the Commune provided the lurid and violent background against which the institutions of the republic were devised and consolidated" (Joughin, *Paris Commune*, p. 11).

36. The remark, which appears in Bismarck's memoirs, is quoted in Maurice Beaumont, *Bazaine: Les secrets d'un maréchal* (Paris, 1978), p. 159. Similarly, the *Times* of London for Nov. 9, 1870, asked when France's soldiers would learn to say that they had been vanquished and not that they had been betrayed (p. 159). See also Moltke: "The French need a traitor at any cost to explain the defeat suffered by their nation" (Edmond Ruby and Jean Regnault, *Bazaine: Coupable ou victime?* [Paris, 1960], p. 304).

37. Quoted in Ruby and Regnault, *Bazaine*, p. 304.

38. Philip Guedalla, *The Two Marshalls: Bazaine—Pétain* (London, 1943), p. 232.

39. Quoted in Beaumont, *Bazaine*, p. 283.

40. Klaus Rudolf Wenger, *Preussen in der öffentlichen Meinung Frankreichs, 1815–1870* (Göttingen, 1979), pp. 37–38.

41. Louis Veuillot, quoted in Wenger, *Preussen*, p. 222.

42. In comparison, the change of mood in 1914 Germany after England's entry into World War I ("Let God punish England!") was also intense but less fundamental and shorter-lived because there had never been even a trace of erotic undertones in Anglo-German relations.

43. H. D. Schmidt, "The Idea and Slogan of 'Perfidious Albion,'" *Journal of the History of Ideas* 14 (1953): 604–16. On the Carthage topos, see Frances Acomb, *Anglophobia in France, 1763–89* (Durham, 1950), p. 9.

44. Wenger, *Preussen*, p. 42.

45. These are the words of Charles Gravier Vergennes, foreign minister under Louis XVI, quoted in Jean-François Labourdette, *Vergennes, ministre principal de Louis XVI* (Paris, 1990), p. 89.

46. The French conceit of having won a "moral victory" over its opponent was much in evidence at the end of the Seven Years War. In 1763, after the signing of the treaty of Paris, which ceded much of France's territory in the New World to England, two plays were staged in the French capital to great popular success. The comedy *L'Anglais à Bordeaux* by the popular playwright Charles-Simon Favart has an English lord, who otherwise embodies all the negative characteristics of his nation (arrogance, coldness, calculation, and greed), being won over as a prisoner of war on the estate of a French chevalier by his host's charm, generosity, and nobility. Likewise, the patriotic melodrama *Le siège de Calais* (1765), in which the heroic citizens of Calais shame the English victors, makes abundantly clear who the moral victor is. Diderot and Voltaire, who doubted that the celebration of defeat could awaken patriotic sentiment, were proved wrong. The marquis de Croy better caught the spirit of the times when he concluded about the Calais melodrama: "The nation, in need of edification, found it in this brand-new genre." On the two plays, see Acomb, *Anglophobia*, pp. 55 ff. On Diderot and Voltaire's divergent opinion, see *Encyclopaedia Britannica*, 11th ed., s.v "Dormont de Belloy."

47. For these formulations, see Jeismann, *Vaterland der Feinde*, p. 201, and Marieluise Christadler, "Zur nationalpädagogischen Funktion kollektiver Mythen in Frankreich," *Nationale Mythen und Symbole in der 2. Hälfte des 19. Jahrhunderts*, ed. Jürgen Link and Wulf Wülfing (Stuttgart, 1991), pp. 201–02.

48. Quoted in Jeismann, *Vaterland der Feinde*, pp. 191–92; emphasis added. The dates of these statements are Sept. 17, Sept. 5, and Sept. 9, 1870. (The quotation that serves as the title of this section is also from Sept. 5.) Jeismann has effectively captured the sudden transformation at the moment of defeat of France's self-perception from *active* bringer of civilization to passive keeper of the flame. This is the overheated rhetorical ideological equivalent of the "trope" in battle, which causes morale to plummet and the soldiers to give up the fight and flee en masse.

49. Victor Hugo, *Oeuvres complétes, Politique* (Paris, 1985), pp. 882–83, 896.

50. Thomas Carlyle, *Critical and Miscellaneous Essays in Five Volumes*, vol. 5 (New York, 1904), p. 54.
51. On the interpretation of the war by the German intelligentsia, see Gerhard R. Kaiser, "Der Bildungsbürger und die normative Kraft des Faktischen: 1870–71 im Urteil der deutschen Intelligenz," *Feindbild und Faszination: Vermittlerfiguren und Wahrnehmungsprozesse in den deutsch-französischen Beziehungen, 1789–1983*, ed. H.-J. Lüsebrink and J. Riesz (Frankfurt, 1984), pp. 55–74, and Hein-Otto Sieburg, "Die Elsass-Lothringen-Frage in der deutsch-französischen Diskussion von 1871 bis 1914," *Zeitschrift für die Geschichte der Saargegend* 17–18 (1969–70): 9–37. On Strauss, see Claude Digeon, *La crise allemande et la pensée française, 1870–1914* (Paris, 1959), pp. 189ff. On Mommsen, see Lothar Wickert, *Grösse und Grenzen*, vol. 4 of *Theodor Mommsen* (Frankfurt am Main, 1980), pp. 170–79. The open letters from July and Aug. 1870, "Agli Italiani," are reprinted in *Quaderni di storia* 4 (1976): 197–247. On Schulze-Delitzsch, see "Drei Briefe an die italienischen Patrioten über den deutschen Krieg und seine Folgen (November/Dezember 1870)," *Hermann Schulze-Delitzschs Schriften und Reden*, ed. F. Thorwart, vol. 4 (Berlin, 1911), pp. 648ff.
52. *Revue des deux mondes*, Jan. 1, 1871, p. 28.
53. *Revue des deux mondes*, Sept. 15, 1870. Quoted in Jeismann, *Vaterland der Feinde*, p. 238.
54. "En campagne," *L'illustration*, Sept. 13, 1870, quoted in Jeismann, *Vaterland der Feinde*, p. 236.
55. Quoted in Wilhelm Windelband, "Der Nationalismus in der französischen Geschichtsschreibung seit 1871," *Deutsche Rundschau* 176 (1918): 174.
56. Warning the victor of 1870–71 against hubris was, like so much of the French reaction to Sedan, an echo of the rhetoric that French public opinion had used to console itself after the Seven Years War. In that conflict, England's victory was deemed doubly Pyrrhic: economically, since the industrialization and colonial expansion that would come with Britain's vastly enlarged empire was certain to destroy the natural harmony of the land, and morally, since victory would remove the last barriers to the "universal rule of the shopkeepers." For the physiocrats—who believed economics should obey natural law—English industrialization was "a harbinger of decadence" (Acomb, *Anglophobia*, p. 66). In contrast, the self-conception of physiocratically balanced France is paraphrased by Acomb as follows: "Her power was 'natural,' for her economy was balanced: her commerce was not overexpanded, and her debt remained, it was supposed, within bounds. . . . If France had lost territory abroad, she

was not beset with imperial problems, while her metropolitan resources in soil and population were many times those of her rival" (pp. 60–61). France considered itself the victor on the moral score as well. One French writer, reacting in 1777 to the humiliation of the treaty of Paris, used a rhetoric that anticipated that of 1789, indeed that of Victor Hugo, to announce France's ambition to lead humanity: "O France, *ma patrie!* Europe has your light to thank for the discovery of human rights and citizens' duties, for insight into its true interests and the revelation of the social order and the laws that govern the lives of men as well as nations" (Le Trosne, quoted in Acomb, *Anglophobia*, p. 65).

57. Hugo, *Politique*, p. 754. The quotations that follow are from pp. 755–56.

58. This characterization of *revanche* was first advanced by Paul Rühlmann, *Die französische Schule und der Weltkrieg* (Leipzig, 1918), p. 3. Rühlmann goes on to call the religion of *revanche* a "substitute for the lost unity of church affiliation."

59. Henry Contamine, *La revanche, 1871–1914* (Paris, 1957), treats only a few of the military doctrines leading up to World War I and—except for a couple of remarks in the foreword—ignores the whole psychological complex of *revanche*.

60. Nietzsche's definition of gratitude as "a milder form of revenge" is relevant here (*Human, All Too Human*). The same idea of the gift as a "flat usurpation" that occasions revengelike ressentiment and compulsion in the recipient and that is redressed through formulas for expressing gratitude, or a countergift, appears in Ralph Waldo Emerson's essay "Gifts" (*The Works* [Boston, 1914], p. 413). On the anthropology of gift giving and exchange, see the still unsurpassed classic by Marcel Mauss, *Essay on the Gift*.

61. Robert A. Nye, *Masculinity and Male Codes of Honor in Modern France* (New York, 1993), p. 26.

62. "A somewhat too direct stare" (Jean Bodin, *Discours contre les duels*) and "a glass of lemonade" (Le Febvre d'Ormesson, *Journal*) are quoted in François Billacois, *Le duel dans la société française des 16è et 17è siècles: Essaie de psychosociologie historique* (Paris, 1986), p. 127. On the choreography of the duel, V. G. Kiernan remarks that the procedure of the duel was "almost as highly stylized as the minuet, and a product of the same social atmosphere" (*The Duel in European History* [Oxford, New York, 1988], p. 97).

63. Billacois, *Duel*, p. 351.

64. On the crisis of confidence, see James C. Riley, *The Seven Years War and the Old Regime in France: The Economic and the Financial Toll*

(Princeton, 1986), p. 192. On the claim to political and moral leadership by the aristocracy in the years leading up to the Revolution, see Guy Chaussinand-Nogaret, *The French Nobility in the 18th Century* (Cambridge, 1985). Chaussinand-Nogaret sees the opposition formed after 1763 as a long-term result and/or revival of Frondist resistance: "Naturally the nobility was the particular opponent of government, and it was to be expected that nobles should want a say in redefining it. . . . Such redefinition of power sprang from the thought of those whom power had most affected, those most wounded by a scandalous authority answerable to none, without limits. . . . It had robbed them of one justification for their existence and at the same time destroyed their fundamental rights: the right to advise, the right to check, the right to govern" (p. 12).

65. Quoted in Simon Schama, *Citizens: A Chronicle of the French Revolution* (New York, 1989), p. 25.

66. Roland Mausnier, *Paris: Capitale au temps de Richelieu et de Mazarin* (Paris, 1978), pp. 235–36.

67. It was only with the return of the republicans to parliamentary power in 1879 that the National Assembly and the government moved back to the capital.

68. Thomas A. Kselman, *Miracles and Prophecies in Nineteenth-Century France* (New Brunswick, 1983), p. 123. In the widely read apocalyptic prophesies of Abbé Latour, *revanche* against Prussian Germany—predicted for 1876—was only the first in a series of events including the restitution of the pope's former rights, the subjugation of Turkey, and a crowning triumph over England (Latour, *L'avenir de la France* [Toulouse, 1871], p. 52).

69. Blanc de Saint-Bonnet, *La legitimité* (Tournai, 1873), pp. 68–69.

70. Saint-Bonnet: "Protestants are undoubtedly delighted in this hour by the successes of the kingdom of Prussia and its sin against France and Christianity. . . . So, too, will they partake of the joy of the prodigal son upon first seeing his father's house again" (quoted in Otfried Eberz, "Die gallikanische Kirche als Werkzeug der Révanche," *Der Nationalismus im Leben der dritten Republik,* ed. Joachim Kühn [Berlin, 1920], p. 160).

71. On the *sacré-coeur* as a symbol for counterrevolution, see Raymond A. Jonas, "Restoring a Sacred Center: Pilgrimage, Politics, and the Sacré-Coeur," *Historical Reflections/Réflexions historiques* 20 (1994): 96 ff. See also Jonas's "Sacred Mysteries and Holy Memories: Counter-Revolutionary France and the Sacré-Coeur," *Canadian Journal of History* 32 (1997), and "Monument Ex-Voto, Monument as Historiosophy: The Basilica of Sacré-Coeur," *French Historical Studies* 18 (1993).

72. Quoted in Jeismann, *Vaterland der Feinde*, pp. 154–55.
73. Quoted in Schama, *Citizens*, p. 744.
74. Hugo, *Politique*, p. 758; *Choses vues*, p. 107.
75. Quoted in Kühn, *Nationalismus*, p. 22. Blanqui quoted in Henri Gallichet Galli, *Gambetta et l'Alsace-Lorraine* (Paris, 1911), p. 50.
76. Gerd Krumeich, *Jeanne d'Arc in der Geschichte: Historiographie, Politik, Kultur* (Sigmaringen, 1989), p. 130. My depiction of the Joan of Arc cult is based, unless otherwise indicated, on this study.
77. Quoted in Krumeich, *Jeanne d'Arc*, p. 12.
78. Michelet is again most explicit. On the triumphant Joan of Arc: "Jeanne took the lead in the popular battle . . . and obliged France to become conscious and free." And: "With centuries of hindsight, the Parisians stormed the Bastille rediscovering the temerity of the soldiers of *La Pucelle*"(quoted in Krumeich, *Jeanne d'Arc*, pp. 64, 65). And on the silent martyr and savior: "The people . . . saw in all of this a form of the Passion, and in their eyes this painful end consecrated La Pucelle, for whom until then they had felt only admiration. . . . The pious tears of La Pucelle regenerated France. . . . The funeral pyre at Rouen was the end of the Middle Ages but also the beginning of modern times. Joan of Arc, the last of martyrs, is also the first patriotic figure" (p. 71).
79. A. Arnou in *Revue de Paris*, Nov. 1949, cited in Krumeich, *Jeanne d'Arc*, p. 162.
80. Kselman, *Miracles and Prophecies*, p. 117.
81. Krumeich, *Jeanne d'Arc*, p. 159.
82. It is unfair, of course, to compare an allegoric and emblematic figure like Marianne with a historical one like Joan of Arc. Nonetheless, in the eighty years after 1792 the figure of Marianne accrued so many levels of meaning that its "appropriation" by various factions of republicanism—from the conservative republic of Adolphe Thiers to the Paris Commune—was not dissimilar to the hotly contested appropriation of Joan of Arc. To name only the most important iconographic variants: the passionate, forward-storming goddess of liberty; the reigning state deity, Minerva; the republican Athena in armor and helmet; the people's goddess, replete with symbols of fertility; the laurel-wearing goddess of victory. Even the iconography of the Phrygian cap—its omission (on account of its connection with the Jacobin terror) and its emphasis (in the Revolution of 1848 and the Commune)—is a long story of its own. See Maurice Agulhon, *Marianne au combat* (Paris, 1979), and its sequel, *Marianne au pouvoir* (Paris, 1989).
83. Christian P. Amalvi, *De l'art et de la manière d'accommoder les héros de l'histoire de France* (Paris, 1988), p. 92.

84. The comparison was popular in the 1870s. In "Le prisonnier," a poem written in 1875 on the occasion of Bazaine's escape from prison, Victor Hugo compares the traitorous marshal not only to Ganelon but to Judas.

85. Léon Gautier, ed., *La chanson de Roland* (Paris, 1872), p. cc.

86. See Amalvi, *De l'art*, pp. 106–07, which compares Lavisse's textbooks of 1876 and 1882.

87. "Like Christ, he saw himself abandoned and forgotten. From his calvary in the Pyrennees, he shouted and blew his horn, . . . he called, and the traitor Ganelon de Mayence and the insouciant Charlemagne did not want to hear" (quoted in Harry Redman Jr., *The Roland Legend in Nineteenth-Century French Literature* [Lexington, 1991] p. 100). Recall, too, Michelet's Christlike image of Joan of Arc (n. 78, above).

88. Maurice Bouchor, 1895, quoted in Redman, *Roland Legend*, p. 197; Robert Francis Cook, *The Sense of the Song of Roland* (Ithaca, 1987), p. 99. The idea of the insignificance of the enemies' weapons also applies to the second version of Roland's demise, namely, his death in an enemy-triggered avalanche, which was used in various nineteenth-century treatments of the story.

89. "Roland perished, but France triumphed" (quoted in Redman, *Roland Legend*, p. 98).

90. Charles Lenient, "*La chanson de Roland* et les Niebelungen [*sic*]," *Revue politique et littéraire* (1872): 291–98.

91. Lenient's political agenda shines through clearly in this passage. Departing from his remarks on the *Nibelungenlied*, he continues: "Everyone, from the king who looks covetously upon the billions of his neighbors, to the sentimental Gretchen figure who asks her fiancé to bring her some golden earrings after the sacking of Paris, to the standard-bearer in whose heart is hidden not a medal, not a cross, but an iron obligation to appropriate from the French peasant his capacity for hard work, they all dream in their own way of the treasure of the Nibelungs" ("La chanson de Roland," p. 294).

92. Christadler, "Funktion," pp. 201–02.

93. Claude Billard and Pierre Guibert, *Histoire mythologique des français* (Paris, 1976), pp. 174–75.

94. Herbert von Nostitz, *Bismarcks unbotmässiger Botschafter: Fürst Münster von Derneburg* (Göttingen, 1968), p. 160. Among the scores of diplomatic memoirs, two are particularly worth noting; although separated by fifteen years, they describe exactly the same mood. In September 1870, a few days after Sedan, Metternich, then Austrian ambassador in Paris, wrote: "A pretense of menaces and at heart an immoderate desire of peace, if I am not mistaken, . . . represents the real state of

public opinion. People wish to lay down their arms, without having the courage to avow it" (Carroll, *French Public Opinion*, p. 37). In the late 1880s, the German ambassador wrote: "The anti-German incitements only find an echo when the word *war* is left unspoken. . . . Every Frenchman harbors the wish for '*revanche*,' for a '*guerre sainte*,' but the thought that the realization of that wish could be at hand is deeply unsavory to the majority and causes people to shake their heads and warn of dire consequences whenever it is uttered" (*Die grosse Politik der europäischen Kabinette, 1871–1914*, vol. 6 [Berlin, 1927], pp. 143–44).

95. Max Nordau, *Paris: Studien und Bilder* (Leipzig, 1881), p. 261.

96. We have Paul Déroulède, the founder of the most important organization for celebrating *revanche*, the Ligue des patriotes (1882), to thank for recording Ernest Renan's famous answer to a request to support the undertaking: "What is the need for all this verbal agitation, these irritating fits and this superfluous excitement? . . . Young man, young man, France is perishing; don't disturb it in its death throes" (Bertrand Joly, *Déroulède: L'inventeur du nationalisme français* [Paris, 1998], p. 72).

97. Gambetta never used this precise formulation. It is an ex post facto contraction and paraphrase of the words "There is a dignity of the vanquished when they are felled by fate and not through any fault of their own. Let us protect this dignity and let us not talk any longer of the foreigner; but let it be understood that he is always on our minds. . . . Then you will be on the right path toward *revanche*" (quoted in Galli, *Gambetta*, p. 51). Another variation: "Let us not talk of *revanche*, let us not speak the frightening words, let us gather our strength" (Joseph Reinach, ed., *Discours et plaidoyers de Léon Gambetta* [Paris, 1903], p. 87, quoted in Matthias Salm, *Deutsche Rundschau*, Feb. 1917, p. 200).

98. These statements can be found in Gambetta's letters to his political confidante Juliette Adam, quoted in Amson, *Gambetta*, pp. 343, 320. From a 1876 conversation with the English politician Grant Duff: "I more and more doubt whether there will be any *guerre de revanche* at all. The fact is nowadays, when peace is once made between two coterminous nations, so many joint interests grow up and become rapidly strong that, with every month that passes, the chances of war are lessened" (quoted in J. P. T. Bury, *Gambetta and the Making of the Third Republic* [London, 1973], p. 350).

99. Quoted in Amson, *Gambetta*, pp. 263–64.

100. Charles Maurras, quoted in Galli, *Gambetta*, p. 249, speaks of Gambetta's "comedy of revanche." George Sand is quoted from a letter to Juliette Adam in Amson, *Gambetta*, p. 258.

101. It makes no difference whether Gambetta pursued this aim consciously or instinctively, although statements of his argue for the former. See, for example, Gambetta's letter to Juliette Adam on the fourth anniversary of September 4, 1870: "Despite the incidents that marked that day, I could not keep the cruel thought from my mind that we did not overthrow the empire with our own hands but saw it succumb to the blows of foreigners" (Amson, *Gambetta*, p. 182).

102. General Trochu, quoted in Amson, *Gambetta*, p. 208.

103. *Revue des deux mondes*, Mar. 15, 1871, pp. 405, 408.

104. Take, for example, Hugo's epic poem "La libération du territoire" (1873):

> The task today is to let ourselves grow
> Quietly, and to shut our hatred away
> Like a virgin in a cloister
> And to nourish our black resentments.
> What is the point of deploying our regiments so soon
> And what is the point of galloping before a hostile Europe?
> To avoid stirring up dust uselessly
> Is wise; the day will come to burst out;
> It's better not to act in haste.

105. Jean-Marie Mayeur and Madeleine Rebérioux, *The Third Republic from Its Origins to the Great War, 1871–1914* (Cambridge, 1984), p. 46.

106. Ibid., p. 130.

107. Zeev Sternhell, *La Droite révolutionnaire* (Paris, 1978), p. 196.

108. Jean Garrigues, *Le général Boulanger* (n.p., 1991), p. 47; Frédéric Monier, *Le complot dans la République: Stratégies du secret de Boulanger à Cagoule* (Paris, 1998), p. 29.

109. The establishment of a press office in the ministry and the creation of a close connection to the Havas press agency (whose employees Boulanger exempted from military service) were among the first measures. It has been surmised that Boulanger was adopting American advertising methods, since a close associate of his, Arthur Dillon, had become acquainted with them during a long stay in America. See Patrick Hutton, "Popular Boulangism and the Advent of Mass Politics in France, 1886–90," *Journal of Contemporary History* 11 (1976): 91.

110. Ibid., p. 64.

111. Garrigues, *Général Boulanger*, p. 74; *Le Figaro*, July 25, 1886, quoted on p. 73, ibid.

112. *Grosse Politik der europäischen Kabinette*, vol. 6, pp. 139, 146, 201. This estimation did not prevent Otto von Bismarck from publicly portraying Boulangism as a threat and using it as a pretense for a military

advance: "I could not invent Boulanger, but he happened very conveniently for me" (quoted in Frederic H. Seager, *The Boulanger Affair: Political Crossroad of France, 1886–1889* [Ithaca, 1969], p. 51).

113. Both poems are quoted in Garrigues, *Général Boulanger*, p. 74. The defensive quality of the eruption of *revanche* sentiment in 1886–87 is taken as a given in contemporary research. For instance, Zeev Sternhell: "Boulanger is the man to slake the thirst for self-respect the whole country feels" (*Maurice Barrès et le nationalisme français* [Paris, 1972], p. 96). Daniel Mollenhauer speaks of the French "analysis of threat . . . according to which Bismarck continued to play the aggressive part" that had to be defended against (*Auf der Suche nach der "wahren Republik": Die französischen "radicaux" in der frühen Dritten Republik, 1870–1890* [Bonn, 1997], p. 338). Even the militaristic science-fiction literature, the genre where the pure aggression of *revanche* fanatasies was allowed to play itself out, reveals the same dynamic. The recurring visions of apocalyptic victories over Germany were simply a compensatory, cathartic playing out of fantasy, an opium of the defeated, as it were. The comparison here with contemporaneous English fantasy literature is instructive: the English literature focuses almost exclusively on military catastrophes and apocalyptic invasions besetting the island kingdom, which was in reality the very incarnation of security. If the analogy holds and militaristic fiction depicts the mirror image of reality, then the French literature of triumph (with titles like *L'art de combattre l'armée allemande*, *La revanche*, *La France victorieuse dans la guerre de demain*, *L'offensive contre l'Allemagne*, *La fin de l'empire d'Allemagne*) would in fact be an expression of a deeply defeatist mood. See I. F. Clarke, ed., *The Tale of the Next Great War, 1871–1914: Fictions of Future Warfare and Battles Still to Come* (Syracuse, 1995).

114. Boulangism was politically and ideologically just as complex and internally inconsistent as the groups that collected around Boulanger, from the extreme left to the reactionary right. The best overview is provided by Seager's *The Boulanger Affair*. On the role of royalist elements, see William D. Irvine, *The Boulanger Affair Reconsidered: Royalism, Boulangism, and the Origins of the Radical Right in France* (New York, 1989).

115. Sternhell, *Barrès*, pp. 365–66. Raoul Girardet describes the same change in mood: "The cult of *revanche* has come back to haunt the existing political institutions" (*Le nationalisme français* [Paris, 1966], p. 16).

116. Arthur Meyer, quoted in Sternhell, *Barrès*, p. 101.

117. Quoted in Saad Moros, *Juliette Adam* (Cairo, 1961), p. 510.

118. Quoted in *Nineteenth Century* (London) 74 (1913): 22–23.

119. Barrès's recollections of the troops returning from Sedan ("This journey embodied everything I was ever to feel about my country") were in fact those not of an eight-year-old boy but of a fully grown man. "Having become a nationalist, these are the childhood memories he most likes to evoke" (Digeon, *Crise allemande*, p. 404).
120. Quoted in Sternhell, *Barrès*, p. 30.
121. Ibid., pp. 29–30. Ten years later, in 1895, Barrès once again said of French-German relations: "The exchange of ideas between France and Germany never ceased. One benefited as much as the other from this fruitful collaboration. . . . It was an uninterrupted mutual penetration of ideas" (p. 33).
122. "M. le général Boulanger et la nouvelle génération," *La revue indépendente*, Apr. 1888, p. 56.
123. The literary character of turn-of-the-century French nationalism has been pointed out by many—indeed most—historians, including Eugene Weber, *The Nationalist Revival in France, 1905–1914* (Berkeley, 1968), who writes of nationalism as a "literary movement," and Sternhell. Along with Barrès, other literati and poets among the fathers of French nationalism were Déroulède, Maurras, and Péguy.

    Before their appropriation by Barrès, the terms *nationalisme* and *nationaliste* were not part of the French vocabulary. In Littré's *Dictionnaire de la langue française* (1873) there is no mention of them. Barrès used the concepts for the first time in 1892. See Michel Winock, *Nationalism, Anti-Semitism, and Fascism in France* (Stanford, 1998), p. 6.
124. Quoted in Digeon, *Crise allemande*, p. 428.
125. Quoted in Sylvia M. King, *Maurice Barrès: La pensée allemande et le problème du Rhin* (Paris, 1933), p. 106.
126. King, *Barrès*, p. 104. The divergent estimations of internal and foreign enemies emerged most clearly in the Dreyfus affair: "The foreign enemy plays above all the role of manipulator and financer of the dark forces that undermine the national organism. But the German is no more hated than the Jew, the Protestant, or the Freemason. On the contary, . . . the German is a brother of race against whom we must fight in order to strengthen the species" (Sternhell, *Barrès*, p. 366).
127. Digeon, *Crise allemande*, p. 404; Sternhell, *Barrès*, p. 64. On the nationalist-racist typology of the German in Barrès's novel *Colette Baudoche*, for example, see Robert Soucy, *Fascism in France: The Case of Maurice Barrès* (Berkeley, 1972), pp. 150–56.
128. Ernst Robert Curtius, *Maurice Barrès und die Grundlagen des französische Nationalismus* (Bonn, 1921), p. 217.
129. Ibid., pp. 216–17.

130. Under the name Agathon, Henri Massis and Alfred de Tarde wrote a programmatic series of newspaper articles and books that appeared under the titles *Sur l'esprit de la nouvelle Sorbonne* (1910 and 1911) and *Les jeunes gens d'aujourd'hui* (1912 and 1913). Once again they enacted the change of generations, which consisted in this case of rebelling against the prevailing liberal-pacifist spirit of the post-Dreyfus age. In retrospect, the Agathon rebellion was a well-planned strategy for establishing literary careers. Starting with a provocative attack on the academic authorities in the first book, they proceeded to a systematic self-portrayal in the second. The public response shows that the time was ripe for such a revision. Not only was the "new generation" suddenly on everyone's tongue but a score of stories followed in newspapers and magazines. See Robert Wohl, *The Generation of 1914* (Cambridge 1979), pp. 5 ff.

131. Quoted in Digeon, *Crise allemande*, p. 441.

132. Julien Benda, *Sur le succès du Bergsonisme* (Paris, 1914), p. 137.

133. Raoul Girardet, *L'idée coloniale en France de 1871 à 1962* (Paris, 1972), p. 100.

134. Along with France, Italy was a leader in the pre-1914 enthusiasm for automobiles and airplanes. Interestingly, France and Italy were also the two major film nations in the world before 1914. As of 1918, America (that is, Hollywood) took the lead with the industrial production methods of its studio system. The traditional French understanding of technology and industry as instruments of emancipation as well as of national prestige—and not as rationally and pragmatically applied methods for increasing productivity can of course be traced back to Saint-Simonism. This emphasis also explains such French-initiated large international projects as the Suez and the Panama Canals.

135. Quoted in Weber, *Nationalist Revival*, p. 113.

136. The best account of the new nationalism is still Weber's *Nationalist Revival in France*.

137. The French response to the Zabern affair in 1913 was, like the whole renaissance of *revanche* for Alsace-Lorraine, an echo of and a reaction to the Moroccan crises. On the fading and functional transformation of the idea of *revanche*, see Gilbert Ziebura, *Die deutsche Frage in der öffentlichen Meinung Frankreichs, 1911–14* (Berlin, 1955), pp. 14–16, 30–32, 160–61 (as well as notes 17 and 18).

138. Along with colonial-imperialistic rivalry, the economic-imperialist challenge from and humiliation by Germany played a major role in the "neo-*revanche*" mood of the years after 1905. Indeed, German colonialism was perceived as less threatening than German economic expansion, which was considered an economic *invasion* and therefore

raised the specter of 1870–71. What was feared was "the most complete and definitive disaster since our defeat during the *année terrible*," a distinct possibility because Germany's "commercial and industrial army now is just as redoubtable as its military army in 1870. It is the same clever organization, with the same attention to details, the same perfection in using resources, the same intelligence agency of spies, extended to the whole world this time" (Marcel Schwob, *Le danger allemand* [Paris, 1896], pp. 1–2). "The pernicious side of the adversary is less cruel in appearance [than the military invasion of 1870–71] but no less deleterious, and every year, in the form of commercial tribute, the vanquished will be paying indemnity for the war" (Maurice Lair, *L'impérialisme allemand* [Paris, 1902], p. 173). One need only look at the titles of the relevant literature to get an idea of the predominant feeling of threat: *La force allemande, La menace allemande, L'expansion de l'Allemagne en France, L'effort allemand, L'impérialisme allemand, La guerre commerciale.* See Digeon, *Crise allemande*, p. 480.

139. Ernest Lavisse, quoted in Aimée Dupuy, *"Sedan" et l'enseignement de la Revanche* (Paris, 1975), p. 13.

140. Howard, *Franco-Prussian War*, p. 16.

141. Douglas Porch, *The March to the Marne: The French Army, 1871–1914* (Cambridge, 1981), p. 52.

142. Quoted in Allan Mitchell, *Victors and Vanquished: The German Influence on Army and Church in France after 1870* (Chapel Hill, 1984), p. 87.

143. *Revue des deux mondes*, Jan. 15, 1871, p. 259.

144. Quoted in *Revue politique et littéraire* (1874): 735. While national enmity continued unabated, the models for purely technical and organizational imitation were the Prussian military reformers whose "hatred of France" was noted, not without sympathy, by the military historian Godefroy Cavaignac, son of the general in charge of the famous June 1848 massacre (*Revue des deux mondes*, Sept. 15, 1890, p. 411).

145. Alfred Rambaud, who along with Ernest Lavisse and Gabriel Monod was one of the most important historians of the early Third Republic, devoted two widely read books to the topic of French fatherhood to modern Prussia: *Les français sur le Rhin, 1792–1804* (1873) and *L'Allemagne sous Napoléon I, 1804–1811* (1874).

146. Ernest Renan, "La réforme intellectuelle et morale de la France" (1871).

147. "The German philosophers before Jena, too, in the tranquil ecstasy of their speculation and labor and the serenity of pure theory, attained a supreme indifference toward their country, which is very often confused with a love for humanity. This kind of blissfully vague cosmopolitanism was singularly like the one from which we were awakened

as if by a thunderball" (*Revue des deux mondes*, Jan. 15, 1871, p. 259).

148. Quoted in Porch, *March to the Marne*, p. 36.

149. Amalvi, *De l'art*, pp. 70–71. This perspective had been advanced for the first time in 1820 by François Guizot: "For more than thirteen centuries France . . . contained both a conquered and a victorious people. For more than thirteen centuries, the conquered people fought to shake the yoke of the victorious peoples. Our history is the history of that struggle" (quoted in Amalvi, *De l'art*, p. 21). The analogy to the English two-class society of Saxons and Normans described by Walter Scott in his medieval novels is obvious. Given the international popularity of Scott, it is conceivable that the division between Gauls and Franks was a translation of the Saxon-Norman dualism.

150. Amalvi, *De l'art*, p. 62.

151. François Corréard, *Vercingetorix, ou la chute de l'indépendence gauloise* (1888), quoted in Amalvi, *De l'art*, p. 69.

152. Quoted in Mona Ozouf, *L'école, l'église, et la République* (Paris, 1963), p. 23.

153. "If political rights outstrip intellectual culture, it is to be feared that people will make the most serious errors in the exercise of those rights" (quoted in Felix Ponteil, *Histoire de l'enseignement de France, 1789–1965* [Tours, 1966], p. 284).

154. In *Elementarschule und Pädagogik in der französischen Revolution* (Munich, 1990), Hans-Christian Harten describes how the idea of reason, which was to a large extent identical to heroism in the First Republic, had no clear equivalent in a concrete educational or organizational program.

155. *Encyclopaedia Britannica*, 11th ed., s.v. "Cousin." Cousin's reforms obliged every community to maintain a public school but without imposing compulsory education or freedom from tuition. Wherever there was already a Catholic school, that was considered sufficient. The influence of the priests and the landed gentry on the curriculum was great, whereas training and pay for teachers were meager.

156. Katherine Auspitz, *The Radical Bourgeoisie: The Ligue de l'enseignement and the Origins of the Third Republic, 1866–1885* (New York, 1982), p. 18. The idea that a fight for education was a fight against the church in favor of a secular, republican substitute is expressed in a statement by republican teachers in 1849 voicing their expectation that "teaching was going to become a veritable mission, and [that] the teacher, the priest of the new world, would be charged with replacing the priest of Catholicism" (Antoine Prost, *Histoire de l'enseignement en France, 1800–1967* [Paris, 1968], pp. 145–46). As a political religion of equality that did not question class society, republicanism saw schools primarily

as instruments for *political* equality and only secondarily as educational institutions. For example, Jules Michelet: "If children rich and poor have sat together on the benches of the same school, if they have been joined in friendship though divided in career . . . they will preserve in their disinterested, innocent friendship the sacred knot of the City" (Prost, *Histoire*, p. 46).

157. Baron Stoffel, *Rapports militaires: Ecrits de Berlin, 1866–1870*, 4th ed. (Paris, 1872), p. 103. Just as Stoffel depicts the Prussian military reforms after the defeat of 1806 as paradigmatic for the later French ones, he also cites as a negative example Austria's behavior after its defeat by Napoleon: "This likeable and sympathetic nation, eager for the finer things in life, continues to go along without any trace of resentment toward its conquerors, without any of those feelings of hatred that, after so many humiliations, are the appropriate reaction of a vigorous race" (p. 189). Stoffel's phrase *nation aimable et sympathique* refers not solely to the Austria of 1805 but also to the France of 1866.

158. The educational trade press in Germany reacted with sympathy, respect, and wonder. The *Pädagogische Zeitung* spoke of the "admirable persistence" of the French reformers (Nov. 29, 1883), suggesting that France "was preparing to steal away one of our greatest achievements, the superiority of our public education system" (July 31, 1879). It was registered, not without some jealousy, that the French synthesis of school education and civic emancipation was superior to the Prussian system of training underlings (*Untertanen*). "In our country the members of the teaching profession find themselves under regulation, so that those liberal-minded teachers who seek truth and openness must unfortunately keep their objectives to themselves or only discuss them in hushed tones. In France, by contrast, these goals are proclaimed by the government itself, and by its advisers, as worthy of pursuit and imitation. That the two countries have swapped roles in the space of a few years is a strange spectacle indeed! And it is admittedly disconcerting that we have abdicated the leadership that France has assumed" (*Pädagogium* 4 [1882]: 149–50).

159. Whether reform propaganda overstated the reality is an open question. In most historical accounts, the republican educational reform emerges as a secular process, and it understood itself as such. Only in isolated cases before 1880 was it conceded that Catholic schools often featured essentially the same curricula and similar moral ideas as public schools; likewise, it was reluctantly admitted that more Catholic than public schools around 1880 were tuition-free. See Raymond Grew and Patrick J. Harrigan, *School, State, and Society: The Growth of Elementary*

Schooling in Nineteenth-Century France (Ann Arbor, 1991), pp. 99, 236–37.

160. Laws making primary education compulsory and waiving tuition for six- to thirteen-year-olds were also passed (1881), as were ones mandating the replacement of religious instruction with *"instruction morale et civique"* (1882). In 1886, the last priests were removed from the system, and the *instituteur* was granted the status of a civil servant.

161. A. Giolitto, *Histoire de l'enseignement primaire au XIXè siècle* (Paris, 1983), p. 150. On the Black Hussars of the Republic, there are only scattered literary and autobiographical sources, for example, Charles Peguy's "L'argent" in *Oeuvres en prose complètes*, vol. 3 (Paris, 1992), p. 801. Another image of the teacher borrowed from the military was that of the "noncommissioned officer of education" (Ozouf, *L'école*, p. 148). As early as 1866, Jean Macé, the founder of the Ligue de l'enseignement, demanded the creation of an "educational *Landwehr* [national guard] as an auxiliary to the regular army" (Sanford Elwitt, *The Making of the Third Republic* [Baton Rouge, 1975], pp. 187–88).

162. Paul Leroy-Beaulieu, *Journal des débats*, Nov. 16, 1871, quoted in Ozouf, *L'école*, p. 20. An informative case study of the renewal of the French discipline of history after 1871 along the German model is provided by William R. Keylor, *Academy and Community: The Foundation of the French Historical Profession* (Cambridge, 1975): "It appeared almost as though the French professors were preparing to reenact the war of 1870, using the modern weapons of scholarship that they had appropriated from their Germanic conquerors in order to reverse the outcome" (p. 241).

163. Report of the Paris Conseil municipal (1890), quoted in Albert Bourzac, "Les bataillons scolaires en France," *Les athlètes de la République*, ed. Pierre Arnaud (Toulouse, 1987), pp. 53, 49; Arnaud, *Le militaire, l'écolier, le gymnaste* (Lyon, 1991), p. 254.

164. Harten, *Elementarschule*, pp. 299, 304.

165. Pierre Chambat, "La gymnastique, sport de la République?" *Esprit* 4 (1987): 24. Arnaud speaks of *"alphabétisation motrice,"* suggesting that the same standardization and normalization took place in gymnastics as in the instruction of standard French idiom, which replaced regional dialects (*Militaire*, p. 253). See Arnaud, "Les deux voies d'intégration du sport dans l'institution scolaire," *Education et politique sportives XIX et XX siècles*, ed. Arnaud and Thierry Terret (Paris, 1995), p. 13.

166. The most important examples are Italy and Bohemian Czechoslovakia (Arnaud, "Deux voies," pp. 14 ff.).

167. Benoit Lecoq, "Les sociétés de gymnastique et de tir dans la France républicaine, 1870–1914," *Revue historique* 276 (1986): 162.

168. Speech of June 26, 1871, quoted in Arnaud, *Militaire*, pp. 59–60. No less militant were the assertions of Jules Ferry, who played the strange double role of being the incarnation of opportunism and the organizer of reform, including the militarization of the schools. On the occasion of the creation of school battalions, he said: "Military education will never completely penetrate our scholarly circles until the instructor himself has become a professor of military exercises" (speech of June 3, 1882, quoted in Arnaud, *Athlètes*, p. 144).

169. Raymond Guasco, quoted in *Nineteenth Century* 74 (1913): 36.

170. Quoted in Michel Caillat, *L'idéologie du sport en France depuis 1880* (Paris, 1989), p. 33.

171. Ibid., pp. 31–32. In Coubertin, the idea of the military instrumentalization of sports approximates that of *gymnastique*, for example, in his remark that "sports are an excellent way of physically 'clearing one's mind,' which should precede entry into the modern army" (1902 article in *Revue des deux mondes*, quoted in Arnaud, *Athlètes*, p. 292). Or even more clearly :"Whoever learns not to shrink from a rugby scrum will not retreat from the mouth of a Prussian cannon" (*Sports athlétique*, Feb. 13, 1892, quoted in Robert A. Nye, *Masculinity and Male Codes of Honor in Modern France* (New York, 1993), p. 230.

172. Robert A. Nye, *Crime, Madness, and Politics in Modern France: The Medical Concept of National Decline* (Princeton, 1984), pp. 328–29.

173. "*Petite machine ailée*": Maurice Leblanc, quoted in Philippe Gaboriau, *Le Tour de France et le vélo: Histoire sociale d'une épopée contemporaine* (Paris, 1995), p. 115. "*Fée bicyclette*": *L'auto*, quoted in *Les lieux de mémoire*, ed. Pierre Nora, vol. 3, part 2 (Paris, 1992), p. 888.

174. Gaboriau, *Tour de France*, p. 116.

175. Richard Holt, *Sport and Society in Modern France* (Oxford, 1981), p. 100.

176. Pre-1914 competitors in the Tour de France were seen as "*soldats du sport*" and as a "*bataillon sacré du sport*" (Holt, *Sport and Society*, p. 23). For example, in a report from *L'auto* on May 20, 1902: "They were climbing Calvary, a long, athletic Calvary, like soldiers drafted by the state going to battle" (Holt, *Sport and Society*, p. 24). The process by which sports gradually accrued a nationalistic meaning in the sense of *gymnastique* is illustrated by the resonance of the Olympic Games of 1912. France's poor results caused "a veritable flood of consternation throughout the country. For the first time, a sporting event profoundly affected the soul of the nation. The press in its entirety commented

on the defeat, . . . expressing the rage of the country . . . and the unanimous will to prepare our *revanche*" (Jean de Pierrefeu, quoted in Caillat, *Idéologie du sport*, p. 49). Sixteen years earlier, Charles Maurras, by then a radical nationalist, remarked self-critically after the first Olympic Games in Athens that he had been wrong to reject Coubertin's idea of internationalism, for Athens had shown that "far from quashing patriotic passions, all the false cosmopolitanism of the stadium does is exacerbate them. I am far from complaining" (Pierre Arnaud and James Riordan, eds., *Sport et relations internationales, 1900–1941* (Paris, 1998), p. 47.

177. Raoul Girardet describes the Algerian occupation as "a limited operation fundamentally directed at lifting the prestige of the restored monarchy in the eyes of outsiders and in popular domestic opinion" (*Idée coloniale*, p. 6).

178. Jacques Valette, "Note sur l'idée coloniale vers 1871," *Revue d'histoire moderne et contemporaine* 14 (1967): 65; Marcel Emerit, "L'idée de colonisation dans les socialismes français," *L'age nouveau* 24 (1947): 103–09. On Algeria as France's replacement for America: "We had in that country a 'Far West' to discover and a California to exploit" (Paul Gaffarel, *L'Algérie: Histoire, conquête, et colonisation* [Paris, 1883], p. 562).

179. The connection of the Far East with the Mediterannean had already been achieved in 1869 with the opening of the Suez Canal, likewise a French project. The fact that both of the great nineteenth-century canals, the Suez and the Panama, were conceived in France suggests a monumental action of compensatory *revanche* for France's demise as a sea power. In the Latin self-conception of French imperialism, the tone was set in part by the idea of a "Latin" *revanche* for England's seventeenth-century displacement of the old colonial powers Spain and Portugal. Prévost-Paradol was already sounding this theme in *La France nouvelle* (1868). Paul Leroy-Beaulieu, the most influential colonial propagandist after 1871, wrote on the occasion of the Italian protest against the French occupation of Tunisia in 1881: "We would hope that the Latin races would be the ones to colonize Africa. They could come together in this glorious task" ("La politique continentale et la politique coloniale," *Economiste français*, May 7, 1881, p. 566). In another passage, Leroy-Beaulieu insisted that the Mediterranean be made "if not a French lake, at least a neo-Latin lake" (quoted in Agnes Murphy, *The Ideology of French Imperialism, 1871–1881* [1948; rpt. New York, 1968], p. 140). On the trans-Saharan railway, see Murphy, *Ideology*, pp. 154–55, as well as A. Duponchel,

Le chemin de fer trans-Saharien, jonction coloniale entre l'Algérie et le Soudan (Paris, 1879).

180. Prévost-Paradol, *La France nouvelle*, p. 418.

181. Quoted in Henri Masson, *Revue française d'histoire d'outre-mer* 49 (1962): 415.

182. Quoted in Girardet, *Idée coloniale*, p. 4. The anticolonial vox populi was summarized by a procolonial author as follows: "Soon we will have been fifty years [in Algeria], and colonialization is still at a rudimentary stage. Millions of us have buried our treasures there and the bones of our children, and here's what we have to show for it: a few artichokes, which were very expensive, and too many insurrections"(Raboisson, *Etude sur les colonies* [Paris, 1877], p. 44).

183. See Charles-Robert Ageron, "Gambetta et la reprise de l'expansion coloniale," *Revue française d'histoire d'outre-mer* 59 (1972): 57.

184. Ibid., p. 203.

185. Gambetta, letter to Arthur Ranc, Sept. 20, 1875, quoted in Ageron, *Gambetta*, p. 169. On exchanging colonies for Alsace-Lorraine, see Peter Grupp, *Deutschland, Frankreich, und die Kolonien: Der französische "Parti colonial" und Deutschland, 1890 bis 1914* (Tübingen, 1980), pp. 78ff., and Sieburg, "Elsass-Lothringen-Frage," p. 32.

186. Ageron, *Gambetta*, pp. 172ff.

187. Raoul Girardet, quoted in Ageron, *Gambetta*, p. 59.

188. Leroy-Beaulieu, "Politique continentale," p. 566.

189. *Le siècle*, May 27, 1881, quoted in Carroll, *French Public Opinion*, p. 90.

190. Open letter to *Le temps*, Oct. 4, 1885, quoted in Leo Haman, ed., *Les Opportunistes—Les débuts de la République aux républicains* (Paris, 1991), p. 174. Jules Ferry, the main target of the accusation that the colonies were a replacement for and thus a betrayal of Alsace-Lorraine, spoke in similar terms before parliament: "There can be no compensation, none whatever, for the disasters we have suffered. . . . The real question that has to be asked, and clearly asked, is this: Must the containment forced on nations that experience great misfortune result in abdication? . . . Should they let themselves be so absorbed in contemplating this incurable wound [Alsace-Lorraine] that they play no part in what is going on around them?" (quoted in Henry Brunschwig, *French Colonialism, 1871–1914* [New York, 1966], p. 79).

191. "How can we" and "an additional weakening": *La nouvelle revue* (1887): 572, 579. *Le temps*, Apr. 7, 1881, described the Tunisian undertaking as a "new Mexican adventure" (quoted in Carroll, *French*

Public Opinion, p. 89). "The breach": quoted in Herbert Tint, *The Decline of French Patriotism, 1870–1940* (London, 1964), p. 43.

192. Ferry the German: Jean Michel Gaillard, *Jules Ferry* (Paris, 1989), p. 14. "For a couple": quoted in Jochen Grube, *Bismarcks Politik in Europa und Übersee: Seine "Annäherung" an Frankreich im Urteil der Pariser Presse, 1883–1885* (Frankfurt am Main, 1975), p. 117. "I see before me": quoted in Mayeur and Rebérioux, *Third Republic*, p. 99. "Ferry has gotten": quoted in Sternhell, *Barrès*, pp. 87–88.

193. "Gold and blood": Girardet, *Idée coloniale*, p. 57. "A successful": quoted in Sternhell, *Barrès*, pp. 87–88. Like the nationalism of the period, the antisemitism of Drumont's *La France juive* was still of the social-revolutionary variety in which Jewishness served as a "metaphor" for high finance. Drumont was an anticapitalist, anticolonialist, and antisemite because all three enemies represented the exploitation of the "little people": "The suffering endured by our soldiers enables the Jews to engage in those operations" (quoted in Girardet, *Idée coloniale*, p. 61).

194. Quoted in Sternhell, *Barrès*, n. 43. A good illustration of the third contention is given by Joseph Reinach, an intimate of Gambetta's and a spokesperson for Opportunism: "Without colonialism, the martial instincts of the French people would turn to bloody confrontation, class hatred, and maybe even civil war" (quoted in Ageron, *Gambetta*, p. 199).

195. Girardet, *Idée coloniale*, p. 85. "From the point of view of the sole imperatives of national interest and grandeur, history appears to have worked in [the Opportunists' and colonialists'] favor. . . . The main arguments of [the anticolonialists and Boulangists] lost most of their significance during the great controversies of the 1880s" (p. 66).

196. Ibid., pp. 36 ff.

197. Between 1871 and 1881, some ten thousand families emigrated from Alsace-Lorraine (Louis Vignon, *La France en Algérie* [Paris, 1893], p. 106).

198. Quoted in Girardet, *Idée coloniale*, p. 65.

199. Porch, *March to the Marne*, pp. 153 ff., 165 ff.

200. Quoted in Girardet, *Idée coloniale*, p. 87. As this quotation suggests, France's self-presentation as a force of liberation usually referred to local, that is, native oppressors. France also styled itself, however, as a benign and unselfish liberator, in contrast to its European imperial competitors, chiefly England. (Worthy of further investigation is the extent to which the memory of France's support for the American War of Independence played a role here.) A similar rhetorical shift took place in Germany after World War I. Following the loss of its colonies,

Germany underwent a reversal of self-presentation from colonial master to vanguard warrior for the colonized peoples oppressed by the Western powers.

If French colonialism is seen as a compensatory mechanism for defeat—that is, as a unique French path to imperialism—further perspectives open up. France fulfills all the conditions for what Winfried Baumgart calls "compensatory imperialism." Traditional, or defensive, imperialism was characteristic of the established colonial and industrial power England, while aggressive imperialism epitomized the ambitious parvenu Germany. According to Baumgart, for the compensatory imperialists (France, Russia, and Italy), colonial expansion was important not so much for economic reasons as, "to a large extent, to restore national prestige" (*Imperialism: The Idea and Reality of British and French Colonial Expansion, 1880–1914* [Oxford, 1982], p. 67). Classic imperialism served both to provide a safety valve for overpopulation and to acquire new markets for industrial production, but these two functions were largely irrelevant to France with its low population growth and comparatively slow industrialization. French investments aboard, too, were made less in the spirit of venture capital, aimed at quickly reaping great financial rewards, than as a kind of "reservoir that could be tapped in times of need" and a "savings account one could draw on in an emergency" (Gilbert Ziebura, "Interne Faktoren des Hochimperialismus, 1871–1914," *Der moderne Imperialismus*, ed. J. Mommsen [Berlin, 1971], p. 91; see also pp. 85 ff.). The extreme social Darwinism of English and German imperialism thus has no equivalent in the Third Republic, for the simple reason that social Darwinist arguments have less appeal for the losers of major wars (Linda Clark, *Social Darwinism in France* [Tuscaloosa, 1984], pp. 161, 180).

201. Girardet, *Idée coloniale*, p. 88.
202. The distinction between the prestige-oriented state colonialism of France and the profit-driven private colonialism of England had its corollary in the realm of culture. If American culture has become the world's mass culture, it is not because of a state-planned export program but rather as the result of the invisible guiding hand of American capital. The anti-American buzzword *cultural imperialism* is a projection of the French mentality of cultural planning.

The Alliance française described itself as "a national association for the spreading of the French language in the colonies and abroad." Among its founders were Paul Bert; Paul Cambon, France's resident minister in Tunisia; and Pierre Foncin. See Maurice Bruezière, *L'Alliance française: Histoire d'une institution* (Paris, 1983), pp. 10, 11. The title of a lecture held at the Alliance in 1885 defined its mission:

"The Struggle of Languages on the Face of the Globe: The Role of the Alliance française" (Bruezière, *Alliance*, p. 20). Unfortunately, there is no study devoted to the institution and its influence other than the uncritical pamphlet published by the Alliance in celebration of its one hundredth anniversary.

203. Quoted in Grupp, *Deutschland*, p. 76. King Leopold II of Belgium spoke of the "twofold revenge" sought by France for the loss of Alsace-Lorraine and Egypt (Baumgart, *Imperialism*, p. 62). Raoul Girardet draws attention to the revival of older traditions of *revanche* (the Seven Years War, Trafalgar) by pointing to its persistence in the French navy, which understood colonial expansion—one of its responsibilities until the creation of a separate colonial ministry—as a form of *revanche* against England (*Idée coloniale*, pp. 11–12).

204. Quoted in Girardet, *Idée coloniale*, p. 100.

205. Pierre Guillen writes of German fears "that a French protectorate in Morocco would mean a weakening of the global position of the empire and would ruin Germany's economic position" (*L'Allemagne et le Maroc de 1870 à 1905* [Paris, 1967], p. 886). On Morocco as a model of and test for German participation in the carving up of the colonial world, see pp. 19, 22, 29, and 125 ff.

206. Max Weber, "Bismarcks Aussenpolitik und die Gegenwart" (1915), *Gesammelte Politische Schriften* (Tübingen, 1958), p. 114.

207. Pierre Baudin, *L'empire allemand et l'empéreur* (Paris, 1911), p. ix.

3: Germany

1. Interview in the *Neue Freie Presse* (Vienna), partially reprinted in the *Berliner Tageblatt*, morning ed., Aug. 3, 1928.

2. Winston S. Churchill, *The World Crisis* (London, 1931), p. 800.

3. Arthur Rosenberg, *The Birth of the German Republic, 1871–1918* (1931; rpt. New York, 1962), p. 239.

4. Quoted in Frederick Maurice, *The Armistice of 1918* (London, 1943), p. 41.

5. Ibid., p. 49. The crusading mentality of the American North during the Civil War and its own "totalitarianism" can be recognized both in Sherman's suggestions as well as in Wilson's universal humanitarianism. Both are the moralizing mirror images of Ludendorff's purely power politics.

6. Erich Ludendorff, "Kriegsführung und Politik," quoted in Joachim Petzold, *Die Dolchstosslegende* (Berlin, 1963), p. 54. It should be recalled that Clausewitz subordinated politics to war only in his later years. In

his "revolutionary" youth, he had distinguished between war as non- or antipolitics, as heroism or national honor, and the private egotism of bourgeois society. He preferred an honorable defeat to a "cowardly subjugation." See Herfried Münkler, *Gewalt und Ordnung* (Frankfurt am Main, 1992), pp. 103–06.

7. Heinrich Mann, *Macht und Mensch* (Munich, 1919), pp. 208–09.

8. Wilfred Trotter, *Instincts of the Herd in Peace and War* (1915; rpt. London, 1953), pp. 204, 184. Emphasis added. Trotter goes so far as to surmise that had the Allies known earlier about this "hysterical" disposition of their enemy, "[Germany's] collapse could have been brought about with comparative ease at a much earlier date" (p. 184).

9. Mann, *Macht und Mensch*, p. 203. See also p. 162: "The counterfeiting of our entire character as a people, boasting, challenges, lies, and self-deception as our daily bread, greed as our only motivation to live: this was the Wilhelminian empire."

10. Frederick Maurice, *The Last Four Months: How the War Was Won* (Boston, 1919), p. 206; Churchill, *World Crisis*, p. 817; George Young, *The New Germany* (London, 1920), p. 4; Henri Lichtenberger, *L'Allemagne d'aujourd'hui dans ses relations avec la France* (Paris, 1922), p. 28.

11. *Hochland*, Dec. 1918, p. 331. Michael Geyer traces the rise of the Ludendorffian mentality to the disappearance of strategy, that is, the setting of strategic goals, in the technocratic totalization of the war as part of the 1916 Hindenburg Program. The replacement of strategic and political goals by an emphasis on the most advanced technology of destruction available enabled the idea of an unrestricted total victory to flourish; anything less would appear to be a failure. See Peter Paret, ed., *Makers of Modern Strategy* (Princeton, 1986), pp. 540ff. The submarine as a "miracle weapon" was a concrete instance of the replacement of strategy with technology. In this respect, it was the immediate precursor of the V rockets of 1944–45 and the various irrational expectations of victory that were projected onto them.

12. Quoted in Rosenberg, *Birth of the German Republic*, p. 251.

13. Martin Doerry, in *Übergangsmenschen: Die Mentalität der Wilhelminer und die Krise des Kaiserreichs* (Weinheim, 1986), characterizes the psychological makeup of the Wilhelminian as combining a fixation with authority with a striving for harmony, conformity, and aggression. Doerry sees their "pale and impotent revolt" against their fathers and grandfathers (Bismarck is their grandfather "who founded the empire over the objections of the despised liberal 'fathers' of 1848") everywhere in evidence in the 1890s: in their program of liberal imperialism,

in their taste for literary naturalism, and in the revisionism of the Social Democratic Party (p. 180).

14. George B. Forgie, *Patricide in a House Divided: A Psychological Interpretation of Lincoln and His Age* (New York, 1979).

15. On Treitschke's role in the political education of the Wilhelminian generation, see W. Bussmann, "Treitschke als Politiker," *Historische Zeitschrift* 177 (1977): 249–79, and Peter Winzen, "Treitschke's Influence on the Rise of Imperialist and Anti-British Nationalism in Germany," *Nationalist and Racialist Movements in Britain and Germany before 1914*, ed. Paul Kennedy and Anthony Nicholls (Oxford, 1981). Among Treitschke's disciples, readers, and acolytes were Friedrich von Bernhardi, Bernhard von Bülow, Helmut von Moltke Jr., Heinrich Class, Carl Peters, Richard von Kühlmann, Alfred Tirpitz, Paul Rohrbach, Maximilian Harden, and even, to an extent, Max Weber. Weber's characterization of the empire's creation as a "youthful prank" of the Germans that would have significance only if followed by further heroic deeds evoked Treitschke's image of Germany as a giant awakening after a long sleep, rubbing his eyes, and scanning the horizon for new possibilities.

16. Treitschke, speech to the Reichstag, Nov. 29, 1871. The elder Helmut Moltke also expected a "Seven Years or Thirty Years War" in which Germany would have to defend the spoils of its victory in 1871 (Gerhard Ritter, *Staatskunst und Kriegshandwerk*, vol. 2 [Munich, 1965], p. 244). After the failure of the blitzkrieg concept, World War I was understood by the educated as a continuation of the Seven Years War, another sign of Treitschke's persistent influence on Wilhelminian elites.

17. Isabel V. Hull, *The Entourage of Kaiser Wilhelm II, 1888–1918* (Cambridge, 1982), p. 44. The phrase *symbolic inflation* can be found on p. 41. On the self-presentation of nation and empire, see Thomas A. Kohut, *Wilhelm II and the Germans: A Study in Leadership* (New York, 1991).

18. On Hindenburg's award, see Bernhard Schwertfeger, *Das Weltkriegs-Ende*, 6th ed. (Potsdam, 1938), p. 60. On Moltke's, see Hull, *Entourage*, p. 41.

19. Albrecht von Thaer, quoted in Siegfried A. Kaehler, "Vier quellenkritische Untersuchungen zum Kriegsende 1918," *Nachrichten der Akademie der Wissenschaften in Göttingen. I. Philologisch-Historische Klasse* 8 (1960): 428.

20. Quoted in *Quellen zur Geschichte des Parlamentarismus und der politischen Parteien. Erste Reihe Vol. 2: Die Regierung des Prinzen Max v. Baden* (Düsseldorf, 1962), p. 44.

21. Schwertfeger, *Weltkriegs-Ende*, p. 142; Secretary of State Hintze, quoted in Schwertfeger, p. 119; Bethmann-Hollweg, quoted in *Ursachen des deutschen Zusammenbruchs von 1918*, vol. 6 (Berlin, 1929), p. 124; Stresemann, quoted in Anneliese Thimme, *Flucht in den Mythos* (Göttingen, 1969), p. 76; Hans Delbrück, in *Preussische Jahrbücher* 174 (1918): 430.
22. Hans von Hentig, *Psychologische Strategie des grossen Krieges* (Heidelberg, 1927), pp. 133, 134.
23. In his article "Ein dunkler Tag" in the *Vossische Zeitung* of Oct. 7, 1918, Rathenau spoke not of a *levée en masse* but—with reference to the anti-Napoleonic movement of 1812–13—of a "popular uprising." See Gerhard Hecker, *Walther Rathenau und sein Verhältnis zu Militär und Krieg* (Boppard, 1983), p. 432. The fact that contemporary commentators and later historians almost exclusively used the French term, which they put in Rathenau's mouth, speaks volumes about the exotic attraction that the idea of popular warfare exerted on the German imagination.
24. Quoted in Prince Max von Baden, *Erinnerungen und Dokumente* (Berlin, 1927), p. 344.
25. Ibid., p. 331.
26. Ibid., p. 455.
27. Quoted in Hecker, *Walther Rathenau*, p. 436.
28. Ludendorff was the driving force behind the creation of the Ufa film studio as a propaganda instrument. A lack of feeling for the mass psyche was evident in the prewar era as well. The "presentation of empire" proved utterly incapable of appealing to a mass audience. The most prominent example of this deficiency was the celebration of the German victory at Sedan, which despite the technical opulence of the ceremonies never became a popular holiday.
29. Max von Baden, *Erinnerungen*, p. 430. Ludendorff made this statement to Philipp Scheidemann. In later discussions, the left would attribute the collapse chiefly to the German leadership's lack of democratic sensibilities. See, for example, Karl Mayr's article "Weltkriegführung und Demokratie," *Sozialistische Monatshefte* (1926): "Democracy contained the only organizational possibility for mobilizing the masses in a defensive war. Democracy could inspire the masses by means of political education and training. This irreplaceable fermenting quality of democracy was what Germany's field marshals were incapable of understanding with either their hearts or their minds" (p. 290).
30. Max von Baden, *Erinnerungen*, p. 495.
31. Albrecht von Thaer, quoted in Kaehler, "Untersuchungen," p. 462.

32. Ibid., pp. 457, 453. Wilhelm, to whom the proposal was addressed, also imagined himself leading the army at its vanguard, but in a completely different sense. According to General Wilhelm Groener, the kaiser intended after the outbreak of revolution "to assume command of the army and order it to do an about-face, attack the Rhine border, and reconquer Berlin and his homeland. He issued orders for me to prepare for this operation" (*Lebenserinnerungen* [Göttingen, 1957], p. 454).

33. Quoted in Gerhard Ritter, *Staatskunst und Kriegshandwerk*, vol. 4 (Munich, 1968), p. 463. The symbolic—even charismatic—power of the fleet in the Wihelminian imagination is evident in the fact that even a realist like Prince Max had similar hopes for a final sea battle: "After a victory by the German fleet, the revolution and capitulation of November 9 and 11 would have been an emotional impossibility. . . . Even if our navy had gone down to glorious defeat, the military and political necessity of the operation would have been affirmed. Such a sacrificial act would have had a shaming power that many of the traitors and cowards would have had a hard time resisting" (Max von Baden, *Erinnerungen*, p. 575).

34. Ernst-Heinrich Schmidt, *Heimatheer und Revolution 1918* (Stuttgart, 1981), p. 292.

35. Thimme, *Flucht in den Mythos*, p. 151.

36. Ibid., p. 163. Scheidemann made similar statements in *Der Zusammenbruch* (Berlin, 1921): "Where were the loyal formations of troops in Berlin? Where were the officers and political leaders speaking even a single word of support for the kaiser? Yes, where were the officers and loyalists? Not one of those who now speak and write such sharp words were anywhere to be seen or heard back then" (pp. 207–08). As an auditor on the committee investigating the causes of the collapse, Hans Delbrück concluded that the characteristic feature of the revolution was "that nowhere did it encounter the slightest resistance. The decisive factor was not one side's power but the other's absolute lack of it. Where was the courage and the feeling of duty, that once created Prussia and the German empire?" (*Ursachen des deutschen Zusamenbruchs. 2. Abt. Der innere Zusammenbruch*, vol. 6 [Berlin, 1928], pp. 79–80). Six months earlier, Max Weber had written of the cowardice and opportunism shown by the Conservatives and National Liberals when Bismarck, who had always been their man, was forced from office: "They did not lift a finger but instead turned toward a new sun. This event is unequaled in the annals of a proud people." Weber diagnosed the "contemptible lack of honor" and "cant," of which German elites perennially accused England, as a pure case of

projection (*Gesammelte politische Schriften* [Tübingen, 1971], pp. 312, 313).

37. Quoted in Petzold, *Dolchstosslegende*, p. 42.

38. Ibid.; Friedrich Hiller von Gaertringen, " 'Dolchstoss-Diskussion' und 'Dolchstoss-Legende' im Wandel von vier Jahrzehnten," *Geschichte und Gegenwartsbewusstsein: Festschrift für Hans Rothfels zum 70. Geburtstag,* ed. W. Besson and von Gaertringen (Göttingen, 1963), pp. 132, 133.

39. Ludendorff's demand for an armistice was often described as the actual stab in the back. Liberal Wilhelminians like Prince Max von Baden, Hans Delbrück, Max Weber, and Walther Rathenau neither used the term nor accused Ludendorff of intentional treason, but they made it clear that they held his peace-through-victory strategy responsible for overtaxing German strength and thus causing the defeat. An explicit version of this reversed stab-in-the-back accusation can be found in the article "Dolchstoss von oben," *Weltbühne* (1920): 406–20.

40. Detlev Peukert, *Die Weimarer Republik* (Frankfurt am Main, 1987), pp. 15, 16.

41. Speech to the Reichstag, Oct. 9, 1878, on the occasion of the proposed Socialist Law (Otto von Bismarck, *Die Gesammelten Werke*, 3rd ed., vol. 12 [Berlin, 1929], p. 9).

42. Quoted in Bernhard Fürst von Bülow, *Denkwürdigkeiten*, vol. 2 (Berlin, 1930), p. 198.

43. Karen Fries-Thiessenhusen, "Politische Kommentare deutscher Historiker 1918/19 zu Niederlage und Staatsumsturz," *Vom Kaiserreich zur Weimarer Republik*, ed. Eberhard Kolb (Cologne, 1972), p. 350.

44. In a sermon delivered in a Protestant church in January 1918, Bruno Doehring referred to striking munitions workers as "cheap, cowardly creatures who have desecrated the altar of the fatherland with their brothers' blood, . . . who . . . have poisoned the virtuous spirit of our people, who have misdirected and herded the unfortunate masses into the streets from their peaceful workplaces, pressed deadly weapons into their hands, and bid them attack from behind their brothers, who are still confronted by the enemy" (quoted in Wilhelm Pressel, *Die Kriegspredigt 1914–1918 in der evangelischen Kirche Deutschlands* [Göttingen, 1967], pp. 305–06).

45. Weber, *Gesammelte politische Schriften*, p. 307.

46. Quoted in Hiller von Gaertringen, " 'Dolchstoss-Diskussion,' " p. 124.

47. Harry Kessler, *Tagebücher, 1918–1937* (Frankfurt am Main, 1982), p. 294.

48. Quoted in Hiller von Gaertringen, " 'Dolchstoss-Diskussion,' " p. 138. The most comprehensive history of the myth's origin after Hiller von

Gaertringen's is Petzold, *Dolchstosslegende*. The English general Frederick Maurice refused to acknowledge his authorship of the phrase. In contrast, there seems to be no doubt as to his authorship of the denigrating remark about Britain's "little army," which wartime English propaganda attributed to Wilhelm II. See Paul Fussell, *The Great War and Modern Memory* (Oxford, 1977). According to another account, the phrase *stab in the back* stemmed from the English general Neill Malcolm, who supposedly used it in conversation with Ludendorff (Petzold, *Dolchstosslegende*, pp. 26–27). The ostensibly English origin of the phrase is remarkable not as a measure of the myth's truth or falsehood but because it has "mercantilist" England—German's former enemy—acting as the arbiter of German honor.

49. Hiller von Gaertringen, " 'Dolchstoss-Diskussion,' " p. 138.
50. Herfried Münkler explains the "victory" of the dagger over the poison metaphor by noting "that in contrast to the dagger, poison could not be incorporated into a mythical story. Therefore it would have symbolized a definitive end, whereas after the dagger, understood as the murder of Siegfried, the story could continue" (Herfried Münkler and Wolfgang Storch, *Siegfrieden: Politik mit einem deutschen Mythos* (Berlin, 1988), p. 93. Münkler recalls here Donoso Cortes's distinction between the "dictatorship of the dagger," that is, revolution, and the "dictatorship of the saber," that is, the old regime (p. 89).
51. Note by von Thaer of Oct. 1, 1918, quoted by Herfried Münkler in Udo Bermbach, ed., *In den Trümmern der eigenen Welt* (Berlin, 1989), p. 259.
52. Quoted in Klaus von See, *Barbar, Germane, Arier* (Heidelberg, 1994), p. 108.
53. Ibid., p. 109.
54. Julius Rodenberg, quoted in Werner Wunderlich, *Der Schatz des Drachentöters: Materialien zur Wirkungsgeschichte des Nibelungen-Liedes* (Stuttgart, 1977), pp. 43–44.
55. Hartmut Zelinsky, in Bermbach, *In den Trümmern*, pp. 201 ff.
56. Walther Rathenau, *An Deutschlands Jugend* (Berlin, 1918), p. 83. On Wagner's influence on the psyche, politics, and culture of Wilhelminian Germany, see Hartmut Zelinsky, "Kaiser Wilhelm II, die Werk-Idee Richard Wagners und der 'Weltkampf,' " *Der Ort Kaiser Wilhelms II in der deutschen Geschichte*, ed. C. G. Röhl (Munich, 1991). See also Zelinsky, *Richard Wagner: Ein deutsches Thema* (Frankfurt am Main, 1976), and Zelinsky, *Sieg oder Untergang* (Munich, 1990).
57. Thimme, *Flucht in den Mythos*, pp. 15, 81. The majority SPD acted in similar fashion. Whatever explanation the SPD offered for its behavior in August 1914 and November 1918 amounted to an abdication of the

fundamental positions that constituted its previous identity. The fact that the right and (former) left were both "broken" after 1918, and were not as self-confident as they had been until 1918 and 1914 respectively, may help explain the political psychology of the Weimar Republic.

58. Edgar J. Jung, *Die Herrschaft der Minderwertigen* (Berlin, 1927), pp. 291, 293. On the radical nationalists' rejection of the stab-in-the-back legend, see Arnim Mohler, *Die Konservative Revolution in Deutschland, 1918–1932*, 4th ed. (Darmstadt, 1994), p. 37.

59. Jung, *Herrschaft*, p. 293.

60. Arnold Bergmann, *Die Bedeutung des Nibelungenliedes für die deutsche Nation* (Karlsruhe, 1924), pp. 22, 14, 21, 23.

61. See Börries von Münchhausen's "Ein Lied Volkers" (1920) (Wunderlich, *Schatz des Drachentöters*, p. 76), which ends as follows:

> We readily lent our sword
> To the king in desperate days
> Still on the most difficult day of all
> Hagen swore Gunther the oath: "Let the blame be mine!"
>
> Therefore, although my heart trembled
> As Siegfried groaned and Krimhild wept,
> You are the hero of my songs,
> Surrounded by horror, my Hagen, my friend!

62. Klaudius Bojunga, *Mittelalterliche Nibelungensage und Nibelungendichtung im Unterricht auf der Obersekunda höherer Schulen*, Deutschunterricht und Deutschkunde, vol. 12 (Berlin, 1928), p. 130. On the reinterpretation of Siegfried and Hagen after 1918, see Francis G. Gentry, "Die Rezeption des Nibelungenliedes in der Weimarer Republik," *Das Weiterleben des Mittelalters in der deutschen Literatur*, ed. James F. Poag and Gerhild Scholtz-Williams (Königstein, 1983), pp. 146 ff., and von See, *Barbar*, pp. 109 ff., 125 ff.

63. Friedrich Altrichter, *Die seelische Entwicklung des Heeres im Weltkriege* (Berlin, 1933), pp. 151 ff.

64. Hermann von Kuhl, addressing the Committee to Investigate the Causes of German Defeat, spoke of "pacifist, internationalist, antimilitarist, and revolutionary foment within the army" and concluded that one should talk "not of a stab in the back but of a poisoning of the army" (*Ursachen des deutschen Zusammenbruchs*, vol. 6, part 2 [Berlin, 1928], p. 39). The nationalist representative Albrecht Philipp, a member of the committee, made a similar suggestion (Hiller von Gaertringen, " 'Dolchstoss,' " p. 149).

65. Wilhelm Groener, *Lebenserinnerungen* (1957; rpt. Osnabrück, 1977), pp. 472, 452. In the *Guidelines for Troop Motivation* of Nov. 6, 1918, "prophylactic inoculations" are recommended to ward off revolutionary agitation (Erich Otto Volkmann, *Der Marxismus und das deutsche Heer* [Berlin, 1925], p. 318).

66. Gustave Le Bon, *La psychologie des foules* (Paris, 1991), p. 74.

67. In the 11th edition of the *Encyclopaedia Britannica* (1910) there is not a single entry devoted to propaganda, which is discussed as part of the entry on the Roman curate. In contrast, in the 12th edition (1922), the article on propaganda stretches over ten pages.

68. Erich Ludendorff, *Meine Kriegserinnerungen* (Berlin, 1919), p. 4; Ludendorff, *Kriegführung und Politik* (Berlin, 1922), p. 188.

69. The same had been true half a century earlier in the American South. See Edward A. Pollard in his second book, *The Lost Cause Regained*: "We find a war tamely expiring, without either of those final experiences almost uniform in history—a last convulsive effort or a resort from the open field to such strongholds as nature or art have supplied. We know of no other instance in modern history where more than one hundred thousand men have laid down their arms in open fields to an enemy, and have ceased from war with a resolution so sudden and complete" (1868; rpt. New York, 1970), p. 18. In the same context, Pollard speaks of the South's lacking "popular will," "the want being, not of material, but of animation."

70. Quoted in Hans Linhardt, ed., *Johann Plenges Organisations- und Propagandalehre* (Berlin, 1965), p. 128.

71. Letter to Karl Lamprecht, quoted in Edgar Stern-Rubarth, *Die Propaganda als politisches Instrument* (Berlin, 1921), p. 108.

72. Paul Rohrbach, *Unser Weg: Betrachtungen zum letzten Jahrhundert deutscher Geschichte* (Cologne, 1949), p. 30; Friedrich Naumann, *Das blaue Buch von Vaterland und Freiheit* (1913), quoted in Rohrbach, *Unser Weg*, p. 31.

73. Paul Rohrbach, *Der deutsche Gedanke* (Düsseldorf, 1912), pp. 6–7, 53. The French idea of *"civilisation"* was for Rohrbach an idea to be admired for other reasons—namely, as a model for cultural world domination, even though the defeat of 1870–71 was the "source of energy" from which it arose (p. 28).

74. Ibid., p. 227.

75. Karl Helfferich, "Die Vorgeschichte des Weltkriegs," quoted in Otto Becker, *Deutschlands Zusammenbruch und Auferstehung* (Berlin, 1922), p. 144.

76. Linhart, *Organisations- und Propagandalehre*, p. 169; Ernst Troeltsch, *Spektator-Briefe* (Tübingen, 1924), p. 318.

77. Paul Rühlmann, *Kulturpropaganda* (Charlottenburg, 1919), p. 6.

78. Ferdinand Tönnies, *Zur Kritik der öffentlichen Meinung* (Berlin, 1922), p. 549. Tönnies identifies precisely the same misconception in a comment by Colonel Walter Nicolai, an aide to Ludendorff: "We needed the mood of confidence we had during the first part of the war." In the same way, Tönnies notes sardonically, "the aged invalid 'needs' the lively strength of youth to achieve again the glories of the past."

79. According to Scheler, Germanophobia was the reaction of the old Western European nations to having been "driven from paradise" by the parvenu Germany with its work ethic, its discipline, and its artificially low prices (*Die Ursachen des Deutschenhasses* [Leipzig, 1917], pp. 63 ff.). Although Scheler does not explore the issue, Germanophobia went hand in hand with antisemitism in the two countries, France and the United States, in which Jewish financiers had predominantly German names.

80. This exceptional German feature can be explained by the marginalization of the Social Democratic movement since Bismarck and the specific SPD public sphere that developed as a result. The mass press in Germany consisted largely of Social Democratic Party organs and was therefore more pedagogic and enlightened than sensationalist in character. As for the tabloid media, even the sensationalist newspapers of the Scherl company were but a pale imitation of their Anglo-American model.

81. Quoted in Hans Thimme, *Weltkrieg ohne Waffen: Die Propaganda der Westmächte gegen Deutschland, ihre Wirkung und ihre Abwehr* (Stuttgart, 1932), p. 42. The extent to which the introduction of psychological warfare on the front in the form of dropped leaflets violated previous standards of military fairness is shown by the initial reactions to the first English sorties. Captured pilots who had dropped bombs on German lines were treated as prisoners of war, whereas pilots who had dropped leaflets were threatened with military execution as spies (Thimme, *Weltkrieg*, pp. 35 ff.; M. L. Sanders, *British Propaganda during the First World War, 1914–1918* [London, 1982], p. 251).

82. Stern-Rubarth, *Propaganda*, p. 72.

83. Ernest K. Bramstedt, *Goebbels and National Socialist Propaganda, 1925–1945* (East Lansing, 1965), p. xiv.

84. Cecil and Buchan quoted in Sanders, *British Propaganda*, p. 252.

85. See Zbynek A. B. Zeman, *Germany and the Revolution in Russia, 1915–18: Documents from the Archives of the German Foreign Ministry* (London, 1958). For a summary see Fritz Fischer, *Griff nach der Weltmacht* (Düsseldorf, 1962), pp. 168 ff., 473 ff.

86. Paranoia about being stabbed in the back can also be understood as a manifestation of another German fear. The *encircling* of the empire, the avoidance of which was the main goal of Bismarck's foreign policy but which by 1905 had become reality, was to be counteracted by entrapment of the enemy armies (Hannibal's Cannae strategy). The so-called Schlieffen Plan envisioned not a frontal attack on France but rather a circling round, then a surrounding, then the destruction of the French army from behind. "Siegfried had maneuvered behind the enemies. Whooping, he swung his horse round and started off along a second lane with his bloody sword." This passage from Rudolf Herzog's novel *Die Nibelungen* (1912) has been seen as an unambiguous reference to the Schlieffen Plan. See Münkler and Storch, *Siegfrieden*, pp. 34, 9.

87. The adherents of French culture ranged from the German princes of the eighteenth century to the American industrial barons of the Gilded Age and the upper middle class of the nineteenth and twentieth centuries. German elites were something of an exception, since to be a Francophile after 1871 was to be part of the intellectual minority, which included Nietzsche, that was dissatisfied with the new imperial German culture. During the First World War, this attitude was radicalized and concentrated among the small colony of émigré German intellectuals in Switzerland.

88. Rühlmann, *Kulturpropaganda*, p. 13.

89. Otto Flake, *Das Ende der Revolution* (Berlin, 1920), p. 83.

90. David Felix, *Walther Rathenau and the Weimar Republic: The Politics of Reparation* (Baltimore, 1971), p. 77. Felix goes on to characterize Rathenau's offer as a "romantic prospect" and a demonstration of the German "perfection of harmlessness" (p. 74).

91. Quoted in Ulrich Heinemann, "Die Last der Vergangenheit: Zur politischen Bedeutung der Kriegsschuld- und Dolchstossdiskussion," *Die Weimarer Republik*, ed. Bracher, Funke, and Jacobson (Düsseldorf, 1987), p. 383.

92. Quoted in Kl. Löffler, ed., *Deutschlands Zukunft im Urteil führender Männer* (Halle, 1921), p. 126.

93. Linhardt, *Organisations- und Propagandalehre*, p. 140.

94. Tönnies speaks of English propaganda's being "kneaded into the masses" and refers to Hermann Oncken's image of a "goal-oriented political will . . . that trickles down from the top to the bottom, . . . becoming ever more powerful" (*Kritik der öffentlichen Meinung*, pp. 518, 517).

95. Theodor Heuss, *Hitlers Weg: Eine historisch-politische Studie über den Nationalsozialismus* (Stuttgart, 1932), p. 129.

96. Hitler writes in *Mein Kampf*: "All propaganda must be popular, and its level must be attuned to the most limited of those at whom it is directed. . . . The more it orients itself exclusively toward the emotions of the masses, the greater its success will be." Compare this with the following two passages from contemporary commentary on how advertisements work: "The effect [of advertisement] on the psyche of the individual or the mass is greatest when it appeals to the most primitive impulses and affectations" (Christof von Hartungen [C. Herting], *Psychologie der Reklame* [Stuttgart, 1921], p. 9) and "The simpler and less argumentative the assertion is, the more authoritative the effect; the masses are always prepared to accept assertions as true and right" (R. Seyffert, *Die Reklame des Kaufmanns*, quoted in Theodor König, *Reklame-Psychologie* [Munich, 1924], p. 175).

97. Derrick Sington and Arthur Weidenfeld, *The Goebbels Experiment* (London, 1942), p. 34.

98. Bramsted, *Goebbels*, p. 22.

99. Nothing would be more misguided than to read Hitler's views on the masses as an expression of disregard or cynicism. His assertions about the "feminine proclivities" and the "primitiveness" of mass sensibilities are the value-neutral opinions of a technical specialist. In contrast, Hitler felt genuine contempt for the educated upper middle classes, as he demonstrates clearly in the propaganda chapter of *Mein Kampf*, where he writes of "pallid little lords" and "literary tea socials" ([Munich, 1940], p. 187).

100. Quoted in Timothy Mason, *Social Policy in the Third Reich: The Working Class and the "National Community"* (Providence, 1993), p. 31. Mason draws attention to the internal conflict within Nazi policies between guns and butter and points out the resulting frictions and contradictions. In contrast to their public claim that the 1918 defeat was the result of "November treachery," the Nazi leaders were fully aware that the collapse was the result of the overtaxing and exhaustion of the people. In 1936, at the beginning of German rearmament, Robert Ley expressed the lesson learned in preparation for the coming war as follows: "If you demand only sacrifices from a people—something the First World War showed us with all possible clarity: Hold out, hold out, stick it out, stick it out!—that's all well and good, but there is a limit to the endurance of every individual, and naturally of every people also. It's just as with an iron girder or any structure that is supposed to support a load. There's a limit and when that limit has been reached everything breaks. And for us, that was 1918, November 9 to be precise. We can be sad about it and embittered, we may curse and swear; but the fact is that the men in power forgot to compensate

the people for the enormous strain of those four-and-a-half years, forgot on the other hand to inject new sources of strength, to pump in new strength again and again" (Mason, *Social Policy*, p. 19).

101. Edward L. Homze, *Arming the Luftwaffe: The Reich Air Ministry and the German Aircraft Industry, 1919–39* (Lincoln, 1976), p. 240. On Britain's paranoia about becoming a target of Nazi air warfare, see Uri Bialer's excellent study, *The Shadow of the Bomber: The Fear of Air Attack and British Politics, 1932–1939* (London, 1980), pp. 143ff. A. J. P. Taylor was one of the first historians to draw attention to Hitler's strategic "war of nerves." Whereas traditional propaganda had played down the extent of actual armaments, the Nazis achieved success by doing precisely the opposite: "Pretending to prepare for a great war and not in fact doing it was an essential part of Hitler's strategy" (*The Origins of the Second World War* [New York, 1983], p. xx). For the bluffing, blackmailing, and psychological steamrolling of the enemy, it was sufficient to have a rearmament "in width, a front-line army without reserves, adequate only for a quick strike" (pp. 217–18). This was what Hitler in fact ordered, in contrast to the rearmament "in depth" favored by military professionals, and he used his small forces to great effect during the blitzkrieg phase of 1939–41. Admittedly, the Nazis themselves eventually became a victim of their own propaganda, in that they came to believe their overestimation of the Luftwaffe. See David Irving, *The Rise and Fall of the Luftwaffe* (Boston 1973), pp. 74ff.

102. Quoted in Karl-Heinz Friese, *Blitzkrieg-Legende: Der Westfeldzug 1940* (Munich, 1995), pp. 431. Friese dismisses the idea that the blitzkrieg was a personal innovation that Hitler pushed through over the objections of the military. On the contrary, military leaders such as Manstein had advocated a highly developed version of shock-troop tactics from the final phase of World War I. It was only after the success of the strategy that Hitler began celebrating himself as the father of the blitzkrieg.

103. See Marc Bloch, *Strange Defeat* (New York, 1968). On the Jericho trumpet, see Friese, *Blitzkrieg-Legende*, p. 432, as well as Peter C. Smith, *Stuka: Die Geschichte der Junkers Ju87* (Stuttgart, 1993), pp. 17–18. After 1941 and the end of the blitzkrieg successes, the sirens were no longer built into planes (Smith, *Stuka*, p. 18).

104. Karl-Heinz Friese, "Die deutschen Blitzkriege: Operativer Triumph—strategische Tragödie," *Die Wehrmacht: Mythos und Realität*, ed. Rolf-Dieter Müller and Hans-Erich Volkmann (Munich, 1999), p. 193. The dropping of the two American atomic bombs on Japan, unlike the German tank advances, owed its devastating demoralizing effect to

the Allies' favorable strategic position. If strategically weak Japan had had the bomb and deployed it against Los Angeles and San Francisco, it seems unlikely that the shock effect would have led to an immediate American offer of peace or surrender.

105. Max Hildebert Boehm, *Ruf der Jungen* (1919; rpt. Freiburg, 1933), p. 43. Walther Rathenau, "Der Kaiser," *Schriften und Reden* (Frankfurt am Main, 1964), p. 251; C. H. Becker, *Kulturpolitische Aufgaben des Reiches* (Leipzig, 1919), p. 5; Hans-Joachim Schwierskott, "Arthur Moeller van den Bruck und die Anfänge des Jungkonservativismus in der Weimarer Republik: Eine Studie über Geschichte und Ideologie des revolutionären Nationalismus" (diss., University of Erlangen, 1960, pp. 128–29).

106. Klemens Klemperer, *Germany's New Conservatism: Its Historical Dilemma in the Twentieth Century* (Princeton, 1957), pp. 76 ff.; Peter Fritzsche, "Breakdown or Breakthrough? Conservatives and the November Revolution," *Between Reform, Reaction, and Resistance*, ed. Larry Eugene Jones and James Retallack (Providence, 1993), pp. 301– 04, 318 ff.). "What would have become of us, had we won the war?" Moeller van den Bruck asked. "Would Wilhelminism not have experienced its greatest and most superficial triumph? Would this triumph not have been credited to the same people who behaved so incomprehensibly on November 9? . . . Who knows whether we wouldn't have experienced a . . . scene at the Brandenburg Gate: Wilhelm II with his paladins in the pose of a monumental statue, receiving the congratulations of a thankful populace" (*Das Dritte Reich*, quoted in Schwierskott, "Arthur Moeller van den Bruck," p. 130).

107. Rathenau quoted in Friedrich von Gottl-Ottlilienfeld, *Fordismus: Über Industrie und technische Vernunft* (Jena, 1926), p. 39.

108. The SPD's August 1914 "betrayal" of its internationalist-socialist ideals can only be understood as part of the yearning to resolve these contradictions. A moving document of the inner struggle between the internationalist tradition and nationalist convictions and aspirations is Konrad Haenisch, *Die deutsche Sozialdemokratie in und nach dem Weltkriege* (1916; rpt. Berlin, 1919): "I would not go through this internal struggle again for anything in the world! This burning desire to plunge into the powerful current of general national enthusiasm and, on the other hand, the terrible fear in my soul of heedlessly following this desire, of giving in entirely to the mood that is crashing and storming all around me! . . . The fear is this: are you going to become a traitor to yourself and your cause?" (p. 110). On the socialist orientation of the wartime economy: "It is beyond question that we are engaged in a gigantic process of reorganizing our entire economy. Likewise beyond doubt is the fact that this reorganization process is moving

in the direction of socialism" (p. 122). A wartime economy is a planned economy, which is essentially socialism.

109. *Fire*, the military term for attacks with guns and cannons, took on a new dimension during the First World War. Its first signs were evident in the nineteenth-century multiplication of *firepower* with the machine gun. After the futility of infantry attacks in the face of blanket machine-gun fire in the Boer War and the Russo-Japanese War, the importance of such firepower was murderously confirmed at the beginning of the world war. As a countermeasure, the *fire barrage*, or *Feuerwalze*, was developed. It consisted of covering fire that preceded an infantry attack in two ways: first, by softening up the enemy lines before the actual attack, and second, by clearing the ground in front of the advancing troops during the attack. The *Feuerwalze* swept forward at the same tempo as the troops, often only a few meters ahead of them. Along with the trenches, it became one of the central symbols of the First World War. This explains why death on the battlefield was no longer associated with the deadly shot but with the inferno of fire. In the jargon of France's soldiers, the word *allumer* (to light) meant "to kill." See Paul Virilio, *War and Cinema* (London, 1989), p. 48. The whole spectrum of fire and front imagery can be found in the works of Ernst Jünger. In his essay "Feuer und Blut" (1925), for example, Jünger speaks of "the glowing hot breath of mechanistic death," "a massive flaming oven," "a glowing wall of fire," "burning waves," "a glowing fire of purgatory," et cetera. In a later essay, "Feuer und Bewegung" (1930), he describes "a zone of flames," "gravity of fiery space," "fire protection . . . under fiery helmets and bells," et cetera. The image of the fire front is that of Purgatory: "Circles of fire, lakes and seas of fire, rings of fire, walls and moats of fire, . . . rivers of fire, rings of fire, and burning mountains and valleys" (Jacques Le Goff, *The Birth of Purgatory* [Chicago, 1984], p. 7). In numerous cultures and mythologies, fire is a symbol of destruction and rebirth. The phoenix rises regularly from the ashes, and Empedocles chooses death in the fires of Etna as the shortest and purest path to salvation. Death by fire is also a "cosmic death" (Gaston Bachelard, *Psychoanalysis of Fire* [Boston, 1964], p. 19). And what does the cherubim's fiery sword blocking the entrance to the Garden of Eden represent if not the prospect of reentering paradise by passing through fire? The idea of a "baptism of fire" existed for quite some time before it became an initiation ritual among soldiers: John the Baptist, who uses water, prefigures Christ, who baptizes with fire and spirit (Matthew 3:11, Luke, 3:16).

110. Ernst Jünger, "Feuer und Blut," *Sämtliche Werke*, vol. 1 (Stuttgart, 1978), p. 518; Jünger, "Das Wäldchen," *Sämtliche Werke*, vol. 1, pp. 472, 442.

111. Friedrich Wilhelm Heinz, *Die Nation greift an: Geschichte und Kritik des soldatischen Nationalismus* (Berlin, 1932), p. 17.

112. Walther Rathenau, *Kritik der dreifachen Revolution* (Berlin, 1919), p. 67.

113. Moeller van den Bruck in *Die Grenzboten* (1920), p. 72.

114. Schwierskott, "Arthur Moeller van den Bruck," p. 128.

115. Hermann Keyserling, *Deutschlands wahre politische Mission* (Darmstadt, 1921), pp. 48–49.

116. In 1923, Eugen Rosenstock characterized Italian Fascism as the conquest of the country by a youth that "had had its eyes opened out there in the field" (*Hochland* [June 1923], p. 229, see also pp. 225–26). Werner Beumelburg does not explicitly describe the march home, but he implicitly invokes it when he writes that Hitler's goal was "to transform Germany's apparent defeat in the war through the mobilization of the new attitude toward life that *had been won out there*. This was to happen in all areas of German life, producing the great, gigantic, awesome truth of a German victory" (*Von 1914 bis 1939: Sinn und Erfüllung des Weltkrieges* [Leipzig, 1939], p. 42, emphasis added). Fredrik Böök, a Swedish literary critic and the author of an account of the collective mood in Germany during the months when the Nazis assumed power, explains Hitler's charisma by nothing that he was the sole surviving "unknown soldier," that is, a living collective monument to the war (*An Eyewitness in Germany* [London, 1933], p. 63; see also pp. 70–74 on Hitler's front mentality in politics).

In conjunction with Hitler and Albert Speer's plans for a monumental triumphal arch in Berlin, Elias Canetti comes closer to understanding the mythological umbilical cord connecting National Socialism and the experience of World War I than most Nazi and Hitler historiography. The *Triumphbogen* was intended to be two things at once: a memorial to the 1.8 million German casualties of the war, whose names were to be chiseled into the structure, and a monument to German triumph in the war of *revanche* that Hitler would conduct in their name. "There is nothing," writes Canetti, "that more concisely sums up Hitler's essence. Defeat in World War I was not to be acknowledged but transformed into a victory. . . . *He* had survived the war but had remained true to it, never denying its memory. Conscious of the many dead, he summoned the strength to deny the outcome of the war. They [the fallen] were his masses, when he had no others. He sensed that they were the ones who had helped him to power; without the dead of World War I, he would have never existed" (*Das Gewissen der Worte* [1981; rpt. Frankfurt am Main, 1994], p. 184). It might be added that without the defeat of 1918 an ex-NCO would never have become Führer since in a victorious Germany there would have been no place for his "movement." Hitler thus owed his rise to the collapse of 1918. A similarly apocalyptic conception of resurrection took hold in the completely different circumstances of April 1945. In his farewell letter before his execution, Helmut Moltke expressed his conviction that it was good that the attempted assassination of Hitler on July 20 had failed since Germany would have to drink the cup of defeat to its very dregs before genuine renewal would be possible. And while the anonymous author of the pamphlet *Why Nazi?* might not have seen the Nazi assumption of power as the work of the front generation of 1918, he does treat it as the *revanche* of the sons, who wanted to reverse the subordination of their unvanquished returning fighter-fathers to the defeatist leadership of the homeland (*Why Nazi?* [London, 1933], pp. 94–95). As the preface makes clear, the author was a German émigré.

117. On "conservative-national socialism," see Christoph H. Werth, *Sozialismus und Nation* (Opladen, 1996), who suggests it as an alternative to the term *conservative revolution*.

118. Ernst Niekisch went the furthest in his murderous fantasies toward liberalism and the West, perhaps as a belated cathartic response to his wartime experiences. For Niekisch, the main goal of world revolution was the destruction of Western civilization, including Western "Communism," which he contrasts with the "Bolshevism" of the East. He not only accepted but promoted the destruction of civilization; his writings anticipate the Morgenthau Plan, which advocated the deindustrialization of Germany: "The uncompromising razing of cities is an essential element of resistance politics. . . . The big cities must fall so that death-defying German men may arise again" (*Entscheidung* [Berlin, 1930], pp. 111–12).

119. Rathenau quoted in Gerhard Hecker, *Walther Rathenau und sein Verhältnis zu Militär und Krieg* (Boppard, 1983), p. 457.

120. The revolutionizing of the "Third World"—including Russia, India, Egypt, Persia, Ireland, and Mexico—against the colonial powers had already played a role in the German strategy for world war (see Fischer, *Griff nach der Weltmacht*, pp. 132ff.). Germany's conception of itself as a "young" nation in contrast to the "old" colonial power England goes back to Treitschke and amounts to a German version of social Darwinism. Moeller van den Bruck's essay "Das Recht der jungen Völker," published in November 1918 and written before the nation's

collapse, can be understood as a bridge between the self-confident demands for power of the prewar and war years and the self-protective conceit of denying defeat in the postwar era. Moeller van den Bruck, who as of 1908 still numbered Great Britain among the "young" nations of the world, now described it as an "old" nation that could not be rescued by victory any more than Germany could be hindered by defeat in its historically predestined road to greatness (Werth, *Sozialismus*, p. 105): "Every war is first decided after the cessation of hostilities. The moment of destiny always comes somehow and from somewhere for young peoples. Luck is on their side. And even when their luck deserts them, destiny is still on their side" (*Das Recht der jungen Völker* [Berlin, 1932], p. 171). This view corresponds exactly with the Communist conviction in the 1930s that every defeat is just a stage in the ultimate victory of class conflict.

121. Hans von Hentig, *Aufsätze zur deutschen Revolution* (Berlin, 1919), p. 38. See also the philosopher Eugen Kühnemann, *Der deutsche Geist und die Revolution* (Breslau, 1918), pp. 34–37.

122. Both quotations are Fried's in *Die Tat*, March 1932, pp. 960, 962.

123. Filipo Bojano, *Ein Faschist erlebt die nationale Revolution* (Berlin, 1933), p. 41. Ernst Günther Gründel, a veteran who became a National Socialist, described the November revolution as a "premature child" who, having languished in the republic's liberal-capitalist incubator, would now be awakened to genuine nationalist revolution (*Die Sendung der jungen Generation: Versuch einer umfassenden revolutionären Sinndeutung der Krise* [Munich, 1933], p. 392).

124. See, for example, Böök, *Eyewitness in Germany*, pp. 9–11, 28. The anonymous author of the pamphlet *Why Nazi?* recapitulates the general expectation that the Nazi assumption of power represented "the promise of 1914 fulfilled" (pp. 16–17).

125. *Neue Rundschau* (1933), p. 709.

126. Martin Spahn, "Die Pariser politische Hochschule und Frankreichs Wiederaufstieg nach 1871," *Die Grenzboten* 79 (1920): 30.

127. Ernst Jaeckh, ed., *Politik als Wissenschaft: Zehn Jahre Deutsche Hochschule für Politik* (Berlin, 1930), p. 182.

128. C. H. Becker, *Gedanken zur Hochschulreform* (Leipzig, 1919), pp. 5, 13. Plenge understood public education to mean organizational training. Since folk community, the state, and organization were just different aspects of one phenomenon, he defined the task of his Academy for Governmental Studies as being to "civicize" German youth (*Das erste staatswissenschaftliche Unterrichtsinstitut* [Essen, 1920], p. 17). For Plenge, "civic renewal" was the cultural reaction that would initiate the revision of defeat: "The victors will be the people who force

through civic renewal with the greatest urgency and thus take on the leading role" (quoted in Löffler, *Deutschlands Zukunft*, p. 120).

129. Ibid., p. 29.

130. It is important, however, not to underestimate the significance of the 1920 reform. Prewar reformist pedagogy, at least as spelled out in the "Guidelines for Primary School Syllabi," was also made binding for all public school instruction, and the requirement that all public school teachers have a higher-education degree ensured the guidelines would be implemented. In contrast, the reform that was considered the most daring and revolutionary, the abolition of preparatory schools for the *Gymnasium* and the introduction of a mandatory four years of primary school, affected higher secondary education more than it did public primary schools. The heated controversy over those four years (the *Grundschulkampf*) seldom if ever made reference to the role of public education in national renewal. Instead it was clearly characterized by the "specific interests of parents from the educated upper middle classes" (Ludwig Friedeburg, *Bildungsreform in Deutschland* [Frankfurt am Main, 1989], p. 226).

131. Werner Picht, *Die deutsche Volkshochschule der Zukunft* (Leipzig, 1919), pp. 12, 15.

132. Enthusiasm for the *Volkshochschule* seized not only the adherents of the movement but also university professors and intellectuals who thought the specialized university had betrayed Humboldt's ideals. This explains statements like "We can [expect] more from the effect of the *Volkshochschule* on the university and its spirit than from any effect of the university on the *Volkshochschule*" (Max Scheler) and "As the truly Humboldtian educational institution, the *Volkshochschule* will pull the cultural carpet from under the feet of the departmentalized university" (Werner Picht).

133. Ludwig Gurlitt, *Der Deutsche und sein Vaterland* (Berlin, 1902), pp. 76, 80.

134. Hans Blüher, quoted in Otto Stählin, *Die deutsche Jugendbewegung* (Leipzig, 1922), p. 11; Peter Wust, "Frankreichs geistige Wiedergeburt," *Hochland*, May 1924, p. 203.

135. Ernst Fraenkel points out another connection between back stabbing and betrayal in the post-1918 German image of America: the German idea that Wilson was guilty of a back stabbing of his own with his betrayal of German trust in October and November 1918 ("Das deutsche Wilsonbild," *Jahrbuch für Amerikastudien* 5 [1960]: 66–120).

136. See Gerd Krumeich, "Le déclin de la France dans la pensée politique et militaire allemande avant la première guerre mondiale," *La moyenne puissance au 20è siècle*, ed. Jean Claude Allain (Paris, 1989), pp. 101–

15. German perceptions of French weakness vacillated after 1871 between satisfaction at seeing the balance of power favorably shifted in Germany's direction and sympathy for history's losers, which Germans had considered themselves to be not so far in the past. A nice example of both is the comparison between the world war and the Thirty Years War made in 1917 by the political scientist Paul Lensch. With reference to the imminent landing of American expeditionary forces in France, he wrote: "The era of the Thirty Years War has come again, only this time France and not Germany will be the battleground for a colorful mixture of foreign soldiers. Mr. Wilson is the Gustav Adolf of the twentieth century translated into the mode of finance capital and Yankeeism. . . . It is entirely possible that France, like seventeenth-century Germany, will suffer more at the hands of its 'liberators' than at those of its enemies" (*Drei Jahre Weltrevolution* [Berlin, 1917], pp. 81–82).

137. Hermann J. Losch, "Sieg Nordamerikas über Europa," *Süddeutsche Monatshefte*, Dec. 1919, p. 363; Eugen Rosenstock, *Hochland*, June 1923, p. 231.

138. Hans von Hentig, *Psychologische Strategie des grossen Krieges* (Heidelberg, 1927), p. 136.

139. The approximate French equivalent of Hentig's comment was André Siegfried's remark that Fordism was just as threatening to postwar France as pre-1914 German technology and economics had been (Ernst Jaeckh, *Amerika und wir* [Berlin, 1929], pp. 16–17).

140. Charles W. Brooks, *America in France's Hopes and Fears, 1890–1920* (New York, 1987), p. 793.

141. See, for example, Firmin Roz, *L'énergie américaine* (1910); Ludwig Max Goldberger, "Die amerikanische Gefahr" (1905); Hugo von Knebel-Doberitz, *Besteht für Deutschland eine amerikanische Gefahr?* (1904); Johann Plenge, *Die Zukunft in Amerika* (1912); Wilhelm von Polenz, *Das Land der Zukunft* (1903); H. G. Wells, *The Future in America* (1906).

142. See Otto Basler, "Amerikanismus: Geschichte eines Schlagwortes," *Deutsche Rundschau* 224 (1930): 142–46.

143. Lothar Burchardt, "Technischer Fortschritt und sozialer Wandel: Das Beispiel der Taylorismus-Rezeption," *Deutsche Technikgeschichte: Vorträge vom 31. Historikertag*, ed. Wilhelm Treue (Göttingen, 1977), p. 54.

144. This development can be traced in the articles and books of Victor Cambon, a glue manufacturer and economics journalist. Before 1914, he was exclusively interested in Germany, seeing in it the model that France should emulate ("L'Allemagne au travail," ca. 1909). During the war, he "discovered America" in the form of Taylorism and saw

France's only hope for salvation in the adoption of scientific management. "Both our prosperity and our future existence depend on Taylorism" (quoted in Patrick Fridenson, "Un tournant taylorien de la société française, 1904–1918," *Annales* 42 [1987]: 1053). Germany owed its prewar superiority, as Cambon came to conclude in 1918, not to its talent for invention and organization but to its imitation of the American model, without which it would much sooner have been defeated in the war (Brooks, *America*, p. 518). In other words, Germany minus America was not a power to be taken seriously. This was the French equivalent of the German interpretation of the Entente's victory.

145. F. Delaisi, *La force allemande* (1905); A. Barre, *La menace allemande* (1908); Marcel Schwob, *Le danger allemand* (1986); Maurice Lair, *L'impérialisme allemand* (1902); H. Andrillon, *L'expansion de l'Allemagne en France* (1909); L. Hubert, *L'effort allemand* (1911).

146. With the conclusion of the last great wave of German emigration to America in 1880, the image arose of a German bloodletting from which the Anglo-Saxon world had profited. About the same time, the myth circulated that German had almost been adopted as the American national language. The idea of "winning back" America also took shape, culminating in wartime German propaganda to the effect that the actual German soul of America had dozed off under Anglo-Saxon influence and could, like Barbarossa or Sleeping Beauty, be reawakened at any time.

147. On the parallels between the Civil War and the events of 1866, see, for instance, Johann Bluntschli: "In both bodies politic, it came to a decisive inner battle that overcame a deeply rooted dualism, and in both the work ethic and energy of the North triumphed over the proud South" (quoted in Ernst Fraenkel, *Amerika im Spiegel des deutschen politischen Denkens* [Cologne, 1959], p. 276). See also August Julius Langbehn's remark on the similar settlement policies of Prussia and the United States: "North America is a Lower German settlement in the West, Prussia the same thing in the East" (ibid., p. 167).

148. Siegmund Hellmann, *Deutschland und Amerika* (Munich, 1917), p. 25.

149. Wichard von Moellendorff, "Germanische Lehren aus Amerika," *Die Zukunft* 86 (1914): 323–32. Whereas Moellendorff saw the Germanic element in Taylor as his pursuit of his studies on time and work independently of or even against the interests of capitalism—"He will socialize capitalism and orient socialism around the aristocracy"—other Taylor adherents considered his methodology his most German feature. Taylorism "should have been a German invention since in the main it is a specific characteristic of the German spirit to organize, allocate,

and classify things in such ideal fashion" (Gustav Winter, *Das Taylor-system und wie man es in Deutschland einführt* [Leipzig, 1919], p. 4).

150. See Rainer Stommer, "Germanisierung des Wolkenkratzers: Die Hoch-hausdebatte in Deutschland bis 1921," *Kritische Berichte* 2 (1992): 36–53. The skyscraper had the potential to be an "Acropolis of labor," but not in socially anarchic America. "Only a socially organized people, pervaded with a socially oriented will to work" (that is, the Germans), could achieve this ideal (Max Berg, quoted in Stommer, "Germanisi-erung," p. 46). Such perceived affinities and ideas of appropriation also underlay the nineteenth-century conviction that *Hamlet* was more a part of German than of English literature.

151. Walther Rathenau, quoted in Gerhard Masur, *Imperial Berlin* (New York, 1970), p. 74; Hermann Ullmann, quoted in Siegfried Kracauer, *Schriften*, vol. 5 (Frankfurt am Main, 1990), part 3, p. 97.

152. Such was the astonished report of Jules Huret, who visited Berlin from Paris in 1909 (*Berlin um 1900* [1909; rpt. Berlin, 1979], pp. 59ff.). On Americans' comfort in Berlin, see Kadmi-Cohen, *L'abomination amér-icaine* (Paris, 1930), p. 33.

153. In an enlightening study, Alexander Schmidt argues that the Wilhel-minian obsession with America can be explained as a projection of the empire's unresolved contradictions (post-1871 industrialization and materialism versus the ideal of culture) onto the United States. On the one hand, the United States represented a "paradigm of a technological-industrial modernism," as Germany aspired to be; on the other, it was seen as the soulless and cultureless image of a modernity that had been uncompromisingly imposed (*Reisen in die Moderne: Der Amerika-Diskurs des deutschen Bürgertums vor dem Ersten Weltkrieg im europäischen Vergleich* [Berlin, 1997], p. 92, see also pp. 186ff.).

154. The storm-troop division (SA) of the NSDAP and the *arditi* of Fascist Italy were the direct descendants of the shock troops in a double sense. Both movements were initially made up of former shock-troop sol-diers, and both considered shock-troop tactics as the most direct and effective means for translating the experiences of the world war into civil war. To what extent the Futurist avant-garde can be described as an aesthetic shock troop before the fact is another question. In any case, the idea of sabotage was central to the avant-garde, as was the desire to use and/or abuse the latest technological and industrial devel-opments.

155. Michael Geyer calls the Hindenburg Program "a comprehensive effort to 'rationalize' warfare much the same way that the German industry 'rationalized' production. The substitution of machines for men forced

the adaptation of the army to the handling of 'war machines' " (*Makers of Modern Strategy*, ed. Peter Paret [Princeton, 1986], p. 541).

156. Speech, Nov. 22, 1925, quoted in Gerald D. Feldman, ed., *Die deutsche Inflation: Eine Zwischenbilanz* (Berlin, 1982), pp. 244–45, 249.

157. The peacemakers of Versailles expected German reparations to lead to a stimulation of their economies similar to the effect the five-billion-franc tribute of 1871 had on the German economy. Only Keynes recognized that—unlike the 1871 tribute, which had been paid from savings capital—the German payments could only be raised by an increase in production, that is, through rationalization, modernization, increased investment, and, above all, higher exports. Before the victorious economies could be paid a single mark in reparations, they had to receive a flood of German exports whose unmatched low prices more seriously threatened their own producers than the German competition they so feared before 1914 ever had. Inflation only augmented this effect. It was both the motor and the price for the German economic upswing of 1919–21, a period of depression for the Allied economies. As recent inflation research has shown, the German middle class was not the only one to suffer. Above all, American investors, who had gambled on a rapid stabilization of the German economy and currency after 1918, saw themselves by 1923 in possession of trillions of worthless paper marks. According to Carl-Ludwig Holtfrerich, American capital exports to Germany during the inflation years were no less than those during the years of stability ("Amerikanischer Kapitalexport und Wiederaufbau der deutschen Wirtschaft 1919–23 im Vergleich zu 1924–29," *Vierteljahresschrift für Sozial- und Wirtschaftsgeschichte* 64 [1977]: 506, 512). Gerald Feldman paints a clear picture of the worldwide readiness to speculate on the mark: "There was scarcely a Scandinavian farmer who did not hold some marks in the expectation that the mark would recover, and thousands of Americans, from lowly busboys to mighty bankers, collectively poured millions of dollars into the German economy in return for marks and mark-denominated assets" (Gerald D. Feldman, ed., *Die Nachwirkungen der Inflation auf die deutsche Geschichte, 1924–1933* [Munich, 1985], p. 387). This speculative optimism can be explained as a continuation of the prewar faith in the capacities of the German economy, which seemed to be confirmed by the upswing of 1919–21. No one was able to predict that economic upswing and currency devaluation could go hand in hand—indeed, that the former could encourage the latter. Stephen A. Shuker, who shows that Germany netted a 5 percent *increase* in national income as a result of reparations, speaks of the American "reparation" to Ger-

many. Shuker compares the German windfall to the financing of the Vietnam War by the world economy: in both cases, the economic superpower unscrupulously exploited its position by printing money to cover debts (Feldman, *Nachwirkungen*, p. 369).

158. See, for example, Hans Delbrück, the most aggressive post-1918 critic of Ludendorff and the first to accuse Germany's military leadership of the actual stab in the back: "The high command gambled away the war intentionally and criminally" ("Ludendorffs Selbstporträt," quoted in *Delbrück's Modern Military History*, ed. Arden Bucholz [Lincoln, 1997], p. 192). On Ludendorff's behavior after the failed spring offensive of 1918: "Ludendorff hoped ... for a deus ex machina, namely, the sudden domestic breaking up of one of the Western powers.... Is that strategy or is it the dream of a man without a sense of responsibility? Is it strategy to have no plans and to hope for the unexpected?" (p. 190). Count Harry Kessler calls Ludendorff an "ingenious specialist idiot who was also an incorrigible gambler, ... the military equivalent of the 'German professor' who in his enthusiasm for his subject strips himself of all ethical decency, indeed of common sense" (*Tagebücher, 1918–1937*, p. 220). Prince Max von Baden, who regarded Ludendorff not as a gambler but as a great field marshal "who is ultimately prepared to bet everything on one card," reports that, when Ludendorff was asked at the beginning of the spring offensive what would happen if it failed, he replied: "Then Germany will have to perish" (*Erinnerungen*, p. 235). The sudden call for an armistice at the beginning of October 1918, which came after four years of obsessively pursuing peace through victory, indicated more the failure of a gambler's nerve than the realism of a professional soldier. Moreover, Ludendorff's justification—"I would feel like a reckless gambler if I did not insist on ... the quickest possible end to the war via armistice" (quoted in Karl Tschuppik, *Ludendorff: Die Tragödie des Fachmanns* [Vienna, 1931], p. 385)—can be understood as a case of psychological denial, that is, as affirmation of what the speaker seems to reject.

159. Feldman, *Nachwirkungen*, p. 388. For Feldman, Fritz Lang's film *Dr. Mabuse the Gambler* is a parable of inflation in which the villainous protagonist preys "upon a world that has surrendered to speculative fever and gambling mania" (p. 386). In another work, Feldman speaks of 1922, the first year of hyperinflation, as "the year of Dr. Mabuse" (*The Great Disorder* [New York, 1993], p. 513). He characterizes the end of inflation and expressionism as the simultaneous disappearance of "expressionist art" and "expressionist economics" (*Nachwirkungen*, p. 390). See also the observations of foreign visitors about the lively

"*rage du jeu*" not only in Berlin but throughout Germany in Ambroise Got, *L'Allemagne après la débacle* (Strasbourg, 1919–20), pp. 78 ff. Permeated with the same fantastic megalomania, lacking any realistic chance of success, and in crass contradiction to Germany's actual situation were the designs for gigantic technological projects published in popular magazines from 1919 to 1922. Examples include a skyscraper on Berlin's Friedrichstrasse, a "world transportation center" in Düsseldorf (*Berliner Illustrirte Zeitung* [1919], pp. 446–47), and the "Air Express Hamburg–New York" (ibid., p. 146).

160. On the "blood pump," see Bernd Hüppauf, "Schlachtenmythen und die Konstruktion des 'Neuen Menschen,' " *Keiner fühlt sich hier mehr als Mensch: Erlebnis und Wirkung des Ersten Weltkriegs*, ed. Gerhard Hirschfeld and Gerd Krumeich (Essen, 1993), p. 61. "The forces of France will bleed to death," said Ludendorff's predecessor in the military high command, Erich von Falkenhayn, as he began the battle of attrition at Verdun (quoted in Robert B. Asprey, *The German High Command at War: Hindenburg and Ludendorff Conduct World War I* [New York, 1991], p. 220).

161. Erwin Vierhaus speaks of a "pseudo-stab-in-the-back legend" among technocrats in Karl-Heinz Ludwig, ed., *Technik, Ingenieure und Gesellschaft: Geschichte des Vereins deutscher Ingenieure, 1856–1981* (Düsseldorf, 1981), p. 292.

162. *Zeitschrift des Vereins deutscher Ingenieure* (1919), p. 224.

163. Ibid., p. 712. A year earlier, while people were still reeling from the German collapse, American superiority was explained by the fact that in the United States "the engineer had all of industry at his beck and call and exercised his influence on every initiative undertaken by the military leadership" (*Zeitschrift des Vereins deutscher Ingenieure* [1918], p. 886).

164. Klaus Braun, *Konservativismus und Gemeinwirtschaft: Eine Studie über Wichard von Moellendorff* (Duisburg, 1978), pp. 52ff., 69.

165. *Technik und Wirtschaft* (1919), p. 341.

166. Ibid. Emphasis added.

167. Gustav Winter, *Deutschland schuldenfrei* (Leipzig, 1921), p. 8. More than a hundred thousand copies of Winter's first publication, *Das Taylorsystem und wie man es in Deutschland einführt*, were sold.

168. Winter, *Taylorsystem*, p. 98. Winter advanced this suggestion during the debate about the socialization of the economy, which he expected to lead above all to inflation. For every 100 percent rise in productivity, he suggested, 50 percent should be reinvested or paid out to Taylorized workers as a bonus and 50 percent used to pay off the national debt and reparations.

169. On France, see George G. Humphreys, *Taylorism in France, 1904–1920* (New York, 1986). Briefly in 1917, Humphreys says, "Taylorism was raised to the level of a national imperative" (p. 249). On Britain, see L. Urwick, *The Meaning of Rationalization* (London, 1929).

170. V. I. Lenin, *Ausgewählte Werke*, vol. 2 (Berlin, 1966), p. 753. On Taylorism in Europe, see Charles S. Maier, "Between Taylorism and Technocracy: European Ideologies and the Vision of Industrial Productivity," *Journal of Contemporary History* 5 (1970): 27–61.

171. Edward Hallett Carr, *The Soviet Impact on the Western World* (New York, 1947), p. 25.

172. Franz Westermann, *Amerika wie ich es sah: Reiseskizzen eines Ingenieurs* (Halberstadt, 1926), p. 99. Quoted in Mary Nolan, *Visions of Modernity: American Business and the Modernization of Germany* (New York, 1994), p. 30.

173. *Berliner Illustrirte Zeitung* (1922), p. 786.

174. Friedrich von Gottl-Ottilienfeld, *Fordismus: Über Industrie und technische Vernunft* (Jena, 1926). Quoted in Helmut Lethen, *Neue Sachlichkeit, 1924–32* (Stuttgart, 1975), p. 21. The idea of the "natural" production of the automobile, its smooth-flowing progression from raw metal to finished product, led to the literary hallucination of the finished product's still being warm, in an almost bodily sense, from the heat of the forge. At the heart of this idea was Ford's claim that eighty-one hours was all it took to produce a car. See Bernard Doray, *From Taylorism to Fordism* (London, 1988), p. 66.

175. Heinrich Hauser in the *Frankfurter Zeitung*, quoted in Ulrich Ott, *Amerika ist anders: Studien zum Amerika-Bild in deutschen Reiseberichten des 20. Jahrhunderts* (Frankfurt, 1991), p. 218.

176. Alexander Friedrich, *Henry Ford der König des Autos und der Herrscher über die Seelen* (Berlin, 1924), p. 24. The literature on Ford repeatedly claims that only the application of "all proven means of American mass suggestion and propaganda" could account for his success, the resonance of his message about service, and the high motivation of his workforce (Helmut Hultzsch, ed., *Ford und wir* [Frankfurt am Main, 1922], p. 19).

177. C. Ibanez de Ibero, *L'Allemagne de la défaite* (Paris, 1919), p. 25.

178. Troeltsch, *Spektator-Briefe*, p. 30.

179. Hans Siemsen, quoted in F. W. Koebner, *Jazz und Shimmy: Brevier der neuesten Tänze* (Berlin, 1921), pp. 14, 18.

180. Ibid., p. 18.

181. R. L. Leonard, quoted in Koebner, *Jazz und Shimmy*, p. 120.

182. Catharina Godwin, "Der Sinn der Tanzwut," *Die Dame* 17 (June 1921): 5.

183. Siegfried Kracauer, "Renovierter Jazz," *Aufsätze, 1927–1931*, vol. 5 of *Schriften* (Frankfurt am Main, 1990), part 2, pp. 390–91.

184. Emil Lederer, *Deutschlands Wiederaufbau und weltwirtschaftliche Neueingliederung durch Sozialisierung* (Tübingen, 1920), p. 47.

185. Jürgen Freiherr von Kruedener, "Die Entstehung des Inflationstraumas: Zur Sozialpsychologie der deutschen Hyperinflation, 1922–23," *Konsequenzen der Inflation*, ed. Gerald D. Feldman, Carl-Ludwig Holtfrerich, Gerald A. Ritter, and Peter Christian Witt (Berlin, 1989), pp. 284 ff.

186. Heinrich Mann, *Essays* (Berlin, 1960), p. 435; Sebastian Haffner, *Geschichte eines Deutschen: Die Erinnerungen, 1914–1933* (Stuttgart, 2000), p. 53.

187. Ludendorff's "nervous breakdown" can be seen in this context as an attack of vertigo—a reaction to the suddenly yawning gap between his previous assumptions and the realities of military strength.

188. *Crowds and Power* (New York, 1963), p. 188. See also Frank Thiess: "The currency devaluation prepared the ground for the destructive desire that ate so deeply into the organs of the body politic as to render it susceptible to every kind of relapse and collapse" (*Freiheit bis Mitternacht* [Vienna, 1965], p. 141) and Pierre Viénot: "During the period of inflation, all Germans existed in an impossible atmosphere that destroyed any sense of certainty. If *that* was possible, anything was" (*Ungewisses Deutschland* [Frankfurt am Main, 1931], p. 67).

189. On the postrevolutionary waltz mania, see Rémi Hess, *La valse: Révolution du couple en Europe* (Paris, 1989), pp. 102 ff. The inflation of the years 1790–96 followed a similar curve to its German equivalent in 1919–23: a slow beginning, with a phase of economic upswing, then hyperinflation. It also yielded the same contradictory picture of impoverishment and prodigious wealth. "Along with misery, there were rich people, speculators, ostentatiously wealthy politicians, theaters that were nearly always full, elegants balls and gambling halls" (Emile Levasseur, *Histoire des classes ouvrières de l'industrie en France de 1789 à 1870* [1903–04, rpt. New York, 1969], vol. 2, p. 237).

190. In this context, the psychoanalytic explanation of dancing seems enlightening. Dance is defined as "a release of nonpleasurable tension" that occurs when the "original solipsistic stasis" of the ego is disturbed by external stimuli. The goal of dancing is to transform this condition of disruption/disease back into the original condition of stasis (A. Stärcke, "Über Tanzen, Schlagen, Küssen usw," *Imago* 12 [1926]: 268– 72).

191. Bernd Widdig, "Culture and Inflation in Weimar Germany," ms. See especially the chapter "Witches Dancing: Gender and Inflation"

(pp. 315 ff.). Joseph Roth called these performances "compositions in militarism and eroticism," quickly adding that the dancers were working in the service of hygiene, not eros (*Frankfurter Zeitung*, Apr. 28, 1925, in Roth, *Werke*, vol. 2 [Cologne, 1990], p. 393).

192. Fritz Giese, *Girlkultur: Vergleiche zwischen amerikanischem und europäischem Rhythmus und Lebensgefühl* (Munich, 1925), p. 141.

193. For Giese, the task of the industrial psychologist resided not in training the producer but in "conditioning" the consumer. The rationalization of consumption was for him identical to the "marketing of wares and goods" that had been synchronized with production, that is, "in the genuine sense of mass production via continual circulation from raw material to finished product" (*Methoden der Wirtschaftspsychologie* [Berlin, 1927], p. 158).

194. Ibid., p. 83.

195. Ibid., p. 17.

196. Westermann, *Amerika*, p. 91.

197. Giese, *Methoden*, p. 98.

198. Kracauer, "Girls und Krise," *Aufsätze, 1927–1931*, p. 321. As sarcastic as Kracauer sounds, he had been fascinated by the phenomenon a few years earlier. "The legs of the Tiller Girls correspond to the working hands of the factory," he wrote in his 1927 essay *Ornament der Masse* (Frankfurt am Main, 1977), p. 54.

199. Giese, *Girlkultur*, p. 82; *Das Tagebuch*, May 29, 1926, p. 773; Adolf Halfeld, *Amerika und der Amerikanismus* (Jena, 1927), p. x.

200. The recontextualization of an enemy's defensive "weapon" into a kind of trophy—in this case an article of women's fashion—follows along the same lines as the social degradation or "humiliation" of the dress of disempowered classes. The most familiar example is the use of aristocratic costume as servants' outfits.

201. Duncan Aiken, quoted in Gerald Critoph, "The Flapper and Her Critics," *"Remember the Ladies": New Perspectives on Women in American History*, ed. Carol V. R. George (Syracuse, 1975), p. 147.

202. From a different perspective, the erotic neutralization of the *Girls* represents a reaction to female sexual emancipation, which had bubbled over in the first years after the war. As Hans Ostwald writes in his "Cultural History of Inflation," "women in many respects completely transformed themselves. They asserted their demands, particularly their sexual demands, much more clearly. In every conceivable way they intensified their claim to experience life more fully and intensely" (quoted in Widdig, "Culture and Inflation," p. 312). This was no doubt a sinister development for a masculine world accustomed to entirely different gender relations. Accordingly, one could consider the sexual

neutrality of the *Girls* as a compromise in which both parties agreed on a functional neutrality because emancipation and liberation were perceived not only as dangerous but also as energy-consuming. For Fritz Giese, all eccentric individual behavior required a high expenditure of energy.

203. A comparison of the Grimms' German dictionary with the *Oxford English Dictionary* (1928) attests to the German fondness for "world" concepts and neologisms. In Grimm, examples for the use of the word *Welt* take up 65 columns, and examples for various *Welt* compounds 219 columns. In the *OED*, the corresponding figures are 15 and 4, respectively. Even if differences in scope are taken into account (31 volumes of Grimm versus 20 volumes of the *OED*), the contrast remains extraordinary. This is true not only of the basic root (*Welt* occurs four times as frequently as *world*) but especially of the compounds. In German, the word *Welt* occurs in conjunction with other nouns 44 times as frequently as the *world*. A comparison with French and other Romance languages is impossible since the word *monde* occurs grammatically in the adjectival form *mondial* as a separate attributive.

204. Quoted in Joachim Heinrich Schultze, ed., *Zum Problem der Weltstadt* (West Berlin, 1958), p. xviii.

205. Jules Huret, *Berlin um 1900* (1909; rpt. Berlin, 1979), p. 33; Martin Mächler, "Die Grossiedlung und ihre weltpolitische Bedeutung: Berlin 1918," *Martin Mächler: Weltstadt Berlin. Schriften und Materialien*, ed. Ilse Balg (West Berlin, 1986), p. 74; D. Rowe, *Urban Studies* 22 (1995): 226. The first mention of Chicago as a world city is in Ernst von Hesse-Wartegg, *Chicago—eine Weltstadt im amerikanischen Westen* (Stuttgart, 1893). The preference for Chicago over New York as a model can probably be attributed to its geographical location in the middle of the United States, a position similar to Berlin's in Germany, and to its large German population.

206. Martin Wagner, "Das neue Berlin—die Weltstadt Berlin," *Das neue Berlin* 1 (1929): 5.

207. Martin Wagner, "Das Formproblem eines Weltstadtplatzes," *Das neue Berlin* 1 (1929): 33.

208. Quoted in Harald Bodenschatz, "Die Planung für die 'Weltstadt Berlin' in der Weimarer Republik," *Hauptstadt Berlin—Wohin mit der Mitte?* ed. H. Engel and W. Ribbe (Berlin, 1993), p. 156. Many were convinced even before 1914 that Berlin was "essentially American," that is, without much of an essence at all, compared with other German and European cities. This perception would seem to be confirmed by a comparison with the American aspects of Paris.

Siegfried Kracauer writes, for instance, that "the bit of America in Paris [seems] quite French" ("Pariser Beobachtungen," *Aufsätze, 1927–1931*, p. 28). Luigi Pirandello declared: "In Berlin one doesn't feel the gap between the old Europe and the new, because the structure of the city itself does not show the contradiction. In Paris, where there exists a historical and artistic structure, and where there is evidence of a native civilization, Americanism jars like make-up on the face of an old lady" (quoted in Antonio Gramsci, *Quaderni des carcere*, vol. 3 [Turin, 1975], p. 2178).

After 1945, the Berlin feuilletons' desire for it to be seen as a world city was fulfilled in a different way and on a different level. Starting in 1933, the intellectual creators of the Berlin-as-world-city fantasy had crossed the Atlantic and penetrated, together with the other remaining elements of artistic and sociological modernism, middle-class American consciousness. With the American victory in 1945 and the establishment of the United States as a superpower, this transfer of culture took on all the characteristics of what I have called "trophy taking." As of about 1960, "Weimar Berlin" became an American metaphor for modernism, in which Americans could recognize themselves, in contrast to Parisian modernism, which remains to this day an export article, a piece of European exoticism. "Weimar Berlin," too, may have contained unfamiliar elements (though far less exotic ones), but American feelings toward it were largely ones of affinity, a sense that the unreflexive technological and materialistic American modernism of Chicago and Detroit first achieved self-consciousness and definitive form in the cultural laboratory of 1920s Berlin.

Theoretically, Paris and London would also have been suitable for this role, but then the trophy element would have been lacking. As a monument to victory, the trophy renders triumph visible, permanent, and omnipresent; and cultural trophies, in contrast to purely military ones, are necessary to confirm the deeper meaning of the victory and the superiority of the victorious system. They are like the torch taken from the loser's hand because he has proven unworthy or incapable of carrying it and transferred to the victor so that its light can be better spread throughout the world. Paul Betts discusses this process with reference to America's appropriation of the Bauhaus idea after 1945 and its transformation into the "International Style." The United States needed a new style of self-presentation befitting its status as a superpower, Betts argues, and Bauhaus fit the bill, first because, along with the rest of European culture, it had been saved by the United States from Nazi barbarism and second because, as a European-American synthesis, it lent an appropriately "Atlantic" style to the emerging struggle against the new barbarism of Communism ("Die Bauhaus-Legende: Amerikanisch-deutsches Joint-Venture des Kalten Krieges," *Amerikanisierung: Traum und Alptraum im Deutschland des 20. Jahrhunderts*, ed. A. Lüdtke, I. Marssolek, and A. von Saldern [Stuttgart, 1996]).

209. Anton von Rieppel, quoted in Peter Berg, *Deutschland und Amerika, 1918–1929* (Lübeck, 1963), p. 102.

210. Thomas Freyberg, *Industrielle Rationalisierung in der Weimarer Republik* (Frankfurt am Main, 1989), p. 355.

211. In contrast to the noun *rationality* and the adjective *rational*, which were used to refer to the increasing enlightenment and objectivity in social relations, Weber's concept of rationalization implies optimization and maximization in the economic sense. When he writes in his essay "Zur Psychologie der industriellen Arbeit" of "the increasing rationalization of the wage system for the purpose of planned increases in output," he marks the transition from an enlightenment-objective to an economic-optimizing definition of rationality (quoted in Hans Wupper-Tewes, *Rationalisierung als Normalisierung: Betriebswissenschaft und betriebliche Leistungspolitik in der Weimarer Republik* [Münster, 1995], p. 38). Before the war only Weber's disciples Wilhelm Kochmann and Emil Lederer used the concept of rationalization.

212. Nolan, *Visions of Modernity*, p. 71.

213. Quoted in Gottl-Ottlilienfeld, *Fordismus*, p. 2.

214. Robert A. Brady, *The Rationalization Movement in German Industry* (1933; rpt. New York, 1974), pp. 3–7; André Fourgeaud, *La rationalisation: Etats-Unis, Allemagne* (Paris, 1929), p. 29. The reception of Fordism and the general acceptance of the concept of rationalization went hand in hand, with the former preceding the latter by about a year. The 1925 edition of the *Handwörterbuch der Staatswissenschaften* does not mention rationalization, whereas the supplemental volume of 1929 devotes 109 pages (pp. 708–817) to the concept. Similarly, the annual *Bibliography of Social Sciences* of the Reich's Department of Statistics has one entry in 1924, 6 in 1925, and 145 in 1926. See Wupper-Tewes, *Rationalisierung*, p. 36.

215. Freyberg, *Industrielle Rationalisierung*, pp. 306, 312, 315.

216. Ibid., pp. 308–09. Freyberg calls rationalization a "formula for consensus and peace that spans all of society."

217. Ibid., p. 306. Emphasis added.

218. Ibid., p. 24. Bruno Rauecker provides some examples of the discrepancy between program and reality in *Rationalisierung und Sozialpolitik* (Berlin, 1926), pp. 14ff. The discrepancy was most evident in manufacturing. Mining and heavy industry, on the other hand, were thor-

oughly rationalized in both the Taylorite-technological sense and the "negative" sense of liquidating unprofitable businesses and branches (Nolan, *Visions of Modernity*, pp. 137 ff.). The main changes took place not in technological-industrial organization but in the concentration of capital and the building of cartels, for example, in the formation of firms like IG Farben and the Associated Steelworks.

219. Brady, *Rationalization Movement*, p. xx. On the New Objectivity of the 1920s as a continuation of the pre-1914 "old" objectivity, see Frank Trommler, "The Creation of a Culture of *Sachlichkeit*," *Society, Culture, and the State in Germany, 1870–1930*, ed. Geoff Eley (Ann Arbor, 1996), pp. 48 off. Old and New Objectivity stand in roughly the same relation to each another as Taylorism and rationalization.

220. *Revue de France*, Nov. 15, 1929.

221. Urwick, *Meaning of Rationalization*, p. 20; Walter Meakin, *The New Industrial Revolution* (London, 1928), pp. 7–8.

222. Brady, *Rationalization Movement*. Emphasis added.

223. Werner Daitz, "Vom Sinn der europäischen Wirtschafts-Rationalisierung," quoted by Charles Roy, *La formule allemande de production rationelle* (Paris, 1929), p. 176.

224. The confidence of the German coal and steel industries, as represented by Werner Daitz, can be explained by their sense of having more leverage than their French enemies. Without coal from the Ruhr region, the steel industry of Lorraine would have come to a standstill, whereas Germany was far less dependent on raw iron from Lorraine. As Guy Greer, a member of the reparations committee, remarked, Germany could "afford to play a waiting game" (*The Ruhr-Lorraine Problem* [New York, 1925], p. 232). The 1923 French occupation of the Ruhr area thus emerges more as an act of desperation than as one of aggression. Probably no more representative than Daitz but still noteworthy was the industrialist Arnold Rechberg, who considered the Treaty of Versailles "not as a political issue but solely as an economic factor, which he saw as being more disadvantageous to the victor than to the vanquished" (Eberhard von Vietsch, *Arnold Rechberg und das Problem der politischen West-Orientierung Deutschlands nach dem 1. Weltkrieg*, Schriftenreihe des Bundesarchivs [Koblenz, 1958], p. 75).

225. Roy, *Formule allemande*, p. 178. The fear that the national independence defended at such enormous cost during the First World War could now be swamped by Germany's overwhelming rationalized economy was specifically French. From the Anglo-American perspective, German rationalization was a welcome contribution to the efforts toward a long overdue modernization of competitive liberal capitalism. If the changeover and transmutation into a more stable system could

be carried out by invoking class- and interest-neutral, technological and scientific rationality, all the better. The definition of rationalization by the American National Industrial Conference Board in 1931 points in this direction: "Rationalization represents the idea of enlightened leadership embracing an entire industry in its relation to other industries and to the national economy" (National Industrial Conference Board, *Rationalization of German Industry* [New York, 1931], p. 7). In other publications, the starring role is given not to rationalization, but to buzzwords like *technocracy, efficiency,* and *managerialism.*

226. Brady, *Rationalization Movement,* pp. 324, 317–18.

227. On rationalization in the Third Reich, see Rüdiger Hachtmann, " 'Die Begründer der amerikanischen Technik sind fast lauter schwäbisch-allemannische Menschen': Nazi-Deutschland, der Blick auf die USA, und die 'Amerikanisierung' der industriellen Produktionsstrukturen im 'Dritten Reich,' " *Amerikanisierung: Traum und Alptraum im Deutschland des 20. Jahrhunderts,* ed. Alf Lüdtke, Inge Marssolek, and Adelheid von Saldern (Stuttgart, 1996), pp. 46 ff. See also Michael Prince and Rainer Zitelmann, eds., *Nationalsozialismus und Modernisierung* (Darmstadt, 1991), especially Hans-Dieter Schäfer, "Amerikanismus im Dritten Reich," pp. 200 ff. On the National Board for Economic Efficiency and the rationalization of mass murder, see Götz Aly and Susanne Heim, *Vordenker der Vernichtung: Auschwitz und die deutschen Pläne für eine neue europäische Ordnung* (Frankfurt am Main, 1997), pp. 300 ff., 312 ff., 322 ff.

228. See Philipp Gassert, *Amerika im Dritten Reich: Ideologie, Propaganda, und Volksmeinung, 1933–1945* (Stuttgart, 1997); Hans-Jürgen Schröder, *Deutschland und die Vereinigte Staaten, 1933–1945* (Wiesbaden, 1970); Schröder, "Das Dritte Reich und die USA," *Die Use und Deutschland, 1918–1975,* ed. Manfred Knapp (Munich, 1978); Hans-Dieter Schäfer, *Das gespaltene Bewusstsein* (Munich, 1983); and Schäfer, "Amerikanismus im Dritten Reich." The Nazis' readiness to learn from America stands in contrast to the reception accorded by European liberalism, which despite its tendency to flirt with American mass culture insisted on the preservation of its individuality. The readiness, indeed the desire, for the total collectivism that seemed to have been achieved in the United States tied the two other great totalitarian movements of the interbellum era, Italian Fascism and Soviet Communism, to National Socialism. It may not be going too far to regard the entire post-1918 totalitarian phase of European history as an attempt to raise Europe technologically and psychologically to the American level by replacing liberal with totalitarian ideology. Lenin and Stalin's expressions of admiration for American's "technical" achievements point in

this direction, as do numerous remarks by European and American intellectuals on the democratic-totalitarian character of American society. See, for example, the Italian anti-Fascist Antonio Borgese: "With the exception of its extreme left, . . . America is totalitarian. The vast majority share the same ideas, the same sentiments. The government is 'administration.' A minority controls all politics" (quoted in Giorgio Spini, Gian Giacomo Migone, and Massimo Teodori, eds., *Italia e America dalla Grande Guerra à oggi* [Lama Umbro, 1976], p. 81). The external appearance, particularly the faces, of Americans struck many Europeans as an especially emphatic sign of standardization. For National Socialist Theodor Lüddecke, the American was "a stable, healthy, unbroken, internally calm type of person. This is expressed in the structure of his athletically controlled body, in his physiognomy, in the stern style of American men's fashion. . . . America has put its stamp not only on the automobile but also on the human face. In general, the physiognomy of the American seems sterner than that of the newly arrived. People have spoken of the 'sporting American face' " (*Das amerikanische Wirtschaftstempo als Bedrohung Europas* [Leipzig, 1925], pp. 19–20). Friedrich Sieburg commented: "Their padded shoulders appear monumental, their uniform faces, six of one, a half-dozen of the other, seem to be masks of iron" (*Die Literarische Welt* 23 [July 1926]: 8, quoted in *The Weimar Republic Sourcebook*, ed. Anton Kaes, Martin Jay, and Edward Dimendberg [Berkeley, 1994], p. 403). Likewise Rudolf Kayser on the "Americanized" European physiognomy of the 1920s: "Beardless with a sharp profile, a resolute look in the eyes, and a steely, thin body" (*Vossische Zeitung*, Sept. 27, 1925, quoted in Kaes, Jay, and Dimendberg, *Weimar Sourcebook*, p. 395).

229. Gassert, *Amerika im Dritten Reich*, pp. 92, 95, 100, 264, 296ff.
230. Erich Welter in the *Frankfurter Zeitung*, Nov. 9, 1941, quoted in Schäfer, "Amerikanismus, im Dritten Reich," p. 213.
231. Nazi communications director Eugen Hadamovsky was equally impressed by the use of the seventy-five thousand "four-minute men" (public promoters whose standardized brief addresses can be seen as the predecessors of the modern advertising commercial) in 1917–18 and the repression of all opposition to the war (*Propaganda und nationale Macht* [Oldenburg, 1933], pp. 43–44, 22–23). The legal foundation for such repression—the Espionage Act (1917) and the Sedition Act (1918)—has been described as the American version of the Enabling Act that suspended the Reichstag and gave Hitler dictatorial power in 1933. The sentencing of the Socialist leader Eugene V. Debs to ten years' imprisonment in the fall of 1918 could be subsumed under this comparison. Charles A. Beard, who found this instance of repression

comparable to those in czarist Russia, commented: "Never before had American citizens realized how thoroughly, how irresistibly a modern government could impose its ideas upon the whole nation and, under a barrage of publicity, stifle dissent with declarations, assertions, official versions, and reiteration" (Charles A. Beard and Mary A. Beard, *The Rise of American Civilization*, vol. 2 [New York, 1930], p. 640). Whether the systematic repression and ultimate silencing of German American culture (all the way down to those with Germanic-sounding last names) in 1917–18 might have served as a model for the discrimination against German Jews in the first years of the Nazi regime is a question that could well be posed in light of Nazi interest in American methods.

232. Quoted in Schäfer, "Amerikanismus in Dritten Reich," p. 214. The Coca-Cola statistics are cited in Hachtmann, " 'Die Begründer,' " p. 39. The institute responsible for researching consumer habits was the Society for Consumer Research under the aegis of the Institute for Economic Research directed by Ludwig Erhard, later minister of economics and chancellor of the Federal Republic of Germany.

233. "The content is utter nonsense," Goebbels remarked of an American film, "but the depiction is very skillful" (quoted in Gassert, *Amerika in Dritten Reich*, p. 177). Hans Siemsen said similarly, "It's always the same. But how charmingly these idiotic scripts are filmed!" Because they depict "thoroughly simple and natural people," he observed, "these American films always make a pleasant impression despite their miserable scripts" (*Die Weltbühne* [1921], pp. 220, 221).

234. Thomas J. Saunders, *Hollywood in Berlin* (Berkeley, 1994), p. 112; Felix Müller, *Der Filmminister: Goebbels und der Film im 3. Reich* (Berlin, 1998), pp. 75–77.

235. Joachim Radkau, quoted in Thomas Kühne, "Massenmotorisierung und Verkehrspolitik im 20. Jahrhundert," *Neue Politische Literatur* 41 (1996): 202.

236. Heinrich Hauser, quoted in M. Bienert, *Die eingebildete Metropole: Berlin im Feuilleton der Weimarer Republik* (Stuttgart, 1992), p. 188.

237. Quoted in R. J. Overy, "Transportation and Rearmament in the Third Reich," *Historical Journal* 16 (1973): 401; Paul Kluke, "Hitler und das Volkswagenprojekt," *Vierteljahreshefte für Zeitgeschichte* 8 (1960): 348.

238. Alexander Friedrich, speaking of Ford's "factory of souls" in 1924, saw in it the aspiration toward total control, beginning with the workers: "The connection stretched beyond the period from 7 a.m. to 3 p.m.; it was not just a matter of one of the seven thousand daily tasks: it concerned the *whole* human being" (*Henry Ford*, p. 19). In addition, he quotes Ford's autobiography: "We need people who are able to form

the formless masses politically, socially, industrially, and morally into a healthy, well-rounded whole" (p. 20). The idea of service was the attempt to extend this total connection to the buyer and the consumer. Hitler was an admirer of Ford, whom he considered the "leader of the growing Fascist movement in America" (quoted in James Pool, *Who Financed Hitler?* [New York, 1978], p. 90). R. J. Overy's claim that Hitler read Ford's autobiography during his imprisonment at Landsberg ("Transportation," pp. 400–01) is unsubstantiated but has been taken up by various others.

239. Kluke, "Hitler," p. 342. The enormous success of the Beetle in the United States after World War II serves as an epilogue to the story. Around 1960, as the market for compact cars began to be tapped, not only the Volkswagen but the British Austin, the French Renault, and the Italian Fiat attempted to answer the call. How is it that the Volkswagen, which was rejected as "Hitler's car" in 1949 when Germany first attempted to export it, soundly defeated its European competition within the space of a few years? Purely economic factors (low price, good service) do not provide a sufficient answer. More to the point, the Beetle's success was tied from the very beginning to the folklore surrounding the car. It was a manifestation of the victor's trophy, pure and simple. In the transformation from "Hitler's car" to "the funny car," the Volkswagen traveled the same route along which a once threatening enemy became a harmless, Chaplinesque comic figure. The fact that Volkswagen consumers came disproportionately from the ranks of the well-educated (60 percent had a college education) argues for this thesis. In line with their other Europe-oriented consumer habits, this group of people should have favored a French compact car like the Citroen 2CV, as their German counterparts did.

240. Eberhard Schütz, in Wolfgang Emmerich and Carl Wege, eds., *Der Technikdiskurs in der Hitler-Stalin-Ära* (Stuttgart, 1995), p. 136.

241. *Frankfurter Zeitung*, Dec. 11, 1938, quoted in Emmerich and Wege, *Technikdiskurs*, p. 142. After a long stay in Germany, Denis de Rougemont comments similarly in a May 1938 diary entry: "In the early days of the automobile, who would have believed that in twenty years men would be capable of driving these machines without thinking of anything in particular, in a perfect state of freedom of spirit? The totalitarian constraints [of driving] keep us hypnotized. Like an obsession, the cars 'drive us,' actually taking away all our freedom. With every thought, I risk an accident. . . . What will happen when these dangers excite only our reflexes? Will we find a new freedom?" (*Journal d'une époque* [Paris, 1968], p. 327).

Index

About the Author and the Translator

Wolfgang Schivelbusch, who has been called "a master of cultural history," is an independent scholar who divides his time between New York and Berlin. His books include *The Railway Journey, Disenchanted Night,* and *Tastes of Paradise.*

Jefferson Chase's translations include the Signet edition of Thomas Mann's *Death in Venice and Other Stories.* He lives in Berlin.